700.—

D0891552

The Paternoster Church History, Vol. IV

General Editor: PROFESSOR F. F. BRUCE, M.A., D.D.

# THE GREAT LIGHT

*In the Same Series:*

# THE GREAT LIGHT
## Luther and Reformation

*by*

### JAMES ATKINSON
M.A., M.Litt.(Durham), D.Theol.(Münster)

*Professor of Bibical History and Literature in the University of Sheffield*
*Canon Theologian of Leicester Cathedral*

THE PATERNOSTER PRESS

SBN: 85364 084 x

*Copyright © 1968 The Paternoster Press*

AUSTRALIA:
*Emu Book Agencies Pty., Ltd.,*
*511, Kent Street, Sydney, N.S.W.*

CANADA:
*Home Evangel Books Ltd.,*
*25, Hobson Avenue, Toronto, 16*

NEW ZEALAND:
*G. W. Moore, Ltd.,*
*P.O. Box 29012 Greenwood's Corner,*
*24, Empire Road, Auckland*

SOUTH AFRICA:
*Oxford University Press,*
*P.O. Box 1141, Thibault House,*
*Thibault Square, Cape Town*

*Made and Printed in Great Britain for*
*The Paternoster Press Paternoster House*
*3 Mount Redford Crescent Exeter Devon*
*by Cox & Wyman Limited Fakenham*

# CONTENTS

# PREFACE

THE REFORMATION HAS A SIGNIFICANCE THAT IS PERMANENT, FOR IN that century the Reformers everywhere in Europe challenged a faithless, secularized Church with the authority of the original Gospel, a challenge that is relevant at all times and in all places to both Protestant and Catholic alike. This volume deals with Luther's fruitless struggle to find a gracious God, through which agony God found him; his consequent reformation of the Church by this rediscovered evangelical theology of faith in Christ only; his stand against Pope and Emperor on the unshakeable ground of the Bible, conscience and common sense; his establishment of the evangelical Church in Saxony. There is recounted the brief, tragic history of Zwingli, and his somewhat Erasmian reformation of Zürich and the surrounding region. The story turns to Calvin and his establishment of the then disorganized rabble of the Reformation into an invincible and international army by the sheer power of his pellucid and profound theology. Some account is given of the English *via media,* an estimation of the timely success of John Knox in Scotland, concluded by the settlement which the Elizabethan divines had established on the death of Elizabeth in 1603.

It is a story of success and failure, a story not yet finished. The saddest feature of the Reformation saga is the resistance to the truth of the Gospel the Papacy and allied princes made. Never was the Papacy more unready for a Word from God, never more immoral, frivolous, irresponsible and irreligious, never more deaf to God and the Gospel. Of all the times when the Papacy has failed God and the Church, this occasion was the most glaring, the most disastrous, the most costly.

A Christian man should remind himself that God's judgments are unsearchable and His ways inscrutable, and as he reflects on the course of events, he meets at the heart of things a paralysing paradox of seeming irrationality. This experience should sharpen his awareness that meaning lies not in his understanding of events but rather in what God is doing in these events. When men sang the Birth of Christ, Herod sought His death. The Incarnation was fulfilled in the Crucifixion. Likewise, the Reformers all met resistance, many of them death. Luther himself taught a theology of the Cross. If the cost of division has been high, its rewards are higher, for men suffered disunity, persecution, even death, rather than that the truth of the Gospel should perish.

7

We stand at a moment when many Catholic men, realizing that the Reformers were sent by God, are humbly and penitently waiting on God to restore the years that the locusts have eaten, and equally, when many evangelical men are humbly and penitently aware that where the Protestant movement has not ossified it has dissipated into division. Perhaps God is leading all His people through a painful renewal into a unity of truth greater than we have ever known.

I express my thanks to my old friend Professor F. F. Bruce for reading the typescript with his customary care and for making suggestions with his usual quietness and humility; to Mr. Howard Mudditt for unfailing patience and courtesy; to the printers for their speed and efficiency; and to Mr. Bernard Lane who, under a physical handicap that would daunt the bravest of us, typed the whole manuscript faultlessly.

# PART ONE

*Luther and the German Reformation*

# CHAPTER I

# LUTHER'S DISCOVERY OF EVANGELICAL THEOLOGY

THE REFORMATION IS LUTHER AND LUTHER IS THE REFORMATION. Therefore, the acid test of any work on this period is whether the author understands, and has the capacity to lay bare, the fundamental concerns of Luther. If this prior task be executed in workmanlike fashion, the reader is at once set on a vantage point from which he may judge and assess all the men and movements of this period. Without this prior investigation and understanding no Reformation study is properly understood: it would be like trying to interpret the Synoptic Gospels without St. John's Gospel, or the Book of Acts without St. Paul's Epistles.

If Luther's concern is understood, the reader can at once see for himself whether in fact Luther's protest for an evangelical, scriptural theology, consonant with both a sound Patristic and historical judgment as well as with reason and common sense, was a legitimate and true protest against the theology and pastoral practice of his own church. The reader is also in a position to assess and relate the work of all the other reformers, on the Continent of Europe as well as in England and Scotland. He will have grasped basic principles which will enable him, liberated from emotion and prejudice, to judge more properly the claims of Rome. He will be enabled to understand and limit the significance of the great humanists of the period, Erasmus in particular, and grow aware of that vital distinction Luther made between those who preach God and those who preach man. He will also develop a kind sensitivity towards that long thin line of radicals, enthusiasts and devotees whose zeal led, and continues to lead, them away from the more classical formulations of Wittenberg, Geneva or Canterbury, sometimes to a more sensitive awareness of the significance of the Reformation than their more orthodox brethren. And finally he will be in a sounder position to assess the oecumenical debate today: he will be able to estimate the immense advance certain Roman Catholic theologians have made for their Church; he will be able to understand the evangelical criticism of Senarclens who argues that modern Catholicism is too mediaeval and modern Protestantism too humanist, and see the direction in which he, Barth and others would have us go. All these will be given to the person who first finds out what Luther said and why he said it.

Gordon Rupp in his *The Righteousness of God*,[1] Part I, gives an excellent discussion of the problems attending the man who seeks to differentiate the Luther of history from Luther the myth, and shows how Luther has been understood and misunderstood both in England and on the Continent these four centuries. Mountains of books have been written wherein Luther is depicted in all kinds of lop-sided ways. In some he is the man who broke the unity of the Great Church; in others the uncouth blusterer, the Germanic Hercules, the fly in the healing ointment of the Renaissance, the renegade monk who married a runaway nun, or the man who sold the Church to the princes. The pictures are legion and the reader can recognize them all. But the present book will simply present a view of Luther's work in the Reformation and relate it to the whole Reformation movement as it finally resolved itself in England at the death of Elizabeth (1603). It will seek to show that Luther had the mantle of reformer thrown over his shoulders when he was confronted with the stark reality that though he had given up all to find God and to save his soul by entering the monastery, the Church could in fact neither reconcile him to God nor assure him of salvation. Luther recoiled from this horrible realization as might a child given a scorpion for a fish or a stone for a loaf. In this humiliating and devastating experience, in this abysmal hell, he cried to God, he hammered on the doors of Scripture, he pored over the Fathers and Doctors. After years of struggle he was eventually hauled out of this abyss of uncertainty and doubt. God made it clear to Luther that the Church had not only largely lost the gospel and God's righteousness but could not even say where it could be found. This realization carried with it the obligation to convey and communicate it to the Church and the world: to restore the Church to her early commission, and man to the God to whom he belonged.

It is important to state at the outset what Martin actually rediscovered. Born in the Saxon village of Eisleben on November 10, 1483, of sound, God-fearing yeoman stock, Luther had two great advantages. He was brought up in the dignity of godly poverty and under the discipline of having to fight every step he took. This clever boy was singled out by his independently-minded father for a career at the university where he was intended to qualify as a lawyer. His father paid for him both at school and university, where he distinguished himself. It was after graduation that Martin seems to have had a distressing disagreement with his father, for whom he had much respect and affection. It was almost certainly because of his father's strong and clear views both on his future career and on marriage, that Martin returned to the university upset, disturbed and uncertain. It would appear, though there is some uncertainty about details, that he and his companion were overtaken by a violent storm, when

[1] E. Gordon Rupp, *The Righteousness of God: Luther Studies* (London, 1953), pp. 3-77.

Martin had the horrifying experience of seeing his friend struck dead by lightning. Certainly there was some extraordinary experience. In this Luther believed he saw the hand of God in His wrath; and in great fear, and gratitude for his preservation, he immediately and unreservedly offered himself to God and His service. In those days that meant only one thing, entering a monastery. Without reference to his father, whom he utterly mortified by this decision, he returned to Erfurt, not as a student but as a monk. He chose the Augustinian Eremite monastery, famous for its learning and its severity, and entered there on July 17, 1505, in sure and certain hope of delivering his soul from all its present conflict and of gaining eternal salvation.

He was put in a hostel so that the state of his soul might be observed. In September, 1505, he received the tonsure and took the cowl. As a clerical novice he was taught all the prescribed acts – to go about with eyes downcast, never to laugh, never to eat or speak except at prescribed times, to do domestic chores, and to beg for bread in the streets (for spiritual not economic reasons). He enjoyed a single cell of nine by six feet, in which were one chair, one table, one candlestick and a straw bed. He ate twice a day, once only on fast days (of which there were a hundred in the year). He had no heating in his cell – a very severe discipline in a German winter.[1]

For a time his disquiet was allayed owing to the total filling in of his time by an external authority. Yet a monk is in far greater danger of falling into sin and guilt than a man occupied with the normal activities of his daily work. Luther had entered the monastery because he was in anxiety about the state of his soul, but found that the spiritual life served only to sharpen his anxiety without allaying it. He knew he could never be certain of having confessed his sins in their entirety, and therefore could never experience forgiveness, for there was always this load of unconfessed and consequently unforgiven sin and the ensuing wrath of God to face. His spiritual mentor reminded him that forgiveness meant total forgiveness, and that it was not a case of God being angry with Luther but Luther being angry with God. Luther's protestations were true; his spiritual father's remonstrances of the mercy and forgiveness of God were true. But the assurances of the mentor did not speak to the heart of the sufferer. The trouble was much deeper, and the father confessor could not diagnose it.

Catholic practice had grown Pelagian, and preached a theology and pastoralia that led to justification by works, merit and effort. It was a kind of spiritual dystrophy, so long-standing, so chronic, that the patient no longer remembered what it was like to be healthy. Martin needed the

---

[1] The monastery was severely damaged by aerial bombardment in 1945, but it was almost completely restored when the author visited it in 1965, including Luther's cell.

Divine Physician's remedy of the Gospel and tossed painfully in his sickness of soul, knowing that his disease was beyond his doctor's practice. His doctors tried to comfort him by saying that he was quite well, and that in time under their spiritual care and direction, he would achieve normality and walk cheerfully again with his brother monks. Luther knew they were wrong and, imprisoned in this holy hell, cursed God that He should cause this wretchedness and misery to one who had turned to God only to find that God had turned against him.

He soldiered on. In September, 1506, he professed the vows of poverty, chastity and obedience, and in May, 1507, he was ordained priest. He found he was not to work in silence for the salvation of his soul but was gently guided into a life of study and teaching. He studied deeply the Occamist theology of his day, but still found no answers to his doubts. Suddenly, in the autumn of 1508, the young scholar was called to the new University of Wittenberg. There he taught Aristotle and the Bible and it was there he qualified to hold a university chair. Before he could read his inaugural lecture he was recalled to Erfurt, still in the same spiritually disturbed state of mind. On his return (1509) he taught at Erfurt. At this time there was a general desire to reform the Augustinian order by bringing the lax houses up to the standards of the strict houses. Erfurt was a reformed and strict house and Luther was assigned to accompany a senior monk to take the appeal to Rome to allow Erfurt to maintain its own high standards rather than be obliged to conform to any generally accepted lower standards which would be imposed on the entire Order.

Contrary to his high anticipations, the four weeks in Rome turned out to be a time of grave disillusionment. The simple, devout, learned monk hoped for spiritual and pastoral guidance from the Eternal City but all he met were ignorant priests unable to hear a confession, much less one so demanding as his. When he celebrated mass, his slow reverence created a bottle-neck in the production-line, and he was pushed on by mass priests anxious to gabble through their quota, crying, "Passa! Passa!" ("Get a move on there! Get a move on there!"). He went through all the pilgrimages available, running "like a mad saint through all the churches and catacombs." He crawled on his knees up the twenty-eight steps of the *Scala Sancta* (the staircase Christ was believed to have ascended to Pilate), saying a Pater Noster on each step and kissing each piously. This performance was guaranteed to free a soul from purgatory at one stroke. Luther's doubts were quickened. He was also shocked at the profligacy of the Papal curia, as well as at the conduct of the common people whom 1500 years of Christianity had seemingly left untouched and who would perform their natural functions in the street like dogs. The two brothers began their long silent walk back to north Germany in January 1511 when Luther at

least enjoyed the loveliness of spring in southern Europe, even though he
was brooding on God's ways with him.

Two things he learnt from his visit to Rome. First, his suspicions about
mediaeval Christianity clarified into a conviction that Rome had lost the
keys of the kingdom. She would neither enter nor suffer anybody else to
enter. "Like a fool," he later said, "I took onions to Rome and brought
back garlic." Because he faced this disillusionment, and refused to consider
garlic as onions, he broke through to a re-understanding of the gospel.
Second, he learnt what it was to stand alone against the majority. Both
lessons gave him an enormous spiritual advance, he strengthened his
integrity and increased his authority. For his loyalty, the good Staupitz
transferred him to Wittenberg once more. The world will ever remember
the despised Nazareth of Wittenberg, men will always look up attentively
and respectfully when that university is mentioned, for it was here on this
"miserable heap of sand" that this unknown scholarly monk lifted Christendom off its hinges and re-hung it straight.

John Staupitz, his Vicar-General and a Professor of Theology at
Wittenberg, convinced Luther that his mission was to be a doctor and a
preacher, and to this office he was commissioned in June, 1512. He was
allocated the room of his predecessor Staupitz, a room which remained
his study till his death thirty-four years later, the room from which he
stormed the papacy, guided the Reformation, and prepared his lectures for
the university as well as his sermons for the Church. To use his own words,
he still "did not know the light." He had gone through dark days during
the last seven years. The next seven were to prove much worse, except
that they were to produce that sweet reward of doubt, an adamantine
faith, when all his fears were swallowed up in hope.

Countless men and women, before and since Luther, have entered the
cloisters to put themselves right with God, to put themselves utterly and
unconditionally at His disposal, to find salvation and avert damnation. As
in Luther's case, the occasion (though not the cause) is often some deep
emotional confrontation with death and judgment, or even with sin.
In the same way as Luther, countless numbers, not known to the world,
have gone through agonies of doubts, scruples, misgivings, faithlessness.
The only point at which Luther differs from all the rest is that none of the
prescribed, proved and accepted methods ever resolved his. Discipline
deepened despair. He found himself unable to accept on authority teaching
which did not authenticate itself in his own experience. He stood theologically against his teachers, and held out, against the certainties of his
contemporaries, with the faith of a Lavoisier, a Newton, a Darwin, that if
theology is to be sound it must answer to human experience. In other
words, if a doctrine is taught as true, it must be able to be verified by every
man in the same experience where it was originally proved true. He

started from the simple empirical beginning of what worked in life and what did not. What evidence was there for God and his activity in the world? What was actually wrong in a world of war and want, sin and selfishness, coarseness and greed? What was man for? What purpose or meaning was there to life? He stood quite simply as an empiricist and experimentalist. He knew he existed. He knew he was a sinner, half-blind, half-success, half-failure. Did God care about it all? If so, how? How did he handle His creation? Was the Church right in her handling of souls? Was she right in her theology? Had she her original commission straight? Was she aware of her true mission to the world? By his slow resolving of these painful questions, won in the first instance by a refusal to accept half-truths or to be intimidated by authority, Luther broke through to what was the new evangelical theology, which in its turn the world came to know as the Reformation. Nevertheless, it should always be remembered that none of this happened by dint of personal pressure on the part of Luther. He was by nature as quiet and reserved as Jeremiah and as unwilling to come forward as Jeremiah was in his day. Luther had the hand of the Lord laid upon him, and all his immense energy, power and flash were a divine communication. He heard the word of the Lord and it was that word that he declared. All along, Luther knew that it was never his own message he gave: his commission was God's. He once said that when he preached it was the one activity he need never apologize for: he was God-possessed.

The most important means of bringing peace to the troubled soul was the confessional. Luther had been taught that the moment the priest whispered, "I now absolve thee," all sins were driven from the soul (except, of course, original sin). This was the very declaration of which Luther could not be certain, for he did not know this forgiveness as a real experience. He turned to all the well-tried means: private chastisement, fastings, vigils, prayers. He sought to propitiate God by doing extra, even to compel God to remove his sense of sin. The nearer he got to God the more terrifying he found Him in relation to his own frailty, finitude and sin. He ruined his health with his much striving. His bones stuck out like an old nag's. There hovered over him in his helpless plight the threat of God and the day of judgment. He felt an overpowering fear of God, a trembling awareness of Him as the destructive power over against a sinner. He was like the moth longing for the flame and about to be scorched to death by its desire. Was God about to scorch him to death? "When I looked for Christ it seemed to me I saw the devil," he said. Modern man finds this difficult to understand, but so intense was his awareness of the holy God in all His eternal majesty, and so intense his own frailty and sin, that he knew that if ever he were to encounter God, he would be met by God's annihilating reaction against sin. Later he attributed the chief cause of his distress to the Occamism of the theology of his day, which taught that a man could prepare his soul for union with God by his own acts, his own asceticism, his own prayers, his own meditation and his own meritorious acts.

A Christian man will at once protest, "But had he not heard of grace?" Yet we have to remind ourselves that in Luther's day both spiritual and academic teachers alike taught that a man had first to earn grace by establishing "congruent merit," in other words by doing "all that in him lay." This sharpened Luther's anguish. How could he or any man ever be certain that he had done "all that in him lay"? How can any man know that he has done enough to "merit" grace? Any decent man is "harder" on himself than a friend would be, any Christian man is "harder" on himself even than a forgiving God. What Luther's problem shows is that the late mediaeval theologians were putting the wrong questions and therefore working with wrong answers.

Luther could have snatched at the straw of "gallows repentance." He could have accepted the teaching that even if pure contrition were never attained the Church would accept attrition and seek to upgrade it in the penitent. He could have accepted Biel's "hangman's doctrine," a desperate theology that taught certainty of salvation if Bernard's method were pursued to the death.[1] Luther questioned whether God ever meant to put a human soul on the rack like this. He thought there must be something wrong somewhere, and believed it must be with himself. All this theological theorizing broke down before the acid test of experience. Luther knew nothing of this transition from the fear of hell and judgment to the rapturous enjoyment of the love of God alleged by his contemporaries in their mystic flights. He, too, had scaled the heights by the ladder of mysticism, but when he reached the summit he found there was nothing there. He struggled on doggedly, surrendering nothing.

Luther began to invest his hope in the Bible. At this time he seems not to have realized that he was tormented by problems posed not by the Bible, but by scholastic theorizing and contemporary pastoral practice. Working on these presuppositions he saw only a demanding God, angered and estranged by his sin, not the forgiving God, the gracious and merciful Father. His lop-sided view of God coloured his concept of Christ. When he finally broke through, Luther was to synthesize these twin concepts of the wrath of God and the love of God into the unity of the gospel.[2]

There was in Luther's character a saving strain of conservatism. He would let no dogma go, not even a scholastic opinion, simply on the grounds that it seemed contrary to his own experience. He clung

---

[1] *Cf.* G. S. M. Walker, *The Growing Storm* (London, 1961), pp. 134 ff.; G. H. W. Parker, *The Morning Star* (Exeter, 1965), pp. 136, 162.

[2] See pp. 28–9.

tenaciously to his authorities and blamed himself, not them, for his plight. It was this that made Luther a prototype not of liberal Protestantism but of Catholicism reformed. It was his indomitable conservatism and his loyalty to his authorities that eventually caused him to break through. It was the authority of the Bible that invalidated the uncritical, usurped authority of church tradition. He simply held on – in faith.

He was drawn to the Augustinian view of predestination at this time, a view which seemed best able to explain his own experiences as well as the Biblical teaching. Current theology made sometimes the divine and at other times the human element the determining factor in man's salvation. Augustine's bold and clear view was that any reason for the divine choice was a mystery beyond accessibility to the human mind, though nevertheless it was a choice made in perfect justice. It was a choice not only to grace but to eternal glory. It depends not on human acceptance but on the eternal decree of God, and is therefore infallible without violating man's free will. This doctrine is in itself one of great comfort, but not when admixed with human presuppositions or qualifications. Luther was in a state of spiritual torture at this hour. Even hell is not too strong a word for it: and so he described it. Luther was long unable to free his mind from the spiritual axiom that a good God is bound to accept a good man doing all he can. It began to emerge that this was taught neither by the Bible nor by the main fathers. God became for him a being incomprehensible in His nature, unknowable in His work. He grew fatalist, almost determinist. He felt impotent to change the fate decreed for him from all eternity, and what was worse, unable ever to know for certain whether he belonged to the elect or to the reprobate.

In this state of mind God was for Luther all dread. He felt he stood accused of God and accused of life, certain he could escape neither. This was a particularly painful experience hemming him in, for he was a man of exuberant spirit, joyous wit and high-hearted happiness. At times, wild hatred of God welled up in his heart. Yet he knew perfectly well that as a creature he had no claims on the Creator, and none against Him. He knew and never doubted that God existed and was holy. He knew that he himself was a sinner. He knew that in no circumstances could he, as he was, make himself acceptable to God as *He* was. So long as he analysed the relationship on such moral principles he could never arrive at an answer, for the relationship is one that is not and cannot be reducible to moral relationships.

Staupitz had helped Luther at this time in the summer of 1511 at Wittenberg to work out his own salvation. Staupitz truly believed that no man could ever will, know, or do good by his own reason or strength. Staupitz believed that if a man belonged to the elect and was to receive continually the heavenly medicine of grace poured in through the sacraments, then increasingly the ability to will, to know and to do the good is granted him. Not that a man could be certain of his election, rather the sacramental signs were appointed to nourish that hope and to drive out despair. He argued that a faithful and diligent use of the sacraments would overcome anxiety in the matter of predestination. Further the good Staupitz was deeply read in the Bible. He very sensibly steered Luther clear of his torments by arguing that he could never seek peace with God on his own good resolutions (which he would never have the strength to carry out), nor on his own good deeds (which could never satisfy the law of God), but in His forgiving mercy only. Staupitz sought to turn Luther's mind away from the system of penance to the reality of repentance, to the depth of an inward change and conversion. He taught Luther to see God in the perspective of Christ whom God sent not as a condemning judge but as a living and redeeming Saviour. Yet, when all this is said of Staupitz, his theology contained a great deal more than this, and this extra served to becloud the former. He did rely on the merits of Christ, but he also relied on the merits of the Virgin and of the saints. He spoke of reliance on Christ only, yet he had always believed, and believed till the end, that a man had to earn, or at least do something to deserve, his salvation. He never really understood the mighty battle raging in the soul of Luther. He comforted Luther by his kindliness and godliness, he helped Luther by dwelling on the Cross. But Luther knew he had to part from Staupitz as he had to part from mediaeval tradition and practice. Luther turned to the Bible. As a theologian Luther from now on began to go it alone.

It was his work on the Bible that saved him. He was working on his lectures on the Psalms in the summer of 1513 when the familiar phrase of Psalm 31, "deliver me in thy righteousness" began to disturb him. He had always thought of the righteousness of God in its obvious meaning, the righteousness of the holy and pure God. But it was this very idea that gave him all his disquiet. Wherein lay the "deliverance"? Surely, if a righteous God met unrighteous man there could be but the annihilating reaction of God. He thought the lying lips of the Psalmist must mean those who establish their own righteousness and therefore made God a liar. The lie was in thinking it possible to achieve righteousness, that is without Christ. He pored over the Bible to find if that, after all, was its real intent. Romans 1:17 excited him: "Therein is the righteousness of God revealed from faith to faith: as it is written, 'The just shall live by faith.'" He still read this through scholastic spectacles, and thought righteousness now meant a righteousness still more qualitatively righteous in view of Christ's revelation. And then, as he wrestled, he realized that Paul was arguing another case, namely, that a man was not justified in God's sight by his own works, or merits, or righteousness, but by faith in Christ: in other words, by accepting Christ's work and not setting about one's own; that salvation was no longer a case of man and his works but God and His work; that it was no longer a matter of man's righteousness but God's righteousness. This righteousness was not the punitive righteousness of God, valid as this is in the old aeon of Adam, but rather the forgiving righteousness of God which sets a man in a new relationship by setting him in the aeon of Christ, not because of his works and merits, but simply because God in His righteousness and mercy elected so to save man. He saw this righteousness of God as the righteousness which reached out for a soul which, if left to its own devices, would be utterly lost. It was not a case of God being far off in His righteousness and of man straining to reach Him; it was a case of man being far from God and of God moving all the way to him, not because of man's goodness but because of God's goodness. "When I realized this I felt myself absolutely born again. The gates of paradise had been flung open and I had entered. There and then the whole of scripture took on another look to me. . . ."[1] Luther sensed that the Church had grown further and further away from the gospel and had lost it in favour of a powerful secular institution and a humanized philosophy-cum-theology. He made nothing new yet made everything new. He simply restored the gospel. He innovated nothing but renovated everything.

Luther never made the error of trying to impose on the Church some idealized external primitive pattern of life from the early Church, as the Independents and Radicals were to do later. Nor did he seek to force upon the Church a literal application of rigorous primitive biblical doctrine and church order as the Puritans were to do. He rediscovered and revived the primitive evangelical faith in God as first expressed in its original purity, and, in the world and place in which God had set him, accepted all that God had done in fifteen hundred years, seeking in that changed and changing world to re-establish the true gospel and to demolish the false ideas devised by man. Unlike many other religious leaders he never claimed for his message the dubious support of petty miracles, visions, dreams, prophecies. Luther's soul was saved by an unyielding and un-compromising faith in the Bible. He wanted every man to look again with fresh eyes at God's work for man as recorded in the Bible: to see the facts for himself in the light of plain common sense; to verify for himself whether this did not accord with his own experience, and to see whether this did not give a meaning to his own life in that raw secular condition in which and out of which God had called him. Such self-authenticating theology at once set the layman on his own theological feet and rang the death knell for the sacrificing priest mediating his mysterious powers. The call was for an educated ministry who could teach, preach and minister the treasures of Christ's gospel. Luther's experience was a matter of sensitized

[1] Introduction to Latin edition of *Works* (Wittenberg, 1545). WA. 54, 186.

insight, and not a matter of special visions or ecstasies. Religion was not to Luther some special rare quality that a poet or musician might have. Every point and every proof Luther made were open for all men to test and prove by the evidence of history, sound scholarship or their own experience. Luther compelled men to look again and look for themselves. In so doing most men were convinced or converted. All that Luther sought to do was to point to Christ and His gospel.

Luther's protest should not be seen simply as a particular protest at a particular moment, but rather as a protest in which Christian men in varying degrees are perpetually involved. The fifteen centuries that had corroded the gospel provide but a long example of what goes on in every breast in every age and in every church. Our own sloth and sin, the conservatism common to every institution with the desire to preserve and perpetuate itself, the corroding claims of the world, all serve to force the Church to preach herself rather than to preach the gospel. This is what Luther saw. He saw, too, the gospel transmuted into a judaistic system of works and merits. He saw the glorious kingdom of all believers submerged under a quasi-spiritual tyranny. He saw the glorious liberating Christian theology utterly lost in a human scholasticism which was but idolatrous intellectualism. He saw countless souls lost and dying for want of the saving theology the Church had been established to convey. What Luther saw in a striking form at the beginning of the sixteenth century is what is always happening everywhere, *mutatis mutandis*. The Church will always be tempted to preach herself rather than the gospel, under the condemnation of which she always stands, yet above which she is always tempted to set herself. The wisdom of the world is always ready to persuade the Christian of its wisdom, and the Christian message is slowly transformed into human reasonableness, its Gospel into a law and an ethic. The Church will ever be more wordly than spiritual, and will ever seek her glorification and flee her crucifixion. Men who understand the Reformation know that the Church always needs reformation. The *ecclesia reformata* is always the *ecclesia reformanda*.

The years 1513–17 were formative for Luther, for during these four precious years he had a very light teaching load of about two lectures a week (though he had other duties and preached three sermons a week) and he used every second of them to strengthen his theology. When Luther showed his hand in the matter of the indulgences scandal of 1517 it was no zealous youth who had got excited but a massive man wearing a great weight of learning, with a known unimpeachable life and of granite integrity, who could hold his peace before God and man no longer.

It is of great interest to note how, during these four years, though he used all the current scholastic terms to express his thought, all these terms began to carry the evangelical insights that were later to play such a determinative role in the Reformation. We find him using the scholastic term for original sin and related terms, but his interpretation of sin was the Augustinian self-centredness which destroyed the capacity freely to will and to do good. Luther saw the will as enslaved to the self, which bondage compelled a man to save his own self and his own interests and blinded him to the claim of God and the claims of his brother. When such a man thought of religion he thought in terms of his own decency and goodness (acceptable enough *per se*) and thought to draw nearer to God by means of these. This was subtle idolatry, and was in fact, from an evangelical point of view, unbelief in Christ. To Luther unbelief was the basic sin.

All the terms he touched are seen to be in a living process of change. With the scholastics he talked of grace, but whereas they seemed to regard it as some kind of ecclesiastical proprietary medicine administered by priests through the sacraments, he regarded it in the New Testament way, as a personal living experience of Christ by which divine encounter a new creation was born. He showed that in Christ God had graciously shown His hand. Just as across the pages of the New Testament men were re-born when they heard of a God who had so loved the world as to give Christ for us men and for our salvation, so again when this gracious gospel was proclaimed God called faith out from the heart of a hearer and freely reconstituted him in Christ. It was not, and never was, a matter of works, but solely a matter of free grace. When a man saw that he was nothing and had nothing in himself but sin, repentance was kindled and faith in the grace of God grew. It takes little seeing to become aware of the difference between grace in the New Testament as taught by Luther, and the contemporary doctrine of "infused grace," poured into a man like milk into a jug. To this was closely related Luther's teaching on faith. Faith was no longer a human achievement or effort, a putting of works and efforts into a bargain with God, but the gift of God (Eph. 2:8). It is the opening of the eyes which the preaching of the gospel effects. It is the birth of a new hope, the confirmation of the promise, the creation of a sober trust in God, and a glad buoyancy in the soul. It is a justification by faith apart from any works or merits. No other formula has so succinctly summed up the gospel.

It was a spiritual engagement of this kind that compelled the centrality of the Word of God in his thinking. It was the preaching of the Word rather than the administration of the sacraments which Luther saw as the chief mission of the Church, for the Word not only gives the Church her commission, but preserves the Church and governs it. The sacraments to Luther were the "visible word." When the Word was preached Christ was active and operative, and it was Christ's active presence that effected new believing men, not so much a passage of scripture itself. A man was only what he heard from God.

This kind of theology gave him a fresh biblical conception of the Church. The Church was the company of believers, the elect who had heard the Word. This was an invisible and spiritual community known only to God and not in any place coterminous with the visible Church. Yet in spite of this bold advanced Augustinian theology, Luther never preached against the Church. The Church was God's; the gates of hell would not prevail against it; it had played, and was yet to play, a further part in the providential ordering of God. Despite its wrong theology, despite its worldliness and corruption, the Church had never been forsaken by God nor had ever lost the gospel utterly. Luther was a great churchman. He had no sympathy with the sectarians who sought to found a new, holy, gathered Church, nor with the enthusiasts who appealed to their own special revelations, despising the Church, the gospel, even Christ in favour of the spirit. To Luther the sacraments were derivative of the gospel; the Church had been founded in Abraham at the beginning of time: neither Church nor sacraments are normally dispensable but are part of God's saving plan.

The thoughtful reader will have discerned in the lectures and disputations of these four quiet years[1] Luther wrestling with all the basic themes of his later Reformation theology. Luther's break-through was not the burst of a single intense experience but rather the growth of years that one day proved overwhelming. Already he is discussing good works, which he sees as the natural outcome of faith. A man cannot do good before he is made good. Luther dismissed outright the idea of certain prescribed ecclesiastical works in the doing of which a man earned merit and favour. The only good works were those commanded by God in the station of life in which a believing man found himself. Scholasticism taught that only the negative prohibitions of God were always binding: the positive commands were binding only on the occasion of their being given. The scholastics had done exactly as the Jews had done before them and cluttered up the commands with a vast casuistic system, at the top of which was the standard expected of monks and spirituals. Luther knew that a sin of omission was as serious as a sin of commission, and that the law of God was good and unchangeable. The law clearly commanded that we love God with all our heart and that we do good to all men, friend or foe, good or evil. The qualifications, modifications and dispensations of scholasticism had no authority, indeed no meaning. The distinction between the commandments which are binding and evangelical counsels which are not, between mortal sin and venial sin, were meaningless and harmful distinctions. It was bogus to speak of a "higher" morality for monks,

[1] See pp. 25 ff.

priests, nuns and spirituals, and of a "lower" standard for married folk and
people "in the world." It is not the occupation that is determinative for
morality but the nature of the relationship with God. When that relationship is right a man behaves towards his brother rightly: the watchwords
were – faith towards God and love towards neighbour. If a man is justified
by faith he fulfils that in the calling given him by God, whether he is
peasant or prince, potter or priest. It is in this natural, normal sphere only,
not in some holy devised performance, useless alike to God and man, that
a man is called to obey all the commandments and counsels. And when he
fails, he starts again as a forgiven man. This theology was the germ of his
emphasis on the priesthood of all believers.

There is in his lectures, too, at this period a remarkable freedom in
criticizing his great contemporaries. Luther did not confine himself to his
texts but showed an awareness of world events and world personalities,
and a freedom to criticize that is surprising, to say the least. He expressed
sharp criticism of the corrupt Roman curia and the institution of the
Church, the Pope for his war-mongering, Duke George for his bigoted
papalism, Archbishop Albrecht[1] for his worldliness, even his own beloved
Prince Frederick the Wise[2] for his absurd interest in relics. Lazy artisans,
cunning merchants, drunken peasants, ignorant astrologers all came in for
their share of astringent criticism, as also did the theologians and the
hawkers in indulgences, with all their stress on popular superstition. All
this criticism, however, was accepted as normal and natural in a theologian
and was consonant with good catholicism. It is important to remind ourselves that when Luther received the call to the Chair of Biblical Theology
it constituted a call to the pulpit. We have no sermon as it was delivered or
written by Luther, but the preservation of over 2,000 of them in shorthand
by his hearers is sufficient testimony to his achievement on that divine
square yard in Wittenberg.

By about 1515 there is evidence that Wittenberg students had noticed
the theology of his lectures and the difference when he preached. Yet in
1514 when a Benedictine, Lange by name, compiled a *Who's Who* of
German university life, Professor Luther of Wittenberg does not receive
a mention. Nevertheless, Saxony knew what it had got; so did the students. Spalatin, the court chaplain, and a friend and contemporary of
Luther at the University of Erfurt, supported Luther in his efforts to
abolish scholasticism and restore the study of the Bible and of Augustine
to the curriculum. The humanists, too, were beginning to take note of
this new scholar, but this uneven partnership between humanist scholarship

---

[1] See pp. 41 ff., 72.
[2] Saxony was at this time divided into Ducal and Electoral Saxony, the former being ruled
by Duke George (1500–39), the latter by the Elector Frederick the Wise (1486–1525), both of
the house of Wettin.

and evangelical theology was destined to collapse by 1524 when Erasmus finally stood on the side against Luther. Luther knew as early as 1516[1] how sharp the distinction between Erasmus and himself was, when in correspondence with Spalatin he showed that Erasmus was unaware of the nature of Pauline theology as well as of Augustinian theology. Luther was shocked at Erasmus's preference for Jerome to Augustine. He admired him as a linguist but found him unhelpful in the knowledge of Christ: to fail here was to fail everywhere.

Further, Luther had some success with his academic colleagues. In 1516[2] he had engaged in a disputation attacking Occamist theology on the ability of man by dint of his own will and reason to fulfil the commandments of God. After some resistance he finally won over his colleagues, and with this victory began the fall of scholastic theology at Wittenberg and the rise of the Bible and Augustine.

University regulations demanded he should lecture on the Psalms and the Epistles, and he threw himself into this task. After his monastic duties were performed he worked into the long hours of the night in that silent cloister till even the mice grew impatient at his intrusion into their hitherto unrestrained nocturnal liberties.

He had a simple method of teaching. He instructed his printer to print the text on a quarto page with wide margins and widely spaced lines. He "glossed" the text by means of linguistic and grammatical comment, by relating it to other texts, by reference to other authorities and by any aid at hand to explain the plain literal meaning of the text. These notes he dictated to the students. In addition, he offered a scholion which is continuous comment on the text covering its theological and spiritual meaning. In the case of the Psalms we have Luther's own text, but in some cases we are dependent on a student's notes. His lectures at this time covered: *Genesis*, October, 1512–July, 1513; *Psalms*, August, 1513–October, 1515; *Romans*, Easter, 1515–September, 1516; *Galatians*, October, 1516–March, 1517; *Hebrews*, March, 1517–March, 1518, and *Psalms* again, April, 1518–March, 1521.

A brief glance at the content of those early lectures shows the intrinsic worth of Luther's work at this time, but shows, too, flashes of the powerful evangelical theology which was soon to reach every corner of Christendom. A little attention to the Luther of these early days rescues the reader from the all too prevalent view of the one-sided Paulinism of Luther pursuing his own bull-headed iconoclastic way. The truth of the matter is that he mined his theology from the Psalms and from Genesis in those early days and first discovered what the Bible was about and where it was all leading. It was this that made him aware of the theological error and

---

[1] WA. Br. I, 27.    [2] See p. 63 f.

the moral obliquity of the Church of his day. From here he studied Church History, and saw the decline of theology over the last 1,000 years and its petrification under the long, slow deposit of human thought and ideas. It was only then that he found that in fact this is exactly what the protest of the whole of Scripture had always been, and how Paul succinctly summarized the whole in his mighty epistles.

Roman Catholic scholars (Denifle, Grisar, Moreau are examples) have taken the view that at this time Luther in his lectures on the Psalms stands on solid catholic doctrine and practice. They accept his criticism of the scandals and seem prepared to accept his theology at this time, yet an evangelical reader reads the matter very differently. If modern Roman Catholic scholars are prepared to describe Luther's teaching at this time as acceptable catholic doctrine, then they are not in agreement with the Curia of the early sixteenth century which resisted it. Modern Roman Catholic scholars accept Luther's criticism of the abuses of the Church of his day. Luther speaks of the abysmal spirituality of the Church. "Throughout the entire Church the spirit is enfeebled and sins abound." No peace or harmony exist in the Church "because of dissensions, sensual pleasures and all the other wretched extravagances with which the ablest and the best in the Church are involved." He speaks of the "heavy odour of scandals everywhere," of "foul corruption," of churchmen who preach not a true theology but a human scheme of things, of the clergy "filled with carnal vice, fornicators and adulterers" and producing from the pulpit opinions and fables, questions and nonsense.[1] He disapproves of the monks' concern with their own petty righteousness rather than with true penitence, "men who do not understand that it is in Christ alone they will be justified, and not by their own works"; men "who seek to be saved without Christ." He argues against those "who want their sins remitted by God on account of their own works and merits, and to be justified by their own works."[2] Such people he dismisses as Jews, as heretics. He argues that the true humility is not the crawling humility of the monk, but the Biblical humility of a man who before God has no righteousness of his own and attends only on the mercy of God. True humility is derivative of faith.

Further, the themes of these lectures resolve themselves continually into the major theme of Christ and faith: "the prophet [i.e. the psalmist] is speaking from beginning to end of the person of Christ."[3] "The Psalm (41) refers to the advent of Christ, and the revelation of the gospel and his grace. . . . The human race receives Christ not according to its righteousness but according to the mercy of God. . . . He is given not as a result of the work I have done in getting ready for Him, but as a result of the

---

[1] On Psalm 38. WA. 3, 216. 24 ff.    [2] On Psalm 32. WA. 3, 172. 30 ff.
[3] On Psalm 89. WA. 4, 43. 7 ff.

covenant of God."[1] Or later in Psalm 119: "All things are given us not according to our merits but issuing from His promises."[2]

The theme of the Righteousness of God constantly breaks out, and Luther refers to Paul to expound the meaning of the psalms. He speaks of the "alien work" of God shown in judgment, so that his "proper work" in the redemption of man in Christ may be shown.[3] It was this conception of Christ's work that impelled a man to faith, the sole ground of our justification. "The righteous" of the psalms are those "justified by faith in Christ."[4] "The shadow of the law has been removed. Out of the womb of the law has Christ been born, that means faith in Christ and His gospel. For the shadow and darkness of the law were holding this same faith hidden within."[5] The "truth" of the Psalmist is "the new evangelical teaching."[6] So strong is this evangelical theology in his interpretation of the Psalms that he frequently describes the Psalms as "a word from Christ," and frequently refers to Christ as speaking and as prophesying in the Psalms. "Every word of the Bible peals forth the name of Christ."[7]

To read these lecture-notes on the Psalms is to see Luther wrestling with all the great theological ideas that were later to be the essentials of his evangelical theology. Justification of the sinner is ever before his mind. "The fact that God shows mercy towards me in itself justifies me. His mercy is my justification."[8] The idea of a catastrophic intellectual lightning streak of spiritual illumination is always attractive, for it dramatizes in one moment what was a long spiritual and intellectual struggle over the years, and provides the student with a catchword. Luther's pilgrimage was not unlike Paul's, and just as Paul's theology of Gospel and Law needs the whole Pauline corpus to explain it and a knowledge of Judaism to show its sharpness, similarly Luther's theology needs to be seen as a long intellectual and spiritual journey out of mediaeval scholastic theology into evangelical New Testament theology and a vast corpus of writing to sustain it. Luther's theology is a line rather than a point, a process rather than an explosion. Luther was experiencing a deep inward spiritual agony which only a religious man can understand. He was in a state of seething rebellion against God who had set him a task he could never accomplish. Luther wrestled with this kind of blasphemy, with predestination, wrath and the mighty Biblical themes, and not with the non-existent problems of many holy men who tend to make their own problems instead of wrestling with those which life sets a man. Not for him the ways of a St. Benedict rolling his naked body in thorns to quell lust, nor of a St. Cuthbert standing all night in that ghastly cold water off the Northumberland coast to subjugate the flesh. Luther roundly remarked, "Women

[1] WA. 4, 329. 19 ff.            [2] WA. 4, 343. 34.            [3] On Psalm 77. WA. 3, 546.
[4] On Psalm 140. WA. 4, 438. 3.            [5] On Psalm 43. 3. WA. 3, 243. 22–244. 2.
[6] Gloss on Psalm 42 (43). WA. 3, 244. 2 f.            [7] WA. 56, 414. 17 f.            [8] WA. 3, 43. 9.

never bothered me. I was always concerned with the really knotty problems." In his search for assurance in the matter of predestination he cried, "Nobody could help me." Yet Staupitz sought to reassure him by liberating him from the scholastic ideas of grace being given in proportion to works and merit and showing that the first moment of repentance brought the wholeness of God's salvation.

There began to grow in Luther's mind the idea of a God working on his behalf in Christ, whose work he saw as a kindling of faith in the heart. With this there grew a deeper sense of his own sin, what scholastics called an accusation of self. Luther described this as humility, in contradistinction to the monkish idea of humility, a humility which grew into a passive waiting on God. This merged into a trust in the Lord and a jettisoning of all and every kind of self-justification face to face with the bounty and mercy of God. This dimension of faith began to play the master rôle of subsuming all other theological ideas into it during those four silent years.

Similarly, the Gospel-Law tension began to take shape as the two ways God handled man. "The law is the word of Moses *to* us, the gospel on the other hand is the Word of God *in* us. The former abides without, it speaks in figures and visible forecasts of things to happen. On the other hand, the latter comes to us within, and speaks of inward and spiritual things and of truth. The one speaks in us, the other speaks to us."[1] He relates this to human experience, and shows how the righteous suffer and the ungodly prosper, and explains this "contrariwise" handling of God of his people on the basis of the Cross: that God kills to make alive, He destroys the natural man that the spiritual man may be born. This is another way of expressing the relation of the Law to the Gospel. Our salvation is not by our own efforts, as Israel's was not by her arms. A Christian man is cast down in the eyes of the world but in his conscience and spirit he knows he is accepted and glorified. Quoting the Psalms, the Apostles and Augustine he writes: "It is the alien work of God, that He might work His proper work. He destroys in order to save, he condemns according to the flesh, that he might glorify the spirit."[2] Unlike many theologians who were to seize on this law-gospel tension, Luther never depreciated either the force or attractiveness of the law.[3]

Luther's full theology of the Wrath was to come later, but he held a clear Augustinian doctrine of the Wrath at this time. He was anxious to distinguish the Wrath from any and every human idea of God being angry as a man is angry. More nearly it meant the Pauline sense of God simply "giving a man up" to the wrath of his own creatureliness, when God turned his back on a soul and allowed it "to go it alone." To Luther the consuming anger of God was when God showed none at all, when a soul simply was left pursuing its own interests. "God does not afflict a

[1] On Psalm 85. WA. 4, 9. 28.    [2] On Psalm 44. WA. 3, 224-6.    [3] See WA. 3, 71. 1.

man by drawing near to him to do so, but by withdrawing from him and abandoning him to the natural world."[1] He carefully safeguarded the merciful nature of wrath. Luther saw a "hidden God" behind the Wrath. He heard under and above the "No!" of God, as he once expressed it, the deep secret "Yes" that God speaks to a man. "The wrath of His mercy is one thing, the wrath of His severity is another ... the former only the saints experience, the latter, only the non-believers."[2] Into the wound the good hand of Christ pours wine to cleanse and oil to heal and soothe. The Wrath should never be explained away in psychological terms but understood in biblical categories as Luther did. Nor must it be dismissed as an appendage to Luther's thought. This biblical category remained a constituent part of Luther's theology throughout his life. He never looked at it but as a constituent part of the Old and New Testaments, confirmed and borne out in his own experience, the only sphere in which theology may be proved true or false.

[1] On Psalm 2. WA. 3, 35. 20.          [2] See Rupp, *Righteousness of God*, pp. 155-7.

CHAPTER II

# LUTHER TEACHES EVANGELICAL THEOLOGY

## 1. Lectures on the Epistle to the Romans 1515–16

IT IS UNIVERSALLY ASSUMED THAT THE EPISTLE TO THE ROMANS WAS THE textbook of the Reformation, but it is almost impossible to believe that Luther's great commentary on it lay unpublished, unknown and unread for four hundred years. It was not until 1908 that the manuscript was found and hurriedly published, and not until 1938 that the text received a critical edition.[1]

Luther at once argues the doctrine of justification by faith as the door to the gospel, showing the profound error of contemporary scholasticism in seeking its own righteousness and in not seeing that the gospel destroys any and all righteousness of our own and creates a wholly other righteousness, a righteousness not of our own making but of God's making.

> The sum total of this epistle is this: It is to tear down, and pull out, and to destroy all wisdom and righteousness as man understands them. This is to happen whatever regard they may have in men's judgment, even in our own convictions, and no matter with what deep sincerity they are done. After that its purpose is to set and establish, even to magnify sin, no matter if we used to think that it was not there and could not be there. . . . God does not want to save us by our own personal and private righteousness and wisdom. He wants to save us by a righteousness and wisdom apart from, and other than, this: a righteousness which does not come from ourselves and is not brought to birth by ourselves. It is a righteousness which comes into us from somewhere else. It is not a righteousness which finds its origins on earth. It is a righteousness which comes from heaven. Therefore we must be instructed in this external and alien righteousness in every possible kind of way. That is why the first task is to pull out our own personal and petty righteousness. . . . As men without anything we must wait for the pure mercy of God, for Him to reckon us as righteous and wise.[2]

He who believes in the gospel must become weak and foolish in the eyes of men so that he may become strong and wise in the power and wisdom of God.[3]

In the doctrines of men it is the righteousness of men that is revealed and taught. In other words, they teach who is righteous, in what way he is righteous, and how he may become righteous, in his own judgment and that of his fellows. But the righteousness of God is revealed only in the gospel: in other

---

[1] WA. 56. The scholia are translated by Wilhelm Pauck in L.C.C. (1961).
[2] WA. 56, 157–9.      [3] WA. 56, 169. 29 ff.

words, who is righteous, how he is righteous, and how he may become righteous, in the sight of God. This comes about by faith alone: by that faith with which the Word of God is believed. . . . The righteousness of God is the cause of salvation. . . . According to Aristotle, righteousness follows from and arises from doing good works. But according to God righteousness precedes good works and works spring from righteousness.[1]

It is not because a man is righteous that he is therefore reputed to be righteous by God, but because he is reputed to be righteous by God he is therefore righteous . . . apart from Christ no one is righteous, and no one keeps the Law.[2]

As long as I recognize that I cannot be righteous before God. . . . I then begin to ask for righteousness from Him. . . . The only thing that resists this idea of justification is the pride of the human heart, proud through unbelief. . . . It does not believe because it does not regard the Word of God as true. It does not regard it as true because it regards its own understanding as true and the Word of God runs counter to that.[3]

Luther carefully safeguarded this teaching against two misunderstandings. First he guarded against the confusion of faith with mere assent:

This is what the Apostle means when he says a man is justified by faith. It is to believe that this is spoken not only about the elect, but rather about yourself, and it is to be appropriated by you yourself: that Christ died for your sins and gave satisfaction for them.[4]

Second, he warned against the insidiousness of making faith into one's own work, something we put into the bargain, a state of mind we achieve. Luther argues that it is not a matter of faith but faith in Christ.

People who presume on this faith believe that they can have access to God without Christ, as if it were sufficient for them to have believed. They believe that they can have access to God by faith alone. They will not go through Christ but alongside Christ. It is as if they no longer had any need of Christ after having received the grace of justification. . . . These people who approach God through faith and not through faith in Christ actually move further from God. . . . Wherefore both must happen together: through faith, through Christ.[5]

Through and beyond, over and above these motives can be heard the deep diapason of sin, but not seen as a man stands in his own eyes or in the opinion of his fellows, but as God sees him.

Every saint is a sinner and prays for his sins. In this way the justified man is in the first place his own accuser. . . . It is the wonderful and most tender mercy

[1] WA. 56, 169–72.    [2] WA. 56, 22. 5 ff.    [3] WA. 56, 226. 7.    [4] WA. 56, 370. 11 ff.
[5] WA. 56, 298–9.

of God that regards us at one and the same time as sinners yet non-sinners.[1]

The error lies in believing that this disease can be cured by means of our own works. All experience proves that whatever good work we effect there remains in it that concupiscence toward evil, and nobody is free from it, not even an infant a day old.[2]

Closely related to this teaching on sin was the clear analysis that the law had no answer to this plight of man and that the gospel was God's original and final purpose. The law as a method of salvation was the preference of the natural man, who if he was going to be saved at all knew how to do it himself. It was a Pelagian "do-it-yourself" salvation or perhaps an Occamist perversion of it. Luther turned heavily to Augustine at this point.

This is a Pelagian opinion. . . . They think that if they have the will to do good, quite infallibly they will receive the grace of God infused.[3]

Luther argued that it was a profound error to think a man draws near to God by dint of much striving. It is not a case of man striving to attain God but the other way round: a merciful God who came and who comes all the way. As the Jews failed to understand the gospel, so do the scholastics and for the same reason: the Jews stuck to the law, the scholastics make the gospel into a new law. But Luther never disparaged the law, nor the deeds of the law: he criticized them only in that the natural man sets up the law against the gospel. He taught that it was only the evangelical man who saw the pure spirituality of the law and its abiding claim on all men, Jews and Christians alike.

The young students at Wittenberg must have been thrilled when they noted these words of their professor:

In the new law all things are free and nothing is necessary for those who believe in Christ. Love is all that is necessary. . . . It does not belong to the new law to set aside some days for fasting but not others, as was done by the law of Moses. Nor does it belong to the new law to select certain kinds of foods and distinguish them from others, such as meat, eggs, etc., as again the law of Moses does (Lev. 11:4 ff., Deut. 14:7 ff.). Nor does it belong to the new law to designate some days as holy and others not. Nor does it belong to the new law to build this or that kind of church, or adorn them in a particular way or sing in them in a particular way. Nor that we must have organs, altar decorations, chalices, images and all other things we now find in places of worship. It is not even necessary to have priests and religious men wearing tonsures and going about in distinctive clothes, as they did in the old law. All these things are but shadows and tokens of reality. Indeed we have outgrown them. Every day is a holiday, every kind of food is permitted, every place is holy, every time is fasting time, every garment permitted. Everything is a matter of free choice, as long as moderation is kept in these things, and love, and the rest of the virtues the Apostle teaches.[1]

The Pauline emphasis on man's incapacity to fulfil the law, on his inability to do the good he knows, convinced Luther of the bondage of the will and the necessity of a gospel rather than a law.

The natural man seeks himself and his own interests in all things. He never seeks God. . . . This is scriptural teaching, which describes a man as curved in upon himself to such an extent that he refers back to himself not only physical but also spiritual goods, and seeks his own interest in everything. This curvature is a natural crookedness: it is a natural defect and a natural evil.[2]

The natural man enjoys everything with reference to himself and uses everybody else for the same purpose, even God Himself: in everything he seeks himself and his own interests.[3]

This saving truth about man is revealed only by God. To Luther the important point is not what man thinks about God but what God thinks of him. In fact the only path to grace is the broken will, which alone can accept God in Christ. This beggarly humility is very close to what Luther means by faith. It is a movement, a direction, an activity, a working out rather than a static condition. It moves from faith to faith.

A man's existence is always in a state of Non-Being, Becoming, and Being. . . . He is always in sin, in justification, in righteousness. Always a sinner, always penitent, always justified.[4]

Closely related to his emphasis on the bondage of the will is Luther's emphasis on predestination, a theme he was later to develop in his controversy with Erasmus.[5] He pushed aside the scholastic handling of this doctrine and returned to Paul. To Luther, as with Paul, the doctrine is always held within the framework of the graciousness and mercy of God as shown in the Gospel. The doctrine was one of assurance and comfort, the perfect salvation from any and every kind of human or religious righteousness. It preserved the theocentricity of the Gospel whilst destroying the anthropocentricity of religion.

To the elect and those who have the spirit, predestination is the sweetest of all doctrines. But to the worldly-wise it is the bitterest and hardest of all. . . . The reason God saves in this way is to show that He saves not by our merits but by election pure and simple, and by His unchanging will. . . . We are saved by His unchanging love. . . . Where then is our righteousness? Where our good works? Where is our free will?[6]

It is surprising how at this early stage Martin the monk could have such

[1] WA. 56, 493. 15 ff.     [2] WA. 56, 355. 13 ff.     [3] WA. 56, 361. 13 ff.     [4] WA. 56, 422. 15.
     [5] See pp. 78–81.          [6] WA. 56, 381. 18 ff.

strong feelings about the follies and ignorances of the monks, about the corrupt practices of the Church, the squabbles between princes and pre-lates, above all the sordid materialism of the clergy.[1] "The monks are really Pelagians. They trust in themselves and their own works, and consequently undermine both the Church and faith."[2] He saw the whole Church undermined by Pelagianism. The spiritual rulers "are guilty of pride and wantonness ... who foster extravagance, greed, luxury and strife."[3] "My distress compels me to speak out, and my office demands that I do."[4] He refers to the scandalous collapse of the papal curia (of Julius II): "It is the most revolting cesspool of filth of every kind, luxury, pomp, avarice, ambition and sacrilege."[5]

The war-mongering of Julius II and the confusion of secular authority and spiritual authority in the minds of the papists caused Luther much concern. Luther made the same distinction as Paul. The State was a servant of God whose authority and responsibility had to do with secular affairs only, the maintenance of law and order and the protection of society from the criminal within and the enemy without. The Church's task was to preach and teach, and care for its people as Christ did. When Luther is blamed for putting the Church in the hands of the princes, whatever we feel about later history, certainly Luther expected from his "godly prince" (the great Reformation ideal) a man who respected the distinction between the rôles of Church and State, who would seek to play his part as well as to protect the Church so as to allow her to play hers.

It is self-evident that in these early years Luther had found a firm theology. He knew what it was to be justified by faith in God's wondrous love and mercy shown in Christ. He knew what it was to be overwhelmed by this mercy, to be predestined to dwell in it. He knew what it was for the righteous God to accept him in his unrighteousness. He had a glorious and fearsome awareness of the great and terrible God, and would not have God treated "as the cobbler does his leather." He had seen through the Pelagianism of his day, and felt that the Church had lost the gospel and was not aware that she had lost anything.

## 2. Lectures on Galatians and Hebrews

The same themes recur in his lectures on the Epistle to the Galatians (October, 1516–March, 1517). With his lectures on the Epistle to the Hebrews (March, 1517–March, 1518) the same evangelical themes are plainly discernible, but the different nature of the epistle drew forth other emphases.[6] Most striking is his teaching on the person and the work of

[1] WA. 56, 417. 27 ff.    [2] WA. 56, 501. 17 ff.    [3] WA. 56, 478. 30 ff.
[4] WA. 56, 480. 3 f.    [5] WA. 56, 480. 10 ff.
[6] Translated by James Atkinson, *Luther's Early Theological Works*, L.C.C. Vol. XVI (London, 1962), pp. 19 ff.

Christ: it is Luther's Christology that set him apart from his contemporaries, and it is his Christology that is the dynamic of his theology. At the outset on the text *When he had purged our sins* (1:3) he writes, "... it was He who purged our sins and it is not we ourselves." "He makes short work of all notions of righteousness and every idea of penances which the natural man holds."[1] He argues that Christ's righteousness is that of God and wholly other than man's righteousness which he interprets as a kind of self-love, even at its best. In fact sin seems to be interpreted in this epistle as a love of self which prevents a man loving Christ and therefore from believing in Him.

Another striking feature of these lectures is his summing up of the argument of the epistle at the beginning of every chapter, an argument which he analyses essentially as law versus gospel, an idea never far from his mind in the text proper:

> In the law many works are enjoined and all external, but in the gospel there is one only, an internal work, namely faith. For that reason the works of the law make a righteousness which is external, but faith makes a righteousness hidden with God. (On Heb. 2:3.)[2]

> God promotes and perfects his proper work (the gospel) by means of his alien work (the law). (On Heb. 2:14.)[3]

> The sins, righteousnesses, sacrifices, holy things, promises, doctrines and priests of the old law all pertained to the flesh. They did not sanctify as far as the conscience was concerned but only as far as the body is concerned. But now, under the dispensation of the Gospel, our sins, righteousnesses, sacrifices, holy things, promises, doctrines and our priest are all operative in the sphere of the spirit, and sanctify in matters of conscience. (On Heb. 9:8.)[4]

Never far away is his primacy of the Word of God.

> A man may be said to depart from the living God when he departs from His Word which is living and makes all things live. In fact, the Word is God Himself. Therefore, when men depart from the Word, they die. He who does not believe is dead. (On Heb. 3:12.)[5]

Faith, of course, receives its expected emphasis, but there is an interesting passage where Luther discusses faith in relation to the sacraments:

> If they believe and trust that at the sacraments they will receive grace, then this faith alone makes them pure and worthy. Such a faith does not put its trust in these works just described, but puts its trust in the most pure, most holy, most reliable word of Christ, "Come unto me, all who labour and are heavy laden, and I will refresh you" (Matt. 11:28). (On Heb. 5:1.)[6]

---

[1] *Op. cit.*, pp. 33 f.
[2] *Op. cit.*, p. 45 (WA. 57), 113. 21 f.).
[3] *Op. cit.*, p. 59 (WA. 57), 128. 13 f.).
[4] *Op. cit.*, p. 166 (WA. 57, 205. 19–23).
[5] *Op. cit.*, p. 81 (WA. 57, 148. 12–15).
[6] *Op. cit.*, p. 107 (WA. 57, 171. 1–7).

Luther insists that faith be regarded not as ours nor of our making, but solely of God's mercy and grace, never of our earning or meriting it.

> . . . it was of His mercy alone, His grace, and the love He has towards us.[1]

It was as he was commenting on Chapter 11 on the faith of Moses, who on account of his faith was rejected and had to flee for his life, that Professor Luther had to break off and go to the chapter of the Augustinians at Heidelberg (April, 1518).[2] The students watched their professor as he folded his notes and filled the door with that broad back. They watched him set out for Heidelberg. They wondered if they would ever see him again as he disappeared down the road – in faith.

### 3. Pastor and Disputant

But Luther was more than a university professor. In May, 1512, when he had succeeded Staupitz, he had assumed the responsibilities of sub-prior and director of studies. Three years later he had been appointed district vicar of eleven important monasteries, "prior eleven times over" as he described it, a work which he carried out with pastoral care and thoroughness. There are letters extant of this period. Luther is found pleading the cause of a monk who ran away; another letter shows his directions on receiving guests; another refuses to take a particular man; yet another reduces a prior to the ranks for failing to keep his monks in order. One of his loveliest is where he is advising the prior of Neustadt on the true peace in a Christian heart:

> . . . You are seeking the peace the world gives not the peace Christ gives. Are you not aware, my dear father, how God is so wonderful among His people that He has set His peace where there is no peace, that is in the midst of our trials? . . . It is not therefore the man whom nobody bothers who has peace. This kind of peace is the peace of the world. It is that man whom everybody disturbs and everything harasses and yet who joyfully and quietly endures all. You are saying with Israel, "Peace! Peace!" but there is no peace. Say rather with Christ, "Cross! Cross!" and there is no cross. For the cross ceases to be a cross the moment you say gladly, "Blessed Cross! of all the trees that are in the wood there is none such as thee. . . ." Seek this peace and you will find peace. Seek for nothing else than to take on trials with joy. . . . You will not find this peace by seeking and choosing what you yourself feel and judge to be the path of peace. (23 June, 1516.)[3]

It was about this time Luther began to feel that he should show his hand by giving some public academic declaration of his theological views. He drew up ninety-seven theses in a *Disputation against Scholastic Theology*.[4]

---

[1] *Op. cit.*, 154. cf. 174, 210, 222.     [2] See pp. 45 ff.     [3] WA. Br. 17.
[4] See L.C.C., Vol. XVI, pp. 269 ff., where the whole disputation is translated and annotated.

The modern reader would find this document negative and polemical and not communicative at all, but that should not hide its importance. Nor should we forget that a public disputation was the normal method a scholar adopted when he sought to discuss any of those theological problems open for discussion. Luther first argued the bondage of the will:

> The will is not free to pursue in the light of its own reason any good thing that has been made clear to it (Thesis 10).

Luther was arguing against the Scotist theology of his day which had veered away from the evangelical theology of Augustine under Occam and Scotus, even from Aquinas, in favour of granting man some responsibility of choice. Luther argued that the natural man cannot love God, but loves only himself and his own interests:

> For the natural man to love God above all else is a figment. It is but a chimera (Thesis 18).
> The natural man cannot want God to be God. Rather he wants himself to be God, and not God to be God (Thesis 17).

He argued against the Pelagianism of scholasticism. Goodness could rise only from the converted man. Every man was depraved, he argued, redeemable only by God's grace and His eternal election. He argued heavily against Aristotle's disastrous influence on ethics and doctrine, which served only to humanize and intellectualize Christian teaching. He also made a fine plea for men to realize that to love God meant to hate self. Clear too, is Luther's fine distinction between gospel and law. He nailed his colours to the mast, namely, the gospel truth of justification in Christ only, applied to the whole realm of man's life, to the realm of his knowing as well as the realm of his doing, an emphasis which has meant a great deal to Karl Barth. His colleagues seemed to have paid scant attention to these rumblings of the earthquake.

Some weeks later he compiled another ninety-five theses on the scandal of Indulgences, inviting his colleagues to the disputation. None of them in fact went along to the disputation, but if the academics seemingly disregarded them, the world sat up and took notice. Thousands of copies poured from the presses with the results every schoolboy knows. Luther had written far more searching documents than these and said far more disturbing things than these, but oddly enough, for it is by no means a remarkable document, it was this document that caught the imagination of Europe and set Luther on the world stage.

# CHAPTER III

# THE PAPACY REPUDIATES EVANGELICAL THEOLOGY

## 1. *The Ninety-Five Theses 1517*[1]

HISTORY BOOKS DRAMATIZE THE NAILING UP OF THE NINETY-FIVE Theses,[2] and as a consequence generalized simplifications of the scandal are too readily accepted. It is well worth explaining and clarifying the issues.

Mediaeval man had little fear of the eternal punishment of hell but a deep concern for the purgings of purgatory. He believed that if he died forgiven by a priest he would most certainly reach heaven, but he also believed that before he reached that portal where only the purified may enter, he would have to purge every sin he had ever committed, known or unknown. These punishments were called temporal, though most of them would have to be purged after death in purgatory. The point is they are not eternal and therefore come to a temporal end. Purgatory was very real to mediaeval man, and was always regarded with the utmost seriousness.

Indulgences had had an honourable history. Luther's concern, in the first instance, was essentially a pastoral concern with their deterioration and abuse. In the early Church lapse into sin involved separation from the Christian community. Readmission was gained by public confession before the congregation, and true repentance proven by the avowal to make amends by offering certain "satisfactions" – a word found as early as Tertullian (d. 220) and Cyprian (d. 258). These satisfactions took the form of making some kind of restitution for a hurt done, or where not practicable, some discipline of fasting, almsgiving, the manumission of a slave, depending on the nature of the offence and the status of the penitent. They were invariably imposed by the community and always in the interests of the sinner, to realize his salvation. They were relaxed or mitigated by the congregation in the light of a penitent's obvious change of heart or even change of circumstances. These relaxations were called indulgences, and were at this stage wholly honourable and sound pastoral practice.

In the course of time this communal repentance took the form of private confession to the priest as father of the congregation. To arrive at

---

[1] See Walther Köhler, *Dokumente zum Ablassstreit von 1517* (Tübingen, 1934).
[2] Text in WA. I, 233–8. See also Luther's Works, American Edition, Vol. 31, pp. 17 ff.

a common and fair practice, books were compiled to guide priests, indicating appropriate penances for sins committed according to the status of the offender. This came to be called "doing penance." From about the seventh century there developed a system whereby penance could be commuted for money (as a kind of spiritual fine), or by a pilgrimage to a shrine where payment was made to the funds. It was even possible for a servant to do this for his master.

In the year 1030 several French bishops conceived the idea of offering partial remission of penance in the case of a particularly outstanding spiritual service. The idea caught the imagination of the people. By 1063 the Pope particularized this feeling in the instance of engaging on a war against the Turk. By 1187 under Gregory VIII the idea was transmuted into an arrangement whereby anybody unable to go to the wars would pay for the cost of a soldier in his place.

When the Crusades were over, an alternative and equivalent was to be found in the Jubilee Indulgence of 1300 promulgated by Boniface VIII. This indulgence promised a full remission of penance to all who visited the graves of the Apostles in Rome once a day for fifteen days during the jubilee year, a privilege available only once in a century. In 1343 Clement VI reduced the period to once in fifty years and in 1389 Urban VI made it thirty-three, in remembrance of the thirty-three years of our Lord's life. Paul II reduced this to twenty-five years in 1470, owing to the brevity of human life. By 1490 this same indulgence could be purchased simply for money, and by the same time, the Pope had assumed the power of granting plenary absolutions at any time for any purpose. It was a far cry from the days of the primitive community seeking the salvation of the sinner to the pontiff literally selling spiritualities. Penance was now treated as a "commercial commodity" (*merx sancta*) and the administration called "the holy trade" (*sacrum negotium*).

One great drawback of these "sacred commodities" was that they were not available at all times. To meet this the popes, as early as 1294, had begun the issue of confessional letters which a soul of gentle birth might purchase and keep in reserve. These letters enabled the holder to procure complete absolution from any priest of the penitent's own choice once during life, and once "in the article of death as often as it shall threaten." Trade was rather brisk. Such letters were eventually extended to anybody who could pay enough. They were even parcelled out as favours.

The idea of indulgences attracted people, and many began to ask if these favours could not be made available for the dead now in purgatory. The popes at first held out against this but in 1476 Sixtus IV established an indulgence for the dead.[1] These indulgences enjoyed instantaneous success. Further inducements were associated with the purchase of this kind of

[1] B. J. Kidd, *Documents Illustrative of the Continental Reformation* (1911), No. 3.

indulgence. The purchaser was usually granted a confessional letter in the first instance. Second, he received a "butter letter" (allowing him to eat butter, eggs, cheese and milk on fast days). Third, he was granted the right to substitute good works in the place of vows, and fourth, the right to avail himself of the Treasury of Merits.[1] Finally, for a further charge, he was given permission to use illegally acquired goods whose owner could not be found.

There is more to the matter than the depraved wordliness of a secularized and institutionalized church. Three quasi-theological factors complicated the issue: the Treasury of Merits, the elevation of penance to the dignity of a sacrament, and the distinction between *attritio* and *contritio*.

The idea of a treasury of merits was first formulated in the thirteenth century by Alexander of Hales (or Hugo de St. Cher). It was conceived as a vast reserve of merits built up by the saints and Christ, treasured in heaven and available to the Pope to draw on by dispensation. A plenary indulgence was reckoned as transferring enough merit to deliver the recipient from all penalties in purgatory consequent on his sin on earth. It will be readily seen how this served to increase the vague ill-defined "supernatural" power of the Pope. The certificates had all the proper theological qualifications written into them (even Tetzel's had), but in practice these were ignored. Bluntly, they served as a mitigation of penalties in return for money.

When penance developed into a sacrament the natural sequence of sorrow, confession, satisfaction and absolution fell into the perverse sequence of sorrow, confession, absolution and then satisfaction. It was taught that guilt and the eternal pains of hell were avoided by absolution, though the sinner had always to face in full the temporal punishment due to his sin. This temporal punishment was endured on earth in this life and/or after death in purgatory. It was at this point that indulgences spoke, for they claimed to reduce or even remove them.

The distinction that had grown up between attrition and contrition had also a part to play. Down to the thirteenth century it had always been recognized that contrition (the godly sorrow prompted by love) was the one and only thing God demanded of a penitent believer. During the thirteenth century theologians began to accept attrition (a lesser sorrow motivated by fear of the consequences) in place of contrition, on the grounds that the lesser sentiment was capable of being upgraded by the ministrations of the Church. In practice attrition became all that was necessary, and though the best theologians never accepted this, it became common practice and was certainly taught by Scotus and practised by all the pardon sellers. At this lowest level the scheme of salvation came to be attrition, confession, indulgence. The theologians taught that indulgences

[1] See *infra*.

had nothing to do with the guilt of sin or eternal punishment, both of which were handled properly in the doctrine of penance, and that they related only to temporal punishments. Nevertheless, in common practice these distinctions were not drawn: even intelligent laymen such as Dante did not make them. Moreover, the time spans of purgatory were astronomical: the relics of the Castle Church on whose door Luther nailed his Theses were reputed to earn 1,902,202 years, 270 days.[1]

Luther had early shown a pastoral concern with the problem. We have sermons of 1515, 1516 and early 1517 on indulgences. Luther saw that a belief in indulgences resulted in blunting the reality of divine forgiveness in Christ. Luther opposed the false sense of security (*securitas de salute futura*) generated by indulgences by the evangelical certainty of salvation (*certitudo salutis*). This, of course, was responsible preaching of the kind expected of a doctor of the Church. The issue came to a head when Prince Albrecht (though only twenty-three and not of canonical age to hold ecclesiastical preferment), who already held the two sees of Halberstadt and Magdeburg, sought to procure the Archbishopric of Mainz and with that the Primacy of all Germany. To avail himself of this he was compelled by the Pope to pay 10,000 ducats for permission to hold an unlawful number of benefices and in addition 21,000 ducats for the pallium. This figure of course was beyond the means of Albrecht. The Pope met this situation by granting an indulgence on deferred payments over the next eight years, provided one half went to the banking family of the Fuggers who had paid the bill, and one half to the Pope himself towards the rebuilding of St. Peter's at Rome. Four privileges were attached to this indulgence. First, subscribers would receive a plenary and perfect remission of all sins; second, they would be given a letter allowing the penitent to choose his own confessor; third, they would participate in the merits of the saints; fourth, they would relieve the poor suffering souls in purgatory.[2]

Albrecht made appropriate safeguards by demanding auricular confession from a contrite heart, but in the hands of the unscrupulous Tetzel, the Dominican monk to whom the sales were committed, such niceties were brushed aside. In his sermons concomitant on the sales he made heart-rendering appeals in the name of the dead languishing in the agonies of purgatory.

> The dead cry, Pity us! Pity us! We are in dire torment from which you can redeem us for a pittance. . . . Will you let us lie here in flames? Will you delay our promised glory?

[1] I have seen reported recently in the Press of an indulgence of 32,310 years, 10 days and 6 hours granted in Mexico with respect to one single mass (Official Catalogue); see Hillerbrand, *The Reformation in its own words*, pp. 47 ff.

[2] Kidd, No. 6.

He went on to assure his listeners that

> As soon as the coin in the coffer rings,
> The soul from purgatory springs!

He went on

> Will you not then for a mere quarter of a florin receive these letters of indulgence through which you are able to lead a divine and immortal soul into the fatherland of paradise?[1]

So Tetzel preached, and so they believed.

Though Tetzel was forbidden to preach in the Wittenberg area by order of Luther's prince, he was near enough to be dangerous. "I'll knock a hole in his drum" was Luther's ominous remark. He drew up his theses for purposes of normal academic disputation, though he elected to argue them himself. He sent printed copies to his own bishop and archbishop. Luther sensed the gravity of his challenge, yet it should be seen essentially as a criticism on pastoral grounds of the Mainz instruction and of the Mainz indulgence preacher, done in the normal way by a professor of theology. The document[2] was posted on the church door, the normal university notice board, on the eve of All Saints' Day, October 31, 1517, the day the university attended divine service in its official capacity and the day the crowds flocked to venerate the famous relics the good Frederick had amassed.

The first reading of the Theses is disappointing. Strangely uncoordinated, remote and academic, they strike the reader as anything but the stuff of revolution. They were written for academic discussion, and not for public dissemination. Theses 1–4 discuss the nature of true penance as taught in the New Testament. Repentance was not "doing penance" nor had it anything to do with this indulgence business. It was an inward and continuous process of dying to self and rising again to righteousness, a whole turning of the entire man to God. In fact, indulgences worked against this godly discipline, for their motive was to evade punishment. Sorrow and suffering are the divine means to break the sinning heart and to turn it to God, penitent and cleansed.

In Theses 5–7 Luther argues that the Church can remit only the penalties she has imposed: guilt, only God can remove. In Theses 8–29 Luther denies the Pope's power over the dead in purgatory, and in 30–40 argues that the living always have true forgiveness and do not need any indulgence. In Theses 41–52 he contrasts true works of mercy with the rebuilding of St. Peter's. In Theses 53–80 he compares the preaching of

---

[1] Kidd, Nos. 7–10. Translation in Hillerbrand, pp. 41–3.
[2] WA. 1, 233–8.

indulgences with the preaching of the gospel. The closing theses develop the essentials of the gospel and close with four theses on the Theology of the Cross.

Though no academic colleagues came to the disputation within four weeks they had spread all over Germany and Switzerland. Luther grumbled about this, saying that if people had wanted a book on indulgences he would have written something much better than academic theses. He therefore wrote to his bishop an explanation of these theses (February, 1518),[1] but went much further than his theses. Luther actually demanded a reformation, not as the concern of the Pope and cardinals but rather as the total concern of the entire Christian world. He discussed the authority of the Pope which he accepted in external matters of order but not in internal matters of faith. He spoke of true historic catholicism compared with the unfounded claims of Rome. He carefully distinguished between the teaching of the New Testament on forgiveness and the priestly practice of the time. An indulgence could remit only such penances as the Church had imposed, and common practice served to obscure the truth. The Treasury of Merits he dismissed: the Church's only treasure was Christ. Luther was writing to show how contemporary Christianity had tragically defected from New Testament Christianity, and believed that, if the Church admitted this, the necessary reformation would follow. Luther was now showing considerable scholarship and ability, as well as a grasp of canon law, church history and the Fathers.

Luther's archbishop reported him to Rome, and inhibited "this rash monk of Wittenberg," as he described him. Rome ordered Luther's vicar general to "soothe and quieten down the man" and commanded Staupitz to secure a formal recantation. The affair was considered a monkish quarrel.

Staupitz characteristically sought to protect Luther and preserve peace, but the Dominicans were aroused and had a vociferous champion in Tetzel. In January, 1518, the Dominicans held a chapter at Frankfurt-on-Oder where Tetzel debated one hundred and six theses against Luther's ninety-five, theses written for him by Professor Conrad Wimpina of Frankfurt. They reported Luther to Rome for heresy, a clever move, for at that time the influential theologian at Rome was the Dominican Cardinal Cajetan, a scholar Luther was to face at Augsburg later that year. Tetzel had the audacity to send a bookseller to Wittenberg with hundreds of copies of his hundred and six theses, but the agent was ragged by the students in the market place and his theses burned.

The wide circulation of Luther's theses, the fierce counter-thrust of the Dominicans, the various reactions in Germany, the anxieties of Luther's close friends, all served to convince Luther that it was imperative for him to declare his position more precisely. He wrote a courteous letter to his

[1] *Resolutions.* WA. 1. 525.

archbishop[1] explaining that his views were not personal assertions but academic points for further discussion, all based on Scripture, Canon Law and the Fathers. The archbishop made no reply. After some weeks Luther made a move that was to characterize all his acts. He wrote directly to the common man in German on the subject of indulgences and grace, to initiate him into the meaning of these academic issues.[2] This tract penetrated where an academic disputation would never reach. In it Luther went further than he did in the Theses, in disapproving of indulgences or even of any talk about purgatory.

> Let none of you procure tickets of indulgence. Leave that to the lazy Christians dozing half asleep. You go right ahead without them. . . . I know nothing about souls being dragged out of purgatory by an indulgence. I do not believe it, in spite of all the new-fangled doctors who say so. But you cannot prove it to them. The Church has not even made up its mind in the matter yet.[3]

He concludes:

> On these points I have no doubt at all. They are not properly based on Scripture. Therefore, have no doubt about them, regardless of what the scholastic doctors say. . . . I pay no attention to that sort of drivel, for nobody engages on it except a few dunderheads who have never even smelt a Bible nor read any Christian teachers.[4]

If the Latin tract did not stir the bishop the German tract electrified him. He sent a senior abbot scurrying across the country with a personal message to Luther to withhold this document from the people. By now the Elector Frederick was concerned, as was Spalatin. They were positively shaken when Luther calmly announced that he was going to walk halfway across Germany to Heidelberg to give an account of his theology to his fellow Augustinian monks.

Before he set out, or possibly on his immediate return (it is not clear), Luther sent to the printer his "explanations and proofs."[5] In these he develops his theses, courteously and cautiously, but courageously. Throughout there is the deep diapason of reform. He contrasts the early Church with the contemporary Church:

> The Church was not then what it is now, a hydra, a monster of many heads, an underworld of simony, lust, pomp, murder and all the rest of their abomination (on Thesis 72).[6]

He declares in Thesis 89:

[1] WA. Br. I, 110–11, 31 October, 1517.          [2] WA. I, 243.
[3] WA. I, 246. 11–24.                            [4] WA. I, 246. 27 ff.
[5] WA. I. 525–628. Trans. *Luther's Works*, American edition, Vol. 31, pp. 83 ff.
[6] American edition, Vol. 31, pp. 237 f.

The Church needs a reformation: a reformation viewed not as the work of one Pontiff nor of many cardinals, both of which the recent council demonstrated. It is the work of all Christendom. Better still, the work of God alone. Only he knows the hour of this reformation.[1]

Aristotle's influence on scholasticism, the corrupt practices into which the Church had allowed herself to fall, all came up for discussion, but shining more clearly is Luther's developing Theology of the Cross, as he called it.

From this you can now see how, ever since scholastic theology began (play-boy theology, that is what it is, for that is the Greek etymology of the word scholastic), the Theology of the Cross has been emptied of its meaning, and all else has been turned upside down. The theologian of the Cross (that is one who speaks of the hidden and unfathomable God) teaches that punishments, crosses and death are the most precious treasure of all and the most sacred of relics, relics which the Lord Himself, the Creator of this theology, has consecrated and blessed. This he did not only by the touch of His most holy flesh but by the embrace of His most holy divine will. These are the relics He has left here to be kissed, sought after and embraced. Indeed, happy and blessed is the man who is considered by God worthy to receive these treasures of the relics of Christ! Nay rather, who understands that they are given him! For to whom are they not offered?[2]

Large indeed was the hole knocked in Tetzel's drum! The whole scheme collapsed. Tetzel was very severely handled by his superiors. He did not even dare to appear on the streets. The whole affair killed him, and next year, as Tetzel lay dying in Leipzig, ignored, rejected, broken and ill, it was Luther alone[3] who wrote to comfort him, assuring him that he was not the cause of the scandal but its victim (July, 1519).

## 2. The Heidelberg Disputation, April 26, 1518[4]

The triennial chapter of the Augustinians fell at this time and Luther set off from Wittenberg on April 11, 1518. In addition to routine business Luther was to give an account of his stewardship as district vicar as well as lead a disputation. Staupitz asked him to be non-controversial, consequently Luther's Heidelberg theses say nothing about indulgences but handle the themes of original sin, sin, grace, free will and faith.

He set off on foot. But the long journey of nearly 400 miles taxed his strength. All along the way he was treated with deference and respect, and when he was received by the Bishop of Würzburg, that saintly man showed great concern to get the exhausted Luther a lift in a cart. He later

[1] American edition, Vol. 31, p. 250.
[2] WA. 1, 613. 21 ff.; American edition, Vol. 31, pp. 225 f.
[3] During the Leipzig disputation (see pp. 53 ff.).
[4] WA. 1, 353–74; American edition, Vol. 31, pp. 35 ff.

wrote to the Elector Frederick, "Do not let them take away from you this devout Doctor Martin"; for he had learned of plots to dispose of Luther.

It was an ideal audience for Luther and an opportune moment. A theologian before theologians, a man of God to men of God, controversy behind him and expectancy before him, Martin rose to the occasion. With a full ten years' hard study behind him he firmly handled the great theological themes which had been exercising his mind and his soul: the righteousness of God and the righteousness of man; sin, grace, free-will, faith, justification; above all, that stirring Theology of the Cross which he had begun to make his own. Forty theses in all: twenty-eight directed against scholastic theology and developed at some length, twelve more directed against Aristotelian scholastic philosophy.[1]

He begins at once with the vital distinction between the gospel and the law:

> The law of God, that most wholesome doctrine of life, cannot bring a man to righteousness. It is a hindrance rather than a help. . . . How much less can man's works . . . They may look splendid but in all probability they are sins . . . The Lord humbles us and terrifies us with the law and the prospect of our sins so that we . . . seem to be nothing but fools and wicked men. The truth of the matter is that this is just what we are . . . This sense of our own deformity arises in us when God flays us or when we accuse ourselves. This is what Isaiah calls the strange work of God that he may effect His proper work (Isa. 28:21), in other words, to humble us in our own eyes and make us despair of ourselves, so that in His mercy he may exalt us and make us men of hope.[2]

He warns his hearers of the danger of making the gospel a more difficult law:

> It is the sweetest mercy of God that it is not imaginary sinners He saves but real sinners. He upholds us in our sins, and accepts our work and our life, worthy as these are of total rejection. He goes on doing this until He perfects and consummates us . . . We escape His condemnation because of His mercy and not because of our own righteousness. . . . Grace is given to heal the sick not to decorate spiritual heroes.[3]

Next he turns to man's knowledge of God, making the fruitful distinction that justification by faith is valid not only for the sphere of man's acts but within the sphere of his knowledge of God. Men cannot draw nearer to God and know more about him by means of their works and efforts. God is to be known in humility, shame and suffering, in a Theology of the Cross rather than a Theology of Glory. This is one of Luther's great insights. He argues:

[1] For a complete translation with commentary see L.C.C., Vol. XVI, pp. 274–307.
[2] L.C.C., Vol. XVI, pp. 276–84 (conflated).
[3] L.C.C., Vol. XVI, pp. 301–5.

In Christ crucified is the true theology and the knowledge of God. "No man comes to the Father except through me." "I am the door." As long as a man does not know Christ, he does not know God as hidden in sufferings. Such a man prefers works to sufferings, and glory to a cross.[1]

When a man has had that revealed to him he then knows what true righteousness is:

> The righteousness of God is not acquired by acts frequently repeated, as Aristotle taught, but is imparted by faith. . . . The good man knows that the good works he is doing are the outcome of this faith, and are not his own at all but God's. . . . Christ is his wisdom, his righteousness, his all. . . . The justified man is surely the work and instrument of Christ.[2]

The sheer simplicity, the unanswerable common sense of all this shines all the brighter when compared with contemporary scholasticism and mysticism. He rejects their technical vocabulary and turns away from their highly intellectualized mysticism to a stark revelational, incarnational theology. Christ is the author and object of faith: no more, but no less.

The disputation must be reckoned a great success. The Augustinians were with him to a man, save for a few elderly monks who remained aloof, though courteous. The nobility gave him unqualified praise. Bucer, then a young monk, later to play a prominent part in the Reformation, wrote:

> Although our chief men contradicted him with all their might, their wiles were not able to make him move one inch from his propositions. His sweetness in answering is remarkable, his patience in listening is incomparable, in his explanations you would recognize the acumen of a Paul not a Scotus; his answers, so brief, so wise, and drawn from the Holy Scriptures, easily made all his hearers his admirers. On the next day I had a familiar and friendly conference with the man alone and a supper rich with doctrine rather than with dainties. He agrees with Erasmus in all things, but with this difference in his favour, that what Erasmus only insinuates he teaches openly and freely. . . . He has brought it about that at Wittenberg the ordinary textbooks have all been abolished, while the Greeks and Jerome, Augustine and Paul are publicly taught.[3]

Luther's own comment on the disputation was, "I went on foot and came back on a cart."

On his return to Wittenberg, Staupitz strongly advised Luther to write to the Pope assuring him of his orthodoxy and loyalty, a document heavily worked over by a courtier's pen. Tetzel had the audacity to publish fifty theses against Luther, and although Luther gave him a verbal flogging in very expressive Saxon German, he felt he was wasting his shot on such

---

[1] L.C.C., Vol. XVI, p. 291.
[2] L.C.C., Vol. XVI, pp. 293 f.
[3] P. Smith, *Luther's Correspondence* (Philadelphia, 1915), p. 82.

pompous fatheads. When Tetzel sheltered behind "thousands of uncon-
demned teachers" Luther reminded him that his thousands were in fact
three; all the rest copied them. Luther's fire was directed at the destruction
of the authority of scripture which such theology implied:

> I will not put up with it one minute when he handles scripture, our comfort,
> like a sow going at a sack of oats. . . . Every day they invent new kinds of keys.
> What for? To empty all our purses and coffers and then unlock hell and lock
> up heaven. These men are worse than the Turks at the gate, for they are on
> the inside. . . . What they are shouting about has nothing to do with faith
> and salvation, human need and God's law. . . . When these men abuse the
> scriptures and give the lie to the word of God, they call it improving and
> honouring Christianity. But if anybody else teaches that it is not necessary
> to buy indulgences, and that it is not right to skin poor folk of their money,
> that is dishonouring the church and sacrament and vexing Christian folk.[1]

The Dominicans moved. They gave Tetzel a doctor's degree (May, 1518)
and pressed charges against Luther at Rome using Prierias, the theological
adviser to the pope. He dismissed Luther's theses as false and proceeded to
attack Luther with remarkably coarse invective, a sure sign of his basic
uncertainty. This document of charges was sent to Cardinal Cajetan in
Augsburg with a citation commanding Luther to appear in Rome within
sixty days, both of which documents Cajetan forwarded to Wittenberg.
Luther promptly made a simple request: to be tried in Germany and not
Italy, in circumstances and before people beyond suspicion. To the
scurrilous invective of Prierias Luther answered with magisterial command.
He showed that his theology was acceptable catholic theology, and that the
matters he was bringing up for disputation (e.g. indulgences) were subjects that as a doctor of theology he was entitled to dispute as well as to
express an opinion on them. True, his fresh theology was clearly visible
all the time, for example, his view of the church as an organism in Christ
rather than an organization under the Pope. He thought both Pope and
council might err; only the Scriptures were infallible. It was traditional
catholicism to uphold the authority of the Bible and the Fathers, but Rome
disregarded both.

Luther was doing more than writing, he was preaching. The Wittenbergers heard a remarkable sermon on the first Sunday back from
Heidelberg on "The Ban," when Luther said that he "put a bell round the
cat's neck." The ban was originally a disciplinary matter but had now
deteriorated into an instrument of blatant extortion. A man unable to pay
his church dues was banned. On a second offence his whole family was
banned. This meant exclusion from all sacraments and ministrations, even
church attendance, as well as from social and commercial dealings. If a
man died when under the ban his body was thrown into the ground like a

---

[1] WA. I, 391. 16-393. 24.

dead cat. If the ban still failed to bring in the dues, the ban was made to cover all friends and associates, even the entire village. This was iniquitous. At harvest-time the clergy grew very active on this score and these bans "were flying round by the hundred like bats," to use Luther's phrase. Luther argued that all this was a grave spiritual scandal, for the uneducated laity largely believed that to die under the ban consigned one to hell for ever. But Luther had other ideas about who was on this road. The ban, he argued, could only effect an exclusion from outward fellowship, never from the inward fellowship of true believers. No man can put a man in this fellowship, only God: no man can exclude another from this fellowship, only sin. Let the corpse be thrown into the river or torn out of its grave, for him who has died faithful there waits only the crown of life. The folk were electrified. They demanded a public disputation. Luther desisted from this only at the urgent request of his bishop.

Secret agents of the Dominicans were sitting under the pulpit that morning and a twisted, garbled version was hurried to Cajetan at Augsburg. Cajetan sent it on to Rome with a covering letter to the effect that Brother Martin be banned not only for his views on indulgences but for his sermon on the ban. Rome reacted quickly. Luther was declared a notorious heretic, Cajetan was ordered to arrest him, and the Elector asked to "hand over the son of perdition to Cajetan." Further, Volta, the Vicar General of the Augustinian Eremites, was asked to send an Augustinian monk with orders to seize Martin, bind him hand and foot, and cast him into prison. Two days later Volta summoned Martin to Rome.

A political affair stayed the hand of Rome. The ageing Emperor, Maximilian, wanted his young nephew Charles to succeed him. Charles was the last man the Pope wanted as Emperor. Consequently we find that suddenly Frederick, being one of the electors, is courted by Rome. Frederick was sympathetic to the request of his brilliant young professor to be heard on German soil before competent judges beyond any suspicion, and at this juncture astutely wrote to Maximilian defending this request. As a consequence Cajetan received orders authorizing him to command Luther to appear before him for a "fatherly handling not a judicial." Rumour ran high. People were apprehensive. Luther's colleagues at Wittenberg wrote to the papal diplomat von Miltitz defending Luther's orthodoxy, piety and erudition, even though he may have "disputed somewhat too freely" (a nice touch!).

The situation was dangerous for Luther. He remembered John Huss had gone to Constance with the Emperor's safe conduct and yet was burned. "I clearly saw my grave ready, and kept saying to myself, 'What a disgrace for my dear parents!'" Albert the count of Luther's birthplace, begged Luther never to leave Wittenberg, for he had heard in very high

c

places that Luther was to be ambushed with a view to strangling him or drowning him. Luther was well aware of his danger. He wrote to his friend Link at Nürnberg, that the more people threatened, the more he would throw his trust in Christ:

> There is only one thing left, my weak and broken body. If they take that away, they will make me the poorer by an hour of life, perhaps two. My soul they cannot take. . . . I am perfectly well aware that from the beginning of the world the word of Christ has been of such a kind that whoever wants to carry it into the world must necessarily, like the Apostles, renounce everything and expect death at any and every hour. If it were not so, it would not be the word of Christ. By death it was bought, by deaths spread abroad, by deaths preserved. It must also take many more deaths to keep it, or even restore it. Christ is a bloody partnership for us.[1]

### 3. Before Cardinal Cajetan, Augsburg, October, 1518[2]

The human mind dramatizes the historically significant. It remembers with intensity the nailing up of the Ninety-Five Theses in Wittenberg in 1517, and never forgets the stand at Worms in 1521 against Church and State. Yet there is another equally dramatic stand in between, at Augsburg in 1518, before the papal legate, the mighty Dominican, Cardinal Cajetan. When Luther posted up his academic theses of 1517 he stood on the *terra firma* of his own university, among his colleagues and in his anonymity sheltered from the outside world. At Worms he had the immense support almost of the whole world of scholarship as well as the loyalty of half Germany. Different was the case when as a beggarly monk he was summoned to appear before Cajetan at Augsburg in October, 1518. He knew that to the Church and the Empire he was now a marked man and could only guess what was in store for him. Lay friends feared he would never return. Staupitz begged him to escape to academic retreat before it was too late. "Christ rules in Augsburg even in the midst of His enemies" was the terse reply. As he walked through his beloved Thuringian forests in a lovely German autumn he feared he would never see them again, never smell that coniferous fragrance of his boyhood. At Heidelberg German advisers warned him that all that the Italians wanted to do was burn him at the stake, to which he replied with wry humour, "If my cause is lost, the shame is God's." This is indeed a text for Luther's life. It was not his cause but God's and God is faithful to those He calls.

The journey over-taxed him physically and his nerves wrecked his digestion. He collapsed three miles from the city and had to be carried in on a cart. In the city his friend Link lent him a cassock to improve his

[1] WA. Br. 1, 83 (July 10, 1518).
[2] W. A. 2, 6–26; American edition, 31, 255. See also Schwiebert, *Luther and his Times*, pp. 338–57.

appearance. But Luther's case rested on God, not garb. To his astonishment the laymen would not let him appear before Cajetan until written guarantees for his safety were provided by the Emperor's officials then in residence in Augsburg.

A certain Italian court diplomat, Serralonga by name, wise in the ways of the world, called on Luther to advise him to withdraw while he could and not to argue with Cajetan. Luther, wise in the ways of God, cheerfully rejoined that of course he would withdraw if Cajetan showed his case groundless. A little worsted on the first round the gentleman confidentially hoped that Luther was not toying with the illusion that his good prince Frederick would go to war for Luther's cause. "Of course not," was the immediate answer. "Ah," said the worldly counsellor, "where will you be in that event?" "Where I am now," said Luther: "with God."

Cajetan was a theologian in his own right. He was a good Aquinas scholar, devoid of that sickening corruption characteristic of his contemporary ecclesiastics, a man who, in the judgment of his contemporaries, might well have been pope. Being an intelligent man he read some of Professor Luther's works before they met, though he never for a moment intended to discuss theology with "the shabby little friar," as he called him, only to command him to recant.

Cajetan announced that all the Pope required of Luther was three things: to repent of his errors and recant, never to teach them again, and never to disturb the peace of the Church. Luther replied he had not come all the way from Wittenberg to do what he could quite easily have done at home, and asked him what his errors were. With some discernment Cajetan instanced two points, on the Treasury of Merits, and on faith justifying a man, not sacraments. The first put Luther in the position of rebutting a papal decretal, the second is one of those points which require a yes–no kind of answer. Luther responded that Scripture took precedence to papal decretals; Cajetan retorted that the Pope was above councils and Scripture. Luther bluntly denied this. Cajetan broke out into a violent temper, for he had come to command Luther, not to argue with him. The next day Luther maintained that he had not been refuted and could not recant: he was not aware that anything in his teaching was contrary to the Bible, the fathers, decretals or reason. On the third day Luther argued that the Treasury of Merits was Christ and not the notion of a papal chest, and that the decretal quoted by the Cardinal was ambiguous and obscure, contrary to the clear testimonies of Scripture. He also outlined his theology on justification by faith. Though he loved the Church, it was the Babylon of the papists he opposed. High words were spoken between the two men. Haughtily Cajetan said, "Luther will have to come to market with fresher eggs." Spalatin grew afraid. Staupitz was terrified and unsuccessfully combed the town begging money to get Luther to safety in Paris. In great apprehension and fear he released Martin from his vow of obedience and fled the city, saying the fine words, "Remember you have begun this affair in the name of our Lord Jesus Christ."

Luther now stood dangerously alone. He received no answer from Cajetan. Luther wrote to the Pope for a hearing elsewhere than in Rome. He reminded His Holiness that since the Pope himself had narrowly escaped assassination a year earlier there, Rome would hardly be a safe place for him. He again wrote to Cajetan taking formal leave of absence. Again no reply. The air was thick with rumours. Some well-wisher took the initiative. He hauled Luther out of bed, and leaving him no time to put on boots or breeches stole through a side gate at dead of night, set him on a horse and galloped him off all night long to safety. When the horse collapsed some forty miles on, Luther, now in a state of exhaustion, lay down in the stable beside it, unable to crawl to bed, too stiff to move, too tired to care.

Once safely home he wrote a careful account of his interviews with Cajetan,[1] a move characteristic of Luther and the source of much of his support. He always appealed quite openly and confidentially to lay judgment. This served to de-clericalize the Church and make the layman see that it belonged to him. Cajetan moved. He wrote to Frederick, blaming Luther for the breakdown and telling the prince he had no course but to send him to Rome or out of the country. Frederick invited Luther's comment and received a spirited reply. Cajetan, he argued had not pointed out his errors nor shown him to be a heretic, but was merely asking his prince to hand him over. Luther was fighting for his life but made no effort to seek the support either of his university or his church.

> I await my excommunication from Rome any day now. On that account I have set all my affairs in order, so that when they come I shall be ready for them with loins girded. I shall be like Abraham not knowing whither. Yet I am most certain whither I go, for God is everywhere.[2]

He called a farewell supper party. A letter from the prince arrived expressing surprise that he had not yet fled the country. Luther knew, now that his prince had withdrawn his lay protection, that he had no hope at all; yet, before the end of the meal, a second letter arrived asking him to stay. Frederick in his natural goodness had had second thoughts, and decided Luther would neither be exiled nor sent to Rome, but would receive fair trial in his own land. The happiest second thoughts in history.

The delicate political situation forced Rome to continue its courtship of Frederick. The German von Miltitz was sent to court Frederick's support and to observe the Luther affair. He was armed with a wonderful collection of bribes and rewards, even with a veiled offer of a cardinal's

[1] *Acta Augustana*, WA. 2, 1. 6–26. (Partial translation in Hillerbrand, 63–5.)
[2] WA. Br. 2, 253.

hat for Luther, but his hidden purpose was to neutralize Luther. To this end he was given appropriate letters to cover his retreat from Wittenberg to Rome with Luther as prisoner. But von Miltitz was a young, pompous palaverer, and never appraised the seriousness of the issues nor the measure of Luther. He managed to arrange some kind of truce to the effect that both sides would remain silent. At this moment the Emperor Maximilian died (January 12, 1519). As soon as Rome realized that Charles V was to be Emperor after all, the Miltitz manœuvres failed and the Luther affair was left unresolved. Miltitz was to say later that he could never have got Luther out of Germany even with 25,000 men.

## 4. The Leipzig Disputation, July, 1519[1]

It was during this lull in the Luther affair that the redoubtable, even if rather disreputable, theologian John Eck of Ingolstadt launched an attack on the Wittenberg school of theology. Earlier there had been some friendly passage of arms between Eck and Luther on the subject of the latter's theses, and when the two men met at Augsburg on Luther's visit to Cajetan they agreed in a friendly way to hold a disputation at Leipzig. However, when Luther was away from Wittenberg attending the Heidelberg Disputation, Carlstadt had impetuously surged forward and issued four hundred and five theses, which amounted to a radical reformulation of the Wittenberg theology. When, therefore, Eck's theses arrived at Wittenberg, Luther perceived that they were directed at Carlstadt and not at him, save in the one respect of papal authority. Luther had considerable difficulty even in gaining permission to accompany Carlstadt. He realized that alone, the older, slower Carlstadt would be no match for the quick-witted, highly experienced disputant Eck. Meanwhile, Luther engaged on an intensive study of the papacy, and when he arrived in Leipzig he had mastered a mass of historical detail which convinced him that the authority of the papal decretals was questionable, and that the mediaeval papacy was a recent imposition on Christendom.[2]

Eck, who arrived before the Wittenberg theologians, was shown every courtesy by the city authorities. When Carlstadt, Luther and Melanchthon arrived they were discourteously ignored; though when the town council noticed that they were escorted by two hundred students in helmets and halberds they hurriedly mustered the town guard. Great excitement ran through the town, and armed men were stationed in the inns.

---

[1] WA. 2, 254–383; American edition, Vol. 31, 307 ff. See Schwiebert, 384–437; Fife, *The Revolt of Martin Luther*, 327–94.

[2] See G. H. W. Parker's discussion of the Donation of Constantine and the forged Isidorian Decretals in *The Morning Star*, pp. 118 f.

After a slow and pompous start Eck defeated Carlstadt mercilessly in a debate which lasted a week. Eck was masterly in argument, with a ready memory and quick wit. Carlstadt was slow and unable to discuss without books of reference. What was worse, on entering Leipzig the wheel of his cart had broken and Carlstadt suffered the humiliation of being thrown in the dirt and the pain of a broken arm. Eck was in fine form after routing Carlstadt and everybody waited excitedly to see how the young Luther would fare.

Luther argued his case on the authority of Scripture, the authority of the Greek patristic tradition, and on Nicaea, but Eck very cleverly insisted that Luther's theology was simply Hussite and already condemned by council. Eck wanted to know why Luther had not used his ability to attack Hussite heretics instead of attacking the Holy Father. Luther was provoked into saying that many of the views of Huss were evangelical and Christian, and that councils may err. This created an uproar.

Eck believed that he had inflicted a crushing defeat on the Wittenberg school, as did many of the witnesses, impressed by manner rather than argument; but reflection shows that he did not in fact meet the arguments of the Reformers. The demeanour of the two parties was revealing. Eck stayed on enjoying his success, and writing bombastically to the world on how he had routed the Wittenbergers. He was fêted and feasted, enjoying the city's wine and her "voluptuous prostitutes." He trounced another victim at a disputation put on at the university, delivered salvoes here and there against the departed reformers, and returned home "in triumph," as he expressed it. Luther and his friends returned home quietly and immediately. A wise observer remarked that only the learned saw that it was Luther who had won the debate.

Then events changed. The Wittenbergers gathered theological strength and support. The humanists resented Eck's gratuitous attack on the young and scholarly Melanchthon, Luther's colleague at Wittenberg. Oecolampadius delivered him a crushing blow from Switzerland and a humanist poet ridiculed him. Students crowded in at the University of Wittenberg. Eck disparaged that university and sought to organize a bonfire of the Wittenberg publications. Even the universities of Paris and Erfurt withdrew their support of Eck. How surprised would he have been if he had known that in twenty-five years that same Dr. Luther would be invited to that same hall to inaugurate the establishment of the Reformation.[1]

As was Luther's constant practice, he wrote an account of the debate for the German people so that the laity could see the issues and judge for themselves.[2] He argued that the pope's supremacy was but 400 years old and had never existed in the eastern half of Christendom; that the great

---

[1] See p. 115.     [2] Loescher, *Reformationsacta*, III. 222 ff.

councils had formulated the faith knowing nothing of papal supremacy, and that he himself stood in this long catholic line.

The Leipzig disputation helped Luther to see himself more clearly. He now saw that it was not the mere abuse of indulgences that he was attacking but the whole conception of priestly mediation on which mediaeval catholicism was based. Luther in effect denied both the divine right and the divine origin of the papacy, as well as the infallibility of a general council. He maintained three bases: the authority of Scripture, responsible private judgment, and faith, all of them to be attested by sound, rational, historical, informed judgment. The world began to realize that his concern was not a mere scandal concerning indulgences but that he was removing the whole conception of priestly mediation on which mediaeval practice was based. When Luther returned from Leipzig he realized that he had launched the ship of the Reformation on the high seas to find himself at the helm.

Luther's method of working was clear. He simply wrote, taught and preached the Word of God and left the result to God. Looking back on these days he said,

> I simply taught, preached, wrote God's Word: otherwise I did nothing. And then, while I slept, or drank Wittenberg beer with my Philip or my Amsdorf, the Word so weakened the papacy that never a prince or emperor inflicted such damage on it. I did nothing. The Word did it all. Had I desired to foment trouble, I could have brought such bloodshed upon Germany. Yea, I could have started such a little game at Worms, that the Emperor would not have been safe. But what would it have been? A mug's game. I left it to the Word.[1]

He was not only a prodigious writer but wrote with an effectiveness and a readiness and a colour never excelled. He averaged a book a fortnight, and whether it was in Latin or German wrote with a fluent style, full of humour and homely truth, of poetry and simplicity. His power can be very simply traced to its source. He knew that he was called by God and that God had given him something to say. He said it without fear or favour.

Some short analysis of his writings at this time shows his thinking. On his return from Leipzig, Spalatin the court chaplain informed Luther that Frederick was ill from overwork. Luther wrote to his prince a work of spiritual comfort which helped him considerably. It had the odd name of *The Fourteen.*[2] That arose from the fact that instead of inculcating the invocation of the fourteen patron saints, the normal procedure in times of affliction or distress, Luther analysed the problem of sin and suffering in

---

[1] Quoted by Rupp, *Luther's Progress to the Diet of Worms*, p. 99. (To "drink wine" is a German saying which means to do nothing about a particular matter – Luther makes it refer to the humbler beer!)

[2] WA. 6, 104–34. Trans. W.M.L. 1, 130 ff.

relation to the gospel under fourteen headings. Against sin and suffering he set, not the saints, but the inexhaustible grace and mercy and goodness of God, the power of Christ and faith in Him.

So impressed was the Elector that he begged Luther to write a book of sermons for the Christian year. Luther met their request with his *Postills*, and in addition produced a vast number of spiritual tracts and articles on prayer, sacraments, the confession and the ban. He wrote on the economic problem of usury. He published his commentary on the Psalms. He was shaping at this time his views on the sacraments. He began to see that a sacrament was a gift which could only be appropriated in faith: baptism was forgiveness of sins and a covenant with God; the Lord's Supper an inner communion with Christ which grows out of faith in Him and the forgiveness of sins. He gave up the doctrine of transubstantiation but held on to the real presence.

His book *On Good Works*[1] is specially interesting. Good works, he argues, are only good in that God commands them, and are not to be thought of as the good works we choose for ourselves, e.g. fasting and pilgrimages. Christ taught that the first and only work was faith, from which stem all the good works God requires of us. Faith is not something we offer but is a divine gift which takes root in the soul when the gospel has been declared. It is something that was not there before; it is something wholly new: it is something God creates but man cannot create. Anything that is done in response to faith of this kind is a good work. Anything that such a faith does is transformed into a good work. Good works are not specifically "religious". The work may simply be a mother washing her baby, the miller's girl putting the corn on the mule's back, the farmer ploughing, the cobbler at his last, the scholar with his students, the prince governing his people. These are the good works, for these are the works God wants his people to do for one another so that His world may continue in peace and harmony. On this argument, going on pilgrimages, reciting paternosters, saying masses for the dead, and other religious "good works" stand condemned. Moreover, once faith has taken root in the heart, God moves a man to effect His good works. The Ten Commandments guide men who have not attained such maturity and Luther thereupon elucidates their meaning.

The book had an immediate effect and made the old mediaeval idea of a sacred and secular morality meaningless. To Luther, all that a man in faith did was holy. There was no "higher" monkish morality and "lower" lay morality: a man with faith in God did the good works God required of him in the station of life where he found himself. Luther further removed the seat of morality from the intellect to the will, a wholesome Biblical emphasis. Luther dismissed all the self-imposed

[1] See American edition, Vol. 44, pp. 15 ff.

disciplines of mediaeval spiritual practice, as useless as they were un-required: it is in the normal demands of so-called "secular" life and not in the spiritual disciplines of the so-called "spiritual" life that a man takes up his cross and follows Christ.

Luther also wrote a book on the mass entitled *Treatise on the New Testament*.[1] The mass[2] to Luther was evangelical: it was the new covenant, new in that it was now gospel, not law, the essence of which was forgive-ness of sins. "This is my body, this is the cup of the new testament in my blood which is shed for you for the forgiveness of sins." This was God's gift in the first instance. It had now been made into a gift of man to God, a sacrifice, a meritorious work. Where a mass does not exist to proclaim the forgiveness of sins it is otiose. Of the souls in purgatory, it was neither scriptural nor reasonable to believe that a celebration of the mass could release a departed soul from misery. Endowed and paid masses should be reduced, the service rendered into German and made audible. All believers make the sacrifice of themselves and their prayers, and all are priests. (Luther, of course, allowed the place of ordained clergy.)

Luther's mind was now hardening towards Rome and in May 1520 he produced *The Papacy at Rome*.[3] He argued that the Church was not to be identified with that institution Rome had made of it but with that organ-ism created by the New Testament, the congregation of men of faith called of God and sustained by His Word. At this moment Prierias' *Answer* to Luther's views expressed in the Leipzig debate reached him. Prierias blandly asserted that every decision of the Pope on matters of faith and morals was infallible because it was of God, and that everybody had to accept these decisions under pain of temporal as well as eternal death. By now, Luther, who had earlier suspected the authority and authenticity of the papal decretals, had received convincing academic proof from the researches of Valla that the decretals were forged and that the Donation of Constantine to Sylvester and his successors of the papal states and of world supremacy had never existed. It was shown to the world that the authority of the papacy based on these ancient decretals, and on the alleged Donation of Constantine, was based on common fraud and plain deceit. Luther began to think that the Antichrist now ruled in Rome.

The word Antichrist was not merely pejorative. Luther seemed to think of this not in terms of some being to appear at the end of time, nor did he identify the papacy with it. Rather it was a demoniacal power which had infected the court at Rome. Its viciousness lay less in its striving after worldly power and riches, less even in its moral depravity, deplorable as these both were; it lay essentially in the claim to infallibility whereby the

---

[1] WA. 6, 353–78. Trans. W.M.L. I. 287.
[2] Luther and his followers retained the designation "mass" for the Lord's Supper.
[3] WA. 6. 285–324. Trans. W.M.L. I. 327 ff.

papacy set itself above the Word of God and kept captive the minds and souls of men. Further, the closer knowledge of ecclesiastics that recent events had given him, and his deep historical studies, had served to convince him that few if any of the papal agents even believed what they were professing. He was driven to the conclusion that the papal curia consisted of religious nihilists, even atheists. It was this state of affairs at Rome that convinced Luther that he was living "in the last days." Luther began to see this Roman Sodom as an institution of the devil, a city set against God, an enemy of the gospel.

When Luther fully appreciated this and saw that Rome would not reform herself, he turned to responsible laity, and wrote his *Open Letter to the Christian Nobility of the German Nation concerning the Reform of the Christian Estate*,[1] the first of his three great "Reformation Writings." Luther appealed to the lay leaders of Germany, *i.e.* the young Emperor, the princes, the knights, the cities, though warning them that Christendom could not be healed by force of arms. He warned them that they were not dealing with flesh and blood but with powers of hell, who would always fill the world with war and bloodshed but could never be overcome by these. Faith alone met them. He struck at once at the quasi-divine power supposed to be inherent in the Church and in the priesthood, a power which had cowed Europe for centuries. Rome had entrenched herself behind three walls: the claim that her spiritual power was superior to the temporal power of kings; the claim that no one can interpret Scripture save the Pope; the claim that only the Pope can summon a general council. Luther then demolished these three walls.

The Romanists asserted that there were two estates of man, the spiritual and the secular. The Pope, bishops, priests and monks constituted the spiritual estate while the princes, lords, artisans and peasants constituted the secular. Luther argued that it was a disastrous delusion to differentiate a "secular" from a "spiritual" estate. The real "spiritual estate" was constituted not by clerics but by the whole body of believers in Jesus Christ, clerical and lay alike, for God had called all such, and all such were kings and priests by virtue of that calling. Baptism, the Gospel, faith – these alone make a Christian and spiritual people. The clergy are not distinguished by some indelible character given at ordination, but they are set apart to do the particular work of a priest within that community of which they are all alike constituted members by virtue of God's calling. The spiritual priesthood of all believers blasts the first wall of the Romanists.

The second wall tumbles just as readily. To allege that Scripture needs interpreting before it can be understood, and that it is only the interpretation of the pope that is valid, is indefensible. If this were true then we need Holy Scripture no longer, only a Pope. "Let us burn the scriptures and be

[1] WA. 6, 404–69. Trans. American edition, Vol. 44, pp. 115 ff.

content with the learned boys at Rome!" Holy Scripture is open to all and can be interpreted by all true believers who have the mind of Christ and seek the Holy Spirit.

The third wall collapses with the others. There was no historical foundation to the pretension that only the Pope has the power to call a council. The Church itself may do so as it did in Jerusalem in Acts 15, or even the Emperor may call a council, as happened at Nicaea in 325.

In the second part of the book Luther castigates the worldly pomp of the Pope and cardinals, their greed and their exactions. It is a telling indictment and makes dismal reading to Christian men, though many of Luther's contemporaries grasped at the social implications to the neglect of the religious, Luther's sole concern.

In the third part he gave a long and practical list of the matters that called for reform. It was in this context he exposed the Papal Decretals of Isidore as a forgery, as well as the Donation of Constantine. What Luther sought in the main was the abolition of papal power over the state, the creation of a German Church with its own court of final appeal, together with a religious and moral reform of the whole of Christendom. He wrote to Spalatin, "I am beyond injury. Whatever I have done and do, I do under constraint, ever ready to keep quiet if only they do not demand that the truth of the Gospel be quiet."[1] The book had an immediate impact.

At the end of the *Appeal* Luther had promised a further book. This appeared within a matter of weeks, *The Prelude on the Babylonish Captivity of the Church*,[2] a book written for the clergy and the humanists. It is a work of far-reaching consequences for it severs the tap-root of Romanism, namely, the sacramental system by which she sought to control the life of every man from birth to death. It was not that Luther's theology was not sacramental. He opposed not sacramentalism but priestcraft in the guise of sacramentalism.

He first discusses the sacrament of Holy Communion and exposes three main errors of Roman practice as a threefold bondage: the exclusion of the laity from the cup, the doctrine of transubstantiation, and the sacrifice of the mass.

With regard to the withholding of the cup, Luther proves from the Gospels of Matthew, Mark and Luke, as well as from Paul, that early Christians not only partook of the cup but were intended to partake. "Drink ye all of this." It was the Romanists who were the heretics and schismatics in excluding the laity.

Second, he regarded the doctrine of transubstantiation as a product of scholasticism. He could not accept any miraculous change in the substance of bread and wine, but maintained the co-existence of the body and blood

[1] WA. Br. 2, 135. 41 ff. (July 9, 1520).          [2] WA. 6, 497-573. Trans. W.M.L. II. 167.

"in, with and under" the elements. He believed in a real presence, rather in the manner of the Incarnation, not requiring any transubstantiation of the flesh and blood of Jesus. The word consubstantiation does not do justice to Luther: it was a word he never used and implies inclusion or circumscription. Luther thought in terms of an illocal presence. In other words, Christ was present, but that presence was not to be thought of in terms of a place or a thing.

Third, the sacrifice of the mass. This meant the offering to God as a sacrifice again of the body of Christ by the hands of the priest after consecration. It was a repetition in an unbloody way of the atoning sacrifice of the cross. To Luther, the original Last Supper was instituted by Christ to serve as a perpetual and thankful memorial of His atoning death about to take place: to it a blessing and promise belonged, namely the forgiveness of sins, a blessing appropriated only by the believing heart. The burden of the sacrament is the promise of forgiveness and its appropriation by faith. But, of course, this blessing and promise is larger than the sacrament and is not limited to or by the sacrament. It is established and proved in Christ's total ministry, and is true without its confirmation by the sacrament. This is indeed the gospel, and the sacrament is its acted word. It is something God has offered, not something we offer. We have nothing to offer. The Romanists had changed this evangelical communion into a priestly mass, surrounded it with vestments and incense, gestures and ceremonies and made it into a work men do. It is God Himself who is doing the offering, the free gift of undeserved forgiveness and fellowship with Him. All man can do is respond to this with all that he has and is. Luther never sought to abolish the sacrament but to evangelize it and restore its proper significance. He also sought to have the service in the vernacular.

He then turned to the sacrament of Baptism. He was glad that this sacrament had remained unexploited by avarice and unspoilt by bad theology. Luther argued that Rome diminished Baptism by relying on "the second plank" of penance. Instead of placing confidence in the absolution of a priest a man should rely on the forgiveness of sins offered in baptism. A penitent man should return to the faith in his baptism where he received and continues to receive the remission of sins.

Finally, Luther attacked the number of sacraments then held. He holds to two, Baptism and Bread, in that both of these were instituted by Christ, and both promise remission of sins. Penance he considered as a means to return to the grace of baptism. The other four sacraments he rejected on the grounds that they are common to the heathen world and not exclusively Christian, or were not instituted by Christ, or cannot be proved from Scripture.

At this time, although Rome had finally condemned Luther, Miltitz persuaded Luther to write once more to the Pope. This was Luther's third and last letter to the Holy Father. With the letter he sent a book, *The Freedom of a Christian Man*,[1] the third of the Reformation Writings. It is a summary of the Christian life. The leading idea is a dual paradox: The Christian man is the lord of all and subject to none, by virtue of faith; the Christian man is the servant of all and subject to every one, by virtue of love. A Christian man's life is made up of faith and love: faith in relation to God, love in relation to his fellow man. Man is made free by his justification by faith, but that faith is exercised in love to one's fellows and in good works. A man must first have this relation to God, *i.e.* be righteous before he can do the righteous things God requires of him. Good works proceed from a good man. Good works do not make man into a believing man or a justified man. Faith unites the soul to Christ in perfect union, therefore whatever is Christ's is the soul's also. This is more than communion: it is victory, redemption and freedom. It is not sufficient to preach the words and works of Christ in an historic manner, but, as St. John did, to promote faith in Him so that Christ is Christ for us. We must preach why Christ came: He has given us freedom and made us all kings and priests – kings in that we are lords of everything, priests in that we continually stand in His presence.

Luther then turned to his second principle, that a Christian man is the servant of all. Faith issues in works, for a Christian man enjoys that freest of all servitudes in which he serves others of his own will and for nought. He should empty himself and serve his neighbours in the same way as he sees that God has acted and is acting towards him through Christ. A Christian lives in Christ and his neighbour: in Christ by faith, in his neighbour by love. What Luther reproached in the Roman doctrine was that Christian men were there taught to seek merits and rewards, so that in fact Rome turned the gospel into law. The letter accompanying the book destroyed all prospects of reconciliation. He addressed the Pope as an equal and pitied him as a poor Daniel in a den of lions. He made the devastating remark that the Pope was called the vicar of Christ for a vicar is there because someone else is absent, and it was Christ who was absent from Rome.

Earlier this same year (1520) it was realized in Rome that Miltitz had bungled the Luther affair. It was realized equally clearly that in spite of Frederick's unquestioning loyalty to the Pope, he was not going to hand Luther over to Rome. A condemnation of Luther was therefore drawn up in Rome. The gentle and scholarly Cajetan suggested that only a few of Luther's statements need be particularized as indictable, the rest might be described as offensive to Catholic truth and that Luther be given another chance to recant. But the burly Eck prevailed against Cajetan's sensible

---

[1] WA. 7, 20-38. Trans. American edition, Vol. 31, 327 ff.

and kindly course of action and seized the initiative by drawing up a bull of indictment which he submitted to the Holy Father then at his hunting lodge chasing wild boar. The bull began with the fatuous attempt to be relevant, "A wild boar hath entered thy vineyard, O Lord. . . !"[1] From some of Luther's writings they roughly drafted forty-one articles which they condemned as heretical. It was a deplorable effort. Neither the Pope nor Eck had read Luther's writings and even listed as heresies such opinions as that "to burn heretics is contrary to the will of the Holy Spirit," and "secular and spiritual princes would do well if they put an end to mendicancy." Others were torn from their context, others were unintelligible. All rulers were forbidden to believe, teach, favour or defend his views. All Luther's writings were to be burned. Luther and his followers were excommunicated and given sixty days in which to recant.

Eck himself thought little of the final form of the bull, still less of the knowledge the curia displayed. He could not understand why so many harmless articles were included, nor why there was no proper theological refutation of Luther's alleged errors. In any case, the bull was utterly without point at that time. The real interest of the Pope was the wild boars in his reservation: he cared as little about the "wild boar of Saxony" as he did about the Lord's vineyard the boar was alleged to be ravaging.

On July 17, 1520, the Pope appointed Aleander[2] and Eck to execute the bull in Germany. Eck was to be responsible for Saxony, Aleander for the west. Eck proceeded in his blustering fashion and had the audacity to add names of sympathizers to the bull. He received a rude shock when only three places allowed him to publish the bull. Even in Leipzig, where only a year previously he had sunned himself in his "triumph" over Wittenberg, he found disenchantment and coolness. The university refused to publish the bull and he was so roughly handled by the students that he had to flee to a monastery for protection.

This gave great satisfaction to Miltitz who pontificated, "Serves you right! I told you so!" He accused Eck of intrusion and of destroying the delicate rapprochement he had so carefully created when he had persuaded Luther to write to the Pope and when Luther had gone further and included the book we have just described, The Freedom of a Christian Man.

Meanwhile Luther wrote a vigorous manifesto against the bull, and reissued his appeal to responsible laity to call a free general council of the Church.[3] Luther had now the ear of Germany.

Meanwhile, Aleander was faring better in his crusade against the "new Arius and Mohammed." In Antwerp he persuaded the Emperor Charles V to issue an edict against heresy in his Burgundian territory, and in Louvain

[1] Kidd, No. 38. Trans. Hillerbrand, p. 80 ff.
[2] Hieronymus Aleander, papal nuncio at the court of Charles V
[3] WA. 6, 597–612.

arranged a bonfire of Luther's books. In Cologne, the climate was less favourable: the Elector Frederick refused to see him and Aleander was obliged to buttonhole him at church. It was at this time Erasmus uttered his oft-quoted remark in response to the Elector's enquiry as to his opinion of Luther. Luther had committed two wrongs: he had hit the Pope on the crown and the monks in the belly. Erasmus urged further, that it was in everybody's interest to give Luther a fair hearing before expert and impartial judges. He also made the important point that of all the universities only two had condemned Luther and none refuted him.

Whilst Aleander was pursuing his bonfire tactics, Luther made like reply. On December 10, at Wittenberg, Luther's friend and student Agricola made a bonfire of the *Canon Law*, the *Summa Angelica* and some smaller volumes of Eck and Emser.[1] The canon law embodied for Luther the confusion of gospel with law, of politics with religion, the secularization of the spiritual, the setting up of the Pope in the room of God. It was the Alcoran of the Antichrist. The *Summa Angelica* meant the intellectualization of this scheme of things. As they were burning Luther was seen to step forward. He quietly and unostentatiously put the bull on the fire. He watched it burn. He turned on his heel and left the scene.[2]

A thrill went through Europe when it learned that a man with no more weight behind him than his faith in God had burned a papal bull. It was the fiery signal of emancipation. The individual soul had discovered its true value and therefore its authority. If the Reformation can be dated precisely, that date must be December 10, 1520. If eras can be dated, our modern era began at nine o'clock that morning.

## 5. *Worms 1521*

Aleander's plan was to have Luther put under the ban at once and unheard, and he worked hard to effect this. Nobody was happy about Luther going to Worms: the Emperor was not, Frederick was not, their advisers were not, Rome was not. They all knew that a diet[3] was neither an appropriate nor a competent court. Aleander insisted that in the event of Luther appearing, the Lutheran affair was not to be raised with the German national grievances, but Luther was to be summarily called to make public recantation. Only Luther was certain about his course. As he was to say later to a private messenger from Spalatin in Worms begging him not to proceed to the Diet, if there were as many devils in Worms as there were tiles on the roofs he would nevertheless go. He knew he had God's Word: and he knew he had to say it. All his predecessors, Wyclif, Huss and others,

---

[1] Secretary to Duke George of Saxony.
[2] American edition, Vol 31, 379.
[3] A diet was an assembly of the states of the Holy Roman Empire.

had failed in their day. Luther knew that God expected him to stand in this fateful hour. He saw his stand as a part of the pattern of history where error seems in power and truth on the scaffold. "I simply say that true Christianity has ceased to exist among those who should have preserved it – the bishops and scholars." Yet even at this severe hour of testing he continued writing. It was not only powerful polemics against Romanizing adversaries such as Emser and Catharinus, as might be expected in this controversial hour, but fine spiritual writings such as his exposition of the *Magnificat*,[1] his *Advent Postills*[2] and his work on the *Psalms*.[3] In the three months before his appearance at Worms he published fifty works which kept three printers busy, all in addition to his university teaching and pastoral preaching.

When the time came for him to go to Worms the town council generously provided him with a covered cart for the long journey and his university offered him £2 for expenses. For company Luther had the theologian Amsdorf, a fellow monk, and a young noble. With the imperial herald in front, the retinue threaded its way to Worms. In every place "the populace poured out to see Dr. Luther" and in every place he was treated with honour. At Erfurt, the seat of his university and his monastery, the whole university came out to meet him as a body, an experience he movingly described as his "Palm Sunday." Here he was called on to preach (as everywhere), and so great was the crowd that they literally burst down a church wall in the press as Luther preached (on faith and works), a situation he calmly capitalized into the content of his sermon as he continued preaching! In Eisenach, the place of his childhood, he fell dangerously ill, but pursued his journey with borrowed strength. The journey turned out to be a triumphal procession, to the consternation and chagrin of Aleander.

At a late stage of the journey, Glapion, father confessor to the Emperor, and a crafty diplomatic court priest, sought to deflect Luther for a "conference" in the hopes of rendering his appearance at Worms unnecessary. Bucer, too, tried to arrange a meeting with Sickingen and Hutten, two nobles seeking reform though on a humanist and nationalist basis, not a theological. The Bishop of Mainz, too, sought to prevent Luther's appearance at Worms. An imperial messenger informed him that Luther had been already condemned at Worms. The bishop asked Luther if he still wanted to proceed a "condemned man." What would he gain? Why not submit to him at once? It was a shattering moment but Luther had put his hand to the plough and would not look back: he relied on the Emperor's safe conduct – and God in all else. A letter from Wittenberg overtook him

---

[1] WA. 7. 544–604. Trans. W.M.L. III. 117 ff.
[2] WA. 7. 463–537.
[3] WA. 3, WA. 4. See Selected Psalms, American edition, Vols. 12–14.

saying that the Elector had given up all hope of any good coming out of Luther's appearance at Worms. Luther was undeterred, for his strength and courage were of God not man. He set his face to go to Worms. On Tuesday April 16, 1521, at ten in the morning he entered Worms accompanied by a great number of nobles and a hundred horsemen who had left the town to meet him. Two thousand waited to see him. As he entered his lodgings he glanced at the crowd and an eyewitness remembered the deep black flash of his falcon eyes as they swept the crowd. "God will be with me," he was heard to say to himself as he stepped down from the cart. God was.

Worms itself must have shocked the young monk. There were colourful wares and wealth on the streets and gargantuan indulgence in the taverns. There was jousting in the fields by day and drinking in the inns by night. An observer wrote of the leading prelates spending much of their time in banqueting and drinking, Lent though it was: of a prelate who lost sixty thousand gulden at one sitting in gambling. Another commentator wrote that murders averaged three to four a night, even though one hundred folk had been executed for murder. It was a humanist who described Worms during the 1521 Diet in these words: "It goes on here quite as in Rome, with murdering, stealing; all the streets are full of whores; there is no Lent here, but jousting, whoring, eating of meat, mutton, pigeons, eggs, milk and cheese, and there are such doings as in the mountain of Dame Venus." These indirect testimonies show the urgency of the spiritual, theological and moral reform to which God was calling Luther.

It was six o'clock in the evening of the next day that Luther was led into the crowded and suffocating hall where the Diet was meeting.[1] He was asked two questions. First, whether he was the author of the pile of books on the table before them (the Emperor could not believe that one man could have written so many!); second, whether he would renounce them. To the first Luther answered quietly in German and in Latin that he had written them. To the second he asked time to consider, for the question involved faith, salvation and the Word of God, though he would renounce everything that could be proved unsupported by warrant of Scripture. Luther was naturally over-awed, and a little apprehensive, for he knew the whole world was watching that scene and awaiting its outcome. He knew that Church and Empire were against him. Above all he needed time to reflect, for he had come to Worms under the impression that he had been called to present his case, but found himself treated a condemned man given his last opportunity to recant. He was granted a further twenty-four hours, provided he would be prepared to make a verbal answer and bring no written statement.

[1] WA. 7. 815–87; American edition, Vol. 32, 101–131; Hillerbrand, 88 ff.

Luther's reserve did not mean he was contemplating recantation. "Truly with the help of Christ I will not revoke even a dot in all eternity." But he was shy, nervous and alone. He needed time to reflect on the mood of the Diet and how they had decided to act. He longed to talk the matter over with his friends, but even Amsdorf, who had accompanied him, had gone into hiding, for Aleander had threatened him with imprisonment on the grounds that though Luther had a safe-conduct, he had not. All night long Luther worked at his statement, a manuscript we still possess. The next day at four he appeared again and faced the Diet at six. But it was a different Luther: self-composed and reassured. To the same questions he replied fearlessly in German. He apologized for any breach of etiquette he might display, on the grounds of being a simple monk and no courtier. He acknowledged authorship of the works which he subdivided into three classes: (a) devotional works on piety, faith and morals, which not even his enemies would want him to recant; (b) polemical works against the papacy, which he would not recant and the truth of which none could deny or dissemble; (c) polemical works against private persons who defended this papal tyranny and sought to destroy Luther's doctrine. If he had been too vehement, he apologized for that, but it was not his behaviour that was under discussion but the doctrine, and this was Christ's. He begged his critics to show the errors of his teaching, and if he were refuted by Scripture he would be the first to cast his books into the fire.

He went on to say that he was aware of the dangerous dissensions that had arisen from his teachings. But it was the Word of God that had excited the controversy, as Christ had forewarned when He said He had come not to bring peace but a sword. It would be an ill start to the proceedings to begin by condemning the Word of God, for that would bring a flood of evils on the reign of the young Emperor whom he loved next to God. Luther owed it to God to take the course of action on which he had embarked in the interests of Christendom. He had not come to teach his lords but to state his case, and hoped to be judged impartially on the merits of the case, not as his enemies had hatefully depicted him.

The princes and lords were nonplussed. They had not expected Luther to stand before them and ask to be set right. They thought this conduct most reasonable and some were of the opinion that the diagnosis of the plight of Germany and of Christendom was utterly sound. The lords spiritual, on the other hand, argued that Luther had already been condemned by the only competent authority there was, namely Rome, and that the task of the princes was not to hear Luther and make their own judgment, but as guardians of the Church to uphold and put into effect the decision the Church had already made.

In a threatening manner Eck demanded a plain answer to a plain question. It was not Luther's place to call the Church's decisions in question. "Will you recant? Yes or No?"

Luther gave a plain answer that was neither ambiguous nor offensive, as he expressed it. Unless he were proved wrong on the basis of scripture and sound reason (for popes and councils had been known to err and could err again), he was bound fast by his conscience to the Word of God, He could not and would not recant. "May God help me," he added, "Amen."[1]

Eck tartly rejoined that if a council might err then perhaps Luther's conscience might err too, though he carefully guarded himself by saying that a council could err only in matters of order, never of faith. Luther responded immediately, "I can prove it." But the Emperor was not going to listen to any proofs or arguments and signalled for Luther to be taken away. Many in the hall interpreted this as a sign to lead Luther off to prison and a tumult arose. The Spanish underlings called out "To the bonfire!" But Charles had not meant that, and fortunately the Germans could not understand the Spaniards, so Luther was escorted to his lodgings where he cried on entering, "I've come through! I've come through!"

History has dramatized Luther's stand at Worms, as it always does with its great moments. But Luther never thought much of what he did and said there, and often regretted his performance. He had been urged to play for time and study the course his accusers adopted. This had the effect of putting Luther in a straitjacket: Luther was always at his worst when he took the advice of others, at his finest when he was simply himself. Further he had expected an opportunity to argue his case and found they wanted only recantation. It was the wrong kind of court, utterly incompetent to deal with the issues. Luther needed a small court of open-minded scholars who would listen to his case. Be that as it may, Luther stood firm and resisted both Emperor and Pope in the interests of truth. It was one of the world's greatest moments.

There was more to Worms than the official proceedings. With a speed that took their breath away, the Emperor summoned the electors to meet him at eight o'clock the next morning. When they assembled, he asked them what they intended to do next. On asking for time for consideration, the Emperor replied that as far as he was concerned there was nothing to think about: he was prepared to stake his life, his soul, his dominions, his all, on the vindication of the Roman Church. He wished he had tackled Luther earlier, but he now intended to send him back on a safe conduct. A single monk could not be right against one thousand years of Christianity. Charles's mind was made up.[2] But at this stage certain alarming posters

---

[1] The famous words "I can no other! Here I stand!" though published that same year in Wittenberg, and the earliest written statement we possess, may not be Luther's *exact* words at Worms, but they certainly sum up his stand at Worms.

[2] Kidd, No. 43.

appeared declaring that thousands of men were ready to fight Church and State but never to abandon Luther.

Terror struck the archbishop, who begged from the Emperor a hearing for Luther and the chance to win a recantation. The Emperor yielded to the request but Luther did not yield to the pressure. He stood by Scripture and sound reason, and was not prepared to accept the authority of council decisions which denied these. Cochlaeus attempted a compromise whereby Luther might retract the points generally found contradictory to catholicism and leave the other points over to be examined by a competent authority and perhaps removed from his writings. Luther answered that nothing would be gained by a personal recantation. Evangelical theology was not a man but a cause.

There seemed real hope at this stage of agreeing to call a general council as soon as possible, but Luther insisted that all decisions must be submitted to the Word of God. It now became apparent that the dispute was not a matter of church order or church politics but of a fundamentally different interpretation of Christianity.

The imperial messenger then called on Luther to inform him that the Emperor, as guardian of the Roman Church, intended to take action against him.[1] He granted him twenty-one days in which to return to Wittenberg, on condition that he did no preaching, teaching, or writing on the way. Luther thanked the Emperor and his officials. He testified his loyalty to the Emperor to the end of his life but reserved the right and freedom to testify to the Word of God: all he had wanted was reform according to Holy Scripture.

On the way back home, as all the world knows, Luther was "ambushed." He hurriedly grasped his Hebrew Old Testament and his Greek Testament as he was unceremoniously escorted by devious routes through the forest. At eleven o'clock that evening they rode over the clanking drawbridge of the Wartburg Castle, overlooking his beloved Eisenach. Here Luther was received kindly and given two rooms, which he was ordered on no account to leave until his tonsure was overgrown and his beard complete. He was introduced to the staff as "Sir George."

When the drawbridge rattled up behind him that April night it was the curtain to Luther's personal biography. His life was no longer his own, but was to be inextricably bound up with the great evangelical cause he had fathered. At Worms Luther had argued that this was not the affair of a single man but the cause of the Church, and that others had long ago taken it up, as many others were yet to do. The Reformation went on at Wittenberg without Luther. Though many tensions were to arise within the movement, tensions more serious than that between Wittenberg and Rome, nevertheless Luther's purpose was as clear as his theology. He

---

[1] Kidd, No. 45. Hillerbrand, 95 ff.

sought to declare the full meaning of the Gospel: by that he stood. What he had written and taught was "for the salvation of Christianity as a whole, for the benefit of the entire German nation, for the extermination of dangerous abuses and superstititions, and for the unburderning of all Christianity from so many unceasing, innumerable, unchristian and damnable restrictions, hardships and blasphemies."[1] He had shown his hand at Worms and was later to be equally unyielding to the fervour of the fanatics, the fury of the peasants, and the theological indifferentism of the humanists: he gave away nothing either to Rome or Zürich. He simply taught God as God had shown Himself in the Bible, and preached Christ in whom God had declared His hand. It was not that others did not, nor that their lives were reprehensible, but rather that they took it upon themselves to modify what was to Luther the clear mind of God declared in His Word. This was true of all who eventually opposed him: the Romanists in the interests of catholic tradition, the humanists in the interests of academic learning, the enthusiasts in the interests of their inspiration, the peasants in the interests of common justice and socialism, the Swiss in the interests of a liberal reformation. All Luther's opponents were emphasizing justifiable causes, but to give these causes parity to the Word of God was to oppose the supremacy of the Word of God. It was less that Luther was stubborn, more that he knew where he stood and who had sent him. He was no more determined or tenacious or bold than the gentle Jeremiah – and for the same reason.

The true story of Luther's disappearance was not known for some time. A cry of dismay arose from all his sympathizers, and in Worms shock and apprehension followed the news. Dürer the artist wrote "O God, if Luther is dead, who will henceforth expound to us the gospel? What might he not have written for us in the next ten or twenty years?" It was rumoured that the body had been found with a knife in the back. Worms grew tense. Then the ban was promulgated, threatening every sympathizer with extermination. Aleander was delighted. The Pope celebrated the news with a round of carnivals and comedies. Henry VIII congratulated the Archbishop of Mainz on the overthrow of "the rebel against Christ." It was the Englishman Tunstall attending the Diet who reported back to Cardinal Wolsey with sober English realism that there were a hundred thousand Germans ready to lay down their lives for Luther. A letter written by de Valdés, the Emperor's secretary, was still more discerning. He saw Worms not as an end but the beginning of something new. He knew the Germans were exasperated with Rome: he noticed that even in Worms they ignored the Emperor's decree and were selling Luther's books openly. He blamed the Pope for not acceding to Luther's request for a general council and for pursuing his own interests. He saw him blindly

[1] WA. Br. 2, 253 ff.

insisting on the burning of Luther, and equally blindly not seeing Christendom being harried to destruction.[1]

The forebodings of de Valdès were justified. Luther's books were burned in the Low Countries, in England and in Scotland. Yet they prevailed. The world was to hear the rending of the seamless robe in a way more disastrous than the tear of 1054 when eastern orthodoxy broke away from western catholicism.

[1] The dispatch of Contarini, April 25 (Kidd, No. 46(a)) and the letter of the Archbishop of Mainz in July to Leo X (Kidd, No. 46(b)) give further evidence of the support Luther enjoyed in Germany.

# CHAPTER IV

# LUTHER FACES THE PROBLEMS OF THE REFORMATION

LUTHER WAS IN THIS REMOTE CASTLE FOR NEARLY A YEAR, ATTENDED by two pages and an armed guard. He received friends, wrote letters, wandered in the grounds and was well treated, though he was hardly in his natural element. Above all he worked hard in his study, in particular on his translation of the Bible, when he actually completed the translation of the whole New Testament in ten weeks. As a result of his labours he hoped that one day "the German lark would sing as well as the Greek nightingale."

## 1. Latomus – Catholic Reaction

For the next four years Luther faced stormy opposition not only from opponents of evangelical theology but from supporters such as the enthusiasts and the socialists. As early as March, 1520, Luther had answered a combined attack on his theology from the two universities of Cologne and Louvain. Louvain sought to press home the attack. They had long suspected Erasmus as one who sympathized with Luther, and sought either to force Erasmus to declare his position or seek his support for their attack. Erasmus refused to be forced or used, and suggested the honourable and normal course open to every university, to hold an academic disputation and publish the findings. This they declined and one of their number, Latomus, attacked Erasmus and then wrote a book against Luther. This storm was brewing as Luther set out for Worms, and it was in the Wartburg on May 26, 1521, that Luther received a copy of this last-named work. Within one month he had framed his answer.[1] In Part I, Luther answered the attack on his thesis that no man can in fact fulfil the commandments of God, and that sin remains after baptism. In Part II Luther developed his evangelical theology on the nature of sin and the answer of the gospel. In Part III Luther discussed the authority of scripture and tradition with reference to law and gospel. The work is a valuable statement of Luther's evangelical theology in relation to catholicism at the time.

## 2. Carlstadt – Radical Reaction

Meanwhile at Wittenberg the Reformation went on without Luther. The

[1] See L.C.C., Vol. XVI, pp. 308 ff.

university had increased its staff and now included John Bugenhagen, the celebrated humanist, John Agricola and the learned Justus Jonas. Many monks had joined the cause, had left their monasteries and were publicly teaching the new theology: among them were the Franciscan Ebertin, the Augustinian Stifel, and the Franciscan von Kettenbach. Luther found these men too socialist. Luther was disturbed at the news from Wittenberg in that theological and religious reform had been violently thrust aside in favour of fanaticism, radicalism and socialism.

At Wittenberg Carlstadt, the senior colleague of Luther, and the man who had put up such a lamentable performance at Leipzig, assumed the leadership in a manner distinguished more by its zeal than its sense. He was aided and abetted by another of the fiery monks just referred to, the Augustinian Gabriel Zwilling, a man who had a great reputation as a preacher. The gospel seemed to go to the heads of these monks! Carlstadt and his supporters stepped forward as energetic and practical reformers scorning Luther's method of preaching the Word and teaching Biblical theology, leaving reformation to develop under the promptings of God and His Spirit. They thought this method was too slow in yielding results. Carlstadt demanded the abolition of monasticism, the rewriting of the mass and its re-establishment on the lines of the Last Supper, and the making of marriage compulsory by law. Melanchthon, disquieted, sought Luther's advice. In the meantime one-third of the monks at the Augustinian convent had left in a way that made it difficult for those remaining. Luther counselled sanity, and worked out his views in his two books *On the Abuse of Masses*[1] and *On Monastic Vows*.[2]

At this moment the Cardinal Archbishop of Mainz,[3] being heavily in debt owing to his scandalous licentiousness, decided to have an exhibition of relics at Halle to raise money. He claimed he had bones and whole corpses of saints, a piece of Isaac's body, some manna from the wilderness, portions of the burning bush, jars from the wedding at Cana (with wine), thorns from Christ's crown, one of the stones that killed Stephen, in all a total of nine thousand relics. Pious alms were invited and "surpassing" indulgences promised. At the moment of perpetrating this he saw fit to throw into gaol a priest who had sought permission to marry. This roused Luther, for not only was the bishop a notorious evil liver but he also accumulated a small income by issuing licences to priests to keep concubines. Luther wrote a very stiff letter to the prelate discussing the whole scandalous affair, and threatened to make it public if he did not receive a satisfactory answer within a fortnight. Both Spalatin and Frederick were terrified at the consequences such an audacious letter from a monk

[1] WA. 8, 482-563.
[2] WA. 8, 573-669. Trans. American edition, Vol. 44, 243-400.
[3] See p. 41.

to his archbishop would provoke, and Spalatin neither delivered the letter nor disclosed he had received one.

Events at Wittenberg began to disturb Luther more and more. Frustrated by the slowness of correspondence and the non-delivery of what could not pass the court censors, he journeyed secretly to Wittenberg as a knight with an attendant. He stayed three days, unknown to all save a few close friends and returned to the Wartburg disquieted and disconsolate both at the state of Wittenberg and at the fact that the court would not let his writings against the recrudescence of the indulgences scandal be delivered to the Archbishop of Mainz. Yet he knew he would one day return to Wittenberg.

Luther learned two lessons on his secret visit to Wittenberg. He now realized that Carlstadt understood the Reformation in a way fundamentally different from his own, and that the court was rather reserved in its support of Luther. The prince wanted as little as possible changed, Carlstadt wanted as much as possible changed. Luther sensed he could do nothing as yet: in society he was an outlaw, in the Church an excommunicate. He had no choice but to return to the Wartburg and wait on God and events.

Luther saw the issue as one involving the Word of God, and held, therefore, that the only appropriate weapons were words. Luther believed that once the gospel was again made clear to men, the old mistaken forms such as the earning of merits or the repetition of masses, as well as all the accretions and innovations of catholic practices would fall away. He was not concerned about the reformation of external forms: clothes and vestments, performances and postures did not interest him. In fact, he genuinely respected tradition in all its forms – the church building, the minister's robes, the crucifix, the form of service. He sought only to make the gospel ring out once more in the clear tones of Christ and the apostles within that historic and catholic tradition. To Luther the evangelical party belonged to Mother Church.

Luther had at first contemplated no change. He had hoped for a reformation of doctrine and morals within the Church without any division, though he was keenly aware that Christ brought a sword rather than peace. It was borne in upon him first at Leipzig in 1519 and finally at Worms in 1521 that the Church was going to resist him. It was then that Luther realized that he would have to fight the Church in the interests of the new evangelical theology. It was at this critical moment, when Luther was a prisoner at the Wartburg, that the negative aspect of this new reconstruction was violently taken over by the radicals and fanatics. They called Luther the Go-Slow Theologian, Dr. Pussyfoot, the Armchair Theologian. Luther knew that a thing can be undone by being overdone. In any case he was a catholic conservative, seeking to preserve what had never been lost, seeking only to free the gospel from accretion and corruption. He believed that this wild left-wing radicalism was a worse danger to Christianity than corrupt catholicism.

Disturbances first broke out in Erfurt in June, 1521. Twelve hundred students, aided and abetted by ruffians and labourers, destroyed sixty houses where the priests lived, drove these men out of the city and burned the library. Monks and scholars fled. Erfurt never recovered its prestige and the university fell into decay.

In Wittenberg Carlstadt wrote and preached against celibacy, monastic vows and the mass. At Christmas, 1521, he changed the service of the mass, abolished elevation, distributed in both kinds, wore lay clothes to celebrate, and with great publicity married a peasant girl. He denounced images and pictures and stirred up the townsfolk to destroy them. He opposed infant baptism, assailed the fasts, repudiated all his titles and dignities, ridiculed theological learning, and sought to turn the students to farming instead. He threw aside his priestly and academic garb and donned a peasant's smock, appealing most dangerously to his inspiration.

All this had disastrous consequences. Thirty monks left the monastery in an uncontrolled and disorderly fashion in November, 1521, and the remaining ten sought the advice of Luther on their future course. At this time two fanatics, Storch and Stübner, were drawn to Wittenberg, and most ominously were joined by Cellarius, supported by Thomas Münzer, the wildest and ablest fanatic of them all, who was developing the same kind of theology at Zwickau by electing twelve apostles and seventy-two disciples. Whereas Luther had taught humble submission to the Word of God, these men boasted direct revelation from God. They talked with God: they knew the Holy Spirit. Wild scenes of excess were generated by these fanatical mystics.

Without waiting for permission, Luther at unbelievable risk to his person, returned to Wittenberg early in March. There he preached a course of eight sermons from Sunday to Sunday,[1] and by sheer power of godly sound sense prevailed against the fanatics. It was a critical moment for the Reformation. Was the sanity and sense of Luther to prevail, or the wild irrationalities of the fanatics? Order or confusion? Discipline under the Word of God, or indiscipline and spiritual licence? Never has sober eloquence achieved more. He preached the Word of Truth, and without naming those in error, he demolished them utterly. No unkind word, no coarse personal allusion passed his lips. He handled the whole matter like a true pastor under God. The "prophets" retired in confusion: Carlstadt to retirement, Münzer to appear again in the disastrous Peasants' War of 1525.

Luther resumed his labours at Wittenberg at once, both teaching in the

[1] WA. 10. 3, 1–64. Trans. W.M.L. II. 387 ff.

university and preaching both there and in the region roundabout. In company with Melanchthon he revised his translation of the New Testament which gave rise to the peevish complaint of Cochlaeus that "even shoemakers and women ... ventured to dispute not only with Catholic laymen but even with masters and doctors of theology, about faith and the Gospel." As soon as he had finished the New Testament, he began the translation of the Old. It was at this time that he had his disagreeable passage of arms with Henry VIII[1] but his most important work was *On the Secular Power*.[2]

It was the pressure of events that compelled Luther to declare his mind on the relation of Christianity to society. First there was the pressure from radicals, enthusiasts and fanatics, who were violently working to bring about a "kingdom of saints" dependent only on the Holy Spirit for guidance, a kingdom beyond the reach of any secular authority. Then there was the older Romanist view which sought to set the civil government and its authority beneath the so-called higher morality of spiritual authority invested in the Church: this view claimed to have the authority of a thousand years of tradition reaching back to Constantine. Certain Catholic princes supported by ecclesiastics were attempting forcibly to suppress evangelical theology and to ban Luther's writings, in particular his translation of the Bible. Luther sought to restore what in effect was the teaching of Paul, in particular in Romans 13:1-7. Luther saw the State as the minister of God doing the work of God, a work no other authority could do, a work in which a Christian man may properly and lawfully engage, and without which society would disintegrate. This civil and secular authority had the right to legitimate use of force in the restraint and punishment of evil-doers and in the protection of the persons and property of the society against outside attack. Luther raised the conception of civil government (in a way he was later to do for marriage) as a divine order in which and through which a man served God and his neighbour. Nevertheless, he was careful to define and limit the authority of the State to the protection of what is external, *i.e.* person and property. He would never allow the right of private persons or pressure groups to take up arms against the State or to use violence for their ends (even if legitimate). On the other side, he would never permit the right of a state or ruler to invade the province of a man's soul or interfere with his religion: he would never permit the raiding of papers by civil authorities, or the seizing of a man's Bible or his books.[3]

Although Luther's concern was strictly theological, the political situation assumed some importance after Worms. The German people began to

---

[1] See pp. 77 ff.
[2] WA. 11, 245-81. Trans. W.M.L. III. 323 ff.
[3] See *Luther Speaks*, ed. Hans Ehrenberg (Lutterworth, 1947), pp. 5-13.

take a growing interest in the Reformation, and consequently ecclesiastical authorities found it more and more difficult to execute the papal bull and to enforce the Edict of Worms. The Emperor was occupied with an insurrection in Spain, a war with France, and the conquest of Mexico by Cortez. The Turks had overrun Hungary and were threatening Germany. Pope Leo X had died in December, 1521, and was succeeded by Adrian VI. Adrian was a striking contrast to his predecessors, a man of grave moral earnestness, monastic piety and unblemished character. He entered Rome bare-footed. Every day at dawn he read mass, he ate frugal food, slept on a simple bed and led the life of a monk. But this same Adrian was a Dominican opposed to any doctrinal reformation: a man with sympathy neither for the new learning nor the new reformed theology. He had advised the Church to take a firm line against Luther and, when a professor at Louvain, had combined with Latomus in his attack on Luther. Adrian saw the urgency of an ethical and moral reformation: Luther sought a theological reformation which would result in a purified and true church. The papal curia detested its new head.

This was the background to the Diet of Nürnberg which met in March and November 1522. Adrian VI demanded the enforcement of Worms against Luther,[1] but virtually destroyed his case in decrying the scandalous state of the Church in terms as strong as Luther's: "From the head the corruption has passed to the limbs, from the Pope to the prelates: we have all departed; there is none that doeth good, no, not one."[2] He saw the rise of Protestantism as a just punishment on wicked Catholicism, and he promised to remedy the evil beginning with the curia. He effected little for he died too soon, rumour says of poison. Rome rejoiced at his timely demise and saw to it that the next pope, Clement VII (1523–34), would be certain to restore the *status quo ante*.

At the Diet of Nürnberg, Frederick's conduct, in permitting Lutheranism to grow, was deplored; nevertheless, Luther's splendid handling of enthusiasm and radicalism at Wittenberg convinced many of his soundness and reliability. His books were openly printed and sold in the shops at Nürnberg, and Osiander (Cranmer's father-in-law) preached freely. The Diet, though commanding Luther to keep silent, refused to execute the edicts of Worms and demanded a free oecumenical council within a year, repeating the charges of the German people and virtually throwing a shield over Lutheranism.[3] Compromise though the Edict of Nürnberg was, it was yet a step forward for the cause of reformation and marked clearly the beginning of German emancipation from the papacy. The pressure from the Emperor was absent and Frederick the Wise still hoped that Germany and the world would see the truth of Luther's doctrine.

A dark cloud loomed up over these political influences. Clement VII

---

[1] Kidd, No. 58.          [2] Kidd, No. 59, Section LXX.          [3] Kidd, Nos. 60, 61.

had forced through the Diet of Nürnberg an edict which Luther at once suspected as contradictory. It promised an investigation into the Luther affair, at the same time allowing itself freedom to prosecute the Edict of Worms. Archduke Ferdinand of Austria and the dukes of Bavaria, together with twelve bishops from Southern Germany, formed a league at Ratisbon (Regensburg) in July, 1524, for the protection of Roman Catholicism from Reformation theology. Philip of Hesse and John of Saxony[1] formed a counter-league at Torgau in 1526, though the Reformers dissociated themselves from this course, on their basic principle that the Word of God would effect the Reformation without the sword. This action at Ratisbon divided the German people into two camps. Germany was to suffer much from this division: she is still much more divided on this issue than, for example, the British.

### 3. Henry VIII – Political Reaction

Henry VIII was hardly a problem to Luther but he was certainly a type of common catholic reaction opposed to evangelical theology. He had urged Charles V to use force to exterminate the Lutheran heresy and was stirred by Luther's *Babylonish Captivity* to write a defence of the seven sacraments,[2] a book he dedicated to Leo X. In the book he handled Luther with the greatest contempt, treating him as a blasphemer and agent of Satan. He reasserted the authority of the Church against individual freedom and adhered to the doctrine of transubstantiation. Clement VII saw the hand of the Holy Spirit in the work and promised indulgence to all who read it. He confirmed on Henry the title of "Defender of the Faith" given by his predecessor, a title the British monarch retains to this day, though with a somewhat different meaning.

Luther replied in the same key.[3] He abused the king's person mercilessly before the world, dismissed his contemptible theology, and treated the whole matter with scurrilous scorn. Luther made a mistake here. He would have served his purpose better by handling Henry with the dignity and restraint he displayed in settling the troubles of Wittenberg. Henry deserved the treatment, but it did Luther more harm than Henry. In September, 1525, the King of Denmark, hoping for some alliance among countries who had rejected the suzerainty of Rome, persuaded Luther against his judgment that an apology for his personal remarks would open up the possibility of England's friendship. Luther apologized to Henry for

[1] John, Elector of Saxony 1525-32, was brother and successor to Frederick the Wise (see p. 109).

[2] *Assertio septem sacramentorum*: re-edited, translated Louis O'Donovan, 1908.

[3] WA. 10. 2, 180-222. See also *Luther's Reply to King Henry VIII*, trans. E. S. Buchanan (New York, 1928).

his personal remarks though not for his theology. Henry rudely replied that he wanted neither his apology nor his theology, and charged Luther with violating a nun and leading monks to perdition. The Reformation suffered a great blow from this controversy. It is true that Cardinal Pole abused Henry just as violently, though nobody raises this as an argument against Roman Catholicism. All that Luther did was to answer a gratuitous attack in terms of the attack. We blame Luther because we expect more of him.

## 4. Erasmus – Humanist Reaction

Luther faced another problem, the humanism of the Renascence: a movement with which all the Reformers were associated and which at first greatly helped them with its appeal to sources and its revival of classical studies. The problem presented itself to Luther in his controversy with Erasmus, a controversy in which Englishmen tend to side with Erasmus rather than with Luther. It is of first importance to understand why Protestantism turned from humanism, and how Luther saved the Church from humanism.

Erasmus, though quiet and reserved, combined high intellect with a vivid imagination, an almost perfect memory, a rapier wit, a sensitive and refined taste, and a genuine faith. He hated hypocrisy and humbug and loved sincerity and truth. In his own field of classical and biblical learning he towered as a sovereign of intellectual Europe. His mission was to revive Christian and classical antiquity and to make that a reforming power within the Church. He could effect the former but not the latter. He had a reformer's mind though none of the resolution and self-sacrifice a reformer needs. He refused to be involved. "I haven't a drop of martyr's blood in my veins," he once said of himself, and on another occasion, said that if he were ever put to the test he would betray his Master like Peter. Luther later said, when the controversy was joined, that Erasmus had done all he could do. Like Moses he had led the children of Israel to the plains of Moab, but could not lead them into the Promised Land. That Joshua was to be Luther. Erasmus forwarded the Reformation, positively by reviving classical, biblical and patristic studies, negatively by exposing pitilessly with a mordant wit the ignorance and bigotry of the monks as well as the obscurantism of the schoolmen. It would seem that when he had done these two tasks he had no nerve to complete his mission. By about 1524 he seemed to withdraw, and for the remaining twelve years of his life was conservative or reactionary. He was a reformer against the Reformation, and at the end of his life lost the respect both of Protestantism and of Catholicism. Nevertheless, history has always judged Erasmus kindly. He stood astride the mediaeval and the modern period, and like Reuchlin and

Staupitz was a transition man. He was never a Protestant and always showed a scholarly, cautious scepticism about the movement and its consequences. He disliked division, separatism and sectarianism, and enthusiasm in any shape or form, and showed distaste for the strong dogmatic theology of the reformers as well as for their evangelical piety. He thought it a fatal error to leave the Catholic Church and believed that all reformation should remain within it.

He was born in Rotterdam in 1466 (?1467), the illegitimate son of a priest and a physician's daughter. He quickly showed himself a prodigy, both at school at Utrecht and at the academy at Deventer. His good mother died early and left her money for the education of her son. The guardians misappropriated his inheritance and when Erasmus was of age thrust him into a monastery against his will. Erasmus detested every moment of the five years he spent there, a loathing which never left him. He escaped by the subterfuge of ordination, and was later released from his vows to live as a free man of letters. It was then he earned his European reputation. He liked England and made friends of people like Colet, More, Fisher, Wolsey and Warham, Henry VIII not excluded. He held the Lady Margaret Chair at Cambridge where his rooms are still in use at Queens' College. Nevertheless, he made many bitter enemies owing to his trenchant criticisms of the European scene, and withdrew to the quiet and tolerant atmosphere of Basel where he could live and work in peace. When Basel went reformed in 1529 he retired to a Catholic milieu at Freiburg. On returning to Holland via Basel he fell ill and died there in 1536, genial and witty even on his death-bed. He died without a priest and without the last rites, and lies buried by a pillar in the Protestant Cathedral at Basel where a plaque sums up his life.

Erasmus was not a theologian in the sense that Luther and Calvin were theologians. Neither was he a humanist of the frivolous and faithless kind that the Renascence threw up in Italy and France, men who ridiculed the Church. Erasmus was more serious, was concerned about the Church, and was a believing man. He did not mock at religion, but at its pompous performers, its obscurantist theologians, its ignorant and irreligious monks. Oecolampadius said that it was from Erasmus that he learned that nothing but Christ had to be sought after in the Scriptures. He sought to restore the Church to paths of Biblical simplicity and spiritual purity. He wanted to bring dogma to a minimum and to grant to the layman the maximum liberty of belief. He loathed the speculations of the schoolmen which raised questions nobody asked and gave answers nobody wanted. He hated the vices and follies of the monks and clergy, but still more their ignorance and superstitition. Even the papacy he criticized for teaching contrary to the doctrines of Christ.

Erasmus opened himself to criticism in his doctrine of sin, and derivatively therefore his shadowy doctrine of grace. Whereas Erasmus laughed at the folly of the Church, Luther cried. Erasmus never diagnosed the problem and his wit worsened it: Luther diagnosed it and poured out rivers of redemptive theology. At this point Erasmus withdrew with the parting shot of his diatribe on the freedom of the will. As long as reformation was being *discussed* Erasmus went along with the idea. As soon as Luther burned the papal bull and the decretals in 1520, and had taken his stand at Worms in 1521, Erasmus began to withdraw.

It was in the interpretation of the gospel that they differed. Luther drew the distinction between law and gospel that characterizes the preaching of Christ and all the New Testament writers. On this basis Luther would grant no place for merit, not even of the freedom of the will to fulfil the demands of either Old or New Testament. The gospel meant that a man was justified by faith in Christ alone, and could never earn merit nor the mercy of God. Luther graphically describes the attack of Erasmus as "grabbing him by the throat," and thought him unlike his other adversaries, who never saw Luther's theological business but discussed abuses and scandals. To Luther all is of grace: in relation to God a man is nothing, has nothing and can effect nothing to make that relationship.

Erasmus had been a very real support to Luther in the beginning and did not readily oppose Luther later. He had disapproved of the procedure of Worms (quite rightly) and (again quite rightly) was highly critical of the men Rome had chosen to answer Luther, e.g. Cajetan, von Miltitz and Aleander. (The latter he described as a maniac and an evil man.) When Carlstadt went enthusiastic at Wittenberg, and Luther engaged in vulgar controversy with Henry VIII, and when the nationalist von Hutten attacked Erasmus bitterly, Erasmus grew apprehensive. Still, even at this advanced stage, Erasmus counselled caution, gentleness, reformation and the calling of a general council.

Provoked by Hutten, goaded by Louvain and urged by Henry and other Englishmen, Erasmus came out against Luther as late as 1524 on the doctrine of depravity and the bondage of the will in his book *The Freedom of the Will*.[1] Erasmus argued that freedom was essential if moral responsibility existed: a man was free to heed or disregard. The book is courteous and respectful, but shows that Erasmus had never plumbed the depths of evangelical theology. In a paradoxical way his very goodness and decency and refinement served to put him beyond the reach of the gospel. Erasmus could be improved but hardly needed redemption. The words to the good Nicodemus could well have been addressed to Erasmus: "Art thou the master of Israel and knowest not these things?"

[1] WA. 18, 600–787. See *Discourse on free will* [by] *Erasmus* [and] *Luther*, trans. and ed. Ernest F. Winter (1961).

Luther took a year to reply.[1] He related divine foreknowledge and pre-destination, and inferred that everything happens by necessity and that there can be no freedom in the creature. The will has no freedom in its salvation, though it is absolutely free in all other activities. It is driven by God or Satan. The exhortations in Scripture to repentance and holy living were calls which convince us we could do neither, and were meant to convince us of our hopelessness and helplessness, and to throw us on the mercy of God. Erasmus was too superficial. The Augustinian view that man in his totality is a *fallen* creation, is the best empirical explanation of the facts, and is biblical. Man is corrupted, tainted, impure in all he thinks, says and does. It is this root conviction that makes men aware of the glorious dimension of the free unmerited grace of God who, while man was yet a sinner, sought him out for salvation and redemption and new life with Him.

It was not that the Reformers were obsessed with sin, but rather that they treated it with the seriousness of Christ. They had realized that their own good works were getting them nowhere, and when they were once aware of this and the reason, they welcomed the gospel as a prisoner the key of his cell. They realized that it was not they who had chosen Christ but Christ who had chosen them. That they were chosen, and others seemingly not, was part of the inscrutable will of God. They deplored intellectual speculation or explanations of the mysteries of God's workings. The Reformers all taught this bondage of the will to oneself and one's own interests and therefore its inability to effect its own righteousness and salvation. All that they now enjoyed was the direct gift of the grace of God, and it was on Him and not themselves they depended.

Erasmus and Luther were now wholly estranged, and when the dis-astrous Peasants' War broke out at this time Erasmus was confirmed in his worst apprehension. He hated controversy and wanted quiet and good sense to prevail. He now regarded the Reformation as a calamity, harmful alike to the Church and to the new learning. When he was later sum-moned by the Emperor to Augsburg in 1530 to act as his adviser, Erasmus was bold enough to decline. He knew he would please neither side, so stayed away.

## 5. *The Peasants' War 1525 – Social Reaction*[2]

Germany had had a long history of peasants' revolts: 1476, 1492, 1493, 1502, 1513 and a very serious one as late as 1514 in Württemberg. All had been quelled by brute force and all had failed to improve the lot of the

---

[1] Martin Luther, *On the Bondage of the Will*, trans. J. I. Packer and O. R. Johnston (Clarke, 1957).
[2] See Franz Guenther, *Der Deutsche Bauernkrieg* (1956).

D

peasant. Indeed rebellion had always made the position worse. There was some considerable justification for these outbreaks, for the German peasants were little more than slaves. They were ground down by taxation, legal and illegal. The increase of wealth, luxury and pleasure following on the discovery of America worsened their lot. There was a shortage of land owing to an increase of population: there was a shortage of money owing to the drainage of silver coinage in papal taxation. Both in Germany and Holland they organized secret trades unions (as they would now be called). England, too, had had a bitter taste of rebellion in 1381 under Wat Tyler and John Balle, a revolt which issued in a disastrous purge at Oxford of all scholars and teachers associated with Wycliffe's evangelical theology.

Although Luther himself never countenanced rebellion of this sort, nor even the association of socialism with the new evangelical theology, society at large laid much of the blame at his feet. The establishment found it a ready excuse to blame their shortcomings on to the Reformation movement, and even the peasants themselves believed that Luther would be their leader in this just cause. The Reformers attacked papal tyranny on theological grounds but most Germans on economic and political grounds. The Reformers preached evangelical liberty, the supremacy of the Word of God and every man's right to know it. They taught the priesthood of all believers and the dignity and decency of every soul in the sight of God apart from social rank. These theological aspirations were very strong and real, and very naturally stirred up hopes and longings of a social kind together with a deep discontent with their lot. A man cannot find a new freedom and dignity in Christ without yearning for a new order of society. The peasants identified their grievances and hopes for a better and more just society with Luther's work, and looked to him, a man of the people, for leadership. They were not wide of the mark, for he would have made a mighty leader of a peasants' trade union, had God not given him and prepared him for a wholly different task. The peasants' cause was just, and their demands both moderate and fair: their mistake was in identifying the religious cause of Luther with a cause justifiable on wholly different grounds. Further, they had disastrous leadership.

The Peasants' War was related to the radicalism which had broken out under Carlstadt at Wittenberg. Luther abruptly left the security of the Wartburg and settled these disturbances by the sheer weight of sensible teaching and preaching. But the Wittenbergers in their close community and fine tradition of balanced theological teaching were open to conviction in a sense in which isolated, down-trodden, illiterate aggrieved peasants could never be. They responded to Luther and rejected Carlstadt and Münzer outright.

Carlstadt remained in Wittenberg until 1523, after which he retired to a parish near Jena where he brought his radicalism, his enthusiasm and his

learning into effect. He preached the destruction of all images and crucifixes and the total disregard of all authority, civil, political and spiritual,
claiming the direct communication of the Lord for his actions. He taught
polygamy on Old Testament principles, and even Old Testament land
law. He carried the dispossessed with him (though many of his parishioners
were disquieted) and continued to keep in touch with the wild Thomas
Münzer.

Thomas Münzer had succeeded in being appointed pastor at Allstedt.
In solitary communion with God in a lonely church tower he received his
divine revelations. He took it upon himself to establish a kingdom of
saints and taught that to this end he and his followers had the divine
command to kill off all the ungodly (rulers especially), and to destroy all
altars and images in the land. All property was to be held in common,
and if any prince refused to concur he had to be beheaded. He built up a
kind of secret confederacy in which all the "reliable" men were known
(his "saints") and was in constant touch with them by secret emissaries.
Many ordinary folk were disquieted but he had much support from
the down-trodden peasants, hardly for his wild theology, more because
they had nothing to lose but their servility and their poverty. Pfiefer,
the ex-monk, was also fanning the embers of revolt with a lot of hot
air.

In the meantime Luther had declared his mind on the relation of the
spiritual and secular in 1523.[1] He had carefully differentiated between the
life of the soul in relation to God, and the authority and responsibility of
secular government to maintain law and order and to protect its citizens.
The former, God had declared in the Bible; the latter, man had to develop
in accordance with his needs at any time or place and it had never been
the subject of divine revelation. Nevertheless, in performing this task the
State was doing the work of God, a work only the State can do. As a
servant of God the State was to maintain a just and proper society and to
punish evil. The Mosaic code had no authority for society, save in its
moral commands: much of the Old Testament legislation belonged to
another religion and another culture and was in no sense universally
authoritative.

Luther's views were clear and consistent. He sought to safeguard the
civil power against an irregular assertion of religious, biblical and mystical
authority, as he had sought to safeguard it against the overreaching
aggression of the papal hierarchy. At the same time he sought to safeguard
the individual against unlawful encroachments of both powers. To
Münzer's reviling of his person and views Luther never replied. To
Münzer's threat that the spirit was soon to strike with fists, Luther maintained that Antichrist would be destroyed "without hands." If the rebels

[1] See p. 75.

were misguided enough to use force, the secular arm would answer with greater force.

The cool common sense of Luther, and his unanswerable theological stand in comparison with the foolish and fanciful theology of the enthusiasts, reassured the normal run of people but served to provoke the fanatics into wilder fury. Münzer went round the countryside stirring up the peasants, Luther went round warning them of the danger and counselling caution. Carlstadt was ejected from his Chair and Luther reformulated his own views in his book *Against the Celestial Prophets* (1524).[1]

The storm broke at Mühlhausen. Münzer and the fiery ex-monk Pfeifer stirred up the people, who ejected their magistrates and set up what was virtually mob law. People flocked in from the region round about. Rebellion broke out in Southern Germany. The poorer artisans of the towns, dispossessed and oppressed by the new power of capitalism, joined cause with the peasants. These poor folk were now utterly obsessed with the idea of a total reconstruction of society. Had they had a Luther to lead them, or even a sane socialist instead of a mad pseudo-theological visionary, tragedy would have been averted. The movement spread to Austria, Alsace, Franconia and Thuringia. The rebels were destroying the palaces of the bishops as well as the castles of the nobility. They burned down monasteries and libraries, and committed outrages on the person.

The demands of the peasants were drawn up in twelve articles, moderate and modest.[2] It is tragic that such good social sense was confounded by so much pseudo-theological nonsense: both the cause of reformation and the cause of social justice were irreparably damaged. The peasants professed that their claims were Christian. This shows the confusion of thought. No claims can ever be "Christian" claims: Christianity can only serve, minister, give, but never claim. A claim may be just, and therefore demand the support of all just men, Christian and non-Christian alike. The twelve articles were:

1. The right to elect their own pastor.
2. Freedom from the small tithe (though agreement to pay the grain tithe).
3. The abolition of bond service, since all men were redeemed by the love of Christ. They promised nevertheless obedience to their lawful rulers in all things reasonable.
4. Freedom to hunt and fish.
5. A share in the forests for domestic fuel.
6. Restriction of compulsory service.
7. Payment for labour in excess of contract (payment for overtime).
8. Reduction of rents.

[1] WA. 18, 62–125.      [2] Kidd, No. 83.

9. Cessation of arbitrary punishments.
10. Restoration of the pastures and fields which had been taken from common ownership.
11. Abolition of the right of heriot. (Heriot meant originally the restoration of a man's weapons to his overlord at death. It now meant the deprivation of inheritance to widows and orphans on the death of the tenant.)
12. All these demands to be tested by scripture, and, if not in agreement therewith, to be withdrawn.

When the articles reached Luther at Wittenberg in April he wrote his *Exhortation to Peace*.[1] He criticized both the secular and spiritual princes for fleecing their subjects, and warned them that if God allowed the devil to stir up these dispossessed folk into rebellion, it was not Luther's gospel that was to blame but their own sin which was earning the wrath of God. Gentleness, justice and fair-mindedness were to be their guides. To the peasants, though he realized that many were fighting for their rights under gospel colours, he spoke as a friend and brother. He was aware that their godless overlords laid intolerable and unjust burdens upon them, but their demands had nothing to do with the gospel and their conduct showed they had forgotten Christ and His ways. No wrongdoing on the part of the authorities ever justified rebellion and violence on the part of the people. He warned them that if they persisted they would do more harm to the gospel than ever Pope or Emperor had ever done. His final practical suggestion was that leaders from both sides should sit at a table and compose their differences, if not in a Christian spirit, then at least according to law and contract. Luther preached to deaf ears on both sides.

Münzer, now in Thuringia, publicly scorned this "snare of a delusive peace," and began to threaten in a very ugly manner. Events gathered a frightening momentum. By this time cruel and bloody outrages were being perpetrated by the aroused peasants, often on innocent women and children. Once committed to this course they could not desist. They extended the war. They justified the war. Success went to their heads.[2] Imperilling his life, Luther travelled throughout the countryside exhorting the peasants to sanity and sense, and the rulers to firmness. At this tragic moment the old Elector Frederick lay dying. He summoned Luther to his death-bed, but died (May 5, 1525) before Luther could reach him. When the conflict worsened, and Luther realized his appeals to both sides were unavailing, he wrote his attack *Against the Murderous and Plundering Bands of Peasants*.[3] He argued that the responsibility of every able-bodied man

[1] WA. 18, 291–334. Trans. W.M.L. IV. 205 ff.
[2] See a contemporary account in Hillerbrand.
[3] WA. 18, 357–61. Trans. WML. IV. 247 ff.

was to resist them "as long as he could move a muscle." He knew that countless peasants had been dragooned into the devilish conspiracy and begged the nobility, "Dear lords, help these people. Save them. Take pity on these poor men." But the magistrates were to "stab, kill and strangle" as they would a mad dog those who persisted in these wicked outrages. This statement shocked many, and is always remembered against Luther. Luther knew it was harsh, yet in later years, when he often expressed regret for earlier errors, this he never confessed and refused to retract.[1] To Luther the gospel was at stake. The peasants had put themselves beyond the conference table, and to those who would not cease from an outrageous and mutually destructive rebellion, there was only one course open, the choice of a greater force to break it. He spoke with equal bluntness to both sides. The violence of his language is a measure of the issue he believed was at stake. Perhaps, had he stopped short of his final letter, history would have remembered him more kindly, but that still does not make Luther wrong on this rebellion.

The course of the lamentable revolt is too painful and too well-known to recount. Within a few weeks the nobility, Catholic and Protestant alike, joined forces to defeat the common social threat of the peasants, now mustered at Frankenhausen in 1525. Without commissariat, without military leadership, the wretched peasant hordes put up no fight and were literally cut to pieces. Five thousand lay slain on the fields and in the streets. Three hundred were summarily beheaded in the market place. Münzer was taken prisoner, cruelly tortured, brutally executed. Eighteen thousand fell in Alsace. In all, one hundred thousand misguided souls perished in battle. Survivors were beheaded or mutilated. Widows and orphans wailed lamentably and could not be comforted. Convents were burnt, villages wiped out. Cattle were slain, farm implements smashed.

The Peasants' Revolt had been the abysmal failure Luther feared, matched by the princes' inglorious tale of merciless revenge. Margrave George of Brandenburg reminded his brother with some bitterness that if he did not leave some peasants alive he would have nothing to live on. The conditions of the peasants worsened, their grievances remained, the prospect of amelioration was indefinitely postponed and the split in the nation widened. Further there was the harm caused to Reformation theology. The Romanists held Luther responsible for the revolt. Even Erasmus attributed it to the violence inherent in Reformation thinking. Yet Luther alone offered a real diagnosis of such social rebellion, and Luther alone proposed a remedy by removal of the long-standing causes. In Roman Catholic districts the peasantry were forced back into catholic practice. Nobody gained.

.    .    .    .    .

[1] WA. 18, 384 ff. Trans. W.M.L. IV. 257 ff.

There was, nevertheless, one quiet and lovely thing that belonged to the sorrow and turmoil of those years, Luther's marriage. Luther had long taught that vows of life-long celibacy were unnatural and unscriptural and most of the Reformers and many priests and monks had seen the truth of this and married. Certain people challenged Luther that he had not the courage of his convictions in that he remained unmarried. But forty is not an easy age to marry, and is long past the years of youth and courtship. Further, he was both a heretic and an outlaw, and had once said that a man in that state could never marry. In addition he had a full-time university teaching post, some cure of souls, and was the inspiration and guide of the Reformation.

Yet when the tumult and confusion were at its worst he very quietly married Katharina von Bora, a young woman of twenty-six years of age, without beauty but strong, healthy, frank and intelligent. Katharina was a member of the lower nobility who as a child had been put into a convent. Two years before her marriage she had contrived an escape with seven other nuns. They appealed to Luther for help to rehabilitate themselves and it was during this period that Luther and Katharina decided to marry. Many of Luther's friends were shocked when they heard the news, and thought Luther was "lowering himself." Luther did not discuss his decision to marry: "A man must ask God for counsel, and pray, and then act accordingly," was all he said.

# CHAPTER V

# LUTHER'S RECONSTRUCTION OF THE CHURCH IN SAXONY ON EVANGELICAL PRINCIPLES, 1525–32

## 1. Parish Reform

THE PEASANTS' WAR MARKED THE LAST OF THE DESTRUCTIVE TENDENCIES associated with the Reformation, and for the next seven years there was a happier period of reconstruction. Luther never saw it as his rôle to re-organize the Church or to re-systematize its theology: he simply preached the Word of God. He sowed the seed and left it to germinate, certain that the Word of God would not return void, and believing that this Word would permeate and restore the Church.

Luther was right in this, yet it must be remembered that as long as a theological leadership was needed, as it was in the early years, Luther gave this with a brilliance unsurpassed. This theological leadership involved him with other men, with princes and peasants, priests and prelates, monks and merchants, scholars and saints, as well as with social, nationalist, cultural and political causes. The latter were not easy to separate from theological reformation proper, and Luther, tied down in an academic backwater of Europe and holding no ecclesiastical office of any kind, had no power beyond his pen to influence or direct the course of events. In fact, after 1521 the Reformation was largely in the hands of statesmen and princes, not in Luther's hands at all. Consequently, Luther's still brilliant academic and spiritual leadership was seen only by those whose eyes had been opened; for the rest, wordly men led the worldly. The Catholic princes, for example, though seeking to remedy certain abuses, refused to sanction any interference with theology, and were seeking political and military alliances to enforce the dominance of Romanism. Henry VIII, too, had taken a stand against Luther. Erasmus had turned against Luther and towards Rome, though the world was marvelling at the theological weight of Luther's attack against the greatest intellectual of Europe. Erasmus's attitude caused a heavy loss of potential to the evangelical cause of the young Renascence scholars. Further, the nobility who had earlier been on Luther's side in those stirring days of 1520, had been disenchanted by the foolish rebellion of the nationalist von Sickingen against the Archbishop of Trier in 1523 and by the alarming disaster of the Peasants' War. And then there were the internal dissensions caused by the radicals, the fanatics and the sacramentarians.

Nevertheless, Luther's theology had won unqualified victory in Saxony whose prince desired to establish a restored Evangelical Church in his domains. Prussia had gone over entirely to the Reformation, bishops and people alike. Philip of Hesse was also a keen evangelical of a very practical kind, and in view of the combined political opposition of the catholic princes formed in 1526 the League of Torgau, which consisted of Saxony, Hesse, Brunswick–Lüneburg, Anhalt, Mecklenberg and the city of Magdeburg. This had the effect of permitting the evangelical cause in those areas to be established firmly both in idea and in constitution, giving some guarantee against violence from the catholic princes or from the Emperor. It further protected the young reformed evangelical Church from those disastrous theological raids of the fanatics.

Luther therefore worked in a situation wholly different from that of his earlier years. Then, there was all that fire and verve as he fought for his evangelical theology against both Pope and Emperor, while the world watched with bated breath. Now it was a matter of consolidation, of care and guidance, exercised by a hardworked university professor. He was an older man and now married. He spoke less the big language of national and international concerns, and more the language of religious, spiritual and even homely matters. Not that he was a lesser Luther than the Luther who had stood his ground among equals at Heidelberg, before superiors at Augsburg and Leipzig or before his rulers at Worms. If anything, it was a weightier and more seasoned Luther, only now he was outlawed and excommunicated and consequently it was only in remote Saxony that he could exercise any influence in the reconstruction of Church life.

Luther pressed his new and sympathetic Elector, John the Pious, to make money available for reforms in the university, in order to make new appointments and to increase the salaries of the established professors. Melanchthon's salary as Professor of Greek was doubled. It all has a very modern ring about it!

As indicated earlier, now that Luther had a prince who gave unqualified freedom to the new evangelical theology and protected it from the danger of outside attack, he had to give some thought to the kind of church system such theology demanded. The bishops in the area had now given up all attempts to check the new ideas. At Wittenberg, where some changes had been made, the Bible was read and the congregation sang hymns. The Elector wished to put Luther's ideas into practice forthwith, but Luther was not anxious to hurry the folk faster than the Holy Spirit was doing. He was all too well aware that many of the laity were only spectators, and many of the clergy obscurantist and incompetent. Many of the nobles were opposed to reformation and they were supported by their priests who depended on their lords' patronage. There was financial anxiety, too, for there were no longer payments for private masses, and many of the nobility had secularized church property and lands.

In the matter of liturgical reform[1] Luther seemed unwilling to make changes at all, possibly viewing liturgical reform as a derivative of theological reform. It was the extremists Carlstadt, Münzer and Zwilling who had initiated the revolutionary reforms. Luther, in fact, on his return from the Wartburg with characteristic conservatism continued to live in the monastery, wear the monk's habit, and celebrate the mass. The parish of Leisnig sought his advice on the maintenance of a parish chest, and in the course of this enquiry sought Luther's further help on worship. He wrote for them a tract *Concerning the Ordering of Divine Worship*[2] (1523) in which he suggested that the liturgy had been debased. The centrality of the Word had been lost; fables and legends had crept in to replace it; and worship had been considered a meritorious work. In Luther's ordering of daily worship his first principle was the reading and exposition of the Bible, to last about half an hour: this to be followed by prayers and thanksgivings, psalms and antiphons. He thought the whole should not be longer than an hour, and that though it should take place morning and evening in the parish church, only on Sunday could the whole parish be expected to attend. He thought the daily mass could well be discontinued, most festivals abolished, and the legends of the saints demythologized.

If Luther's first principle was the ministry of the Word, his second was to perpetuate the true and purify what had grown corrupt. He sought no changes for their own sake, nor did he cultivate fads as many radicals (and later Puritans) did. He wanted simplicity and integrity, with participation by the congregation intelligently and worshipfully. For his own people in Wittenberg he took a further step in formulating his *Formula of the Mass* (1523),[3] seeking to maintain the divine and set aside the human:

> We assert, it is not now, nor has it ever been, in our mind to abolish entirely the whole formal cultus of God, but to cleanse that which is in use, which has been vitiated by most abominable additions, and to point out a pious use.[4]

In this work he sets the mass in relation to its New Testament origins, and explains the catholic developments which began to incorporate prayers, psalms, kyries, the epistle, the gospel, the gloria, the creed and the sanctus as permissive and desirable. He relates this to legitimate patristic authorities. He considered the fatal error lay in the introduction of the Canon, the making of the mass into a priestly monopoly, its association

---

[1] W.M.L. VI contains *Luther's Liturgical Writings* in translation, his own principles of ordering worship (particularly pp. 83 ff.), and a selection of his hymns. See also American edition, 53. Both are most valuable source books.
[2] WA. 12, 1–30. Trans. W.M.L. VI. 49 ff.
[3] WA. 12, 205–20. Trans. W.M.L. VI. 65 ff.
[4] W.M.L. IV. 84 f.

with money in paid masses for the dead, and the long development of vestments, candles, images and idolatrous practices. He then suggested the shape of a reformed mass:

Introit
Kyrie
Gloria
Salutation
Collect
Epistle
Gradual
Gospel
Nicene Creed
Sermon
(Offertory abrogated)
Preface
(Canon abrogated)
Consecration
Lord's Prayer
Communion
Agnus Dei
Alleluia
Blessing

It is a widespread opinion among liturgical scholars that this was Luther's best liturgical work. The resemblance to other Reformed liturgies, not least the Anglican, is evident.

Owing to external demand Luther wrote his *German Mass*[1] of 1526, a folk mass in German idiom and in the vernacular. It comes as a surprise to most people to learn that Luther was not wholly given to this popularizing of the liturgy into the vernacular. Equally he was very concerned lest the reforming movement be petrified into any kind of uniformity. Fundamentally, his belief was in movement, so that the Holy Spirit could be more operative among the people of God. It is of great interest to see that, when he drew up the vernacular mass, he never sought a mere translation of a reformed Latin rite. He sought a fresh creation expressed in German thought and through the medium of German music for the simple Germans in the pew on Sundays: on weekdays the Latin Mass continued. Some have waxed enthusiastic about this great creation of Luther, but the best liturgical scholarship favours his earlier *Formula of the Mass* (a view Luther himself shared).

In the preface, on a discussion of the nature of worship, Luther classifies worship in three categories: the reformed Latin Mass, the German Mass, and finally the house congregation. Luther's interest seems more concerned with the last than with the other two. Here he envisaged the true

[1] WA. 19. 72–113; W.M.L. IV. 151 ff. complete text translated. Kidd, No. 95.

evangelical assembly gathering for Bible reading, prayer, the celebration of the sacraments, and to determine the pastoral responsibilities. At this point it becomes clear that Luther was more concerned to provide a good catechism for the people than to further liturgical reform.

The shape of the German Mass was:

> Hymn or Psalm
> Kyrie (threefold, not ninefold, and in Greek)
> Collect
> Epistle
> Hymn
> Gospel
> Creed
> Sermon on the Gospel
> Paraphrase of Lord's Prayer
> Blessing of bread and administration
> (Priest facing the people in the pattern of the Last Supper)
> German Sanctus and Elevation
> Blessing of Cup and its administration
> Hymns
> Agnus Dei
> Collect and Benediction.

Luther also engaged on other liturgical activities. He rewrote the Baptismal Service (1523, 1526).[1] He wrote books to advise pastors on the practice of confession,[2] marriage[3] and baptism.[4] He also drew up a Litany,[5] rewrote the Ordinal[6] and composed a few hymns,[7] all solidly biblical and evangelical, and still sung Sunday by Sunday.

From Luther's point of view he wanted to establish church principles based on the basic evangelical principles of justification by faith and the priesthood of all believers. Philip of Hesse convoked a synod at Homberg in 1526 to put these principles into effect, but Luther believed the people were not yet ready as a whole and that such ideas could not be imposed from without only desired from within. Now that he had re-organized the university, Luther pressed his Elector to re-organize parish life and also to overhaul his civil administration. Luther's plans were for every parish to have its own evangelical minister, and for every parish to maintain him. Ministers incompetent to preach, being otherwise of pious life, should be instructed to read the gospel and one of Luther's homilies. The Elector and Spalatin saw this immense task through in two districts and for the rest issued instructions.

In the larger world of the Empire matters were less favourable for evangelical theology. At Pavia, in 1525, Charles finally defeated and captured

---

[1] W.M.L. VI. 191 ff.    [2] Op. cit., 213 ff.    [3] Op. cit., 217 ff.
[4] Op. cit., 241 ff.    [5] Op. cit., 231 ff.    [6] Op. cit., 275 ff.

Francis I, King of France, and in 1526 both victor and vanquished promised together to do two things: to beat the Turk and to beat Luther. Certain evangelical German princes were intimidated, and it was this that caused Philip of Hesse to organize the League of Torgau.[1] Therefore when the Catholics met at Speier (Spires) in 1526 with the intention of effecting the final execution of the Edict of Worms they found they had to agree that until a general council was called, each state was "to live, rule and bear itself as it thought it could answer to God and Emperor."

In his concern for life at the parish level, though he despaired of doing much with the peasants, Luther showed solicitude for their children. He begged the Elector to compel every town and village to provide its own school as it already provided roads and bridges. He also showed concern for the monasteries, and now that the papal yoke had been removed, he begged the Elector, as the only authority available, to take over responsibility for their care and administration. The Elector complied.

At this time Luther was struck with recurrent attacks of the stone, and suffered intense pain and illness to the point of death. A friend and pastor, Leonard Kaiser, had been burnt alive in Bavaria for adhering to evangelical theology, and another, Winkler, had been murdered in Cologne. Erasmus was criticizing Luther, and the Swiss theologians opposing his sacramental theology. The plague struck the university and his home. Kathy was having a difficult confinement. Little Hans lay grievously ill. Luther was under considerable duress and wrote to Jonas:

> Pope, Emperor, princes, bishops, and all the world hate me, and as if that were not enough, my brethren too [referring to Zwingli, Oecolampadius and Erasmus] must needs afflict me.[2]

He felt, too, the burden of his sins, the nearness of death, and Satan raging against him. These he interpreted as the wrath of God to make him humbler and more receptive to His mercy. His great hymn "A safe stronghold is our God" was born of all this agony.

With the abatement of the plague his friends returned to Wittenberg. Melanchthon continued his visitations, and drew up articles for the guidance of laymen.[3] Luther wrote a preface to this work and said that as the bishops were faithless in their duty, the Elector had to carry out these plans as an "emergency bishop." The plans were formulated and considerable progress made, though the visitations showed a grim and distressing picture. Wittenberg, as was to be expected, was satisfactory, but the countryside was in a state of abysmal ignorance. A priest near Torgau did not know the Lord's Prayer or the Creed, but did a brisk business as an exorcist. Priests had to be ejected for gross immorality, drunkenness,

---

[1] See p. 89.　　[2] WA. Br. 4, No. 1168, November 10, 1527.　　[3] Kidd, No. 96.

irregular marriages, and many had to be prevented from keeping public houses and engaging on other work. Poverty and destitution were everywhere, but what grieved Luther most was the gross ignorance of the people the visitations revealed, and the desperate dearth of schools.

Luther's easy and unassuming mixing with the people with all his irrepressible humour, his boisterousness and energy makes pleasant reading. For the clergy he provided sermons for a year; for the people, and later the children, two splendid catechisms.[1] The catechisms were meant to provide simple directions for daily prayer, texts for the home, guidance for living. He exhorted the clergy to teach their folk: he exhorted the father of every household to take over the responsibility for the whole household, to give this teaching, help its members to pray and inculcate in them thankful hearts. These catechisms are magnificent statements of the Christian faith expressed without polemic or controversy.

At the same time as this reconstructive work was being forwarded in Saxony, there were ominous thunderings from the rest of Europe. Erasmus wrote two tracts castigating Luther for ruining the cultural climate and for bringing anarchy in the Church. Emser had procured a copy of Henry VIII's offensive reply to Luther, "improved" it, and published it throughout Germany. The Emperor was making plans to "settle the German question," the papal curia to extirpate Lutheranism. But there were pressures within as well as pressures without, and of these the most distressing was the sacramentarian controversy with the Swiss theologians.

## 2. The Sacramentarian Controversies[2]

The catholic interpretation of Christianity was sacramental and therefore sacerdotal. It had developed into a system marked by seven sacraments which are the means or the occasion through which the priest ministers grace to the faithful from infancy to death. As for the mass, it taught that the sacrifice Christ made on Calvary was repeated by the priesthood daily. Rome went further and claimed that the power of the mass reached beyond death to the souls in purgatory and released them from suffering.

Luther (and all the Reformers) found sacerdotalism of this kind alien to original and true Christianity. To them, all believing men called in the gospel were kings and priests alike. There was only one Mediator and Advocate and all believing men had free and unqualified access by prayer in faith. They rejected the notion of a sacrificing priesthood as non-Christian, and knew of only one Sacrifice, once offered, once for all. The

---

[1] Kidd, No. 97. Full texts WA. 30. 1, 125 ff., 239 ff. Translations in Tappert, *Book of Concord*, pp. 337 ff.

[2] The relevant material, annotated, and with valuable introductions, can be found in the American edition, Vols. 35–8.

theory of the transubstantiation of bread and wine into flesh and blood they rejected as based on Aristotle, non-scriptural, and of mediaeval, not primitive, origin. They emphasized the hearing and appropriation of the Word of God as the normal channel of grace, and saw the sacraments as the Word enacted, the validity and meaning being perceived in the Word though appropriated in the act of the sacrament. The root difference here is a doctrine of grace. Catholic practice had betrayed itself into allowing grace to be thought of almost as a spiritual medicine administered by a priest. Reformed theology was and is stiffly embattled against this (as were and are good catholic theologians), and makes grace the free, un-merited, unqualified, unconditional mercy of God freely offered to sinful man. Grace is not a potion but a relationship to God.

The difficulties in the Protestant world arose in the extent to which they allowed themselves to depart from catholic practice. Luther, for instance, held a very high sacramental theology, insisting on baptismal regeneration and the corporal presence. Zwingli took the view that Luther was scholastic and could not liberate himself from the mediaevalist philosophy of *substantia*, and (with Calvin later) reduced the sacraments to signs and seals of the grace of God. The Reformed theologians sought to preserve the sovereignty and freedom of God to work as He chose, though admitt-ing the sacraments as normal channels of grace, provided faith was there to make their reception worthy. Calvin and Zwingli were not wrong here. Luther had approached the doctrine of grace from the anthropocen-tric point of view of how he should find a gracious God, the others ap-proached it from the theocentric point of view of God's work for man. Luther was a Catholic whose eyes were opened to the reality of justifica-tion by faith: his theology was evangelical and redemptive, and though never anthropocentric, was found and explained in terms of man seeking God.[1] Zwingli, and Calvin even more, began with a glorious and in-fectious doctrine of God's sovereignty and the fiery doctrine of election. They proceeded from this and sought to re-state catholic theology and practice in the light of these first principles. Luther, on the other hand, started as a Catholic and sought by his theology to preserve and purify tradition.

The differences received their sharpest expression in eucharistic theology. Zwingli did not hold any doctrine of the real presence except in a spiritual sense. He rejected outright Roman transubstantiationism as well as Luther's catholic compromise. Zwingli understood the spiritual feeding of the faithful, who by partaking in faith heard the Word of God and received the Holy Spirit. Luther's doctrine of the real presence meant that a believer ate the real body and in this communion partook in faith of the forgiveness and salvation offered by Christ. Zwingli's doctrine of God

---

[1] "When shall I ever find a gracious God?" was Luther's starting quest.

prevented his sharing this "catholic" view: God was sovereign and Christ's body reigned at His right hand. Luther was almost Eutychian in his Christology in that he allowed the divine and human to interpenetrate. He believed that Christ was everywhere present in the sacrament with his once human now transfigured body. Zwingli was almost Nestorian in refusing to see two natures in the elements. Zwingli refused to have Christ objectified. To Luther's insistence that Christ had said, "This *is* my body," Zwingli replied that "is" could mean "represents" and certainly did not imply an equation.

Luther had always thought of Zwingli as a socialist and enthusiast, interested primarily in social and national reform rather than in theological reform. There was some truth in this for Zwingli was never a trained theologian. He had made his reputation as a nationalist and socialist and was to develop into a self-made theologian later. He was in fact a man of sober intelligence who in this controversy behaved much better than Luther. Luther never freed his mind from this prejudice which in fact hardened when a great number of speculative, socialist enthusiasts were giving him (and Germany) a great deal of trouble at home in Wittenberg. Luther wanted to know why they should speculate and theorize. Why could they not take Christ's words "This is my body" in their plain meaning?

Luther retained the deep religious urge which had driven him to seek God in the monastic life. He approached theology with a deep sense of mystery and painful awareness of his own creatureliness, as well as the awareness of the inadequacy of language. He sought a new grammar in an attempt to express the mystery of the gospel in relation to the climate of his day where Christianity was emerging from an effete mediaevalism under the pressure of an over-confident humanism. He sought to hold the mystery of the gospel within its historic biblical and catholic revelation, rather than nationalize it. He would have neither God, the gospel nor the church cut to a size acceptable to man. His obduracy was a measure of his conviction on these theological issues, for he sought to safeguard God against man. He refused to have God measured by man's finitude, to have Him defined by man's understanding, to have Him limited by man's logic. He wanted to let God be God.

Zwingli had little respect for Luther's catholic approach. He knew Luther had severed the shackles of Rome but wondered why he continued to carry them around. He seemed not aware that Luther's Catholicism was not a mere conservatism, but a profound reverence for the continuing work of God in the Bible and through His Church, faithless and undeserving as she might be. Zwingli was wrong about Luther and Luther was wrong about Zwingli. Bucer was the one man who might have explained the one to the other.

A spate of books came out on the subject. Zwingli, self-assured, dismissed Luther's views as catholic, and made the unfortunate mistake of bringing in Luther's views on socialism and his conduct in the Peasants' Revolt. As a result, when the men met at table they met as foes rather than friends. It should not be too quickly assumed that this difference was a squabble among theologians, even though one regrets the whole course of events. There were deep issues at stake. There still are. It involved a doctrine of God, different Christological emphases, different views of worship, different views on the nature of society. The Church in her credal formularies had preserved the idea of the union of the two natures of Christ each retaining the attributes and qualities peculiar to itself. Luther held this intensely: as the Son of God, Christ had died for us and as the Son of Man risen for us, and was now at the right hand of God limited to neither place nor time, everywhere as an illocal presence. Zwingli, though never questioning the divinity, kept separate the humanity and the divinity, which Luther thought of as one reality. It was the fact of these different emphases in the doctrine of God and Christ that caused the differences in their views on worship and the relation of Christianity to society.

Under great duress of illness and personal anxiety, and under pressure from the catholic princes as well as from Anabaptists and fanatics, Luther framed a reply to Zwingli, his *Confession Concerning the Lord's Supper* (1528).[1] It was a thoughtful non-controversial piece of work whereby Luther hoped to bring an end to controversy. In it Luther rejected the doctrine of the mass, transubstantiation, and the withdrawal of the cup. He opposed the scholasticism of substance and accidents though he insisted on the real, substantial presence in the elements. This work made the Marburg Colloquy unnecessary, but Luther was finally persuaded to attend.

The conference began on October 1, 1529.[2] The Landgrave put what he called "the lions" (Luther and Oecolampadius) in one room and "the lambs" (Zwingli and Melanchthon) in another. On the Wittenberg side there were Luther and Melanchthon, supported by Jonas, Cruciger, Myconius, Osiander, Agricola and Brentius; on the Swiss side, Zwingli and Oecolampadius supported by Bucer and Hedio. There were many scholars and noblemen besides, and many more refused admission.

Little that was new came out of the debate. The Wittenbergers were agreeably surprised at the sound theology of the Swiss as well as the quality of their lives. Luther stood by his view of the unambiguous meaning of "This is my body," Zwingli on its figurative meaning. Zwingli thought that differences in non-essentials were nothing to worry about when they

---

[1] WA. 26, 261–509; American edition, 37, 151 ff.
[2] WA. 30. III. 110 ff.

were united in essentials. This was true enough, but Luther would not accept the idea of the real presence as a "non-essential," and thought that Zwingli's liberalism was only indifference. Luther refused the right hand of fellowship to Zwingli, an act which brought tears to Zwingli's eyes. This refusal of the right hand did not indicate churlishness; it meant simply that they could not reach complete agreement. Luther finally yielded to the Landgrave's request to draw up a common confession in German. This consisted of fifteen articles expressing the evangelical doctrines of the Trinity, Christ's person, His death and resurrection, original sin, the Holy Spirit and the sacraments. To fourteen of the fifteen the Swiss assented, and even on the fifteenth there was much common agreement. It was only on the matter of the corporal presence and oral manducation that the dispute was left open:

> In the matter of the fifteenth article we all believe with regard to the Supper of our dear Lord Jesus Christ that it ought to be celebrated in both kinds according to the institution of Christ: also, that the mass is not a work by which a man obtains grace for another, either dead or alive. Further, that the Sacrament of the altar is a sacrament of the true body and blood of Jesus Christ, and that the spiritual manducation of this body and blood is specially necessary to every true Christian. In like manner, as to the use of the sacrament, we are agreed that it was given by Almighty God just as His Word was, and was ordained that weak consciences might be moved to faith through the work of the Holy Spirit. And although at the present time we are not of the same mind on the question whether the real body and blood of Christ are corporally present in the bread and wine, yet both parties shall regard each other in Christian charity in so far as their consciences can ever permit, and both parties will earnestly implore Almighty God that he will strengthen us in the right understanding through His Spirit. Amen.[1]

The articles were signed, and at once printed and circulated. On October 5 they all shook hands, a handshake of friendship, not theological agreement.

Whatever view the reader takes of both sides, he certainly must regret that the Swiss and German parted without reaching agreement. On matters of Church order and government, even on some doctrines notably the real presence, there can never be unity among thinking Christians. Luther always hoped for an evangelized Catholicism, and is always open to charges of scholasticism and theological obduracy. Zwingli was a practical man of the world who had had no theological training. Zwingli had the advantage of simplicity, of being lay in his approach and of allowing freedom and common sense to prevail. He was less subtle, less ecclesiastical, less respectful to Catholicism. Had Zwingli and Luther met today there would doubtless have ensued an eirenic unity. Nevertheless, there is more hope for Catholic unity along Luther's approach than along

[1] Text in Kidd, No. 110.

Zwingli's. The problem for catholic unity was and remains: can Catholicism move far enough and fast enough to contain within it Protestantism? Luther began with Catholicism and sought to evangelize it: Zwingli rejected it and sought to establish a liberal Protestantism. A century later a Lutheran theologian was to plead in the vexatious wars of the seventeenth century, almost in the words of Augustine and Ambrose: "In essentials unity, in non-essentials liberty, in all things charity." It would be hard to improve on that as an oecumenical formula.

Bucer and Hedio continued to bring both sides together in the following years, but when Zwingli lost his life at the Battle of Kappel in 1531 it confirmed Luther in his deep suspicions of Zwingli's motives as a theologian. And then, towards the end of his life, in serious ill-health, provoked by the mystic Caspar Schwenkfeld (1490–1561) and others who had unnecessarily reopened the issue by mischievously declaring that Luther had now gone Zwinglian, he wrote a brief statement entitled *A Short Confession* (1544).[1] He reasserted his own views and violently attacked the Swiss as radicals, socialists and enthusiasts, whose liberalism was but theological indifferentism. Luther thought this more dangerous than reactionary Catholicism, and was known to have said on one occasion that he would rather drink blood with the papists than mere wine with the Zwinglians. It must be seen as regrettable that Luther saw fit to express himself against the Swiss in this way at this time. Nevertheless, it is recorded that Luther once said to Melanchthon that the matter of the Lord's Supper had been overdone, and that he expressed the hope that Melanchthon might bring peace to the Church on this matter after he was gone.

In a work on the Reformation it might be of interest to compare and relate the views of Luther, Zwingli and Calvin on the Eucharist. Negatively, all three rejected transubstantiation, the mass as a sacrifice, and the withdrawal of the chalice from the laity. Positively, all three taught the divine institution of the Lord's Supper, the spiritual real presence of Christ, its commemoration of Christ's atoning sacrifice, its centrality in the Christian liturgy, and the grace attached to a proper partaking of it. They differed on three points. First, the mode of Christ's presence: whether it was a bodily presence located in the elements or a spiritual presence discerned by faith. Second, the mode of partaking: whether by eating, or receiving in the heart by faith. Third, whether all received, or only believing souls.

Since Luther taught a corporal presence "in, with and under the elements," all alike, believers and unbelievers, partook of both, the former to their good, the latter to their hurt. The two substances dwelt together in the same way as the two natures in the Incarnation, and were neither

[1] WA. 54, 141–67.

to be fused nor confused. Luther lived and died a pious Catholic, but parted from Rome in its later doctrine of transubstantiation. He further believed that this relationship between Christ and the elements terminated with the service.

Though Luther was most unwilling to discuss and define these matters he substantiated his views on three main grounds: one, the plain meaning and intent of Christ's words, "This is my body"; two, a belief in the ubiquity of Christ's body (stronger in Lutheranism than in Luther); three, catholic tradition. On one, modern exegetes would be more prepared to grant the force of Zwingli's exegesis. On two, he argued that the ubiquity of Christ was scriptural doctrine: "Lo, I am with you always even to the end of the world" (Matt. 28:20) and "Wherever two or three are gathered together in my name, there am I in the midst of them" (Matt. 18:20). On three, he argued that Christendom had always shown a firm belief in the real presence. He found Zwingli too matter-of-fact, and believed Zwingli was too ready to jettison catholic truth. It is always important to bear in mind that Luther hoped for some healing of the breach with Rome, and was right in realizing that there was some possibility of this with the Wittenberg theology, none with the Swiss.

Zwingli thought of the Eucharist as commemorative, a seal of what the believer was already well aware of on the grounds of the gospel. He could accept no bodily presence, for Christ's body had ascended to the Father. He held a real spiritual presence, teaching participation in faith. His views still prevail in Switzerland and among liberal Protestants.

Calvin, coming a generation later, stood midway between Luther and Zwingli. He shared Luther's deep spiritual approach, but saw the force of Zwingli's realism,. He accepted Zwingli's view of the symbolic nature of the words of the institution, rejecting the ideas of corporal presence as well as ubiquity. He held the real presence as well as the spiritual participation of Christ's body and blood by faith, and with them the benefit of His atoning death and the virtue of his immortal life. The sacrament united the crucified Christ with the glorified Christ in the heart of the believer, giving the redemptive work of Christ and the victorious assurance of that work. He also restored a rôle to the Holy Spirit in uniting the glorified Christ with the believer, an emphasis neither Luther nor Zwingli made.

New Biblical insights are helping us to see the truths which these men emphasized and which then divided Christendom. We should reflect that all doctrine has its authority in Scripture. Today, the Biblical exegetes seem closer than the dogmatic theologians. Perhaps it will be at that point which once divided Christendom, namely Scripture, the foundation common to us all, that she may yet find a unity better than she has ever known.

### 3. The Diets of Speier, 1526, 1529

The conviction had been growing in Germany that the Edict of Worms was not going to be enforced, and when at the Diet of Speier (Spires), 1526, the evangelical princes and the imperial cities had successfully resisted the Catholic party, this conviction gained ground.[1] Two other factors had made the Catholic party uncertain of their power to carry through their plans and had compelled them to yield: first, there was the threat of invasion from the Turk; second, there was disunity in the Catholic camp with hostility between the Emperor and the Pope, and Francis in the background ready to seek his own advantage. Most Protestants felt they could now breathe, and even Luther took Speier 1526 as a kind of acquittal. When the long-promised oecumenical council seemed indefinitely postponed, this view was further established. Nevertheless, it was a misreading of facts on the part of the Protestants. Charles was biding his time, and never for a moment thought of granting the Protestants toleration.

At all events, the exercise of territorial sovereignty and the establishment of separate State churches dates from Speier, *cujus regio ejus religio*. Every Protestant sovereign claimed and exercised the *jus reformandi religionem*, and settled the church question as he thought fit.[2] Saxony, Hesse, Prussia, Anhalt, Lüneberg, East Friesland, Schleswig-Holstein, Silesia, and the cities of Nürnberg, Augsburg, Frankfurt, Ulm, Strasbourg, Bremen, Hamburg and Lübeck supported the Reformation. On the other hand, the Dukes of Bavaria, the house of Austria and the Emperor did not accept this state of affairs. Protestantism paid a high price for the right of toleration. Victory was conceded at Augsburg in 1555 after Luther's death, and finally guaranteed only as late as the Treaty of Westphalia in 1648.

Charles V had not shown his hand at Speier. Earlier in the year he had decisively defeated Francis I of France at Pavia and had imposed on him very firm terms. Francis had never intended to honour these terms and at once entered a league with the Pope against Charles. The Pope paid dearly for this deceit and intrigue. The imperial troops sacked Rome (1527), they plundered all treasuries, libraries, churches and palaces, dishonoured sacred tombs, committed outrages on defenceless priests, monks and nuns, excelling the worst of the barbarian invasions. Paradoxically, Pope and Emperor needed each other, and in the treaty of Cadan Charles agreed to extirpate the Lutheran heresy and in the spring of 1528 sent an ambassador to Germany to arouse interest in the cause.

The Emperor summoned a diet to meet at Speier again in February, 1529,[3] to secure the unity and sole supremacy of the Catholic Church and

---

[1] Kidd, No. 89.    [2] Kidd, No. 90.    [3] Kidd, No. 103.

to find a common policy against the Turk.[1] The Catholic dignitaries appeared in full force, hopeful of final victory over the Reformation. The Catholic Estates succeeded in forcing through an article most harmful to the cause of the Reformation which virtually neutralized the decisions of the former Diet of 1526.[2] It was that those states which had supported the Edict of Worms should be allowed to impose its execution on all their subjects, but that those states which had not supported it should not be allowed any innovations; the celebration of the mass was nowhere to be obstructed; and no member of any state could flee to another state for protection. This decision meant that the Reformation would never be allowed to develop. It would also mean that the Reformation would be cut out in certain catholic areas where it had established itself; mass could be again imposed in evangelical territory and power given to catholic lay lords to coerce evangelical clergy. This was the occasion when the evangelicals entered their famous "Protest,"[3] and therefrom gave the word "Protestant" to the world. The evangelicals refused to accept the decision and denied the power of a Diet to disannul previous decisions save by unanimous consent. Philip of Hesse and others at once thought of a defensive alliance, but Luther argued that the sword could never be drawn in the interests of the gospel. He made clear that the sole concern of the evangelicals was for the truth of the gospel and the removal of the abuses that disturbed catholic and evangelical man alike; that he had always resisted fanaticism and iconoclasm; and that evangelicals had always been by conviction the staunchest upholders of law and authority.

The protest at Worms by Luther in the interests of the Word of God and the responsibility of individual judgment had now exfoliated into the protest of Speier of 1529 undertaken by princes and cities determined to uphold scripture and conscience. It is important to recall that the protest was no negative objection against error, tyranny and popery, but a positive assertion of freedom for the authority of the Word of God and of the individual conscience. The Reformation is wrongly conceived when thought of as a protest against Rome: Rome came in for opposition only when she claimed mastery over the gospel. Evangelical theology can be fully expounded without reference to Rome at all.

The moral force of the unanimous protest at Speier did not fructify the hopes it engendered. Luther and Melanchthon were disturbed by the dissension between the Wittenberg and the Swiss theologians, which Marburg did little to heal. Philip tended to think of military action, and had more interest in the activist Zwingli than in the theological Luther. Meanwhile, Pope and Emperor were seeking reconciliation. The Pope was reinstated on condition that he convened a council. He acknowledged the Emperor's sovereignty in Italy, and the Emperor guaranteed the Pope his

---

[1] Kidd, No. 104.       [2] Kidd, No. 105.       [3] Kidd, No. 107.

temporal possessions. In February, 1530, the Emperor was crowned by the Pope with the crown of Charlemagne as the temporal head of Western Christendom. A few weeks later he crossed the Alps on his way to the Diet of Augsburg, which was convened to determine the fate of Lutheranism in Germany.

## 4. The Diet and Confession of Augsburg, 1530

Charles convoked the Diet of Augsburg in 1530, using in the proclamation conciliatory and courteous language.[1] It is a false reading of history to interpret that as an intention of seeking a *modus vivendi*. Charles's only intention was that Protestantism should accept the terms dictated by him and the Pope, and thereby heal all internal dissension. Protestantism faced a perilous situation: the Diet of Speier had forbidden further progress of the Reformation; Luther was still under the papal and imperial ban and could never attend any conference or diet; Charles and the Pope had restored their relationships and the Pope had crowned the Emperor; the Protestants had failed to unite, a very grave tragedy; and finally, the Turk was threatening Christendom.

The Catholics went to Augsburg with a dual purpose: to defeat once and for all the Protestants as the enemies of the Church and to muster sufficient forces from both sides to defeat the Turk, the enemy of Christendom. The Protestant minority also had a dual purpose: to defend the gospel against the Roman Church and to support the Emperor in his defence of Christendom.

John of Saxony summoned his Wittenberg theologians to prepare a confession of faith,[2] and with them he journeyed to Augsburg, having to leave Luther behind at the Coburg, the nearest point his territory approached Augsburg. Here Luther suffered serious illness, and at the same time his father died. It was a grievous sorrow to Luther that he could not go to his dying father. After two days of prayer he recovered sufficient strength to seek further solace in pursuing his translation of the Bible. To the Elector, to Brück, his Chancellor, and to Melanchthon he gave continuous advice. He wrote a fine book to the clergy assembled at Augsburg[3] warning them of the scandals from which the Church was suffering, and begging them to exercise sense and care how they resolve this matter, asking them to leave the gospel free. He wrote tracts about the Romish abuses. What strikes the reader in all these writings is Luther's inextinguishable faith and invincible confidence. He wrote and talked as a man whose cause would never fail. His doctrine was God's and his gospel Christ's: neither God nor Christ would ever fail him. There is about

---

[1] Kidd, No. 113.  [2] WA. 30. III. 178 ff.; Tappert, 23.
[3] W.A. 30. II. 268 ff.; American edition, 34, 3 ff.

Luther that disconcerting certainty sensed perfectly in the Johannine Christ. He said he was a detached observer watching a cause that could only prosper.

At the Diet the Emperor declared that their first task was to secure support against the Turk,[1] but the evangelicals insisted on the priority of the church question. The Emperor gave them four days to prepare a confession. This was read in German on June 25. But the Emperor, whose German was weaker than his theology, fell asleep in the middle of it, though the Catholics gave it their rapt attention for the two hours it lasted. It surprised the Catholics: the Bishop of Augsburg described it as "the pure truth." The Duke of Bavaria was heard to say to Eck that the evangelicals stood within the Scriptures and the Catholics were outside. At considerable risk to themselves seven princes signed the document: the Elector of Saxony, Philip of Hesse, George of Brandenburg, Duke Ernest of Lüneburg, John of Saxony, Duke Francis of Lüneburg, Prince Wolfgang of Anhalt. These brave confessors were ill-advised when they refused to allow the free cities of Strasbourg, Lindau, Constance and Memmingen, to sign, on the grounds of their Zwinglian tendencies. These four cities submitted their own confession later, the Tetrapolitana.

The Confession[2] was mainly the work of Melanchthon who hoped all along to conciliate the papists and keep the peace and unity of the Church. His gentle and conciliatory overtures were met by threats of putting Wittenberg under the ban, of bringing the Inquisition into Germany, of exterminating Protestantism with fire and sword. Melanchthon's gentleness and his genius for compromise and concession were unavailing. Rome demanded unconditional surrender. Melanchthon was hurt by this, and quite shocked at the malice and guile of the papist theologians. The more vigorous evangelicals were extremely critical of Melanchthon for conceding so much to Rome, but Luther's faith in Melanchthon was complete.

The Roman theologians produced a refutation, and Charles returned it for revision no fewer than five times, so bitter was its tone. A small committee of theologians of both parties sought to reach agreement, and though Melanchthon made concession after concession the Romanists remained adamant on an infallible church, the sacrifice of the mass, and a sacerdotal priesthood, even insisting on clerical celibacy, communion in one kind, and the restoration of all church property.

On September 22 the Emperor ordered the recess of the Diet, and issued his terms.[3] The Protestants had been heard and refuted; they had been given opportunity to reach agreement and had failed. He for his part now granted the Protestants until April 15, 1531, for consideration of his terms: no innovations to be made; no attacks on Catholic faith and worship; the Emperor to be assisted against the Anabaptists; and a promise of a

[1] Kidd, No. 115.    [2] Bekenntnisschriften 33 ff.; Tappert, 23 ff.    [3] Kidd, No. 123.

general council within a year. The Protestants rejected this, and Luther attacked the Emperor's terms on the grounds that they were merely a reaffirmation of Worms.

The Lutheran princes for purposes of self defence formed a defensive alliance, the Schmalkaldian League.[1] Luther disapproved of any taking up of arms. (His warning proved true, for this League issued in the tragic Schmalkaldian War of 1547, just after Luther's death.) Nevertheless, under the threat of Islam, some political unity was achieved for the Empire.

Suleiman II had advanced in April and had inexplicably withdrawn his armies in the September, nevertheless he remained sufficient of a threat to compel the Emperor to arrange a truce with the Protestants at the Diet of Nürnberg, 1532.[2] The Emperor had to reckon with the Protestants. In the now famous words of Ranke, Germany had now "another centre besides the diets."[3] His plea to the Pope for the convening of a council had been given more urgency than ever in the light of this development of a new seat of authority in Germany. Yet, when he went to Rome to plead his cause, the Pope met his urgency with the usual delaying tactics.

The Confession of Augsburg[4] was the first evangelical confession and is the most famous. Of the nature of the early "Apologies," it was a statement of the Lutheran theology in non-polemical terms: it is conciliatory, eirenic, comprehensive, churchly and conservative. In it Melanchthon emphasized the ground common to both parties and showed himself prepared to go a long way to meet the Romanists. He knew that this would be the last occasion when evangelical theology might be contained within Catholicism, and this goes a long way to explain his conciliatory views with regard to Rome but his stiff views with regard to Zürich. Though Luther said that Melanchthon had "danced a few light steps" over the difficulties, Luther realized that if any man in Christendom could bring both sides together that man was the gentle Melanchthon. Melanchthon did not conceive of his task as setting up a final infallible statement, but rather a formula of concord not discord, a *modus vivendi*. For instance, Melanchthon made no mention of the supremacy of scripture, nor of the Catholic abuses such as indulgences, purgatory or supremacy of the Pope: he even blunted the doctrine of justification by faith alone. The Confession failed in its purpose, but has had some influence on Protestantism, even on the Anglican Thirty-nine Articles.

Its historical antecedents were the Articles of Marburg 1529, the Articles of Schwabach drawn up immediately afterwards, and the Torgau Articles of 1530. There are twenty-one articles in all:

[1] An enlargement of the League of Torgau (pp. 77, 89, 93) and so called from Schmalkald in Saxony.
[2] Kidd, No. 125.    [3] Quoted, Kidd, p. 301.    [4] Tappert, 23 f.

1. God – Nicene doctrine.
2. Original sin.
3. Christ's Divine-Human personality.
4. Justification by faith – without the "alone".
5. The Ministry of Word and Sacrament.
6. Christian Obedience.
7 and 8. The Church.
9. Baptism.
10. The Supper of the Lord.
11. Confession – to retain it.
12. Penance – an evangelical interpretation.
13. The use of the sacraments – to increase faith.
14. Ordination – an essential to the ministry.
15. Ecclesiastical rites – to retain wherever possible.
16. Civil Government.
17. The Return of Christ.
18. The bondage of the will and the necessity of grace.
19. The cause of sin.
20. Faith and Works.
21. Worship of saints and the sole mediatorship of Christ.

At the conclusion Melanchthon argued that Lutherans held no doctrine contrary to Scripture, contrary to the Catholic Church, or contrary to the Roman Church as far as was known from the Fathers. He disavowed the charge of heresy and accepted differences of tradition.

Part Two of the Confession discusses those abuses of Rome the Reformers found most objectionable:

22. The withdrawal of the cup from the laity.
23. The celibacy of the clergy.
24. The sacrifice of the mass.
25. Compulsory auricular confession.
26. Fasts and feasts.
27. Monastic vows.
28. The secular power of bishops: not to confound ecclesiastical and civil powers.

Finally, the Confession places the sin of schism squarely on Rome if it refuses to let the gospel be freely taught and the abuses removed. Rome refused both and not until Pope John in our own day has there been any admission of some share in the sin of schism:

> We do not intend to conduct a trial of the past; we do not want to prove who was right or who was wrong. The blame is on both sides. All we want is to say: "Let us come together. Let us make an end of our divisions."[1]

The sequel to the Confession was the Confutation drawn up at the com-

---

[1] John XXIII to the observers at Vatican II.

mand of the Emperor. This Confutation (expressly ordered by the Emperor to be modest in tone) followed the lines of the Confession. It approved eighteen of the Lutheran points: Article Four on Justification is allowed: Article Ten on the Lord's Supper is approved provided the Lutherans would grant the whole Christ in either element; Article Seven on the Church is rejected, along with Article Twenty on Faith and Works and Article Twenty-one on the worship of saints. The second part dealing with abuses is rejected outright, though clerical abuses are admitted and a reformation of discipline promised. The document was given a specious weight with a few ill-selected biblical and patristic quotations. It was no answer to the Wittenberg theologians. Rome has yet to furnish its answer.

These documents were not published, and for a long time men had to be content with the notes and memories of the participants. Even while he sat on the homeward cart Melanchthon began to revise and expand his Apology to his Confession.[1] It is a splendid theological document, seven times longer than his Confession and well written. It is limited in places by an outmoded exegesis and certain patristic errors (common in those days), but it gave splendid support to the Reformation. The document was eventually signed by the theologians at Schmalkald in 1537 and finally embodied in the Formula of Concord, 1580.[2]

The Swiss and Strasbourg theologians, rejected at Marburg and now excluded from Augsburg, made efforts to present their views to the world. Bucer, Hedio and Capito presented their views in the name of Strasbourg, Constance, Lindau and Memmingen (the Tetrapolitan Confession)[3] in the hope of yet finding unity. The Catholic theologians refused to read it at the Diet, penned a refutation of it that was most unjust, and refused even to allow the Strasbourgers a copy of their answer. The Tetrapolitan Confession was more Protestant than Melanchthon's. It took a strong line on the sole authority of Scripture; a more distinctively evangelical doctrine of justification; a clearer call for the abolition of images; and sought to combine the Swiss and Lutheran views on Holy Communion.

Zwingli, in great haste and without being able to consult the others, produced a confessional statement, too. Eck, true to form, treated this with all the scorn and contempt of his rich repertoire. Yet, to read Zwingli's document, with its sheer sense and soundness, its simplicity and integrity, its dignity and courtesy, the reader is filled with a hopeless dismay that responsible men in high office such as Eck could be so misguided as to try to handle men like Zwingli, with God's cause so palpably at heart, in so revolting and nauseating terms. When one considers the

[1] Tappert 97 ff.
[2] Text of all these documents are found in *Die Bekenntnisschriften der evangelisch-lutherischen Kirche* (4th edn., revd.) (Göttingen, 1959), pp. 141 ff.
[3] Text in *Reformed Confessions of the Sixteenth Century*, ed. Arthur Cochrane (S.C.M., 1966), pp. 54–88.

desperate problems exercising Zwingli at this time, and how within months he was brutally to die a lingering death on the field of battle for the cause of liberty and truth, a believing man can but humbly marvel that God did not "give us up"[1] but has stayed with us.

In his confession[2] Zwingli attested his orthodoxy according to the creeds. He taught free and unmerited grace perceived and received by faith alone. He taught the doctrine of the visible and invisible church. Purgatory he rejected. On original sin and the sacraments he made a clear departure from Wittenberg as well as from Rome. He rejected outright the false association of his theology with Anabaptism. Finally, he appealed to all in the interests of truth, and in the light of the grave contemporary situation, to heed his words. Rome and Wittenberg were both wrong to reject Zwingli outright.

[1] Rom. 1:24, 26, 28.
[2] Complete text in *Niemeyer: Collectio Confessionum.* Leipzig. 1840. pp. 16 ff.

# CHAPTER VI

# DEVELOPMENTS TO THE DEATH OF CHARLES V, 1532–58

## 1. Overtures towards Unity

JOHN FREDERICK THE MAGNANIMOUS SUCCEEDED HIS FATHER JOHN[1] AS Elector of Saxony in 1532. He was utterly evangelical, pious by nature, and served faithfully as "the godly prince" of Reformation theology. Supported by his faithful wife, Princess Sybil, he provided Luther with the political stability that made the Reformation a practical territorial possibility. This situation served to change the pattern of Luther's life work: he was now less the dominant European figure and more the professor of theology teaching at the university, preaching at Church, writing books, and guiding the Reformed Church of Saxony. By now the pattern of a protestantism that would not yield and a catholicism that would not change was beginning to harden in Europe.

At the university he began another course on Galatians,[2] and made this exposition his finest exposition of justification in Christ alone:

> One article, the only solid rock, rules in my heart, namely, faith in Christ: out of which, through which, and to which, all my theological opinions ebb and flow, day and night.[3]

He turned again to his translation of the Bible and now completed the Prophets and the Apocrypha. The immensity of this task and the perfection of the result, carried out through tumult and tribulation, trial and temptation, not least grave and painful illness, was an achievement that took heavy toll of Luther. Preaching regularly in the parish pulpit was a further task. In addition he supported the Elector in his scheme of reforming the Church in Saxony. The prince forwarded the Reformation positively in visitations whereby he sought to maintain a decent, disciplined reformed life for lay and cleric alike, negatively by abolishing gross sin and rooting out witchcraft and superstition. In all these reforms Luther showed a biting criticism of the sophisticated immorality of the nobility as well as of the coarse vulgarity of the peasants. Luther never understood how men could

---

[1] See p. 77.
[2] See Martin Luther, *Commentary on the Epistle to the Galatians*, Middleton translation, revised by P. S. Watson (Edinburgh, 1953).
[3] WA. 40. I, 33. 7 ff. (Middleton translation, p. 16).

remain licentious when once the gospel had been declared. Calvin was to face this same problem but he curbed sin by discipline and decree, and was prepared to use sanctions.

The years 1532–46 are not easy to disentangle in the intricacies of the theological, social, political, and personal factors. A secular historian traces the meaning essentially in the social and political events, paying little attention to the theologians. A religious historian sees the importance of the theological battle and relates other events to this. Nevertheless, some clarification must be made, and it is wisest to deal with the religious issues primarily.

Under pressure from the Emperor the Pope reluctantly sent a nuncio to the German princes to explore the possibilities of the oft-promised but oft-delayed free general council. Luther had no hopes of the overtures ever coming to fruition, "muttering in the dark" he described it. Nevertheless he co-operated courteously. Almost everybody wanted some reformation of some kind, only the papal curia opposed it. There were two main ideas on how that reformation should proceed. The first was that the Church should once more be revivified into her pristine splendour, retaining all the characteristics of her sacerdotal hierarchy under the papacy, though disposing of the abuses and discrediting practices. The other idea was that the Church had to go through a theological revivification on the lines of the cardinal reformed evangelical doctrines of the priesthood of all believers, justification by faith, supremacy of God's Word and the other New Testament doctrines, retaining the organic structure of traditional catholicism but freeing it from all its sacerdotalism and secularism as well as its unwarrantable accretions and developments.

Charles desired the former, Luther the latter. Charles wanted to preserve all the mediaeval structure of the Church and maintain the Church monolithic and entire. Luther wanted to preserve the theological entirety of a Catholic Church, but was utterly free of any desire to impose any structural or organizational form on any Church, provided she held the gospel whole and entire. Charles was prepared to accept changes in usage, but not of doctrine, unless clearly proved. In any event no reform or change was to be at the expense of a division in the Church. True, he allowed the postponement of the church question under certain pressures, but it was never his intent to grant any separate existence to the evangelical churches. If the evangelicals could not be induced to return to the fold, Charles's intention was to compel them.

Then there were factors other than theological, even if bound up with them. The geographical area of protestantism was hardening and extending: Anhalt had now openly joined the evangelical cause. But, though Philip of Hesse had openly espoused the evangelical cause he brought into it his own problems. He hated the House of Hapsburg and their dynastic dominance in Germany. The Dukes of Bavaria, though uncompromising papists, had the same hatred of the Hapsburgs in common. The German religious question was made too difficult for Charles, partly by his *a priori* idea of a monolithic settlement, and partly because both the Catholic and the Protestant sides interpreted his actions as dynastic aggrandisement and resented them. There was also the very unpleasant scheming of the Pope who often sought to thwart Charles, creating the paradoxical situation in which the Pope, though hostile to Charles, was essential to Charles.

Luther meanwhile pursued his own theological course, council or no. He was showing some sharp hostility to Rome at this time. In his work *On Private Masses* (January 29, 1536)[1] he argues that both the idea of a private mass as well as the idea of the sacrifice of Christ's body are an utter perversion. He contrasts the mass priest with his sacrifice on the one hand, and the great evangelical doctrine of the priesthood of all believers with its preacher called to minister the Word of God on the other.

A happy feature at this juncture was presented by the attempts to re-unite Christendom, not all of which came from the Protestant side. Characteristically, Erasmus sought to promote unity by exhorting the catholics to abolish abuses and the evangelicals (and other dissentients) to submit to proper ecclesiastical authority in current theological disputes. Luther argued that such a course would serve to strengthen the Catholics, and asked the direct question: What was a man to do who knew that Catholic teaching at certain points was contrary to Scripture? Did Erasmus counsel obedience to the Pope rather than to the Bible on those issues? Erasmus sought mutual concessions but his advice in fact meant unilateral submission. Luther further argued that the evangelicals had always shown themselves prepared to concede (amply proven at Worms and subsequently at Augsburg in 1530) provided the gospel was not allowed to suffer. Luther suspected Erasmus of wanting peace at any price, and thought him a sceptic and an Epicurean at heart.

Not only Erasmus sought unity. That indefatigable ecumenist, Bucer of Strasbourg, renewed his activities at this moment. Luther met him with stolid caution. It is true that, when Luther had actually met Zwingli at Marburg, he had liked him as a person, yet he still disliked his theology. He still continued to regard Zwingli as tending to humanism and socialism, fanaticism and Anabaptism. The latter two charges may be ungrounded, but the former are not. Luther was disinclined to enter into controversy, and even when the Swiss theology was interpreted sympathetically by Bucer, Luther remained unconvinced. And then Luther's worst fears were confirmed when the fanatics imposed their wild ideas on Münster under a rule of saints, a nightmarish kingdom eventually overcome by imperialist

[1] WA. 39. I, 138-73.

forces. All Protestantism was excluded from this once evangelical stronghold, and to this day it is the most catholic of cities.

Bucer was undeterred, in spite of Luther's caution and in spite of events. He wanted some public expression of doctrinal unity among the Protestants. He laboured to persuade the Swiss that Luther was not rigorist in his theology at all. He won Philip over to the view that in fundamentals the evangelicals were one and that both sides were safeguarding different aspects of truth, the Swiss against substantiation in any form, Luther against non-sacramentalism. Philip approached Luther whom he found cordial and sympathetic. Luther wanted a united evangelical front against the arrogant papists, yet he always considered unity as a divine gift issuing from the truth of the gospel, hardly as an end in itself. A conference was arranged to take place on December 27, 1534, at Kassel, for which Luther wrote his *Consideration, whether unity is possible or not*.[1] In it Luther discusses unity on the basis of the Augsburg Confessions and counsels time for reflection.

The new Pope, Paul III (1534-49) seemed anxious to call a council,[2] and to this end sent Cardinal Vergerius to Germany. Vergerius called on Archbishop Albrecht and on Luther. Luther was cautious and reserved. He doubted the sincerity of the Catholics in wanting a council at all, and grumbled that if they did, all they would want to discuss would be monks' cowls, tonsures, diets and suchlike. On this a legate was heard to whisper, "He has hit the nail on the head!" Luther went on with some bluntness that it was not the evangelicals who needed a council for they were utterly sure of the truth of their doctrine based as it was on the Word of God, though he could well understand why papists needed one for they had been led astray under a papal tyranny. Nevertheless, Luther agreed to attend such a council at any place at any time. All the proceedings were marked by cordiality and good-will, helped along by Luther's penetrating and devastating good humour. Vergerius was later to be converted to the evangelical cause.

There were social and political problems, too. George, Duke of Brunswick, began to expel the evangelicals from his territories, a very cruel injustice to innocent folk. Luther expressed himself strongly on this as well as the wider imperial issues. In these he deplored the Pope's political machinations as well as the ill-will and double dealing of Francis I, and yet, remarkably Luther showed a true loyalty to his "dear, good Emperor," a man determined on his personal destruction. And then, that activist and muscular Christian, Philip of Hesse, took it upon himself to oust the usurper King Ferdinand of Württemberg and restore the land to Duke Ulrich, the rightful owner and an evangelical. Luther disapproved of Philip taking the sword on behalf of the gospel, but nevertheless was

[1] WA. 30, 294 ff.          [2] Kidd, No. 126.

very impressed at the quick and positive result of this short, sharp war. Philip routed the usurper ignominiously; demanded from him publicly that he would never again drag a Protestant through imperial courts to regain church property; destroyed the hostile Swabian League of catholic princes; and established the Reformation in Württemberg. Luther mused on Philip achieving so much so quickly by improper means.

In the Empire at large more complex movements were astir. The Emperor was fighting the Turk in North Africa. Francis I was raising claims against Italian territory which issued in two wars. There was revolt in the Netherlands. Relations were strained between Austria and Bavaria. Ferdinand of Austria was showing interest in the Reformation. Though the Pope was now showing some readiness to hold a council, on Italian soil, Charles V was now so preoccupied that he was unable to give attention to religious matters before 1541. In this change of climate the Schmalkaldic League, now a completed organization with its own constitution, invited other states to discuss matters with them in 1535. France and England showed an interest in this development, though Luther distrusted both Francis I and Henry VIII and feared their interest was not in evangelical theology.

Nevertheless the overtures of Bucer, combined with the visit of Cardinal Vergerius, at a time when political events were so favourable, caused Luther to call a conference on unity at Eisenach for May, 1536. Luther fell ill, so the delegates generously called the meeting for Wittenberg. Bullinger declined the invitation, and Luther saw Bucer and Capito privately. Luther thought things were better left as they were to work themselves out, rather than create some unreal unity at a conference. Bucer assured Luther his caution was groundless, that everybody was with him in essentials, a viewpoint confirmed when he produced from Bullinger a most agreeable statement. The outcome of the conference was an apology drawn up and signed alongside the Augsburg Confession.[1] The Swiss found themselves unable to agree to the German formulation, but they expressed unfeigned gladness for the advance so far made, which amounted to unity among German Protestants.

Within a few days of the Wittenberg agreement the Pope announced his intention of holding the council in Mantua the following year. He had not the same purpose as the Reformers. His declared intention was to extirpate the Lutheran heresy. Luther's declared intention was to go to the council and defend the cause of evangelical theology as he had done at Worms. The Elector would not grant him permission to go, but asked him to furnish a list of essential articles of faith. Luther listed justification by faith in Christ alone in the first instance. He condemned the mass as

---

[1] Kidd, No. 127; C.R. 3. 75-7. Most of text translated: Darwell Stone, *History of the Doctrine of the Holy Eucharist*, ii, 46 f.

B

an idolatrous practice, destructive of the evangelical doctrine of justification in Christ. He argued, further, that the Pope was not the head of
Christendom by divine right but in actual fact the Antichrist who sets
himself up against Christ. John Frederick, anxious for his theologians to
reach a common mind at this critical juncture, invited them all to
Schmalkald, where he also invited an imperial envoy and a papal nuncio.
Most tragically Luther was stricken there with an excruciating attack of
the stone, from which agony none of his physicians could deliver him,
and at the point of death, was carefully carried home to Wittenberg. Even
at this moment Bucer, who was in attendance, seized the occasional lull
in the pain to win Luther over to his oecumenical thinking.

In Luther's absence the Wittenberg theologians pursued their deliberations. They decided to decline the Pope's invitation on the grounds that
the situation demanded nothing less than a free general council on German
and not Italian soil. Luther's points were carried no further except that the
Reformers approved the Wittenberg Concord of the previous year and
submitted that to the various princes and cities. At this time Luther wrote
firm but friendly letters to the Swiss, showing himself disinclined to
prolong the debate in the interests of unity and understanding. The
Moravians, too, sought to be active in the oecumenical movement. They
made approaches to Luther who realized that their Wycliffite theology
did not have at its centre his own doctrine of justification, and that
their sacramental theology tended towards Calvinism, nevertheless
Luther developed considerable respect for their views and not least
for the outstanding moral qualities of John Augusta and the Moravian
brethren.

## 2. Last Days of Luther

Luther's illness had warned the Elector and the Wittenberg theologians
that their beloved leader was now ageing and might die and leave them
at any time. Grimly they saw how long and heavy responsibilities had
ruined his health and vigour and natural joyousness. The Elector sought
to reduce his work at the university and increased his salary to make his
life a little easier. It was at this time that Luther began his famous course
of lectures on Genesis where he mined the pure gold of evangelical theology
for nine more years. He continued his regular preaching on Sundays and
weekdays. With his colleagues he revised his translation of the Bible. He
worked towards the hoped-for council, writing in 1539 his well-known
work *On Councils and Churches*,[1] where he made a vigorous defence of
the Church as the world-wide community of faithful men and not an
assemblage of cardinals, priests and monks under a pope.

[1] WA. 50, 509-653; American edition, 41, 3 ff.

Luther had internal troubles in his own church. He was very anxious to hold a full evangelical theology against the antinomian tendencies of Agricola and eventually was engaged in controversy with this old friend. Luther always took the view that the law was to be understood in relation to the gospel, and that to dismiss the law, as certain fanatics sought to do, was to lose the full reality, not only of its moral validity, but of God's purpose in the gospel. Melanchthon, too, changed his ground a little as he grew older, in the first instance on the doctrine of justification by faith by permitting an element of human will, and in the second place by thinking that Luther's insistence on the bodily presence was too rigid and not an essential part of historic catholicism. In Melanchthon's case there was never any conflict. A further anxiety to Luther was a morality among the evangelicals not clearly enough distinguished as markedly Christian. In particular he hated the drunkenness and vulgarity of society. Further, there were threats of united Catholic opposition against the evangelicals, but the Emperor sought peace at this moment and the threats came to nought.

Nevertheless there were favourable developments. On the death of Duke George of Saxony (April 17, 1539), his dominion passed to his brother Henry, a convinced evangelical. On Whitsunday, 1539, Luther had the emotional experience of preaching at Henry's accession in Leipzig in the very place where twenty years earlier he had had his fateful disputation with Eck. Further, in the same year the electorate of Brandenburg went over to the Reformation. At this the Emperor called a meeting at Speier to end "all the wearisome dissension in a Christian manner," a meeting actually held in Hagenau in June, 1540, owing to the plague.

Favourable as these developments were the cause of reformation suffered a deadly wound from one of its most ardent champions, Philip of Hesse. Philip, when very young, had contracted a marriage of convenience, a marriage that had been a failure. About this time he met a lady whom he wanted to marry. The lady would accept only honourable marriage, and Philip sought advice of the Wittenberg theologians arguing that Scripture said nothing against polygamy. The theologians said his case was specious and that marriage could not settle his problem. Starting from the principle that divorce was always wrong, they suggested there might be a case for a special dispensation provided such dispensation was considered private to Philip and was not permitted to hurt or scandalize a third party, and that the marriage be seen not as a marriage but as a permitted concubinage. At once the girl's mother translated this into the "approval of her daughter's marriage by the Wittenberg authorities" to the horror of all parties concerned except Philip, who welcomed the publicity. The evangelicals were scandalized and the Catholics were very quick to take advantage of the scandal. No explanations were accepted, and the whole affair was a cruel and undeserved blow to the cause of Protestantism.

Meanwhile it had been decided at Hagenau to call a further meeting at Worms later that year, when competent, earnest peaceably-minded theologians were to represent both sides.[1] Regrettably, Melanchthon, ill with remorse over the bigamy of Philip, collapsed on the way to Hagenau. Luther stayed by his bedside in prayer. There is a delightful story of his threatening Melanchthon with excommunication if he continued to refuse the food proffered! Meanwhile, proceedings were kept open at Worms and extended to the Diet of Ratisbon (Regensburg), 1541. At this time the infamous and coarse Duke Henry of Brunswick sought to attack the evangelical cause, and in his book *Wider Hans Wurst*[2] Luther stooped just as low in his reply, exposing Henry's immoral life in appropriate language as well as defending Protestantism. Once more grave illness struck Luther, when he suffered intense pain and copious discharge from his ear.

When the theologians eventually met the following year at Ratisbon (1541) hopes of a new unity in the Church ran higher than they had ever done before. In the first place the participants were men who were both theologically and spiritually adequate to the demands of the hour. On the Catholic side, distinguished theologians of proved ability, with a known concern for truth, reform and unity, sat at the table. There was the kind and scholarly Julius von Pflug, supported by the earnest reformer Gropper of Cologne, as well as by Contarini,[3] a man of known evangelical convictions, though the truculent John Eck was also there, largely absentee. On the Protestant side there was the brilliant and trustworthy Melanchthon, known on all sides for his eirenical and conciliatory approach, supported by one of the most active oecumenical figures of all time, Bucer, patient, understanding, mediatorial. There was also the younger theologian, Pistorius. The conference launched into matters of faith at once, on the basis of the *Liber Ratisponensis*[4] and not the Augsburg Confession, and left aside the relatively external matters of order. They tackled the central doctrines of salvation, sin and grace, as well as the more divisive doctrine of justification by faith apart from works. The Roman Catholics conceded much of the Protestant argument. Never had the sides been closer, never have they since been nearer.[5] Luther reserved his support and showed some criticism of the final formula as a "patched-

---

[1] Perhaps John Eck ought to be excepted, though fortunately for the colloquy he was absent through illness most of the time.
[2] WA. 51, 469–572.
[3] Contarini was to face most unfair criticism for his work at Ratisbon on his return to Rome (Kidd, No. 140).
[4] Kidd, No. 136; C.R. 4, 190.
[5] Kidd, No. 137; CR. 4, 199; *cf.* Pole's letter: Kidd, No. 140.

up affair." The Catholic princes rejected the formula of the combined theologians and dashed all hopes to the ground.

The evangelicals refused to be so easily daunted, and made a new move. They brought Luther into their deliberations (Luther was by law excluded from all diets, councils, etc., following the Edict of Worms, 1521). They urged Luther to use his influence to bring about some permanent validity to the agreement God had granted the divided Church at Ratisbon, and to effect some working compromise on those points in which agreement had been denied them. Luther agreed, but added two stipulations: (a) that the evangelical Church be openly permitted to preach those articles on which the theologians of both sides had agreed; and (b) that they be allowed to teach those articles upon which agreement had not been reached. The Emperor agreed to the former, subject to the decisions of the general council all awaited, but would not agree to the second. The Catholic estates showed the same mind as the Emperor. Hopes were once more dashed. Luther again explained his view that there was a fundamental cleavage between the two sides and what was needed was not schemes for unity but a sound evangelical and biblical theology.[1]

Despite the Emperor's unyielding resistance to evangelical theology, Protestantism continued to spread. Halle was the next place to go over to the Reformation. The irony of this transition lay in that the continued licentiousness of the Archbishop, Cardinal Albrecht, forced him to flee his own city. He had earlier been involved in gross scandal when, seriously embarrassed by debt, he summarily ordered his steward to be publicly hanged, a man openly acquitted in court. Albrecht had again run into heavy debt and called on the citizens to help to the extent of 22,000 gulden. The inhabitants retaliated by demanding an evangelical pastor in return for their financial help, and the Archbishop had to submit to the ignominy of withdrawing from his own city and handing its spiritual care to Justus Jonas the Wittenberg theologian. Immediately two other Churches demanded the same. It gave Luther grim satisfaction that "the wicked old rogue" who had precipitated the Reformation with his indulgences scandal of 1517[2] had to submit to the demands of humble laity to be given a godly pastor. Albrecht had the audacity to take all his relics away with him to Mainz, refurbish them, and advertise them as bigger and better than ever. Three tongues now from the burning bush, and a small piece of the left horn of Moses: to visit these relics and leave only one gulden guaranteed a remission of ten years from any sin whatsoever.

Another ecclesiastical problem caused much trouble to the moderate evangelicals. On the death of the Bishop of Naumburg the chapter elected the saintly and scholarly Catholic, von Pflug, who had shown himself an

---

[1] The *Acta* were published by Bucer at Strasbourg at once, 1541, and translated by Coverdale (Geneva?), 1542.　　　　[2] See pp. 38 ff.

earnest seeker after unity at Ratisbon in 1541. This was an excellent appointment, but the Elector, John Frederick, insisted that the right of nomination
was his and his alone, and forced upon the Church the evangelical Nicholas
von Amsdorf, an equally excellent appointment. In Catholic (and some
evangelical) eyes this was invalid and broke the line of apostolic succession.
But to the evangelical, apostolic succession is a succession of doctrine, not
of men. Nevertheless, many thought it was a great pity to jettison this
tradition when there were no compelling reasons such as war, persecution
or enemy occupation. The moderates were right. It is possible, as in
Sweden, to hold an evangelical theology and at the same time to preserve
catholic tradition. This was the method the Anglicans adopted.

In the midst of all this unnecessary acrimony, Luther grew more and
more disquieted about the state of morals at every level of society in
Germany. He felt that religion had little or no hold on the Germans, and
consequently their morals were low. He had expected the fire and fervour
of the gospel to glow in the lives of men and women, and the Holy Spirit
to blow His pentecostal wind through the hearts of all: churchmen,
nobles, merchants and peasants. He felt he had reached some moral and
spiritual impasse. The gospel had been preached, church and university
reformed, but he found so little evidence of faith in God and the power of
the Holy Spirit. Luther further realized he had but little time to live. He
was coming to the conclusion that by and large the nobility were vicious
parasites, seizing church property, money and lands for their own ends,
prepared to go to war if opposed. He found the peasants and artisans
drunken and living little better than beasts. Luther never had any faith in
society: peasant, prince or prelate. His only faith was in God and in those
who had answered God's call in the gospel. Yet he knew that faith should
issue in works. This was a very bitter moment for Luther.

Still, the Reformation spread. Philip of Hesse and John Frederick routed
Henry of Brunswick who was threatening the evangelical stronghold of
Goslar, and as a consequence the people begged the evangelicals to take
over Brunswick. Maurice of Saxony extended the Reformation to
Merseburg, fortunately without bloodshed. In Cologne, the Archbishop
and Elector, Hermann von Wied (who had much influence on the English
Reformation) resolved to introduce the Reformation into his archbishopric
and called in Bucer to help with liturgical reform and Melanchthon with
doctrinal.[1] At first he succeeded, but was later to experience bitter opposition from Gropper[2] and wicked deprivation from Charles.[3] Then the
Bishop of Münster began to attempt some reformation. The Emperor, too,

---

[1] Kidd, No. 142. See Melanchthan's account, CR. 5, 112 f., 148 f.

[2] Gropper, a liberal theologian, member of the Ratisbon Conference, and one time sympathizer of Hermann, was found to be a strenuous opponent of Hermann finally. Later made
cardinal.

[3] See p. 123. See terms of Treaty of Venlo, September 7, 1543. Kidd, No. 143.

showed himself gracious, when at the Diet of Speier, 1544, he promised a
council on German soil. He asked the estates to prepare a general scheme
which would at the same time bring about a Christian reformation yet
preserve unity. Cardinal Albrecht and the Pope reacted violently. The
Cardinal, defeated on every issue since 1517, and having just had the
humiliation of handing his own spiritual cure to evangelicals at the demand
of his own people, knew that a council on German soil would mean clear
victory for the evangelicals, and said so. The Pope was furious with
Charles for his audacity in thinking that any layman could sit and judge
such holy matters!

Charles, however, had the audacious duplicity, in writing to the Pope,
to describe the recent diets and colloquies as a mere blind to keep the
Protestants quiet, and argued that he was merely seeking to stabilize his
political position, from this position of strength to call the long-hoped-for
council, and then, to impose a Catholic unity on the Protestants. He now
knew that German Protestantism was in a position to become the religion
of Germany. Luther was more aware of this than Charles and this realization must have caused much of the bitterness in Luther's soul. He saw a
reformed Christianity in his land as a real possibility, but castigated
mercilessly the faithlessness and immorality of his countryman: the peasants, for their indifference, coarseness and stupidity; the burghers for their
luxury, their worldly values, their selfish ambition; the nobility for their
vulgar greed and parasitic existence; the whole of Germany for its drunkenness, gluttony, immorality and indifferentism; even his beloved students,
for vulgar and loose living. None would respond adequately to the clear
call of God, and Luther mourned his jeremiads of pending nemesis. At
this moment the harmonious understanding Luther had earlier reached
with the Swiss suffered some extraneous and unprovoked attacks and,
now suffering grave illness and in no state of mind for balanced and kindly
judgments, Luther broke out in bitterness of soul into an attack on them
as seditious blasphemers. This was regrettable, for the Swiss naturally rose
to the defence of their Zwingli, now of honoured memory, and relations
were worsened unnecessarily.

There was also the regrettable polemic against the Jews. This was not
the kind of antisemitism that marked the National Socialists in our own
century. It arose from a Jewish attack on the gospel in Moravia, directed
mainly against the doctrine of Christ. To attack Christ was to be guilty of
the ultimate blasphemy, and Luther directed violent salvoes against the
Jews. It was regrettable that Luther also criticized the perennial association
of the Jew with money and business: he ought to have kept to theological
ground only. Nevertheless, an historian must remind the reader that these
final outbreaks of invective against society for its godlessness, the sacramentarians for their bad theology, and the Jews for their opposition to

Christology, should not be explained away as the sourness of age, ill-health and failure. Luther had prior and profound theological convictions on all three. The mode of expression was reprehensible but the principles were sound.

All this time he laboured continually on the improvement of his *magnum opus*, the translation of the Bible. With the help of his amanuenses, Roth and Cruciger, he allowed some of his earlier sermons to be preserved in perpetuity and bequeathed to posterity. Luther never thought much of his work but Christendom can be grateful to these faithful scribes. The author knows of no sermons, not excluding those of the great classical Church Fathers, perhaps not excluding even the great Calvin, which speak so directly to the soul and virtually compel the Holy Spirit to be articulate.

The Emperor's mind was now being increasingly given to the church question which he wanted settled before he died. The Pope on the other hand was increasingly embarrassed in his efforts to stave off a council. No longer able to resist, the Pope eventually relented and conceded the council to meet at Trent in March 1545.[1] Meanwhile, the Emperor freed himself from the Turkish threat by buying them off for an eighteen-month truce.

In response to the Emperor's promises of reformation made at the Diet of Speier in 1544, the Elector John Frederick commissioned his theologians to prepare a scheme.[2] This was to be the last great document of peace designed to unite the Catholics and Protestants.[3] It set forward the great principles of an Evangelical Church, and on the practical side adopted the moderate policy that if the Catholic bishops would concede evangelical theology, and fulfil the proper pastoral duties of their office in accepting and preaching the gospel, the evangelicals in their turn would offer them true and canonical obedience. No mention was made of the Pope and popedom. No mention was made of the evangelical doctrine of Holy Communion over against the Romish doctrine of the mass. Critics were disquieted by the moderation and evasiveness of the document and deplored the absence of the stamp of Luther.

The proceedings suffered a great set-back, when a letter from the Pope to the Emperor was shown to Luther in which the Pope expressed indignant objections to Charles for his audacity at Speier in holding out any possibility of the Pope recognizing any evangelical contingent at any conference at all. Assured by the Elector that the letter was genuine, Luther wrote a violent attack against the papacy, the bitterest he ever penned. Luther argued that the whole idea of a free general council was abhorrent

[1] See the definitive Hubert Jedin, *History of the Council of Trent*. 2 vols. trans. Ernest Graf (1957). Note also the debate on what Scripture and Tradition meant at Trent in *Christianity Divided*, Küng, Barth and others, pp. 3–72. See also Kidd, Nos. 145–7.
[2] Enders-Kawerau, xvi. 113–14. 20 November, 1544.
[3] Given in Sehling, *Die Evangelische Kirchenordnungen*, 1, 209 f.

to the Pope, and the reasons were obvious. The Pope made nonsense of the council in any case, for he reserved the right of veto. Luther accused the papacy of trickery in preventing Charles from effecting peace and unity in Germany as well as bringing about a Christian general council to reform Christendom. The Pope had shown that he was no longer in fact the head of Christendom. Luther questioned the Pope's right to stand above conciliar judgment, and raised the possibility of his deposition by Christendom. In effect Luther rejected both the temporal and spiritual authority of the Pope.

The Protestants could not take part in the Council of Trent. Nevertheless, it is obvious that if they had, the Council would have foundered on the first question raised, the nature and source of authority. The Emperor feigned a concession to the Protestants by promising them a religious national conference to be held in Ratisbon in 1546, at the same time informing the Pope that he could not be ready to make war on the Protestants for at least another year.

It takes little imagination to picture the sore dismay of the evangelicals when all this was made known to them, men to whom God and their religion meant all. The calculating cynicism of the Emperor biding his time to strike them, the double-dealing irreligion of the Pope, religious war impending, their theological champion nearing his end. The council opened in December, 1545, without the evangelicals. The opportunity was lost and has not presented itself these four hundred years. Perhaps the convening of Vatican II, ensuing in new oecumenical relations, may prove the beginning of a new movement.

Luther was buffeted with many trials. In 1545 a fresh rupture with the Swiss broke out. And then he was bitterly distressed that Wittenberg, the very cradle of the Reformation, should bear such meagre fruits of spirituality and morality. It demonstrated how thinly the evangelical theology had penetrated the hearts and minds of his countryman. He sensed he had failed. Luther never reconciled himself to the natural resistance of the human heart to the gospel, nor to the attacks of its enemies. His closing years were darkened with a dismal foreboding of the outcome. In addition to this his health was deteriorating: he suffered acutely from stones in his bladder, his sight was failing him. "Old, spent, worn, weary, cold, and with but one eye to see with" he said of himself at this time. It was during these years that he said that, had not God willed otherwise, death would have been a merciful release. It was a great relief to him when on November 17 he completed his lectures on Genesis, the last he was ever to give. To his students he said:

This is the beloved Genesis; God grant that after me it may be better done. I can do no more. I am weak. Pray God that He may grant me a good and happy end.[1]

[1] WA. 44, 825. 10 ff.

It was on a last visit to his native parts, where he had gone against all advice to heal a difference between the Count of Mansfeld and his brother, that Luther's body finally broke down. He died quietly in the village where he was born, knowing he was passing on, with the words of Christ on his lips: "God so loved the world that he gave His only begotten Son, to the end that whosoever believeth in Him should not perish, but have everlasting life" (John 3:16).

It was a desolate cry of lamentation that went up throughout the evangelical church of Germany. When the news reached Wittenberg, Melanchthon was lecturing to his students. The porter interrupted. In that momentary stillness that final and fatal word was spoken, Professor Luther had died. Melanchthon cried out in a sorrow that could not be soothed, "Alas! the chariot of Israel and the horseman thereof!" The Church had lost its Elijah, Elisha could but cry. He left the students stricken and silent, and was later to say, "And now we are like the forsaken orphans of a beloved father." The Elector insisted that the mortal remains be brought back to Wittenberg and buried there. In the church on whose door he had nailed the Theses a short twenty-nine years earlier, Luther was lowered to his last rest. There his mortal remains still lie, near those of Melanchthon.

### 3. From the Death of Luther to the Death of Charles V

The Reformation in Germany may be said to have reached the end of its first phase when the Peace of Augsburg was signed in 1555,[1] eleven years after Luther's death. The religious revolt hardened in that moment into political Protestantism. The evolution of the reforming movement into a church possessing precise doctrine and formal organization had its counterpart in a political development arising not of theological necessity but from the pressure of national and international forces. When Charles sought to destroy Protestantism the Protestant princes of Germany moved from their religious stand into a collective military force. This movement gave Luther and Melanchthon grave disquiet and filled Luther with foreboding as he drew near to death. At Ratisbon in January, 1546, it grew clear that the Emperor and the princes would be compelled to join war, for Charles was now free from any threat from France[2] and was firmly resolved to crush the German theological rebellion. When Luther died (February 18, 1546) the last obstacle to war was removed.

Within weeks of Luther's death (June 19, 1546) Charles came to terms with the traitorous Maurice, the cousin and rival of John Frederick. He then put Philip of Hesse and John Frederick under the ban of the Empire

---

[1] Kidd, No. 149.
[2] By the Treaty of Crespy, September 18, 1544. Kidd, No 144.

(July 20, 1546) on the grounds that they had violated public peace. Pope Paul III showed his approval by sending a contingent of supporting troops under the command of his grandson, Ottavio Farnese. After a summer of desultory campaigning Maurice suddenly hurled his troops against John Frederick (October, 1546). The latter deserted the Schmalkaldic army to repulse the attack on his own territory, and this desertion had the effect of dispersing the Schmalkaldic army. The Emperor now felt in a strong position. He forced the evangelical Duke of Württemberg to submit. He deposed the evangelical Archbishop of Cologne who was on the point of allying his whole diocese with the Reformation. He entered Ulm, Augsburg, Frankfurt and Strasbourg, and reasserted his imperial authority in these cities which had adhered to the evangelical cause. The Protestant princes now stood without allies: even support from Henry VIII or Francis I was no longer possible for both had just died (Henry, January 28, 1547, Francis, March 31, 1547). Finally, Charles swept down on Saxony (April, 1547) and both John Frederick and Philip of Hesse were defeated and taken prisoner. Wittenberg capitulated, John Frederick was declared a traitor and his territory given to Maurice. Philip and John Frederick were cast into prison where they remained for five years.

Now at the height of his power, the Emperor determined to settle the religious question once for all. But the Council of Trent was now under way, and had handled major theological issues in a way unacceptable to the reformers. Further, Charles and the Pope were again at loggerheads. Nevertheless, Charles determined to do what he could about Germany and decided on a provisional settlement. This was prepared by two Catholics, von Pflug and Helding, in co-operation with one Protestant, Agricola. This document of twenty-six articles was called the *Interim*,[1] and was proclaimed by the Diet of Augsburg on May 15, 1548. By its terms of compromise the liberties and advantages which the evangelicals had gained were annulled. Certain guarantees were made to Catholics living in Protestant territories. The worship of saints and the observance of the seven sacraments were reaffirmed. Communion in both kinds was conceded, as well as the permission for married priests to continue in office. The Pope felt the initiative was taken out of his hands so suspended the Council.

Nevertheless, it was one thing to pass the *Interim* but another to effect it. Changing sides in an effort to redeem his character in German eyes, Maurice of Saxony refused to enforce it, and even had it revised by his theologians and given the new name of the *Interim of Leipzig*. Charles was now ageing and ill, and had not the power or energy to see that his *Interim* was obeyed. At this stage of his life Charles sometimes showed force, as for example in the expulsion of Bucer from Strasbourg; sometimes he

[1] Kidd, No. 148.

took no notice, as in the case of Maurice. Further, though Charles had defeated the German princes in the field he had not subdued the German people in their hearts. The folk hated the foreign imperial troops and were much disquieted when the rumour gained ground that Charles was ready to abdicate in favour of his Spanish son Philip. Maurice, sensing the change, had the effrontery to let the German princes know that he was now clearly on their side and not the Emperor's in this matter. Moreover, fresh troubles of an international kind were now brewing. The new French king, Henry II (1547–59) took over Lorraine by the terms of the Treaty of Chambord, January 15, 1552,[1] and marched to the Rhine. Maurice fell on Augsburg to deprive the Emperor of his bankers' aid, and rapidly hurled his forces on Innsbruck, whereupon the Emperor rose from his sick-bed and fled for his life. The Council at Trent hurriedly suspended itself once more. Charles failed to drive back Henry, so retired to Brussels leaving his brother Ferdinand of Austria to negotiate the Treaty of Passau[2] with the Protestants, August 2, 1552. Finally, at the Diet of Augsburg in 1555[3] the treaty was signed and the Protestants finally compelled Charles to accept the principle *cujus regio ejus religio*. It recognized the right of every ruler, Catholic and Protestant alike, to regulate the religious affairs of his own state and to impose his own religion on his subjects. If the latter would not submit they ran the risk of exile or death. This principle, first formulated at Speier in 1526, formed a new basis of Germanic Law, and sanctioned the triumph of politics over religion. As far as church property was concerned, it was laid down that all property secularized before 1552 should be retained by its present owners, but that for the future any ecclesiastic who went over to Protestantism was to relinquish his properties with his office. Finally, any principality which was to abandon Catholicism might do so by mutual decision of the nobility and the towns of the territory.

It was in this way that the Reformation in Germany received its political constitution. By confirming the virtual partition of the country it sowed the seeds of the long religious wars of the seventeenth century for it was a victory merely for territorialism, not for toleration. It further showed the impotence of imperial authority, and the independence of pocket principalities. The great ideal of liberty of conscience seemingly secured was actually lost: a man had to follow his ruler. Nor was Protestantism as a whole conceded: the theology of Wittenberg was permitted but not that of Zürich, Geneva nor Strasbourg, not to mention the quiet army of independent men who wore no label. It was a shabby victory for such a glorious cause.

[1] Text in Dumont, *Corps Diplomatique* IV, 1. 31 ff.
[2] *Op. cit.*, 42 ff.
[3] Kidd, No. 149. Trans. Emil Reich, *Selected Documents illustrating Mediaeval and Modern History*, 230 ff.

If Luther did not succeed, Charles's failure was crushing. Lutheranism had won its freedom, and ruled in the heart of his empire, a powerful church protected by princes and adhered to by millions of his subjects. He had preserved for Catholicism only Westphalia, the Rhineland and the Alpine region in Germany. Broken and defeated, he solemnly divested himself of all his titles and domains: the Empire he handed to his brother Ferdinand; Spain, the Low Countries, the Italian territories and the empire overseas he handed to his son Philip of Spain. He retired to a monastery in Spain to do penance, seek forgiveness and save his soul. That sad and tortured man devoted himself to prayer and meditation until his death two years later, on September 21, 1558. In token of his eternal humiliation he asked to be buried under the altar at the monastery, in such a way that every morning at mass the priest would stand on Charles's face.

PART TWO

*Zwingli and the Swiss Reformation*

# CHAPTER VII

# ZWINGLI AND HIS BACKGROUND

## 1. *The European Background*

THE RELIGIOUS PEACE OF AUGSBURG, 1555, SECURED THE TOLERATION of Lutheranism within the Empire. For a long time toleration was very grudgingly conceded by the Romanists, who in the Thirty Years' War of the seventeenth century made their last unsuccessful effort under the Jesuits to extirpate Protestantism and compel all Germany to submission to the Roman Church. Nevertheless the settlement lasted and still stands. Yet the Peace did not embrace all Protestants, for the Zwinglians, the Calvinists and that energetic group loosely called the Sectarians, which finally shaped itself into what we now understand as Baptists and Radical Protestants, were all deliberately excluded.

Nor did the Religious Peace end the revolt against Rome. There were countless Lutherans in the provinces of the Catholic princes, whose only freedom was emigration. Otherwise they were to submit. Further, by the "clause of reservation," if an ecclesiastic or a prince broke away to the Protestant cause, all property and income was reserved to the Roman Church. By this means vast areas such as the Archbishopric of Cologne were snatched back just as they were about to enter the portals of Protestantism.

Not all Protestants were Lutherans by any means. By the time of the Religious Peace there had grown up a strong Calvinist movement. Melanchthon was aware of this and sought to bridge the difference. Theologically he was most successful, but the greatness of Luther overshadowed the German Protestants, who sought to maintain the deposit of truth left by Luther, and the Lutheran theologians turned against Melanchthon. Consequently, large districts transferred their theological allegiance and were lost to the Lutheran Church in Germany after 1555. The Church of the Palatinate was the first to separate and in 1563 published its Heidelberg Catechism.[1] Bremen followed in 1568. Anhalt abandoned Luther's Catechism and Lutheran church order. Hesse-Cassel went over in 1605. Many smaller places followed suit, and lost the protection the Peace of Augsburg afforded.

There were two principal differences between the Evangelical Church (Luther) and the Reformed Church (Calvin). Fundamentally, of course, they are alike Protestant and Reformed, but in the doctrine of the sacrament

[1] See Cochrane, *Reformed Confessions*, 305-31.

and in the matter of church government the Reformed Church felt sufficiently strongly to separate. The Lutheran view of the corporal real presence now supported by a doctrine of Ubiquity, they found too closely related to the mediaeval idea of *substantia*. This had been Zwingli's objection, and Calvin now argued that substance was an idea more related to power than to an object in space. They also rejected Luther's idea of consistorial government of the Church as again being mediaeval and secular, and sought to establish an idea of church government derived directly from apostolic times.

In this connection not only was the Reformed Church excluded from Augsburg, but also the radical Anabaptist wing, and therefore there hardened out in Germany, in addition to the Reformed Church, what might be called the Radical or extreme Protestant movement.

And then, for a complex variety of historical, geographical, social and political reasons, other countries in Europe, which had throbbed with both the Renascence and the Reformation movements, had begun to develop their own idea of how the Reformation should be effected. Doubtless, the best grasp of the Reformation can be found in a firm hold of the issues of the Lutheran Reformation, and from that to assess the other Reformers, Zwingli, Bucer, Calvin and the distinguished host of the lesser Reformers throughout Europe. Nevertheless, though the Reformation took a different course almost in every land, outside of Germany it had one thing in common different from Lutheranism, and that was a type of theology which is often called Calvinist or "Reformed."

This type of theology crystallized out in the distinctive confessions of the different countries, and was marked by a refusal to accept Lutheran dogma on the one hand, and by a much more marked departure from the mediaeval Church than ever Luther made. Their national confessions were inspired by Zürich and Geneva rather than Wittenberg,[1] and there is clearly to be discerned throughout them all the refusal to accept Lutheran sacramental theology as well as the positive assertion of an apostolic system of church polity.

This reformed ideal of ecclesiastical government meant that the Church was a theocratic democracy, and was to be ruled by an authority which lay in the converted community. Whilst Luther sought to reform ecclesiastical rule and wanted the whole system to continue, but purified, the Reformed theologians sought to cut out the whole structure root and branch, and to start a renewed Church on the principles clearly shown in the New Testament and in the early church. Nevertheless, in practice this was always considerably qualified, for society at large showed as much

---

[1] England was an exception in this respect. The author believes that there were certain theological and historical affinities between England and the Lutheran Reformation, and clear antipathies towards Zürich and Geneva. See pp. 199 ff.

apprehension of an earnest presbyter as they had done of a devoted priest. Consequently, much of the rule of the Church passed into civil hands, as in Zürich and Geneva: nevertheless, if the civic authority was a converted authority, Reformed theologians found this acceptable. Luther worked with a "godly prince" by theological conviction, and clearly differentiated the spheres and responsibilities of Church and State. But the Reformed theology is the theology which spread throughout Europe, and owing to nationalist and intellectual movements, was not prepared to allow the return of any kind of ecclesiastical tyranny, authority or abuse, whether of priest or presbyter. In most places the crown took authority in all matters, except in certain areas of doctrine. Further, civil lawyers had just discovered the Codes of Justinian and Theodosius, and they were pressing urgently everywhere for the substitution of civil law in the place of canon law. These lawyers never accepted the idea of an independent church disciplined and governed by its own membership. To them the Church was a department of the State answerable to the law of the State. This produced the anomaly that in all those lands where the secular authorities were sympathetic to the Reformation, the Church became more or less subject to the State. Although Luther had insisted that the *jus episcopale* belonged to the magistrate, and although he is loosely accused of "handing the Church over to the princes," in practice the civil authorities of the Reformed countries, Switzerland, the Netherlands, the Palatinate, etc., had a tighter control of the Church in their countries than ever a Lutheran prince sought or desired.

The Reformed churches shared another characteristic in common, and that was a stronger influence of humanism. Certainly England under Henry VIII sought some reformation in life and morals which would leave untouched the fundamental doctrine and structure of the mediaeval church, almost as Erasmus desired it. Certainly Zwingli began as a humanist. It was Erasmus and not Luther who caused him to study the Bible and the Church Fathers, and it was his reading of Augustine on St. John's Gospel together with the publication of the Pauline Epistles in Erasmus' New Testament, that brought him to a Reformed theology. In any case, his reformation was humanist, intellectualist, socialist, nationalist. Zwingli sought for a clear understanding of the Holy Scriptures, the removal of idolatry and superstition in popular religion, and the formulation of a reasonable, clear understanding of intellectual belief.

Humanism, too, strongly influenced the "Meaux Group." Their pursuit of a middle course between stubborn Scholastics and thorough-going Reformers was not crowned with success, nevertheless it produced William Farel and Calvin. Calvin blossomed out as a first-class humanist and a classical moralist in his early days, and his classical learning and high morality remained characteristic of the Reformed churches.

True though it is that the Reformation sprang up everywhere without the influence of Luther, and in many places long before Luther was born; true though it is that Reformed theology developed its own ethos; nevertheless the influence of Luther on the Reformation must be admitted as the greatest single force within the movement. He was indeed the "monk that shook the world." In fact, he quietly took the Church off its hinges and re-hung it. He showed the world what religious courage and conviction meant. After a long, painful struggle for redemption, God gave him the clear redemption of the New Testament, and in the strength of this conviction he broke the priestly yoke, made the layman free, gave him direct access to God and put the Bible in his hands. Luther was intensely religious and had solved all man's religious conflicts on the battlefield of his own soul: he spoke as a victor to men seeking victory. His very freedom from the intellectual humanism of his day made him speak to every man's heart. There was nothing wild, nothing irrational about him. It was a mature scholar that quietly struck at the one scandal that every man knew was a disgrace. He wrote, spoke and acted as the mighty religious genius of his day. He stripped Christianity of all its excrescences and showed to every man, woman, and child the glory and mystery of God: what it meant to have an unwavering trust in God who had given Himself in Christ; what it meant to say "I believe in God." He had been along every road on which men blunder after God, and could speak mighty certainties to men who were less certain of where they were going with a sympathy and a power that literally moved men. That is why, as long as Luther lived, evangelicals were labelled "Lutheran": it was only about the end of his life when the genius of Calvin began to be felt in Europe, that the name ceased being used in this way.

Certain Reformed historians are apt to rate Zwingli higher than Luther on the grounds of a first-class intellect, a first-rate humanist equipment, and the foresight to make a cleaner break with Rome. These judgments are true enough, but Zwingli never had the passionate upsurge of Luther, nor his religious genius. This can be shown in the attitude of the two men to indulgences. Zwingli laughed at them with his derisive wit. Luther wept, and taking lost men by the arm, with love and pity directed them on the real road to pardon. Luther knew that the vast crowds buying their indulgences, tramping miles to shrines, kissing relics, did this because they sensed a need for pardon. Luther felt as the people felt, where they had gone wrong he had gone wrong, where they had dreaded the wrath of God, he had dreaded it too. Luther not only knew God at first hand but the comman man too. That was why the whole of Europe listened to him and marvelled. He shouted from the house-tops what they had but muttered in the streets. Men took the greatest risks and paid dearly to possess his tracts and treatises: cautious Scottish merchants, university students in every city, Spanish traders, all men in all countries read these writings, and in a very real way Luther shaped the Reformation.

It is important to recall that Luther never sought to effect a *Lutheran* Reformation. The Reformation according to Luther ought to be a reformation of traditional catholicism worked out in the natural institutions of life, i.e. in a family, in a particular country, in a particular job, at a particular time. The Reformation throughout Europe was inspired essentially by the same principles, but it worked itself out quite differently in every country. Compare, for instance, how England worked out her reformation in a Wycliffite fashion modified by humanism, Continental theology, and conservatism, with the independent way the Netherlands and the Swiss set their own house in order. Reformed theology was always more oecumenical than Lutheran, perhaps because Calvin came a generation later when there was much persecution, which served to make Reformed theologians think of themselves as an international comity of theologians. Be that as it may, the course of the Reformation has virtually to be described country by country, although each story is the same theme with variations.

## 2. *The Swiss background*

The Swiss background was utterly different from anywhere else in Europe. There had developed a long tradition whereby independent cantons formed a very loose federation. For centuries the Swiss had fought for this kind of communal independence,[1] sometimes against their neighbours, sometimes against larger forces such as Austria. Concomitant with this there grew up a reputation that they were the finest soldiers in Europe.[2] More and more foreign powers hired these men, actually vying one with another for their services, going to the extent of bribing magistrates. This produced a serious internal problem in Switzerland. Young men returned to their villages and hamlets with quickly earned gold which produced resentment in the breasts of craftsmen and farmers living in primitive simplicity or near poverty. When the mercenaries returned home there were wild drinking orgies and vulgar festivals and fairs. Zwingli was to oppose this human traffic later at some cost to himself, though he was involved in it at first as a paid agent of the Pope.

As for the position of the Church, there were the usual plethora of monasteries and shrines produced by mediaeval piety, now grown lax, and top-heavy with the usual wealthy prince-bishops and their courts. Nobles sought the rich canonries for their sons. There were the usual pilgrimages,

---

[1] Kidd argues that it was this independence which caused the Reformation to grow in Switzerland, p. 365. See Doc. No. 150, The Diet of Baden, August 11, 1512, and Doc. 151, The League with Appenzell, December 17, 1513.
[2] Kidd, No. 152

the usual indulgences, the usual cult of relics. There were also the occasional rays of saintly protest. Yet in many places, particularly at the level of city council, the layman made his voice heard and criticized the ways of his Church leaders.[1]

Their geography, their history and their social structure gave the Swiss a love of liberty, a ruggedness of character, a tenacity of purpose, a courage, sometimes an obstinacy that is clearly marked, even though generalizations are unsafe. He was a hard worker, dogged, determined and opinionated. He did not like being handled, or being organized. William Tell is a type of the Swiss, and Zwingli himself shared quite strikingly the characteristics of his people and was recognized by them as their leader.

Born on January 1, 1484, six weeks after Martin Luther, in the hamlet of Wildhaus, high up in the Toggenburg Valley near the eastern end of Lake Constance, Zwingli[2] enjoyed a good well-to-do background and home-life. The splendid wooden chalet-house where he was born stands to this day: his father's study, the noble living-room, the large dark kitchen, the interesting bedrooms looking out on to the lovely Swiss mountains, are exactly as they were used by the large Zwingli family, eleven children and servants. To move through the rooms, to sit on the bench at the door, to look at the mountains and breathe the high cool air, is a salutary experience for men of an urban civilization. His father and his grandfather were each what we might call a town-clerk and mayor combined in one office, the town official.

The boyhood of Zwingli was happy and normal.[3] But educational opportunities were limited for a boy like Zwingli in the hamlet of Wildhaus, and at the age of five, when he had already having shown a sharp mind and musical gifts, the father reluctantly sent Ulrich to school at the lovely lake-side town of Weesen some twenty miles away, where a scholarly uncle was parish parson. The house of his uncle and the walled garden, where the young boy lived, learned and played are still there today. So bright was Ulrich that he was sent to Basel where he was taught by the famous, kindly scholar Bünzli (1494–8). By then Zwingli had grown beyond his teacher and was sent to Berne to be a pupil of the famous humanist Lupulus, a disciple of Erasmus and a reformer at heart. In Berne he lodged in the Dominican convent, and showed such musical ability he was almost persuaded to become a monk, but his level-headed parents

[1] See Goldli's defence of his practice of buying and selling livings, Kidd, No. 156; the admissions of Canon Hofmann (December, 1521), Kidd, No. 156; Zwingli's own admissions, No. 178, and Hillerbrand, 115 f.
[2] For information on Zwingli consult the authoritative Oskar Farner, *Huldrych Zwingli*, 4 vols. (Zürich, 1943–60).
[3] The author picked up from a Swiss monk in the area the apocryphal story that when Zwingli was being baptized he emptied his bowels into the font and that so devilish was the smell that the Church could not be used for eight days! This was taken for an omen as to what Zwingli was to do for the Church, and actually did!!

rescued him from that and sent him to the University of Vienna (1500–02). In 1502 he returned to Basel where he took his B.A. in 1504 and his M.A. in 1506. It was here that he came under the influence of Thomas Wyttenbach, the humanist and reformer, teacher alike of Capito, Pellicanus and Leo Jud, reformers all.[1]

Already discernible are the striking differences that marked him off from a Luther (or a Calvin for that matter). In Basel he enjoyed a comfortable background, was well educated by first-class humanists, fell in with the plans of a family with strong clerical connections, took life easily, had no moral scruples, and entered his vocation in a careless, unconsidered way. He had none of the urgency of Luther or Calvin for strong personal religion, none of their moral earnestness, none of their God-mastered theology. He became a Reformer because he was a trained humanist with a liking for Augustine and the New Testament, and this, allied with a frank honesty, brought him into conflict with all shams and hypocrisies. He was a Reformer of the head rather than the heart. Nevertheless, he developed into a religious Reformer of abiding significance and should not be underestimated.

### 3. Zwingli at Glarus and Einsiedeln

From the University of Basel he went to Glarus,[2] hurriedly ordained to qualify as vicar (1506). The great church at Glarus has long been used by both Reformed and Catholic congregations, though at the moment of writing (September, 1964) the Catholic congregation are about to break this long and valuable tradition (on practical grounds, not religious) to move into their own new church. In the church the chalice of Zwingli can be seen, a sight which brings those troublous days so much nearer. There is still found on the streets of Glarus, and in its common memory, a tradition of a faithful, popular, preaching parson in its own Zwingli.

Zwingli worked hard in this onerous cure. In addition to the normal responsibilities, he pursued his own studies as well as founded a school. He developed a great interest in Erasmus[3] and made interesting liturgical discoveries on the subject of the mass.[4] By now Zwingli had been made aware of the evils of indulgences, the authority of the Bible, the power of atonement in the Cross and the reality of faith as the key to heaven. The people knew that they had a good parson, and his ministry was most effective. Nevertheless, they were not aware of the moral conflict and scandal in his heart, nor of his increasing concern on the subject of mercenary war.

At Glarus he was secretly involved with loose women. Admittedly, it was a time of gross scandal, when Pope Innocent VIII publicly and

[1] Kidd. No. 159.    [2] Hillerbrand, 110 f.    [3] Kidd, No. 160.    [4] Kidd, No. 161.

extravagantly married off his daughter to a Medici, when Pope Alexander VI confessed to six natural children when he mounted the papal throne and practised the same liberty afterwards and when the abbot of Engelberg publicly maintained a wife and numerous children. Nevertheless, there were clergy and laymen alike who were deeply concerned about this and not involved in such scandal at all. Later at Einsiedeln Zwingli was again involved with a notorious girl, thrown out by her father the barber for loose living. Zwingli painfully and frankly admitted his frailty: he first blamed himself, and then blamed the folly of the imposition of celibacy on a man. The wrong was grave, yet God proved greater. He showed Zwingli how frail the human will was, how powerful God was. His torment of soul shattered his pride, and it was a broken man who realized the healing power of forgiveness in Christ.

There was another shadow over his life. From Glarus he had twice accompanied his men to the wars as an army chaplain. His experience convinced him of the evil of this practice of paying men to fight other people's wars, and of the grave social evil of the life these men led on periods of leave. The sight after the battle of Monza (1515) when he saw ten thousand young men dead on one field on a beautiful September day, and another fifteen hundred maimed in the rude hospitals of Milan and the canals choked by dead horses, fired a conviction that never left him. Why should "the booted Pope" (Julius II) unleash such massacre? On his return he powerfully denounced wickedness of this kind, though in so doing he incurred such odium among the influential in the parish, on the grounds that he was wrecking the flourishing trade of exporting soldiers, that he was forced to leave Glarus.

While in the torment of his own impurity and the conflict of mercenary warfare, Zwingli deepened both his Patristic and Biblical learning, and spent his military pay on books. In these years there was a strong influence of Erasmus on Zwingli, in addition to that of Augustine and the New Testament.

It was at this time that Zwingli was offered the post of people's priest at Einsiedeln,[1] the famous monastery and pilgrimage resort (April 14, 1516), and with a very heavy heart left Glarus in the care of a curate. Einsiedeln is a typical Catholic pilgrimage town, packed with shops selling trinkets, rosaries, charms, images, pictures, ikons and candles. It was famous in Zwingli's day for the same reasons, though spiritually dead. There were only two monks there at the time: the abbot, now nearly eighty and more interested in hunting than in the cloister; and the administrator a conscientious, good man, who struck up a great friendship with Zwingli and eventually died by his side on the tragic field of Kappel.

At Einsiedeln, in addition to the normal pastoral duties, Zwingli

[1] Hillerbrand, pp. 112 f.

studied the Bible and the Fathers, but also gained a great reputation as a preacher. It was his knowledge of the Bible and the theology of the Fathers that showed him the wide gulf that yawned between the New Testament and the Early Church on the one hand and the church life of his own day on the other, and it was this awareness that made his preaching so effective. When Samson, the notorious seller of indulgences, came trafficking his wares, Zwingli sharply rebuked him from the pulpit.

At Whitsuntide in 1518, fifteen hundred men of Zürich went to Einsiedeln on a pilgrimage to the Blessed Virgin, and noticed Zwingli on account of his preaching. When the post at the Great Minster fell vacant they pressed the canons to appoint Zwingli. The canons demurred somewhat, owing to the ugly rumours of Zwingli's morality, but when Zwingli openly confessed the nature of his lapses and his views on his former conduct, they were considerably reassured, particularly in view of the fact that the other possibility for the post had six illegitimate children and was in possession of numerous benefices! The canons had no idea they were inviting a Reformer to take over the Minister. On Christmas Day, 1518, Zwingli preached his last sermon at Einsiedeln, and on December 27 took over office at Zürich with consequences that were to have a lasting effect on Europe. To walk round his church the *Grossmünster* where the Reformation in Switzerland began, to go inside and read his Bible, to stand on the bank of the Limmat and gaze at that fine noble figure standing there, Bible in one hand and sword in the other, to study his books, manuscripts and letters in the library, to see in the museum his sword and his helmet with its gash speaking eloquently of his early and tragic death, to walk on the field of Kappel in the silent countryside where he was slain and where cruel enemies cut his body in pieces and then destroyed them by fire, is to take part in the history of Europe.

# CHAPTER VIII

# THE REFORMATION IN SWITZERLAND

## 1. Zwingli in Zürich

NO PLACE WAS MORE SUITED TO ZWINGLI THAN ZÜRICH. ZÜRICH WAS an imperial city, which had developed around the Great and the Little Minster, into what was the centre of a trading, banking and manufacturing area. It had grown up strongly independent of Papal and ecclesiastical authority owing to the help Zürich had provided in the Pope's wars and also because its bishop lived in Constance in what was virtually another country. It was also strongly lay, democratic and self-governing. The young scholar, with his desire to simplify religion and turn to essentials, was readily accepted in this independently minded city.

The city liked him at once.[1] One of the first things he did was to preach against Samson the seller of indulgences and then to persuade the council to forbid Samson to lodge in the town. It is interesting to mark the reaction of Rome to Zwingli's protest and compare it with their reaction to Luther's protest. Rome simply ordered Samson to go and not to upset the Zürichers, yet it had launched into Luther with all its fire and fury. The main reason for this difference lay in that Zwingli, rather like Erasmus, laughed and ridiculed the whole affair,[2] whereas Luther not only struck at the moral abuse but went much deeper. He struck at the whole theology of priesthood claiming to pardon sin and claiming to mediate between God and man: Luther cut to the nerve, Zwingli showed them what they could no longer decently conceal. Ranke expressed the difference in his usual eloquence: "while in the one case, we see the highest and most august powers of the world in agitation, in the other it is a question of the emancipation of a city from an episcopal power."[3]

It was at this moment that Zwingli discovered the theology of Luther and is found reading and recommending Luther's works, an influence he later sought to modify or even disclaim. To a startled chapter he announced he was going to preach through the entire Gospel of Matthew and not follow the usual scholastic *Evangelia dominicalia*. As Bullinger expressed it:

> He wanted to interpret the Scripture, and not the opinions of men, to the honour of God and His only Son, our Lord Jesus Christ, as well as to the true salvation of souls and the edification of pious and honourable men.[4]

[1] Though he faced much opposition from the chapter and from the friars. Kidd, No. 165.
[2] See the letter of Beatus Rhenanus on indulgences, December 6, 1518. Kidd, No. 163.
[3] Quoted Kidd, p. 387.     [4] Hillerbrand, pp. 118 f.

Bullinger went on to describe Zwingli's preaching at this time:

He praised God the Father, and taught men to trust only in the Son of God, Jesus Christ, as saviour. He vehemently denounced all unbelief, superstition and hypocrisy. Eagerly he strove after repentance, improvement of life, and Christian love and faith. He rebuked vice such as idleness, excesses in eating, drinking and apparel, gluttony, suppression of the poor, pensions and wars. He insisted that the Government should maintain law and justice, and protect widows and orphans. The people should always seek to retain Swiss freedom.

The people flocked to hear such preaching, and Zwingli actually preached in the market-place on Fridays so that the country-folk from the villages might hear him.

One further experience served to bring Zwingli to some sense of religious conversion. In the summer of 1519 the plague ravaged Switzerland, and Zwingli returned from holiday into the city to fulfil his pastoral duties to the sick and dying. By September the dreaded disease had struck him and he lay at death's door. But his robust rustic constitution saved him. Slowly he staggered through a shaky convalescence to receive the shattering blow that his brother Andrew, a brilliant young man and beloved of Zwingli, had succumbed to the plague. The illness had a very serious effect on Zwingli, and his writings during the illness and convalescence show a man matured by affliction, all too aware of the nearness of death and the horror of dying in sin. The whole experience made him much more religious, and when he eventually returned to his duties, men noted that affliction and grief had marked his physical frame, but had cleansed and purified the spirit. God was working on Zwingli.

## 2. Zwingli becomes a Reformer

When Zwingli announced to the astonished chapter that he was to begin his work by expounding the whole of St. Matthew's Gospel beginning at verse 1, he announced the foundations of the Reformation in Switzerland. The centre of the life of the Great Minster now moved away from the mass and mediaeval tradition to the living Word of God expounded from the words of Christ, the apostles and the prophets. When the reactionaries criticized this practice he replied he was following the practice of Augustine and Chrysostom, and during the next twelve years of his life he stuck to this course. After Matthew he expounded Acts, 1 Timothy and Galatians. When attacked for his Paulinism and his Lutheranism, Zwingli was to say, "I preach the way Paul writes. Why do you not call me a follower of Paul? Indeed, I proclaim the Word of Christ. Why do you not call me a Christian. . . ? Why do you ascribe the teaching of other men to Luther, when he himself ascribes everything to God?"[1]

[1] Hillderbrand, p. 126.

He expounded I and II Peter, followed by Hebrews in 1522. In 1523 he turned to St. Luke, in 1524 to St. John, in 1525 back to the Pauline texts and then for the first time he turned to the Old Testament.

These sermons are all simple, homely, extempore, free from dogmatic polemic. He simply sought to change his hearers' heart. Two very simple illustrations of this preaching are given by Rilliet.[1]

> The essential in my religion, says God, is that you should obey me. (On Jer. 7.)

> On Isaiah 1:17, *Defend the fatherless, plead for the widow*: These are the works which are pleasing to God. You must cast off the burden of sin and then at once the joy of a good conscience will fill your life. If anyone bears a heavy burden and asks, "How shall I manage to dance?" he is mad. We likewise: if we bend under the weight of sin and if we try by means of ceremonies to please God and to gain peace of conscience, we are fools.

He was known to offer homely and saucy comment from the pulpit. He advised a priest to keep his oil for his salad rather than unction: "We became blessed through faith, not through oil, otherwise it would be containers that would be happiest."

A strong attack was made on the existing ecclesiastical system when Zwingli preached a sermon against tithes, but a more shattering blow was struck when some of Zwingli's sympathizers, working overtime to publish an edition of St. Paul's Epistles for the Frankfurt fair, and being tired and hungry, ate meat during Lent.[2] When official action was taken Zwingli openly supported the action on the grounds of evangelical liberty,[3] and, showing much courage against what can only be called ecclesiastical jobbery, he secured a compromise decision.[4]

At this time the Pope asked Zürich for a force of soldiers, promising not to use them against the French in whose ranks were many Swiss mercenaries. Zwingli opposed this with much energy, and finally prevailed, though many Zürichers smarted at the financial loss incurred in Zwingli's policy. Six thousand of his townsmen joined up of their own accord but when they returned home without money and without honour Zwingli's views had won over the people. This action of Zwingli virtually meant a break with the papacy, a break effectually made with the publication in August, 1522, of his *Architeles*,[5] his first and last word to the Pope. The book was in fact an apologia of Zwingli's programme. In this book he staunchly rebutted the charges of being a heresiarch, claiming but to have preached the New Testament only and to have sought the

---

[1] J. H. Rilliet, *Zwingli: Third Man of the Reformation* (London, 1964), pp. 60, 61, 62.
[2] Kidd, No. 171.     [3] Kidd, No. 174.     [4] Kidd, Nos. 175–7.
[5] Künzli, *Zwinglis Schriften*, pp. 42–53.

unity of the primitive church. He advocated the liberation of believers from episcopal and papal control.

All the Reformers, from Luther on, had one characteristic in common, to allow the common man to judge for himself the truth of the evangelical theology by means of public disputation. The papists or Romanists everywhere resisted this practice, preferring their traditional authoritative control. Zwingli persisted, but by now the Great Council had been won over to Zwingli's views, and so he gained permission to hold a public disputation in the Town Hall on January 29, 1523, to settle the controversies in religion.

Zwingli promulgated Sixty-Seven Theses[1] for discussion. Their theme was to establish the primacy of the Word of God, to be received on its own authority and not that of the Church. Running through most of the theses was the centrality of Christ as Redeemer. They attack the primacy of the Pope, the Mass, the invocation of saints, the idea of the acquisition of merit by means of good works, fasts, pilgrimages, Purgatory and sacerdotal celibacy. They are unlike Luther's ninety-seven, which were couched in anti-scholastic, academic terms, and shine out in clear, short assertions designed obviously to win the mind of the laity. In this they succeeded. The case for the opposition virtually went by default: none had the courage to defend it. The outcome of the debate marked the first stage of the Reformation in Zürich in that the Council agreed that Zwingli was no heretic and gave open approval to his ministry.

Zwingli showed great common sense and prudence. His method was not to initiate changes but to teach, instruct and publish, and to leave it to the civic authorities to institute any change. He had shown strong views on images and revolutionary views on the Mass. Some enthusiasts had ventured to destroy the images, and thereupon the Great Council called the second public disputation in October, 1523.[2] The decision was the sensible one that the images were to be removed properly and officially, and all rioting was condemned[3] (the rioters were pardoned, except for the leader, who was banished for two years). On the subject of the Mass, Zwingli argued that it was not a sacrifice but a memorial of the death of Christ, and urged that all the abuses associated with the Mass be abolished. The Council asked for further deliberation by appointing a small commission to go into the matter and report and asked Zwingli to write to all the clergy, and deputed preachers to inform the laity of the canton of the proceedings of the debate. It was in the *Instruction*[4] which Zwingli sent to all the clergy in the canton of Zürich that he outlined his theology, a task he was later to do in his *Concerning True and False Religion*[5] (1525). In the *Instruction* he considered sin, law and the gospel; condemned images and

[1] Cochrane, p. 33.  [2] Kidd, No. 197.  [3] Kidd, No. 198.
[4] Kidd, No. 200.  [5] Künzli, pp. 193–243.

pictures in church; and concluded with a discussion on the Mass. Here he argued that the main idea of the Eucharist is its faithful remembrance and not a repetition of the sacrifice of Christ, and that it was the false doctrine of Rome that was responsible for introducing the corruptions and superstitions into the Mass.

Zwingli's victory at the debate and the inability of the Romanist contingent to refute him marked the beginning of the Reformation in Zürich. Leading laymen began to press for reforms. The farmers objected to giving tithes to maintain futile customs. People argued that the clergy ought to be fewer and engaged on service to the people. Within a year liturgical reform was well under way: baptism was held in German, and the Mass rewritten. Zwingli's own view of the communion was now taking shape. He dismissed the idea of a repetition of the sacrifice and emphasized the idea of a memorial. The bread and wine proclaim Christ's redeeming death and render it present to the believing heart. He dismissed all speculation on the transubstantiation of the elements. As a consequence of this simplicity of doctrine, all the abuses and scandals fell away as meaningless, though Zwingli retained many of the externalities such as vestments, acts of reverence and traditional music.

The tempo was suddenly increased when Leo Jud, a distinguished scholar and associate of Zwingli, preached a strong sermon against images and after ugly demonstrations an artisan pulled down a famous crucifix. Public tension mounted. A second disputation was held at which Zwingli counselled the leaving of decisions to the authority of council in deliberation. His good sense prevailed. Within a few months the council produced a responsible decision urging the people "to turn from idols to the living God". On Whit Monday, when a pilgrimage of fifteen hundred people would normally have gone to the Virgin of Einsiedeln, not one mustered for the pilgrimage and not one saw any reason why he should. The council organized the skilled and orderly removal of all images everywhere, and when the appointed smiths and masons and woodworkers had done their job in ordered precision, they had denuded the churches to that bare austerity which still characterizes them today.

Zwingli had strong views on social justice. On June 24, 1523, he preached a striking sermon on divine and human justice, characterized by his usual robust sense. He spoke against injustice as well as the limits of justice. Zwingli was no revolutionary; he warned peasants as well as kings. The thinking was in accordance with Luther and largely based on Romans 13. He cut into ecclesiastical wrong particularly. It caused him concern that twenty-four canons as well as their chaplains were living on the tithes of the people, and now that masses had been abolished had no *raison d'être*. He sought to convert the revenue into the building of a theological school for the training of evangelical clergy and hospitals for the care of the poor. It must have given much satisfaction to Zwingli when the majority of the canons accepted his argument; the laity, of course, did so entirely. His plans were submitted to council and approved. The revenues were to pay the pastors to perform their pastoral duties. No successors were to be appointed to deceased canons. A school developed at the Minster as well as a theological faculty, in which Zwingli was the chief of four professors; each village had a pastor appointed; hospitals for the poor were built; convents and monasteries were suppressed (many voluntarily),[1] and their revenues diverted into social service.

During Holy Week, 1525, the council decided that the Mass should be discontinued and the holy apostolic table set up in church.[2] Astonished worshippers found Zwingli facing them over a table, without music or ceremony, assistant ministers distributing bread and wine to the laity after the saying of prayers and the reciting of scripture. People who still had scruples went to those churches where the mass was continuing to be said until about 1528.

A remarkable feature of the Reformation in Zürich is the quiet order with which these immense changes were carried through. The secret was that Zwingli never initiated anything: he simply taught evangelical truth, the force of which persuaded lay authority of their responsibilities in carrying through reformation. When he had convinced the lay leadership he then showed them the necessity of schools and universities to provide a continuing educated leadership. After Zwingli had removed the superstitious practices, converted the monasteries and nunneries into schools and hospitals, built up an educated evangelical ministry, and finally converted the mass into the holy communion, he had in effect established the reformation in a large part of Switzerland.

## 3. Zwingli's Theology

At this stage we might sketch an outline of Zwingli's theology. In March 1525 he wrote his *Commentary on True and False Religion*,[3] a work which summarizes his thinking, thinking which had previously been worked out under the necessity of events.

At once he opens his thesis with the doctrine common to all reformers, that true religion has its source in the Word of God, false religion is no different from superstition. He concedes some slight natural knowledge of God but argues that God is an unknowable mystery revealed only by Christ. Face to face with this God, Zwingli confronts the creature man in the form of Adam in bondage to his own sin and self-centredness and facing eternal death. God called to Adam and asked him how he stood,

[1] Kidd, No. 204.    [2] Kidd, Nos. 205, 206.    [3] Künzli, pp. 193–243.

and in this question of concern and mercy, "Adam, where art thou?", Zwingli sees the birth of all true religion. Zwingli wrote:

> Love of God and trust in Him, or what we call religion, is this: God brings man to recognize, as he did Adam, his disobedience, his betrayal, his pitiful plight. When he realizes this a man utterly despairs of himself. At that moment God opens wide for him the heart of His goodness and mercy. Man who previously was in utter doubt and confusion, sees with certainty and conviction that his Creator and Father still has for him limitless resources of grace and favour, that nothing can ever separate him from Him in whose grace he hides himself. This dependence on God is the faith that loves: this is religion.[1]

True religion adheres to such a God only, and listens only to His Word given in the Scriptures: on Him alone must man direct his eye, to Him alone his ear. Zwingli argues that the papists have never tasted, never even had a lick, of this religion. And then he moves into a discussion of Christ, arguing in simple lay language against current scholastic theology to a patristic handling of the first Adam and the last Adam. With a warm evangelical fervour, in crystal-clear language, he sets Christ the Redeemer in the centre of all theology. The word Zwinglian is used as a term of abuse in certain quarters of the Church, but passages such as this belie all such criticism. Courvoisier,[1] in his chapter on Zwingli's Christology, argues (with Locher and against Wernle and others) that the axis of Zwingli's thinking is his Christology. The writer finds himself in complete agreement, and would go on to say that this was the underlying strength of all the reformers.

Zwingli then turns to the gospel and penitence, law and sin. The gospel is the forgiveness of sins in the name of Christ. With forgiveness is the call to repentance and new life. The gospel he relates closely to law in Pauline fashion. The will, freed from the ancient curse by the new certainty of forgiveness, now freely seeks the will of God. Nevertheless, it is a life-long struggle, the certainty of the victory resting not in himself but in Christ's victory. There is a splendid robustness about Zwingli's emphasis of the certainty of salvation alongside the frailty of the human heart.

Zwingli then turns to the power of the keys, the Church and sacraments. To Zwingli the keys meant not a power invested in a priest but the power of the gospel offering forgiveness in Christ. The power of the keys to Zwingli meant the power of the word of the gospel. He sought to equate the keys with Christ's liberating message given and promised, an indicative not a subjunctive. The keys are not an authority conferred on man by God. Christ defines the keys as the faith by which man believes in the

---

[1] Künzli, p. 202.
[2] Jacques Courvoisier, *Zwingli – a Reformed Theologian* (Richmond, Virginia, 1963), p. 38 ff.

message of the gospel. When the disciples were received by unbelief they were commanded to leave and shake off the dust from their feet. This is what "binding" means: to leave in error. Zwingli made clergy ministers of the word rather than priests.

It was a natural step to argue that the Church was not the hierarchy but the community of believing and called men. Zwingli ruled out any possibility that the papists belonged to this church, and is in this respect, unlike Luther, inclined to sectarianism.

Zwingli's view of sacraments is important in this connection and tends to be dismissed as memorialism. This is an injustice. Zwingli took the clear line that no *thing* of itself, whether it is bread or wine, water or oil, has any effect on the soul at all. God alone works on the soul, and in the manner of the evangelical principles already argued. To Zwingli the bread meant the gospel, to eat meant to believe. The transference of these words to the communion service had for centuries produced utter confusion. (In this connection Zwingli dismissed masses for the dead.) Zwingli wanted a complete break with the mass, and rejected both the transubstantiation of Rome and the consubstantiation of Wittenberg.

Zwingli proceeds to discuss confession, marriage, vows, invocation of saints, images, prayer and purgatory. The only confession Scripture knows, Zwingli argues, is to hear Christ in the gospel, who freely offers forgiveness and absolution. Auricular confession is only a kind of consultation to help a soul to find peace in Christ. Confirmation, unction and ordination belong to the category of customs, and marriage is no sacrament. In this connection he approves of marriage for the clergy and rules out the taking of monastic vows of celibacy and poverty. This was to promise what God does not want, and what is not in man's power to promise. The monks are severely criticized for their avoidance of work and the responsibility of full citizenship. He dismisses the invocation of saints as a heathen practice, and recognizes one mediator only, Christ. Zwingli's objection to images and pictures was that veneration is spiritually dangerous. Where images were not actually venerated (as, e.g., in stained-glass windows), Zwingli would leave them where they were. He believed that any representation of God was sacrilegious. He even objected to crucifixes on the grounds that if they are supposed to express Christ's divinity they cannot; if His humanity, then that should not be adored. Zwingli was more radical than Luther here, and only from a religious, not an artistic, viewpoint. The merits of the saints Zwingli dismisses on the ground that all merit, all good works, spring from Christ's activity in us and not of ourselves: our faith is of God, likewise our works. Zwingli hated the exploitation of prayer in its association with money and made a plea for prayer as the lifting up of the soul to God. He condemned the idea of monks being segregated for prayer and the rest of mankind for work. He condemned

F

outright the exploitation of purgatory for gain, and dismissed the idea as unscriptural.

## 4. Church and State

Some authors criticize Zwingli, alleging that he confuses Church and State. This echoes criticism of Luther, who saw in Zwingli the spirit of socialism and enthusiasm. Two important considerations present themselves. It must be understood that Zwingli saw the problem of society as arising from the sin of man and he sought a theological, still better rather a Christological, answer to the problem. Though at root his theological answer was unrealizable he did not think it therefore irrelevant, and sought to maintain the dialectic of a redeemed Christian community within an unredeemed society. The other consideration is that the words Church and State do not belong to the sixteenth century and in this context they need not mean what we mean by them today. There was at that time a single Christian society, *corpus christianum*, of which minister and magistrate were essential members. It is not that Zwingli confused Church and State, but rather that in Zürich he was "the prophet" of the secret council. His rôle was, as a man of God, to advise a council that *sought and wanted* the judgments and advice of a man of God.

At root Zwingli saw the problem of society as the problem of sin. This God had met in Christ, and even if men did not know this, even *before* it was known at all, it was still true. Man is utterly unable to live as Christ taught, in forgiveness and love. Yet in spite of this the remedy for sin was still valid. To Zwingli society was viable only if Christ was at work in it, and viable only if relying on God's Word. Zwingli almost made the law into gospel.

He spoke of two kinds of justice, inward and outward. Inward justice meant the righteousness of the guidance of the Spirit, the pattern given by Christ in the Sermon on the Mount. This is what Zwingli meant when he said that Christ made the law sweet: but only Christ could live in this way. Therefore, Zwingli made room for his idea of outward justice, or human justice. This idea of justice had to be observed by all, believers and unbelievers alike, though it could never bring salvation nor the kingdom of God. If divine justice obtained there would be no need of human justice, but because of the sin of man human justice is necessary. As executants of human justice there are judges and governors, and these are very properly called God's servants or ministers, to whose authority all must submit. In the case of weak or evil government, a good man must resist out of obedience to God but never to the extent of murder, war or rebellion. Zwingli went so far as to say that a bad ruler arises when a people have no faith or goodness, for the answer to tyranny is the collective morality and resistance of the people.

Zwingli clearly taught that the minister was not a ruler, but a minister of God's Word, and his diligence and watchfulness in this ministry before governors and governed alike presented constantly the meaning of human justice in relation to divine. Similarly, the magistrate must act according to Christ's rule and God's Word, and does fulfil a spiritual office, a divine function.

Nevertheless, what Zwingli expected of human justice was not simply that law, order and peace may be obtained. Valuable as that attainment was, it was yet but a stage towards something more abiding, and that was a state where the gospel may be freely preached and salvation offered to all its members. The good human society affords the true basis on which the eternal society may be envisaged and proclaimed. It is at this point that magistrate and minister meet: this dialectical relationship gives the meaning to Zwingli's views. It is not that Zwingli confuses them: he relates them. In this respect Zwingli's views reached their fruition in Calvin's Geneva.

## 5. *The Reformation beyond Zürich*

The Reformation was spreading elsewhere in Switzerland. In Basel a number of distinguished scholars were at work. Capito had been teaching there since 1512 and had been showing that many of the usages and ceremonies of the Church were unscriptural. Oecolampadius, a supporter of Luther, had been teaching there since 1522, the effects of which were that the people of Basel demanded a public disputation. Two were held in December, 1524, the consequence of which was that Oecolampadius was set up by the town council as the town preacher and given authority to refashion the Church in accordance with Scripture.

In Berne, too, the Reformation began to take hold. There the council granted freedom to preach according to the Word of God, but forbade any changes in worship. The effect of such preaching was to increase the number of Christians, and once they were in the majority on the council (1527), they too called a public disputation. The council undertook this in a most impressive way. All four diocesan bishops (connected with Berne) received invitations, as well as a goodly number of Romanist theologians, all with promises of escort and safe-conduct. But all the Romanists invited showed great reluctance to appear, and many Romanists viewed the consequences with grave anxiety. Charles V took the council to task for its temerity in summoning a public disputation. But the Bernese were undaunted and pressed forward with their work. With the invitations they sent out Ten Theses for disputation, in Latin and French.[1]

[1] Kidd, No. 217.

1. The Holy Catholic (*Christiana*) Church, of which Christ is the only Head, is born of the Word of God, abides in this Word and does not hear the voice of a stranger.

2. The Church of Christ does not establish laws and statutes apart from the Word of God, and consequently all human traditions which they call church ordinances do not bind our consciences except in so far as they are founded on the Word of God and are agreeable thereto.

3. Christ is the one and only wisdom, righteousness and redemption for the sins of the whole world; therefore to confess another way of salvation or another satisfaction for sin is to renounce Christ.

4. It cannot be proved from Holy Scripture that the Body and Blood of Christ are essentially and corporally present in the bread of the Eucharist.

5. The Mass, as it is today in use, in which Christ is offered to God the Father for the sins of the living and the dead, is contrary to Scripture and a blasphemy against the most holy sacrifice, passion and death of Christ, and is therefore an abomination before God.

6. Since Christ alone died for us, and since he is therefore the only mediator and advocate between God the Father and ourselves as believers, He alone ought to be invoked; therefore, to conceive for worship other mediators, existing apart from this life, is repugnant to the foundations of the Word of God.

7. That there is some place after death where souls are purged is not found in Scripture; therefore all services instituted for the dead, such as vigils, masses for the departed, funeral rites, funeral masses on the third, seventh, and thirtieth day and the annual anniversary, the burning of lamps at the grave, of dark candles round the body, and all that kind of thing, are vain activities.

8. The making of images for the purpose of worship is contrary to the entire Old and New Testament; therefore, if there is danger of their being worshipped, they should be destroyed.

9. Marriage is forbidden to no estate of man in the Scriptures, but for the sake of avoiding fornication and impurity it is both commanded and permitted to all estates of man.

10. As it is clear throughout Scripture that the fornicator must be excommunicated, it necessarily follows that wantonness and fornication among monks and priests are much more scandalous and pernicious than among other men.

The council of Berne had sent invitations to leading evangelical theologians also, among whom were Bucer, Capito, Oecolampadius and Zwingli himself. Zürich allowed Zwingli to go only under a guard of three hundred men-at-arms. When the famous Züricher arrived at the gate and marched up the arcaded main street to the Cathedral in the centre of his guard every arcade was jammed tight with sightseers, every window full of faces eager to see the great reformer. If the Reformers welcomed the disputation and marched to it in quiet certainty and a God-given courage, the Romanists on the contrary showed a very uncertain front. In fact their leading theologians refused to speak, on the grounds that such weighty matters must not be discussed in the vulgar tongue. The matters were debated from January 15 to 26, 1528, with the consequences that the Mass was abolished and replaced by a sermon; images were removed from the churches; and the monasteries were secularized, their funds being used for education as well as to replace the now abolished papal pensions.[1]

Zwingli impressed the Bernese with his preaching. The President of the Republic declared himself for the evangelical faith, and his son, a priest and excessive pluralist, destined to be Bishop of Constance, gave up all his benefices to lead a simple lay life. He was often later to play the rôle of the gentle adviser to the fiery and tempestuous Farel.[2] The republic of Berne not only accepted the Reformation for itself but sent messages and messengers to propagate the evangelical cause in all the territory under their control. This was carried out under instructions from Berne. Although these instructions clearly enunciated that the content of the preaching was to be evangelical and scriptural, careful safeguards were made in the avoidance of controversy, particularly on Lutheran theology, and for the maintenance of some tolerance of Catholic practice. When an area univocally accepted the Reformation, the Ten Theses were accepted as the doctrinal norm, supported by instructions for the conduct of Baptism, Communion and marriage. The German-speaking areas accepted the Reformation at once, the French-speaking areas rather more slowly (even reluctantly?). Biel and St. Gallen followed suit; only Luzern in the German-speaking area held out against the Reformation.

The Romanist party sought to resist the Protestant movement. As early as 1522 the Bishop of Constance had asked the Swiss Federal Diet meeting at Baden to prohibit the preaching of the Reformation, and in the following year (September, 1523) the Diet issued a declaration that all who practised these new religious ideas should be punished. The first move to persuade the political power to practise religious persecution came from the Romanist side. In the Bernese Oberland Catholics actually crossed the frontier and committed armed aggression. Zwingli saw the danger here, and realized that the Reformed movement ought to seek a real unity with a view to defending itself one day.

In the meantime the great evangelical preacher Ambrose Blaarer had converted Constance to Protestantism, and the Bishop had the humiliating experience of feeling compelled to withdraw from his own city, followed by his cathedral clergy. Constance, in fear of immediate attack from Austria, appealed to Zwingli. Zwingli asked that Constance be admitted to the Swiss Federation, a request that was not granted. Whereupon Zwingli entered into a league with Constance,[3] a league which Berne (June 25, 1528),

[1] Jacobus Monasteriensis gives an eye-witness description of the rout of the old religion in Kidd, No. 218.
[2] See pp. 152, 161.
[3] Christian Civic Alliance, December 25, 1527. Kidd, No. 220. (See Kidd, pp. 467 f., for detailed references.)

St. Gallen (November 26, 1528), Biel (January 28, 1529), Mühlhausen (February 17, 1529), Basel (March 3, 1529) and Schaffhausen (October 15, 1529) eventually joined. Strasbourg, Hesse and Württemberg joined later.

Ferdinand of Austria made a counter-league under his command, calling it the Christian Union. The Christian Union sought to preserve the mediaeval faith and to allow reforms under proper ecclesiastical control. Tension mounted, and when Catholic Schwyz caught and burnt a Zürich pastor, war was inevitable. Zwingli drafted the plan of the campaign as well as the treaty which would follow the war. The treaty demanded freedom to preach, the abandonment of papal pensions, and the payment of a war indemnity to Zürich. When the soldiers actually faced each other on the field of battle they had little inclination to fight what after all were their fellow countrymen, and without fighting, Zwingli's conditions were met. These amounted to the dissolution of the Catholic bloc; no persecution for religious belief; mutual acceptance of Catholic and Protestant; abolition of religious wars; abolition of mercenary military service; and a financial indemnity to Zürich.[1] Zwingli was disquieted about this cheap peace, and distrusted the *ex animo* acceptance of the Romanists, for he felt that they would interpret the peace settlement as the right to pursue their own way.

Zwingli had then to attend the Marburg Colloquy,[2] knowing in the depths of his heart that the peace was but a truce. When he returned, his students were waiting for their lectures, the council waiting for his advice, his family waiting for his return, and his vast congregation waiting for him to tell them the results of the Colloquy. Zwingli knew the sands were running out, and sought not merely the unity of the Swiss, but also the unity of like-minded powers such as France and Venice. In the meantime Zwingli had been excluded from Augsburg as well as from the Schmalkaldian League, which exclusion caused him to distrust the Emperor and to feel uncertain about the Germans. The Romanists had no intention of observing the terms of the truce of Kappel and Zwingli counselled war as the only immediate course open to establish these rights beyond dispute. Berne demurred. Zürich then imposed economic sanctions, though Zwingli advised in church and council that the only course was war. He felt that the Romanists were resisting the preaching of the Word and of the gospel, and that it was incumbent on the Protestants to see this and to break it. He sought to strengthen Berne in their uncertain support of his course of action. Berne would not give unqualified support, and for the first time some members of the Zürich council did not agree with Zwingli. Zwingli resigned. Feeling ran high. The Romanists mobilized and declared war, and a force of Zürichers, greatly inferior in numbers, faced a battle on the heights of Kappel in an unfavourable position and in hurried

---

[1] Kidd, No. 222.                    [2] See pp. 94 ff.

unreadiness. Outnumbered four to one the men of Zürich faced an ugly situation and were brutally overwhelmed. Zwingli received two lance wounds in his thigh and a fatal blow on the head. His armour, his sword and his helmet, with his name on the front and the gash in the side give silent tribute in the museum of Zürich to his tragic end. When the enemy found his body the next morning, in spite of protests from a former canon colleague, they quartered it, mixed the pieces with dung and burnt them on the battle-field. In the silence of the Swiss countryside on a green mound near the church where he prayed before joining battle stands a simple granite monolith inscribed with the bare historical facts.

It was a ruinous defeat. Zürich had lost her finest sons, some twenty-four (?) of her pastors, and the chief shepherd of them all. The level-headed Bullinger gathered up the broken pieces and sought to preserve the reformation and the good name of Zwingli. Nevertheless, the leadership passed from Zürich into the hands of Geneva as we shall see in the next section. A still more important consequence was that men saw that the Reformation, though it could not be defeated, was unable to win the whole of Christendom, a truth which the German Reformation endorsed. Men realized that Catholics and Protestants must live alongside one another,[1] and Zwinglianism began to move into Calvinism.[2]

## 6. The Reformation in Geneva

Geneva rose to be the great fortress of Reformed Christianity. Its history and its geography fitted it supremely for this rôle, and when Calvin lodged in Geneva on that fateful night of late July or early August, 1536, it was manifest to Calvin, and eventually to history, that he was the man of destiny, fated to assume the awesome rôle of reformer.

By ancient constitution there were already established three authorities in Geneva: the Prince Bishop, sovereign of the city; the Count, the supreme justiciary; and the Free Burghers. In the century previous to Calvin the House of Savoy had managed to wrest the office of count and bishop into the family, and the Genevans smarted under the sight of small boys and bastards occupying the episcopal throne. This led to war and rebellion, a situation resolved in 1530 by the agreement to rule Geneva by means of three councils: the Council (small), the Council of the Two Hundred, and the Council General comprising all the burghers. Berne had assumed the rôle of patron to towns or districts inclined to reformation, but remained aloof in the case of Geneva because, though many Genevans

---

[1] The Second Peace of Kappel, November 20, 1531. Kidd, No. 227.

[2] In 1566 Bullinger concluded with Beza the *Confession Helvétique Postérieure*, a confession signed by the Zwinglians and the Calvinists, and later recognized by France (at La Rochelle, 1571), countersigned by Scotland in Glasgow in 1566, by the Hungarians at Debreczen in 1567, and by Poland in 1570. See Cochrane, 220-301.

desired the Reformation there was nevertheless a stubborn majority who opposed it.

Suddenly in the summer of 1532 a religious earthquake shook Geneva. Pope Clement VII, utterly blind to the motions of the Spirit, or even to the signs of the times, published an Indulgence within Geneva. The city woke on the morning of June 9 and with astonished eyes gazed at placards nailed by a "certain nombre de mauvais garçons" on every church door with the evangelical words:

> Plenary pardon would be granted to every one for all their sins on the one condition of repentance and a living faith in Jesus Christ.[1]

The storm broke. Priests rushed out to tear the placards down. Laymen stepped forward to prevent them. In the clashes a canon of the cathedral was wounded. A deputation came from Freiburg complaining of the placards and about the evangelical literature circulating in Geneva. The Papal Nuncio, in a state of alarm, wanted to know if it was true that Lutheranism was being taught everywhere. The Papal Nuncio received an evasive letter, Freiburg assurances that the Genevans were not seeking innovations and meant to live as their fathers lived.[2] That autumn the tempestuous Frenchman Farel arrived in Geneva and at once that storm-petrel brought in his wake the tumults that were the first beginnings of new ideas. The Reformation had arrived in Geneva.

Farel had been recognized as the ablest theologian at the Berne Disputation 1528,[3] and had been based in Aigle to further the cause of reformation in French-speaking Switzerland under some kind of protection from the Berne Council.[4] His main activity lay in preaching and teaching throughout the district, and whenever possible to arrange for a public disputation with the Romanists. The Romanists risked public disputation only under great public pressure and were always seen to fail before the informed zeal of the evangelicals. Farel built round him a group of missioners (hand-picked by Farel himself), men who went into all the countryside, where they received a kind reception from the people generally but hostility from the authorities. These preachers, all fiery Celts like Farel, often ran into very great personal danger. Their zeal outran all normal discretion, and they often found themselves attacked, beaten, stoned or imprisoned. Often women attacked them, stormed churches where they were preaching, screamed and shouted during the sermon, while men beat drums at the church door. Nevertheless the cause of the Reformation spread and many of the missioners were invited to stay on and undertake the pastoral care of a church and village.

The affair of the placards had caused Farel to decide to evangelize

---

[1] Herminjard, II. 382.    [2] Kidd, No. 248.    [3] See pp. 147 f.
[4] November 30, 1526. Kidd, No. 228.

Geneva, but he was bound to proceed cautiously, and sent his faithful disciple Froment.[1] Froment at once began to succeed, to the extent that certain Roman priests were provoked to resist, even to fighting in the streets. The Council wished to grant liberty to preach the gospel, but warned against provocative insult. When the evangelicals met to celebrate the Lord's Supper a riot broke out. Armed priests suddenly broke out from the Cathedral and attacked a group of known evangelicals, three of whom were severely wounded. Several of the priests wildly rampaged down the high street and attacked another group of evangelicals. Many were wounded and in the fracas the leader of the priests was killed. This rogue was now acclaimed a martyr of the Catholic cause and his death was to be the signal for a massacre of the protestants. Only an appeal to Berne saved the evangelicals.

Great tensions developed in Geneva, not only of a religious kind, but between the ruling authorities of Council, Count and people. Turbulent priests and bellicose canons intrigued with monks and nuns to restore the authority of the Bishop and the House of Savoy. In the meantime a strong unknown quantity was emerging, the evangelicals. Berne sought to procure toleration of Protestantism and urged Geneva to hold a disputation. It so happened that in Advent 1533, Furbiti, a renowned Roman Catholic preacher from the Sorbonne, came to Geneva to preach a course of Advent Sermons. He vigorously condemned evangelical theology, using the Decretals and Thomas as his authority. At the end he made a derisive comment about the evangelical theologians hiding behind the skirts of the women and afraid to challenge him. He had not measured his enemy. Froment called out in church that the teaching was false and that the preacher was speaking the words of the Antichrist: far from hiding behind the skirts of the women he challenged him to open, public debate. The preacher was dumbfounded at the consequences of his foolish rhetoric. A violent commotion ensued. "To the fire!" the catholic faithful roared, and a certain nun writing later in her diary was proud of the way the women launched into Froment with stones from the street. Froment escaped but his companion was caught and exiled under pain of death. Berne wrote a fine protest complaining of the treatment of the Evangelicals and demanding the immediate arrest of Furbiti.[2] They followed up the letter by sending Farel back to Geneva and a deputation to see the matter through. Geneva played delaying tactics, but Berne was immovable. Furbiti was compelled to face Farel and Viret before the Council and answer for his wild accusations. At that hour the Catholics organized another riot and stabbed an Evangelical to death. The common people had had all they could stand. The murderer was dragged from the Cathedral where he was hiding (in safety as he imagined) and summarily hanged the next morning. The

[1] Kidd, No. 249.    [2] Kidd, No. 251.

houses of the rioters were searched and incriminating evidence of a plot to seize the town and massacre the evangelicals came to light. The deputies of Berne pressed for a renewal of the proceedings against Furbiti. In debate[1] it was realized that his theology was based not on Scripture but on Thomas and the Decretals. Beaten in debate he promised to recant from the Cathedral pulpit on the following Sunday, a promise he failed to honour.

The bishop, foiled in his schemes, made the fateful decision to unite with the Duke of Savoy and reduce the city to subjection by war.[2] Their forces ravaged the countryside and laid siege to Geneva, to Geneva's great hurt. But men cannot gather grapes of thorns. The bishop was found to be on the side of the city's old enemy, aided and abetted by priests, monks and nuns. It had the effect of compelling Catholics to go against their country for the sake of their religion, a rôle Catholics were too often forced to play, a rôle that has done untold damage to the Catholic cause.

When the evangelical pastors manned the fortifications, shared the watches and strengthened the defenders, the common man saw the mettle of the two contenders. After the siege was raised the Genevans continued to suffer acutely for the enemy held the countryside. Meanwhile the Evangelicals grew.

The ruin of the Roman Catholic party came about in a sordid way. The cook in the house where the three great evangelical preachers, Viret, Farel and Froment lived, attempted to poison them. The subsequent trial implicated Roman priests. This created a situation where the Council agreed to a public disputation, the trump card of the evangelicals. Five *Thèses Évangéliques* were drawn up and everything done to encourage even foreign Roman Catholics to take part. When the Disputation opened (May 30, 1535)[3] no Roman Catholic debater appeared, and it was only after four weeks of exposition by the evangelicals that two Roman champions, Jean Chapuis and Jean Cachi, took up the challenge. But they were conspicuous failures before the ability and conviction of the evangelicals and were compelled to apologize publicly for their lack of learning. The common man had now proof positive and realized why Rome's answer had been fire or sword, and saw reasonable disputation as the one way to end all strife. Farel followed his victory in debate by mastery in the Genevan pulpits.[4] The people grew restive. They contemptuously jostled the priests in the streets. They pulled down and desecrated the images. All hope of Catholicism was lost, hastened to its ignominious end by a sordid tale of war, persecution and poison, unable finally to give an account of its stewardship.

The Council was disturbed and summoned Farel before it. He gave a magnificent defence, stating he would face death if it could be shown that he had taught anything but scriptural truth. He ended on his knees with

[1] Kidd, No. 254.     [2] Kidd, No. 256.     [3] Kidd, No. 260.     [4] Kidd, No. 261.

one of his famous perorations of prayer. The Council was much moved and the next day the Council of the Two Hundred summoned not Farel but the monks, to show why the Mass and the worship of the saints should be continued.[1]

Nevertheless, the two Councils were in a delicate political position, even if the laity were of one mind. Their enemies were still in the surrounding countryside. Berne seemed unable to effect much help. It was the political uncertainty that caused the Genevan leadership to play safe, for they feared that if they moved too boldly into reformation they would dangerously increase their all too many enemies. When the Roman Catholic clergy eventually faced up to disputation (November 29, 1535) the monks one after another declared that they were unlearned men unable to discuss these matters whilst the secular clergy said they wanted to continue in their old ways and hear no more evangelical theology. The Council was appalled at the lamentable failure of both monks and priests, and directed them to discontinue saying mass until further orders. The Reformation was established in Geneva. When war broke out, Geneva found herself supported on all sides. The army of the Bishop of Geneva and the House of Savoy was dispersed without formal battle, and the victory of the republic brought deliverance not only to Geneva but to Lausanne and other municipalities. The democracy of Geneva fell heir to the episcopal as well as the ducal rights and became an independent republic.

Geneva experienced a liberation: it had secured political and religious independence. True, the Romanists were still strong but the worst feature of the situation was not the numerical strength of the Romanists but the disorder and demoralization that it had caused in the common life. Dissolute, bastard and sometimes boy bishops, coupled with the dissoluteness and ignorance of the clergy had wreaked grievous harm on church and state. Farel saw the immensity of the task that confronted him in building Geneva as the citadel of Reformed religion. He founded schools and hospitals, and sought to re-kindle some moral integrity into the life of the Genevans. Yet Farel knew that he was not ideally suited for these constructive tasks: his fiery, ardent, holy zeal made him a better missionary, a pioneer, an evangelist, a crusader. Farel needed Calvin. At this fateful hour the young Calvin, though on a different journey, was compelled by the exigencies of war to stay the night in Geneva. Farel descended on him with frightening fatality.

[1] Kidd, No. 262.

# PART THREE

*Calvin and the Establishment of Protestantism*

# CHAPTER IX

# CALVIN'S LIFE AND WORK

### 1. Calvin's Early Years, 1509–36

CALVIN WAS BORN ON JULY 10, 1509, IN THE LOVELY CATHEDRAL TOWN of Noyon in Picardy, a countryside well known to the soldiers of two world wars. His father was a lawyer of considerable social standing, married to a beautiful and pious woman. Calvin shared the education of the local gentry with whom he later went to university in Paris.

Calvin enjoyed many of the characteristics of the Picards: he was independent and anti-clerical, possessing a determined kind of uneffusive enthusiasm, not unlike our own Lollards. He also enjoyed all the polished grace of a refined and educated Picard and had a marked gentlemanly reserve. The father saw the boy's brilliance, and his social position allowed Calvin to enjoy, at the early age of twelve, certain benefices to advance his education, in return for which he adopted the tonsure and paid for a curate to do the work.

In August, 1523, he went to the University of Paris where he enjoyed the inestimable benefit of the great teacher Cordier, who was an evangelical at heart. Calvin was removed from this "dangerous influence," but history shows that the seed bore fruit. Nevertheless, in his new college he again had distinguished teachers, Béda and Tempête, and Calvin rose to outstanding academic distinction.

In the meantime Calvin's father had quarrelled with the ecclesiastics at home in Noyon. The quarrel was grave and the father refused to yield. When the ecclesiastics excommunicated him, the father responded by removing his son John from Paris to Orleans in 1528[1] to study law. Gérard Calvin knew that his son had no prospects in the Church, but evidence also shows that Calvin himself found the decision agreeable. He certainly accepted his father's advice without demur. He studied at Orleans for one year under the renowned lawyer Pierre de l'Estoile and then advanced to Bourges to study under André Alciat, the famous law reformer. Calvin benefited from these intellectual changes, for Orleans had as strong humanist as Bourges had Protestant tendencies. During his stay at Orleans Calvin actually set himself the task of learning Greek from the German Melchior Wolmar, a known Lutheran. There is no evidence that Calvin

---

[1] Calvin left as Loyola began, but we do not know if they ever met.

picked up any evangelical theology from Wolmar, for at that time he showed himself a Catholic humanist and no more.

The death of his father (May 26, 1531) enabled Calvin to pursue his natural bent, and turning his back on both Law and Theology he returned to Paris as a young man of letters. He attended the lectures of the humanist professors, learnt Greek and Hebrew, and aroused not a little suspicion from the Sorbonne. Within a year (April, 1532) at the astonishingly early age of 23, he published his first book, a commentary on Seneca's *De Clementia*. The book was the work of an accomplished scholar of the total range of classical learning. That was staggering enough. But, with the brilliance of a leader born, he published it at the moment when Francis I was persecuting the Huguenots. In his preface he made a bold attack on the procedures at courts and the administration of justice.

In Paris Calvin was now a known Protestant, the friend of Roussel the evangelical preacher, Margaret of Navarre, Léfèvre, Farel and the "group of Meaux." Calvin said that God drew him from the perversion of the papacy by "a sudden conversion,"[1] though the present writer sees a good deal of evidence for a gradual maturity which one day was to overwhelm by its sheer weight.[2] The conversion was no more sudden than Luther's: it was the result of a long period of growth. Calvin was most reluctant to break with Rome.

The issue came to a head in Paris when the reactionary theologians objected to the new humanism infecting the university, tracing its origin to the court of Margaret of Navarre. The Rector, Nicolas Cop, publicly repudiated this conduct and sought the help of Calvin. In a fine oration, wherein the crowds heard the voice of Cop but traced the hand of Calvin,[3] Cop read an eloquent defence of evangelical theology in particular on the gospel and on justification by faith.[4] Much of the thinking had obviously originated in Erasmus and not a little is directly quoted from Luther, and from the structure and content of the discourse the author shows his belief in a reformation of the Church which would find room for both men. The distinguished humanist, with his belief in the greatness of man, was now the theologian emphasizing the corruption of man and his alienation from God. All this was Calvin's doing. To those who taught free will and human autonomy Calvin now proclaimed man's total dependence on God and his doctrine of election and predestination. To men who hardly deigned to concern themselves with sin, Calvin spoke of sin as the determining reality in man's knowledge of God. The Sorbonne reacted violently. Their theologians accused the author of heresy

---

[1] Hillerbrand, 175 f.; Kidd, No. 268.
[2] It almost certainly falls between his taking part in the chapter at Noyon on August 23, 1533, and his return to Noyon to give up his benefices in May, 1534.
[3] Cf. Gen. 27:22.
[4] Kidd, No. 269(b).

and called the King to act in accordance with the papal Bulls directed against the Lutheran heresy.[1] Calvin had to flee the country, taking refuge in Basel in 1535.

It was there at the early age of 26 that he completed his brilliant *Institutio*, 1536. In one act he assumed the rôle of leader of the Reformation, and in one book converted reforming men from a rabble into an army. In that mighty preface to the book he wrote with some warmth to Francis I, who in his double-dealing way was seeking abroad an alliance with the German Protestant Princes, while at home he was persecuting French Protestant Christians. Calvin pleaded that those he persecuted were true Frenchmen and true churchmen, not seditious Anabaptists, as the persecutors alleged.

He had two purposes for the book.[2] First, he took the view that the work would enable men to read and understand the Scriptures, and secondly, would vindicate Reformation theology against its calumniators. He based the book on the Apostles' Creed, the earliest statement of doctrine in the Church, and moreover a statement that had developed out of the Church and was not devised by the Church. The first part is on God the Creator; the second on God the Son, the Redeemer; the third on the Holy Ghost and Grace; the fourth on the Catholic Church.[3] During this time he set himself to master the study of theology, and there is evidence of a deep study of Scriptures, of the Fathers, of Luther, Melanchthon and Bucer, as well as of the scholastics. Much of the teaching is directed against the *mediaevalism* of Catholicism in favour of the true catholic, biblical and patristic Catholicism. He argued that the evangelicals were true Catholics, the Catholics false, innovating, mediaevalist-bound Catholics. There was no new theology preached, no new Church founded. All his theology was founded on Scripture, a theology that had been known to the faithful all down the ages. This is just what Luther had said. Calvin brought all the evangelical theology into one superbly written book. He revised the *Institutio* in 1539 and 1559, and in 1541 translated it into French himself.

After a short visit to Italy to visit the Duchess of Ferrara, known for her interest in the reformed religion, he set out for family reasons to visit Paris and then Strasbourg, where he intended to settle down to the quiet life of a scholar. Owing to the exigencies of war Calvin's course was diverted to Geneva, where he intended staying one night. When Farel heard that the young Calvin was in Geneva he virtually attacked Calvin with the fire of an emissary of the Holy Spirit. Farel knew that the failure of the Reformation in Geneva lay in that it was introduced there partly from political motives, and he knew that the one man in Christendom able to give the movement a sure theological foundation was the theologian

---

[1] The King's letter to Parliament. Kidd, No. 270.
[2] The best translation is L.C.C., Vols. 20, 21.
[3] See pp. 183 ff.

Jean Calvin now before him. Calvin heard in the trembling emotional voice of Farel the voice of God commanding him to assume the rôle of leader of the reformed cause in Geneva, and when it was expressed in those terms he could but hear and obey.[1] Calvin now turned his back on the deeply desired life of the quiet scholar to pilot the ship of the Reformation through the turbulent uncharted waters,[2] though the only post he agreed to accept was Reader in Holy Scripture.

His life was now to fall into three distinct parts. The first was his first stay in Geneva as professor of theology and preacher, July, 1536, to March, 1538. Next came his stay at Strasbourg, where again he was professor of theology and preacher from September, 1538, to September, 1541, and where he developed a warm friendship and admiration for Melanchthon, and studied appreciatively more of Luther. It was at Strasbourg that he wrote some of his finest works: the Letter to Sadolet,[3] his commentary on Romans,[4] and his treatise on the Lord's Supper.[5] The third phase was his second and last stay in Geneva, September, 1541, to May 27, 1584.

## 2. First Stay in Geneva, 1536–38

The Council thought very little of the frail young Frenchman on his first appearance. In their minutes they refer to him as "that Frenchman"![6] He at once began his labours by expounding St. Paul's Epistle to the Romans daily in St. Peter's, and made such a profound impression on the city that the Council was compelled to revise its opinion forthwith. But he was soon to stagger even his friends and admirers. Berne had compelled Lausanne to hold a public disputation (October 1–8, 1536),[7] and some four hundred clergy, all the monks of some thirty-eight monasteries and both cathedral chapters were invited to refute the Ten Theses of Farel and Viret.[8] Some three clergy and one monk ventured to take part and though Farel and Viret were the actual protagonists it was when one of the Romanists had the temerity to assert that the Protestants neglected the ancient Fathers on the grounds that they feared their authority did not support them, that the young Calvin rose to his feet. He suggested that the Romanists might read the Fathers before they mentioned them, and quoting one Father after another in exact context, he argued his case with unerring certainty. Men realized that there stood in their midst not a man

[1] Kidd, No. 274.
[2] Kidd, No. 274; Hillerbrand, 179 f.
[3] L.C.C. Vol. 22. 219–56. Also J. C. Olin *A Reformation Debate* (1966).
[4] Calvin Translation Society. Vol. 37 (1849), ed. John Owen; new translation.
[5] Calvin's Treatises II, ed. Henry Beveridge (1849).
[6] "Ille Gallus." Kidd, No. 275.
[7] Kidd Nos. 277, 278.
[8] CR. 37. 701; Kidd, No. 278.

who had memorized catenae of the Fathers but one who had read them, understood them and set them in their proper relation to true catholicism.[1]

Yet the real need in Geneva was organization and instruction, and he met both as no one else could have done. As well as his daily exposition he prepared a programme of reform covering four main issues: Holy Communion, public worship, religious instruction of children and marriage. Calvin encouraged the weekly celebration of the Lord's Supper in true apostolic tradition. He taught that it ought to be the strength of believing men wherein they were partakers of the body and blood of Jesus, His death, life and all benefits including the Holy Spirit. With this he carefully developed the right and importance of excommunication of unworthy men. Calvin was not seeking to build a "gathered church of the elect" but to found a living community, a kingdom of Christ upon earth. Secondly, he advocated the singing of psalms in worship as training in true prayer. Thirdly, he urged the careful instruction of children in the faith so that they would grow up in purity of doctrine. Fourthly, he made a plea for simple rules agreeable to the Word of God to be laid down for marriage, disfigured as it had been by the unscriptural laws of the Papacy.

Calvin sought with single zeal to restore the Church to the life and discipline of its first three centuries. Study had convinced him that the Holy Communion was the centre of the religious life of the early Church and the height of her worship. He saw that the early Church had held this simple rite in the very centre and by discipline and excommunication sought to keep off profane and sinful hands. Calvin sought to regain for the Church weekly communion, discipline and excommunication. Historians often charge Calvin with seeking to regulate private lives by municipal and national laws. They are wrong. Such practice was the norm in that period. Every mediaeval town had its laws against drunkenness and revelry, cursing and swearing, gaming and dancing. What was new with Calvin was the *church* discipline. He opened himself up to criticism in this regard by insisting that the secular power should enforce the censures of the Church. Many people were opposed to Calvin in this: they had had enough of excommunication on Roman lips and many laymen resented the infringement of their office by church officers. They tended to take the line of the German Swiss reformers, Zwingli, Bullinger and their successors, namely that the practice desired by the Frenchman was admittedly the practice of the early Church, but the Church was then in a pagan environment and not under the protection of a Christian magistracy. The German view was that the ministry was the servant of society and therefore of its elected representatives: the French view was that the magistrates were servants of the ministry. Calvin's view did not prevail in Switzerland and was to meet opposition everywhere.

[1] Kidd No. 278(b).

Calvin's *Catechism*[1] was published in 1537. It expounded the Ten Commandments, the Apostles' Creed, the Lord's Prayer, and the Sacraments. In practice it was found too difficult for children and Calvin published a revised version in 1541. The *Confession*,[2] which was a kind of summary of the *Catechism*, was accepted by the magistracy after some delay, but when they sought to submit it to the populace they met with widespread opposition. The Romanists opposed it and many Protestants took the view that they wanted to live in their liberty not be constrained to it. Many objected to the new popery.

Then other anxieties overtook Calvin. The Anabaptists presented their wild theology.[3] Further, Caroli, a former friend of the Meaux group, gave acute pain to Calvin by arguing that Calvin's Christology was Arian.[4] At this stage, Berne, in a desire for political control over Geneva, sought to impose on Geneva an ecclesiastical conformity by way of preparing the ground for political suzerainty. Berne was still a theologically divided city, and the Romanists cannot be absolved from the charge of fishing in the troubled theological waters of Geneva. Farel and Calvin attended a Synod of Lausanne (April 4, 1538) where it was decided to adopt the usages of Berne: baptisms to be celebrated in stone fonts at church doors; unleavened bread to be used at the Holy Supper; and four religious festivals, Christmas, New Year, the Annunciation and the Ascension, to be observed annually.[5] The Council of Geneva had been working independently of Farel and Calvin, and presented a demand to them to put these usages into practice forthwith under pain of expulsion.[6] Calvin argued that he had no objection to the usages, but would have to present them properly to his people for consideration and approval, and that in no case would he accept the fiat of the Council in such a matter.[7] The question was unimportant but the principles underlying it were vital. Calvin and Farel were sent into exile as soon as new appointments could be made.[8]

Calvin always remembered the agony and tumult of those days: how he was insulted in the streets, and fireworks were put in his door, while lewd louts sang obscene songs in his window at night.

## 3. Calvin at Strasbourg, 1538–41

Calvin and Farel journeyed to Berne. Berne received them with courtesy, and disapproved of the conduct of the Genevan Council on such an external matter.[9] A Synod made the request to Geneva to receive back her ministers, a request that was refused.[10] Calvin had only one desire: to return

[1] See page 168. CR. 50. II. See also Thomas F. Torrance, *School of Faith* (1959), pp. 3 ff.
[2] L.C.C. 22, pp. 25–33.    [3] Kidd, No. 287.    [4] Kidd, No. 288.    [5] Kidd, No. 281.
[6] Kidd, No. 293.    [7] CR. 49. 223 f.    [8] Kidd, No. 294.    [9] CR. 38. 193.
[10] Herminjard V, No. 713, n.2.

to the quiet life of the scholar, in Basel for preference. His experiences at Geneva had now utterly convinced him of his unsuitability for this kind of public life. Strasbourg pressed Calvin to accept the pastorate of the French Reformed congregation, but Calvin gave a resolute refusal. Bucer was not the man to accept refusals. With that friendly tenacity characteristic of him he pursued Calvin with letters, even sent friends as emissaries. Eventually, with the technique of Farel, he virtually commanded Calvin to return to Strasbourg, and the reluctant Calvin once more took on the responsibility of professor and preacher there in September, 1538.[1]

This interval gave Calvin the temporary rôle of an oecumenical theologian,[2] as well as his normal work of preacher and scholar. His first task was as pastor of the exiled Reformed congregation. He organized the worship and sought to establish an effective discipline. He was at once appointed to the Chair of Exegesis, and this gave him the opportunity of producing those brilliant Pauline commentaries that grace his name, Corinthians and Romans, as well as his commentary on St. John's Gospel. He worked on his *Institutio* (*Institutes*), converting it from a catechism to a manual of dogmatic theology. At this time, too, he wrote his famous *Letter to Sadolet*,[3] a book warmly appreciated by Luther. Cardinal Sadolet had invited the Genevans to return to the bosom of the Church, but Calvin answered that the true Church was not that of Rome but the one in which the pure gospel was preached. He also published the French version of his *Institutes*, as well as his *Treatise on the Holy Communion*[4] where he showed his own interpretation of the Biblical evidence in relation to Roman, Lutheran and Zwinglian interpretations.

At this time Calvin made several journeys to attend the various colloquia which Charles V called in Europe to heal the breach of Christendom.[5] He attended Frankfurt (February, 1539), where he formed a deep friendship with Melanchthon. Between the two men there were differences of views, though not so much on the essentials of Reformation theology as on matters of liturgy and discipline and how the Catholics should be handled. Again, he was at Hagenau (1540) and Worms (1540–1); and finally at Ratisbon (1541) came the last of all the efforts. Much progress was made and both sides made concessions, for on each side were men both learned and godly. Calvin (like the compulsorily absent Luther) showed penetrating perspicacity during this conference and was far and away the quickest to uncover the motives of the protagonists as well as their theology. Calvin was less prepared than Melanchthon and Bucer to concede a theological position for the lesser prize of unity. Calvin thought that the Germans underestimated the importance of church discipline. The liturgy of the Germans he considered too dependent on Catholic tradition and

[1] Herminjard V, 729, 743, 767.  [2] Letters, CR. 38. Nos. 164. 169.
[3] See p. 162.  [4] L.C.C., 22, pp. 140–66.  [5] See p. 116.

too unreformed in the light of New Testament usage. Calvin criticized the German practice (not Luther's), by which the princes strove to bring the Church within their orbit of administration. Calvin sought not independence but autonomy and freedom.

It was here in Strasbourg in August, 1540, that Calvin was persuaded to marry,[1] largely owing to the organizing zeal of Bucer: the lady was Idelette de Bure. Unlike Luther in this respect, Calvin tells us nothing of his wife, but if paintings are sufficient to judge by, she was a fine and handsome woman.

### 4. Return to Geneva (1541–64)

In the meantime, things were going on in Geneva very much as before, except that many of Calvin's friends struck a non-co-operative note with the authorities, and disharmony and disunity reigned in the city. Much pressure from both Council and Farel was again brought to bear on Calvin to return.[2] Strasbourg did all it could to persuade him to remain and Calvin himself dreaded all thought of return. Eventually, Zürich, Basel and Geneva begged him to return,[3] not only to save the Church, but the Republic of Geneva. Bucer argued that he owed it to the Church Universal to return. In the end Calvin relented and returned on September 2, 1541.[4] Friends spoke of a triumphal entry, and writers often speak as if Calvin returned the master of Geneva. The truth is more sober. Calvin entered reluctantly and against his own judgment.[5] It took fourteen years of hard struggle before he really established himself.

When Calvin returned to Geneva he faced the master problem of his life: how could the Church be made not simply an institution for the worship of God but into an agency for the making of men fit to worship Him? He was only thirty-two, but he was a young man utterly certain of his theology, terrifyingly certain that God had called him to this task and would not fail him in it. He sought to build up a true Church on the basis of Reformed theology, giving the closest attention to the theology that was to create and sustain that edifice. If the first part of the task may be described as ecclesiastical, the second part was theological. Calvin sustained a determined fight for orthodoxy, which in other words was a battle for the integrity of the Word of God.

The magistracy granted him a house, No. 11, Rue des Chanoines, which he occupied till his death. His first task was to demand a commission to go into the matter of the ecclesiastical constitution. Within a week Calvin had completed his *Ordinances*,[6] but the magistracy were a little difficult. Though they respected Calvin's authority in the church they were most

---

[1] Hillerbrand, 184 f.       [2] Herminjard VI, No. 900.       [3] Kidd, Nos. 298, 299.
[4] CR 39. 214, 217, 246; CR.59. 25–7.   [5] CR. 39. No. 355.   [6] CR. 38. 5 ff.; Kidd, No. 302.

sensitive to any infringement of their civil power. Calvin found himself compelled to give way on the frequency of Holy Communion, the form of appointment of pastors, discipline of pastors, appointment of schoolmasters and certain matrimonial regulations. Some concern was felt at Calvin's claims for spiritual jurisdiction which the magistracy felt were, or could be, an infringement on their civil jurisdiction. The magistracy did not object to a spiritual control or even spiritual authority as such, but feared that excommunication would have serious repercussions on their temporal jurisdiction. But to Calvin the disciplinary right of excommunication was the cornerstone of his edifice. Calvin persisted and won the battle, but only after inserting a paragraph to the effect that excommunication was to be effected without prejudice to the exercise of the civil jurisdiction. This compromise, interpreted differently by both sides, was to be a source of conflict for fourteen years, when eventually Calvin won his right.

After one month's work the *Ordinances* were published on November 20, 1541. Even with the modifications forced on Calvin, Calvin felt he had properly established an ecclesiastical policy founded on the gospel. He believed Christ was the Founder and Master of the Church and that He had left behind Him rules for its government. The Church was the body of Christ, of which each and every member has its place and function under the Holy Spirit. Four ministries he distinguished for its well-being, ministries instituted by Christ: pastors, doctors, elders, deacons. The pastors were to be chosen by the church and the magistracy, and were to be subjected to the most rigorous tests of doctrinal and moral integrity. Calvin had early realized that the Reformed faith could live in a democratic city only by an enlightened pulpit speaking to enlightened citizens, and that an educated ministry needed an educated laity, and for this purpose set the teachers as an integral part of the total ministry. The elders had essentially the responsibility of the cure of souls and the care of the weaker brethren. The deacons had the care of the sick and poor. Arrangements were carefully made for the administration of the sacraments, marriage, burial, visitation of the sick and of prisoners. Parents were under obligation to send their children for instruction in the catechism, and only when knowledgeable were they admitted to communion.

It is often said that Calvin founded a theocracy and that he confused the rôle of the State and the Church by dominating the State. The truth is other. Calvin distinguished Church from State and realized the essential partnership that exists between them. Each power, Church and State, was autonomous, proceeding from the divine will, and each responsible for its own half of the total law. The Church had to interpret revelation and to exercise spiritual authority: the State had to conduct temporal affairs and protect in peace both Church and State. That the magistracy was Christian meant that each owed the other mutual support. Calvin never interfered in a political matter: when pressed for his views he spoke for Calvin, not for the church. There was friction in practice but unanimity in theory.

Calvin's liturgical[1] and ecclesiastical[2] reforms went through smoothly. With these he simplified and revised his *Catechism* of 1542,[3] later to exercise considerable influence on Calvinism, indeed on Protestantism everywhere, save Lutheranism.

From now on Calvin's life-work was clear. He devoted himself to making Geneva a city and a church of the pattern shown him on the mount. Daily sermons were provided for the populace, theological lectures for a potential pastorate, schools for general education. Calvin, with characteristic industry,[4] wrote a treatise on free will against the Catholic Albert Pighius, a commentary on Jude, a new edition of the *Institutes*, a treatise on relics, and the first of his writings against the Nicodemites.

For all this work Calvin had built around himself a team of workers. These men were devoted to their master, yet Calvin's sense of divine mission caused him to set himself apart from other men, and occasionally difference of opinion broke the harmony. An instance of such breakdown was the case of Castellion.[5] Castellion was the head of the school, but on his seeking to take holy orders, Calvin failed him at the interrogation. Calvin was at pains to show that the difference was not one of false doctrine or of immorality, merely unsuitability for the pastorate, and that he wanted Castellion to continue as schoolmaster. Castellion would not be mollified. He attacked the committee of pastors who had examined him, the final outcome of which was a request by the magistracy for Castellion to leave. Castellion's departure had a deleterious effect on the school.

We now notice a quickening of the activity of the consistory in disciplinary matters, as well as of the magistracy, and the reading of the reports of the proceedings are startling if only for the triviality of some of the offences.[6] Calvin forbade the inns and replaced them with abbeys wherein guests were provided with supervision and Bibles. The profane theatre was prohibited and later there was even an attack on personal names which were not biblical.

It is obvious that legislation of this kind produced exasperation and indignation in the hearts of most Genevans.[7] A member of the Council

---

[1] *Tract on the Eucharist*, CR. 33. 458 ff.; *Genevan Liturgy*, CR. 38. 213.
[2] Kidd, No. 302.
[3] CR. 34. 1 ff.; L.C.C., 22. 83–139.
[4] Kidd, No. 306; Torrance, *School of Faith*, pp. 3 ff.
[5] Kidd, No. 309.
[6] Walker, pp. 304 ff., and Koehler, Vol. II, 580–8, give details. Dancing, singing, jesting about a sermon are among the foolish charges. There are, of course, serious offences as well. Examples are given in Hillerbrand, 195 f., and Kidd, Nos. 307, 310–13.
[7] Hillerbrand, 197 f.

attacked Calvin. Calvin took this as an attack on God's honour. He would accept no apology short of total submission, and when the populace saw a city councillor compelled to walk round the entire city bareheaded, wearing only his shirt and carrying a lighted torch, and after that present himself to the tribunal and cry to God for mercy, they realized the authority Calvin wielded. When a country parson criticized Calvin he was summarily unfrocked. Nevertheless, the consistory showed neither fear nor favour, for in support of the Reformation even patrician families found themselves summoned before the court. For this uncompromising integrity there was in the magistracy a patrician swing against Calvin and the consistory. The patricians were accused of libertinism, but the evidence shows them good men, even Calvinist men, but with a different conception of ecclesiastical authority. In fact they often came to the support of Calvin.

Then Calvin's hand was strengthened by a flow of French refugees whose number was inversely proportional to their intellectual and theological weight. Among these were Beza, who was to succeed him, Laurent of Normandy, the family of Budé, Guillaume de Trie and others. It is interesting to note that, loyal as these refugees were, it is from them Calvin received the first attacks on his doctrine. Bolsec, an ex-Carmelite, found Calvin's doctrine of double predestination neither Biblical nor Augustinian, arguing that it made God the author of sin. Calvin at once gave answer both from Scripture and Augustine. He later answered formally, and Bolsec was banished. It has to be recorded with regret that Bolsec took ignoble revenge in producing a calumnious biography of Calvin,[1] a book Calvin's enemies were to use for two centuries. To Calvin's deep pain others joined in. Calvin remained immovable.[2] He argued that the responsibility for sin lay with man not God, and showed his ground to rest on Scripture not his own views. This view Council later endorsed. But the disputes were harmful, for there grew up in Council a strong anti-Calvinist movement. It was in this critical situation that the tragic case of Servetus erupted.[3]

In 1531 as a young man of twenty, Servetus had been in controversy with the Reformers on the matter of the relation of the Word to the man Jesus as well as on the treatment of heretics. At that time he published two works on the Trinity wherein he expounded a monarchian view, but at Strasbourg their sale was forbidden.[4] He later qualified as a brilliant physician, but his time was largely spent in writing secretly a massive book on the restitution of primitive Christianity. Servetus saw in the work of the Fathers, in the development of Roman Catholicism, and now

---

[1] Extracts given in Hillerbrand, pp. 210 f.
[2] *Concerning the eternal predestination of God*, ed. and trans. J. K. S. Reid (London, 1961). See also Kidd, No. 314.
[3] Kidd, No. 315.
[4] *Two Treatises on the Trinity*, trans. E. M. Wilbur in *Harvard Theological Studies*, xvi (1932).

in the Reformation, the falsification of primitive Christianity. There is a great deal of speculation on the Word as the primordial reason and essence of all things, and some Gnostic talk of emanations. Original sin he rejected but saw the Church's ministry as a means of cleansing from later sin. He developed also in the book his views on the Trinity. The printer was suspicious of the book when he read it and sent extracts to Calvin, who promptly condemned them and advised the author to read the *Institutes*. Servetus sent back a heavily annotated copy of the *Institutes*. The affair was believed closed, but seven years later Servetus managed to get his work printed, and when its authorship was revealed by the Inquisition, Servetus, then physician to the Archbishop of Vienne, had to flee. Most foolishly and unaccountably he travelled to Geneva, possibly counting on support from the anti-Calvinist party, and when he arrived there in August, 1555, Calvin demanded his arrest. So grave were the charges that the magistracy itself prosecuted, even refusing to extradite the heretic to Vienne.

Servetus seemed unaware of the gravity of his position and is reported to have behaved with arrogance and discourtesy. He demanded action against Calvin on grounds of heresy, his expulsion from Geneva and the award of his goods to himself as recompense. Everybody felt that they had had all of Servetus they could stand. On October 26, 1555, he was condemned to the stake, a sentence carried out the next day, in spite of frantic last-minute efforts of Calvin and others that Servetus be executed humanely and not by fire.[1]

Modern man is appalled at the thought of Calvin being involved in the barbarous execution of a man whose only crime was heresy. This is a measure of our emancipation. We should do well to remember two things. Both Catholic and Protestant authorities believed that it was right to sentence heretics to capital punishment. Calvin was convinced that a Christian magistrate was obliged to execute blasphemers who kill the soul as they executed murderers who kill the body. Calvin received strong support for his conduct. The other point to bear in mind is that we should avoid applying modern judgments and enlightened moral criteria to issues of the past: sixteenth-century issues and sixteenth-century men should be assessed by sixteenth-century criteria. The root charge against Servetus was not mere heresy but blasphemy: blasphemy made worse by having his work printed secretly and spread abroad to harm the Church. Christian men can see further into this matter than non-Christians, for they know that the centre of all Reformation theology lies in its doctrine of Christ, and to impugn this by any kind of anti-Trinitarian teaching is a dagger at the heart. When Castellion was to raise his voice after the death of Servetus no one paid any attention. Calvin came out of the affair with his

[1] See L. Verduin, *The Reformers and their Stepchildren* (Exeter, 1966). pp. 50 ff.

reputation enhanced: he had played the rôle of defender of the faith, but it was the magistracy that had conducted the prosecution.

Yet the struggle was by no means over. A year earlier the consistory had excommunicated a certain anti-Calvinist, Berthelier by name. Berthelier conceived the cunning move of petitioning the Council and not the consistory for restoration to communion. This implied the right of the magistracy over excommunication.[1] Calvin protested, yet the request was granted. Calvin refused to yield and preached a farewell sermon. Berthelier yielded by not presenting himself for communion, but it took still longer for the Calvinist party to win the day.

Calvin's doctrine of the Church made him concerned not only with orthodoxy but with oecumenicity. Calvin sought the unity of Protestantism and made considerable efforts to bring Lutheranism, Zwinglianism, and Anglicanism within the peace and unity of a Church Reformed. One might have expected a ready unity with Zwinglianism in that Calvin carried through the Helvetic Reformation, yet it took ten years of hazardous negotiations before agreement was found in the *Consensus Tigurinus*[2] of 1549, which established a common ground of twenty-six articles on the sacramental problem.

At this time Calvin encountered criticism from the Lutherans, perhaps engendered on the grounds that Calvinism could come to any agreement at all with the Zwinglians. It was occasioned in 1552 by Westphal, a former student of Luther at Wittenberg, who attacked the Calvinists as well as the Zwinglians for their alleged muddled thinking on the Eucharist. He followed this up the next year with a dogmatic study of the words of institution. The Reformed congregations in his own area (Hamburg) took exception to the work, and eventually, in 1555, Bullinger persuaded Calvin to publish an answer in defence of his own theology of the sacraments. Calvin treated Westphal contemptuously, and Calvin's work was the begetter of a violent counter move. Westphal accused Calvin of being a disturber of the peace of the Church, and of denying the real presence. Calvin appealed to Melanchthon (Luther being now dead), and to all the other good and true ministers of the Gospel in Saxony (1557). Still more polemics were engendered from other disputants. The dispute spread and infected certain divisions already showing among Lutherans as well as serving to alienate the Zwinglians from the Lutherans. The supporters of the protagonists bandied about the stronger language of their leaders, all of which served to confuse the issue and divide the Church. Calvin was exasperated with this fruitless debate, and had neither the health nor the strength, still less the desire, to pursue it. He asked Beza to continue the debate while he completed his thinking in his final revision of his *Institutes*.

[1] Kidd, No. 316.                    [2] Kidd, No. 319.

Calvin's mind was on another undertaking, the establishment of the Academy. All the Reformers were educationists: the Reformation was founded in universities by great scholars and nourished there. The men that Calvin established in sound learning and godly discipline came from many lands and went back as ministers of the struggling Protestants in the Netherlands, England, Scotland, the Rhineland and France. They were learned and godly, fearless and devoted, and what these unnamed apostles did for the cause of reform may never be known.

Calvin knew that he now had but a short time to live, or rather in Calvin's case, to work. As far as he was able, he perfected his work and appointed Beza as his successor. On February 6, 1564, he mounted the pulpit for the last time. In prescribed order he paid his final farewells, first to the councils and then to the pastors.[1] Farel hastened to the death-bed, and Calvin died in pure faith and in living hope on May 27, 1564.[2] So frail was he on his death-bed, that Beza said nothing seemed left but his spirit. He did not achieve what he and Cranmer always hoped for, and what he had once said he would cross ten seas to accomplish: the union of all the Protestant Churches. Yet he left a priceless heritage in his theology. His grave is unmarked as he desired. He did not want men to honour him alive or dead, but to heed his voice which spoke only of his sovereign Lord and His work for man in Christ. To a brief examination of Calvin's theology we must now turn.

[1] Selections from Beza in Hillerbrand, pp. 206 ff.
[2] Kidd, No. 318.

# CHAPTER X

# CALVIN'S THEOLOGY

## 1. The Transcendence of God

THE DIFFICULTY OF GIVING AN ACCOUNT OF THE THEOLOGY OF LUTHER or Bucer or Zwingli is universally recognized, for such a task requires the mastering of an immense corpus of theological works, commentaries, correspondence and other source material, as well as the careful assessment of what period and to whom and to which controversy the writing was designed. In Calvin's case it is utterly different. Calvin came on the scene one generation later than the pioneer Reformers. All the questions had been raised, discussed and answered. Calvin's task was to stand on the shoulders of his illustrious predecessors and to formulate a full dogmatic of Protestant theology. This he did in the form of the *Institutes* with his brilliant French genius and refined precision of thought, on a background of culture and knowledge none has surpassed. So well did he perform this task, revising the book to his dying day, that he played and still plays, an authority little short of apostolic in the Reformed tradition.

As has been stated earlier, the book falls into four main parts: God the Creator; God the Redeemer; God the Holy Ghost and the means of Grace; the Holy Catholic Church. From the structure of the book, as well as from Calvin's other writings, it is crystal-clear that Calvin's theology began from the conviction of the absolute transcendence of God and therefore of His total otherness in relation to the creature man. If Luther found his liberation in the doctrine of justification by faith alone, Calvin found that same liberation in a passionate theocentrism, in a terrifying certainty of being mastered by God. Calvin, if not God-intoxicated, was certainly God-possessed. This doctrine of the unqualified sovereignty of God, related to the consequent equally unqualified creatureliness of man, lies at the heart of Calvin's experience and theology. It further dominates all of Calvin's exposition and is the stumbling block his critics never negotiated.

The first question then to ask is how such a transcendent God may be known, a God "hidden in majesty, remote from all senses."[1] Calvin's answer is direct. Only as He has condescended to reveal himself in Scripture. No man can know God except through the Scriptures. Not that it

[1] *Inst.* i. 5. 1.

173

was enough to read the Scriptures. There must be a change of heart and mind. To the believing man the Holy Spirit sets his seal and proof. The divine revelation God intended in the Scriptures is Christ, and this must be the goal of all who read. God is of necessity a God hidden from sinful man, but He has chosen to reveal Himself in the history of his people, a revelation given in the Bible and fulfilled in Christ, and made plain only to a converted man waiting on the Holy Spirit's guidance. The bond between the Scriptures as a book and a history on the one hand and the believer on the other hand, is that that same Spirit who inspired the history and the events is the same Spirit who now opens up their meaning authoritatively. The Spirit uses now exactly what He used in olden times: the prophets and apostles, and He opens up these and these only, and this is the burden of His message now. At once Calvin gives a firm answer to the authority of interpretation claimed by Rome, as well as to the enthusiasts in their claim to possess the Spirit outside His earlier revelation. Further, the Holy Spirit adds nothing new: He only declares what is already there. The Spirit seeks out and gives and certifies the Word contained in Scriptures. It was this approach which made him see the Old Testament as equivalent in value to the New Testament. Or to express this differently, it was because both had been given by God and both gave him Jesus Christ that he considered them equally necessary and important. Calvin was not a literalist: he claimed infallibility for the spiritual not the literal content.

It is not that Calvin denied any and all natural knowledge of God. He conceded a knowledge of God in the natural man which he could discern in nature, in the natural evolution of things, and in the history of mankind. But this knowledge causes men to evolve their own ideas of God and generates idolatry, for fallen man cannot know God by the guidance of nature alone. Only in Christ can man see. (This showed a marked contrast to the humanists, even to Zwingli.) There is no course open to fallen humanity other than to embrace the revelation that has been given him of Jesus Christ.

In Chapter 13 of the first book, Calvin turns to the doctrine of the Trinity. Servetus, with his anti-trinitarian speculations, had compelled Calvin to be more specific. Calvin was well aware that much of the Trinitarian vocabulary was extra-Biblical. He defended it not primarily for its own sake but because he saw that this framework preserved the divinity of Christ and therefore his doctrine of saving faith in Christ as well as the authority of the Holy Spirit in His relation to God and Christ. Calvin held the orthodox doctrine of the unity of the essence in the Persons of the Trinity at the same time as the distinction between them. Both Luther and Calvin were passionately Christocentric: the theology of both is primarily a Christology.

Calvin turned from the knowledge of God to the knowledge of man, beginning with the doctrine of Creation. Calvin saw the divine creation and providence as general knowledge of God given by Scripture, but distinguished it from that special knowledge of God experienced as the Father reconciled to sinful man by Jesus Christ. He argued that it was this special knowledge that gave meaning to the general; indeed that Christ gave both, and therefore it is by Christ the Word of God that all things were created.

In that God *created* the world, we have an argument that God alone is eternal. Calvin saw the whole purpose of creation as centring on man and fulfilling its purpose in man as its end. This graciousness and foresight of God Calvin proclaimed as evidence of the mercy of God and therefore interpreted it in an evangelical sense. God's purpose of love served to underline the horror of Adam's sin in relation to God who had done so much, and made him declare that the sovereign aim of man is to glorify such a God.

Although Calvin thought of man in two parts, body and soul, he conceived the soul as existing in its own right and not as an aspect of the body, an argument he substantiated from the Scriptures and from psychological and philosophical speculations. He did not argue that the soul was immortal of itself, but that immortality was a gift of God, which, if not granted, meant that the soul would perish and return to nothing, as did the body. Man has a privileged place in God's creation for he is not only a dweller on earth like the animals but an inheritor of the Kingdom of Heaven. He is in the image of God, as the angels are, which means that man has imprinted on him the integrity and righteousness which were the attributes of Adam when created by God fresh in the Garden of Eden, the true image of which is found in Christ, the second Adam.

## 2. Providence

Calvin then argues that to have a Creator means that we have a Governor and Preserver, and that not in general terms, but in the particular sense of the continuous action of God in the midst of his creation, "sustaining, nourishing and caring for every creature, even the sparrow."[1] This is not a providence by which

> the Deity, sitting idly in heaven, looking on at what is taking place in the world, but one by which he, as it were, holds the helm and overrules all events.[2]

This view of Providence in its total depth and total range is a view that only a believing man can understand. Calvin sharply distinguishes his

---

[1] *Inst.* i. 16. 1.        [2] *Inst.* i.16. 4.

teaching from ideas of fate, fortune or chance, bringing Basil and Augustine in support of his point.

Calvin enlarges on the doctrine with a view to strengthening and consoling the faithful:

> ... the Providence of God is to be considered with reference both to the past and the future; and, secondly, that in overruling all things, it works at one time with means, at another without means, and at another against means. Lastly, the design of God is to show that he takes care of the whole human race, but is specially vigilant in governing the Church ... [1]

One by one Calvin raises the objections of his critics: those who object *in toto*; those who argue that Calvin's views are his own and not Catholic; those who argue that Calvin makes God the author of evil; those who argue that man therefore is not responsible for his sin. He meets each of them on a basis of Scripture and sound experience. To him the belief in God's Providence removes a man utterly from the atmosphere of fear and anxiety and care, and commits him to that glorious freedom in which he knows that nothing can happen to him except what a loving Father has sent, and no event or person can harm him by alienating him from God.

Yet Calvin sees Providence in operation not only within the activity of believers and of the elect, but in the area of the reprobate. The devil and the wicked operate only by divine permission: every creature is an instrument in the hands of God. Their wickedness lies in their being turned away from the will of God: their wickedness God uses for His providential purpose.

> The sum of the whole is this – since the will of God is said to be the cause of all things, all the counsels and actions of men must be held to be governed by his providence; so that He not only exerts his power in the elect, who are guided by the Holy Spirit, but also forces the reprobate to do him service. [2]

## 3. Of God the Redeemer, Christ

### (a) The knowledge of man and of sin

If Calvin taught that God can be known only in Christ and that Christ can be found only in the Scriptures, he also taught that man can know himself only in so far as he contemplates in the same Scripture, what he is, and where he stands, and where he is going. It is in Scripture that he learns that man was made in the image of God, and it is in Scripture that he learns that his own faithlessness and pride voluntarily brought his own ruin and estrangement. Calvin argued that man in himself was but mud, even before the Fall, and all that he had before the Fall was of God, and all

---

[1] *Inst.* i. 17. 1.        [2] *Inst.* i. 18. 2.

that he had received since the Fall was the bounty of the same God of mercy and of grace. Not only was the good lost in the Fall, but after the Fall the consequent perversity, disobedience and faithlessness were a source of more and contrived sinning, an infected well that poisoned the whole of man's being – thought, feeling and will. In losing the spiritual gifts of faith, righteousness and integrity man had shut himself off from heavenly things and could of himself not even imagine what these things were. Faith, love, holiness are all now alien to him, so that man neither knows nor wills anything but what is bad, perverse and tainted. He still possesses will which operates on a lower level, but cannot will to do good except by God's grace. Many critics at this point have demanded of Calvin how, if that be the case, any responsibility for sin can be levelled at man. Calvin firmly replied that it could. He argued from his own experience that in no case was he ever compelled or constrained to sin of necessity, but that he at that moment voluntarily committed himself to it. Critics of Calvin at this point argue that he slips out of a metaphysical difficulty by a psychological escape; nevertheless, Calvin may well be right.

If this be man's plight, then salvation in Christ could but be the rectification and reorientating of our will. The elect experience this in their conversion, a process which goes on the whole of one's life and works out in a ceaseless warfare against sin. Yet Calvin allowed that the greatnesses and virtues of the pagans were indeed greatnesses and virtues, only they availed nothing in the one vital matter of justifying a man before God. In any case all these pagan virtues derived from God of His mercy, and no man could take credit for them. This position is not the Erasmian view and is far removed from the Zwinglian view which was ready to concede the virtues of the pagans as signs of their election.

Calvin concedes far more to the natural man than is generally realized. In the matter of politics and government, economic life and liberal culture, Calvin portrayed man as competent and law-abiding, even reasonable. The philosophers and ancient jurists excited wonder in Calvin, but Calvin saw through all this wisdom and learning a merciful God who had granted these gifts: unlike Zwingli, he did not allow his admiration of this ancient body of learning to blunt his abiding awareness of human corruption. To Calvin, Adam represented the whole human race. It was not that Adam's sin was transmitted but rather that in Adam we are all corrupted.

## (b) The Law

Calvin saw the law, by which he meant the Mosaic dispensation, as an integral part of the covenant once made with Abraham, the historic guarantee of God's concern for His chosen people. The value of the law, and its sole difference from the civil and religious legislations of other

G

peoples, was that it was wholly orientated towards Christ. Deprived of this, the law is empty and a spiritual encumbrance. It was valid in its entirety for the Jews, but since the coming of Christ it was no longer valid in the same way for Christians.

Calvin divided the function of the law into three parts. First, it was a mirror of sin. It showed man how sinful he was, and condemned him, but it condemned man only to show his need of God's mercy. Second, it was a restraint to the evil one, a deterrent that compels a kind of forced righteousness. Third, and most important of all, it has a function to play in the lives of believers. It will serve to make the believing man more certain what the will of God is and quicken him in obedience to God. Though he dismissed the political and ceremonial laws of the Old Testament as no longer binding (even if significant typologically), Calvin did not modify the moral laws. Calvin distinguished here between the moral law as instructing the conscience and subjugating the conscience. The law was not abrogated by Christ but the slavery to it and the curse attaching to its disobedience were broken by Christ.

Calvin later developed this liberation. He argued that no man can trust in his own capacity to keep the law, and therefore stands condemned under the law, or turns to Christ and accepts the mercy of God. In this deliverance from the threat or curse of the law, man can then turn to the law with fresh eyes and new hope, and actually desire of his own will to be obedient to it: the law merges into the gospel in the believing heart. This glad deliverance saves a man from making into matters of conscience indifferent points of clothing, diet and the like.

## (c) The Old and the New Testaments

Calvin had opened himself to the charge of setting the Old Testament and the New Testament on the same level, so in 1539 and again later in 1559 he extended the *Institutes* to explain the similarities and the differences between the Old Testament and the New. Calvin explained his views basically in seeing the Old Testament as a promise and the New Testament its fulfilment: the new covenant was essentially the re-establishment of the old broken covenant. He taught, as Luther before him, that Christ dominates both Testaments. The substance of both Testaments is identical, even the sacraments, only the manner is different. As Luther argued, he taught that the thinking of the Old Testament is directed primarily to earthly happiness, and therefore is of prime importance in the inculcation of vice and virtue now in this life and their reward. Nevertheless it was a heavenly blessedness to which God was leading men through these earthly blessings. He taught that the Old Testament presented truth by images and had only the shadow rather than the substance; e.g. priesthood and worship are figurative of Christ and His redemptive work, and not ultimates.

He argued that the opposition of law and gospel was only to emphasize the abundance of grace at the hands of the same legislator. Calvin warns against assuming that "none had been converted to Him (by the law),"[1] arguing that there were many true believers in the old Israel. He contrasted the freedom in Christ with the bondage of the law. "Bondage is applied to the Old Testament, because it begets fear, ... freedom to the New Testament, because it is productive of confidence and security."[2] The Old Testament filled the conscience with fear and trembling, the New inspires it with gladness. Another contrast he drew was that in the Old Testament God had confined Himself to one people, in the gospel He reveals Himself to other nations.

### (d) Christ and His Work of Redemption

Calvin is always described as theocentric, but this should not be understood as opposed to Christocentric: his Christocentrism was as central as Luther's.

> The case was certainly desperate, if the Godhead itself did not descend to us, it being impossible for us to ascend.[3]

Calvin saw man's sin as having two effects: first, making him an object of horror to God; and conversely, filling the sinner with a horror of God owing to the fear of His righteousness. Only the incarnation could meet the plight of man; only Christ could mediate in this dilemma. At this point Calvin clearly distinguished between the divinity and the humanity, but equally certainly defined the essential separateness of the two natures and the maintenance of their respective characteristics.

If this be the nature of Christ, Calvin summed up His work of redemption in the three offices of prophet, king and priest.[4]

> The purpose of this prophetical dignity in Christ is to teach us, that in the doctrine which he delivered is substantially included a wisdom which is perfect in all its parts.[5]

His office as king is to bring us into a spiritual not an earthly kingdom, a kingdom which is heavenly and eternal, membership of which brings "righteousness and peace and joy in the Holy Spirit" (Rom. 14:17), and eternal life with certain victory over all evil. But if this kingship embraces all believers, this same king will one day break the rebellious as a potter his pots. His office as priest is seen as the voluntary sacrifice of himself in perfect obedience, the mediator who obtained the divine reconciliation.

[1] *Inst.* ii. 11. 8.     [2] *Inst.* ii. 11. 9.     [3] *Inst.* ii. 12. 1.
[4] J. F. Jansen *Calvin's Doctrine of the Work of Christ* (London, 1956) minimizes the importance of these three offices in Calvin's theology.
[5] *Inst.* ii. 15. 2.

The sum comes to this: that the honour of the priesthood was competent to none but Christ, because by the sacrifice of his death he wiped away our guilt, and made satisfaction for sin.[1]

Calvin then turned to the mode of obtaining the grace of Christ. In the manner of participation he argued that there was no obtaining the benefits of Christ's redemptive work save in a personal union with Christ, but that saving union is a creation of the Holy Spirit.

The Holy Spirit is the bond by which Christ effectually binds to himself.[2]

And it is in the gift of faith that the Holy Spirit grafts us into this indispensable communion: the Holy Spirit is almost the mediator between Christ and man, as Christ was between God and man. Calvin distinguished carefully, as did Luther, between historic faith and saving faith: by the former a man believes that God and Christ exist, by the second he believes in God and Christ. This meant not only trust in God but a certain knowledge of God's good will towards us. We no longer have a judge in heaven to condemn us but a Father who justifies: and we have the Holy Spirit who regenerates us.

Our regeneration or sanctification consisted in Christ's taking hold of our whole being. There were two aspects of it: the mortification of the old man and participation in the new life, which arise from the believer's sharing in the death and in the resurrection of Christ. Both of these are life-long processes, in fact Calvin thinks in terms of war, but it is a battle which the believer will ultimately win. He closely relates this to the reality of election, and argues that we are chosen by God to live a holy life, and the reason for our election lies in that, while we were once servants of sin, we are now in the service of God. In this call God awakens the power to sanctification; He gives a new heart to the elect that they may in fact walk in His ways. Arguing that we are not our own and therefore none of our own ends or desires may be sought, he says:

... we are God's; let us, therefore, live and die to him (Rom. 14:8). We are God's; therefore, let his wisdom and will preside over all our actions. We are God's; to him, then, as the only legitimate end, let every part of our life be directed.[3]

A real practical consequence of regeneration was the liberation from self to serve God: this denial of self is the basis of Calvin's ethics – and Christ's too. But only by the gift of faith is the believer led to penitence and renunciation. Calvin is positively splendid when he discusses the evangelical *imitatio Christi* and what it means to live the Christian life by taking up daily the Cross of Christ and ever lifting up the heart in the certain hope of eternal glory.

[1] *Inst.* ii. 15. 6.     [2] *Inst.* iii. 1. 1.     [3] *Inst.* iii. 7. 1.

(e) *Justification by Faith*

Calvin, as Luther, held this doctrine central to Christianity, "the main hinge on which religion turns."[1] It meant the acceptance of a sinner by God as if he were righteous, and consists in the forgiveness of sins and the imputation of the righteousness of Christ. But this imputation is made possible only by our union with Christ. Calvin places regeneration in juxtaposition to justification in the *Institutes*, but he saw neither a casual nor a chronological connection between the two. They are benefits both that issue from the foundation of all benefits, Jesus Christ. Justification is perfect from the moment it is given, but sanctification is a process incomplete at death. Justification and sanctification are two graces of equal value to Calvin. Calvin held, as Luther, a doctrine of double justification, which only means a clarification of the fact that when the sinner is accepted, his works after adoption are still sinful, but nevertheless his first justification means that his justification continues and is not dependent on the value or lack of value of his works after justification. As Luther used frequently to say that it is not faith that justifies but Christ, Calvin too argued that faith acquires value only in relation to its content, Jesus Christ.

> Faith justifies not because it merits justification for us by its own worth, but because it is an instrument by which we freely obtain the righteousness of Christ.[2]

## 4. *Predestination*

It is too readily assumed that predestination is the centre of Calvinism. It is much rather the ultimate consequence of faith in the grace of Christ facing the enigmas of experience. He early accepted the doctrine as taught by the other reformers, and it was in the later editions of the *Institutes* that he began to change its place in his system and even enlarge on it. Calvin never discussed the idea within a metaphysical framework, but in order to find a surer basis to the doctrine of justification by grace alone and a clearer theological basis for ecclesiology. Calvin, unlike Luther, never feared to meditate on the doctrine, or to consider it in the light of difficulties and objections. He thought that men were bound to raise these. Calvin saw that the fundamental difficulty lay in man's refusal to see the full cause of his salvation in God alone, and raised no objections to man seeking to know.

Calvin made a careful distinction between predestination and foreknowledge, a distinction Augustine and Luther confused. Foreknowledge to Calvin meant simply that no event is either future or past to God: He knows all at any one moment. But predestination was the eternal decree of

---

[1] *Inst.* iii. 11. 1.　　　　[2] *Inst.* iii. 18. 8.

God by which He decided what He would do with each man: "some are preordained to eternal life, others to eternal damnation."[1] Election, like reprobation, was a free act of the divine will.

In this matter, God's will cannot be defeated, grace is irresistible. Here Calvin follows Augustine. The elect soul cannot resist God. He is an instrument of the divine will. This does not mean that such a man has no will, but rather it is liberated to serve the will of God. It is important to say again that the doctrine of predestination only takes on its meaning when it is seen as grounded in Jesus Christ. The relation between election and union with Christ was steadily in the forefront of all his teachings, "we are written in the book of life if we communicate with Christ." The calling of the elect, and their justification, carried the marks and evidences of election, and a sure sign of our adoption was the taking to heart of the doctrine preached to us. The assurance of our election is our faith in Christ and union with Him, and secondly, the gifts that God grants in sanctifying us.

There is a counterpart to predestination and that is reprobation. "There could be no election without its opposite reprobation."[2] Here Calvin diverges from Augustine, in whose theology the elect alone are the subject of a special decision which withdraws them from the *massa perditionis*; the reprobate are simply abandoned to the consequences of their sin. But to Calvin all mortal flesh is subject to death as the Scripture clearly declares: this is a "horrible decree,"[3] but a divine decree, and therefore righteous and necessary. Calvin stubbornly argues here that God created everything that was good and that man sins of his own volition: God predestinated, but the cause and matter of it is man himself.

> Though by the eternal providence of God, man was formed for the calamity under which he lies, he took the matter of it from himself, not from God, since the only cause of his destruction was his degenerating from the purity of his creation into a state of vice and corruption.[4]

Reprobates sometimes do not know their own state, still less can believers classify them with any certainty, save in clear cases of heresy and sin. Calvin taught church discipline to the extent of excommunication, but always to retrieve souls, not to banish them. Calvin never abrogated to the Church the judgments that belonged to God alone.

## 5. The Last Things

Calvin closes the third book with a discussion on the final resurrection. He

---

[1] *Inst.* iii. 21. 5.     [2] *Inst.* iii. 23. 1.
[3] *Inst.* iii. 23. 7: Latin, *decretum quidem horribile, fateor* ("a decree indeed to make one shudder, I confess").
[4] *Inst.* iii. 23. 9.

is Augustinian in his emphasis that believers are not citizens of this earth but strangers and pilgrims travelling to the celestial kingdom of joy and peace and fellowship with God and the saints. This hope Calvin closely weaves with faith, for in this life the believing man finds the assurance of the experience of the ultimate promise and hope. The conditions of access are two: the immortality of the soul and the resurrection of the body. Calvin sensed human difficulty in the second and dwelt on the infinite power of God and the example of Christ who in the fulfilment of His mortal life was made immortal, a sure pledge of our own immortality. Christ's resurrection was the type of every believing man's resurrection. As for the soul, Calvin taught that that was already immortal, and after death awaits in joy its future glory in Christ when he finally appears in judgment. This state was a rest but not a sleep: it was a conscious sharing in the kingdom of God. The day of judgment would see the Lord's coming again and the separation of the faithful from the reprobate.

Calvin is discreet on the fate of the elect and reprobate, and confines himself to Scriptural indications. He does not take the imagery associated with the blessed nor that associated with the reprobate in any literal sense. As the kingdom is full of light and joy, felicity and glory, even that is beyond our intelligence, until that hour when the Saviour comes and makes it all real. Similarly with the fate of the reprobate. Calvin argues that no image of darkness, gnashing of teeth and undying worms gnawing eternally at a soul are equal to the misery of a man separated from God and the terror of facing the Eternal Judge. They are not descriptions but warnings.

## 6. The Eternal Means

The last book of the *Institutes* treats of the external means or helps by which God invites us to fellowship with Christ, and keeps us in it: Church, Sacraments and Civil Government. Calvin's doctrine of the Church is of central importance in the understanding of his theology. He argues that God intended the Church to teach and nurture the gospel, for which purposes He instituted pastors and teachers to whom He has committed the sacraments. "To those to whom God is a father, the Church must also be a mother,"[1] Calvin repeated in the patristic tradition of Cyprian and Augustine, adding that this was as true for the Old Testament as it was for the New Testament. Calvin sought the collective sanctification of the church community by establishing among them what he called "the consent of faith." As God had had recourse to the Incarnation of his Son to effect reconciliation between fallen mankind and Himself, so he used earthly means to sanctify those to whom he had given faith. God is not

---

[1] *Inst.* iv. 1. 1.

limited by or bound to His church, but he constrains us to use the means He has appointed: "Beyond the pale of the Church no forgiveness of sins, no salvation can be hoped for"[1] (Isa. 37:32; Joel 2:32).

The Church to Calvin was more than the visible community of believers but comprised all the elect, living and dead. Further, Calvin did not constitute the Church by the quality of its members but by the means of grace instituted by Christ.

> Wherever we see the Word of God purely preached and listened to, and the sacraments administered according to the institution of Christ, we must not doubt that there is the Church.[2]

None of the early Reformers held the doctrine of the Anabaptists and related sects by which the Church was regarded as an ideal community of saints.

Calvin saw the necessity of discipline over the members as well as the constant self-examination of the Church itself if error was to be avoided and the purity and truth of the Gospel maintained. He distinguished three kinds of discipline: first, against heretics and schismatics; second, against shameful conduct; third, and subsuming all three, excommunication, practised for the purpose of redeeming souls in sin or error. Nevertheless, discipline was not a mark of the true Church (as Bucer made it), but simply a matter of organization.

Calvin is sometimes distinguished from Luther in his views on the organization of the Church. True, he sought to make church life and organization scriptural whereas Luther made it also dependent upon time and circumstances, yet Calvin would not limit the Church to scriptural modes only, but allowed her some freedom to develop her own forms and organization in the circumstances historical and geographical in which she found herself. He distinguished four ministries, even here departing from New Testament precedent, for there were other ministries in the early Church, e.g. prophets, apostles and evangelists. The four ministries were: pastors, doctors, elders and deacons. Yet even they could be fused into one person, in certain circumstances. The two most important are the pastors and the doctors. The preconditions of any man's election to office were the prior call of the Holy Spirit and the subsequent ratification by the community of his sound doctrine and saintly life. The chief task of the "lay" ministry of the elder was the exercise of discipline, and that of the deacon (also "lay") was the care of the sick and of the poor.

Calvin taught that the Church had a spiritual power in a way parallel to the State's possession of temporal power. The Church's teaching power was limited to formulating and explaining Scriptural doctrine and defending it against its enemies. She had no power whatever to formulate any

---

[1] *Inst.* iv. 1. 5.     [2] *Inst.* iv. 1. 9.

doctrine, only to declare the Word of God. The Church cannot claim, by virtue of her being ruled by the Holy Spirit, any authority over and above Scripture.

In the matter of the legislative power of the Church Calvin sought the Pauline principle of doing everything decently and in order (1 Cor. 14:40), and to this end laws were necessary as "a kind of bonds."[1] But these laws were not "necessary to salvation" neither must they be imposed as obligatory on the consciences of men, as the old canon law attempted.

Calvin gave to the Church a juridical power, not the repressive and authoritarian and disciplinary power of the magistracy with its fines and imprisonments, but one of maintaining order. Calvin made even the magistrate subject to this spiritual jurisdiction as Theodosius himself had once submitted, but this was only necessary because the magistracy was not always Christian. Calvin did not set the magistracy in any sense as competing for the Church's power and responsibility: he sought to make the two administrations co-operate, and make one the complement of the other. It is wrong to accuse Calvin of attempting to establish a theocratic régime in which the temporal power would be subject to the spiritual power. He sought a state of affairs very close to what Luther wanted but Lutheranism never achieved, where ministers showed what society required and where the magistracy protected the Church.

It is true that when Calvin spoke of the Church he envisaged the communities he had experienced in Geneva and Strasbourg and elsewhere, yet he had a powerful ecumenical sense of the Church Catholic. When Cranmer wrote to him (April, 1552) seeking the meeting of the leaders of European Protestantism he replied:

> Would to God that we might have learned and serious men, taken from the principal churches, come together to discuss the articles of faith and to hand down to those who will follow us the certain teaching of the Scriptures, as is common to all. It must be counted among the worst evils of our epoch that the churches are thus separated one from another, so much so that hardly any human society exists among us, still less that holy communion between the members of Christ which all profess but very few sincerely cultivate in reality.[2]

This ecumenical approach arose from his firm basis in fundamentals and his refusal to be divided on inessentials which do not impair the theological principles of Christianity. As the churches may never break their unity in dissension over inessentials, neither may a church member separate himself from his church and thereby break the communion of the congregation.

[1] *Inst.* iv. 10. 27.
[2] Joannis Calvini . . . *Epistolae atque Responsa* (Amsterdam, 1667), Vol. IX, p. 61. No. IX dated (1551?).

## 7. Sacraments

The sacraments to Calvin were secondary and supplementary to the gospel, a kind of confirmatory visual aid conceded to our weakness. He followed an Augustinian tradition of viewing a sacrament as a visible form of invisible grace. He suggested two definitions:

> an outward sign by which God seals on our consciences the promises of his good will towards us, to confirm our feeble faith . . . a testimony of the grace of God towards us, confirmed by an external sign.[1]

The sacrament consisted of the Word plus the external sign, a principle Luther expounded and which all Reformers accepted. Calvin refuted the Zwinglian view that sacraments add nothing, for, because our faith is always weak, God had chosen to work with sacraments as a means of strengthening it. He also opposed the Roman Catholic view that sacraments justify and confer grace provided we interpose no obstacle of sin or unbelief, by arguing that the Word is received by faith alone:

> He who would have the sign with the thing, and not void of its truth, must apprehend by faith the Word which is there enclosed.[2]

Or later:

> we gain nothing, unless in so far as we receive in faith.[3]

It will be recalled that, together with the criticism of the idea of the Treasury of Merits, this same view was selected by Cajetan at Augsburg as one of Luther's erroneous views.[4] Calvin made it sharper even than Luther for to Calvin only the elect are able to receive faith. Further Calvin was aware of the organic relationship between the sacraments of the Old and the New Testaments: the former prefigured the promised Christ, the latter testifies that he had already been given.

Calvin retained only two sacraments, Baptism and Communion, the only two attested by Scripture. They testify Christ to us, he argued:

> Baptism testifies that we are washed and purified; the Supper of the Eucharist that we are redeemed. Ablution is figured by water, satisfaction by blood. . . . Of this the Spirit of God is a witness.[5]

### (a) Baptism

Baptism first of all attests the forgiveness of sins. Calvin leads away from the visible element of water to turn attention to Christ alone. Calvin argued that baptism was not a thing of the past but for all life, and that this constant mercy of God was offered to repentant sinners only. Secondly, baptism shows us our mortification in Christ and our new life in Him.

---

[1] Inst. iv. 14. 1.    [2] Inst. iv. 14. 15.    [3] Inst. iv. 15. 15.    [4] See p. 50 ff.    [5] Inst. iv. 14. 22.

This was in no sense the mediaeval idea of mortification: it meant the dying to sin and the rising again to a new life in the Holy Spirit. The third benefit is that we are united with Christ and partakers of all his blessings.

> The fulfilment of our baptism is in Christ . . . all the divine gifts held forth in Baptism are found in Christ alone.[1]

Calvin rebutted the Roman doctrine of baptism in that it argued that baptism restored a man to the original state of Adam. Calvin related the doctrine to justification, which assures us that God has remitted our sin and its punishment and imputes the rightousness of Christ to us.

Having explained the religious content of baptism and conceded the value of the sacrament as a public confession before men, he turns to another aspect of it as a confirmation of our faith. He argues that in baptism it is Christ Himself who is the agent, not the minister, and that it is He who cleanses us from our sin, clothes us and justifies us, and this not as "bare show" but actuality. The admission of the taper, of chrism and exorcism, of spittle and other follies, Calvin saw as satanic corruptions of the pure idea of Christ's conception of baptism by water alone, and dismissed them as theatrical pomp.

It is on infant baptism that Calvin has his real difficulties. Luther stood with Augustine in thinking that children had a faith of their own but accepted the practice mainly on traditional grounds. Calvin sought biblical foundations and found them in the "sacrament" of circumcision: circumcision and baptism conveyed the same promise, the difference lay only in "the outward ceremony." Children were heirs of the promise, why exclude them from the outward sign which marked that membership, he asked the Anabaptists, especially when history records no time when it was not practised. Baptism was normal but not necessary to salvation: he rejected outright the idea that unbaptized children go to Hell (or limbo). Calvin adds, very powerfully, in his last paragraph, of the glory of the divine goodness, that desires to care for the children of men:

> God acts towards us as a provident parent, not ceasing to care for us after our death, but consulting and providing for our children.[2]

## (b) Holy Communion

Calvin owed something to Augustine among the ancients and to Luther and Bucer among his contemporaries for his views on the Holy Communion, and seemingly nothing to Zwingli. He saw the sacrament under three headings: the meaning, which lies in the promises; the matter, by which he understands Jesus Christ with his death and resurrection; the effect, by which he understands redemption, righteousness, sanctification, the life everlasting and all the benefits brought to us by Jesus Christ.

[1] *Inst.* iv. 15. 6.          [2] *Inst.* iv. 16. 32.

In the mystery of the Supper, by the symbols of bread and wine, Christ, his body and his blood, are truly exhibited to us, that in them he fulfilled all obedience, in order to procure righteousness for us – first that we might become one body with him; and, secondly, that being made partakers of his substance, we might feel the result of this fact in the participation of all his blessings.[1]

The promises Calvin sees in the words of institution when Christ gives Himself to us, dwells in us by faith, and gives us eternal life. The matter, Jesus Christ, Calvin believed was offered with the elements, but not in the sense of being identified with them nor included under them: simply given at the same time as the elements. He meant that the soul fed upon the substance of the body in order to be made one with Him. The effects meant to Calvin all that Christ communicated to a believing soul.

A further problem was the understanding of the real presence. Luther had defended the ubiquity of the glorified body of Christ, and had used this as an explanation of the real presence in every eucharist simultaneously. In controversy with Westphal Calvin would not admit this and argued that it was an unnecessary hypothesis. For Calvin the Holy Spirit was ubiquitous: Christ had promised that he would send the Holy Spirit, and that excluded any necessity of the corporal presence of Christ in this world. In any case, the body of Christ was in heaven above all elements. The Lutherans have no cause to argue for the enclosing of Christ in the bread, since they confess that they have Him equally without the Supper. In the last analysis, Calvin always saw Christ as beyond and above the sacraments, and independent of them. Union with Christ is attained by other means, prayer, preaching and Bible reading. It is difficult to avoid the conclusion that the sacrament was not an integral part of his system: it seems to subserve or complete the Word.

## 8. Secular Government

Calvin regards the State as fulfilling its appointed rôle in relation to the service of Christ's dominion. Calvin was not concerned about the State, nor about the Christian State. His concern was with Christ, and the significance the civil power had in relation to this fellowship with the Lord. It is most significant for Calvin's thinking that when he had considered the place of the Church, the Word and the Sacraments as outward aids by which God helps us to communion with Christ, he turns to the secular government as a further means to this same end.

"Secular government rests upon God's providence and sacred prescription."[2] Rulers and magistrates are instituted by God, and as representative of God are His servants and His officers. Calvin exalted rulers and yet

---

[1] *Inst.* iv. 17. 11.          [2] *Inst.* iv. 20. 4.

abased them: they were not co-rulers with God but His servants. He was Lord of all, and all were in His hands. They exercised God's power mediately. Calvin saw Christ as the eternal King, and all rulers took on their significance in relation to Christ: "His heavenly voice both for governors and their subjects is the one rule for living and dying."[1] Magistrates and princes were all subject to Christ and His rule, and their government is nothing but a service under this one Lord.

There is no conflict with the spiritual rule of Christ for secular rulers have a different task:

> to look after and protect the outward side of church worship, to defend the pure doctrine appertaining to the true worship of God and to secure the stability of the church, to establish social harmony, to shape our conduct as citizens according to the law, to bind us to each other and to maintain the common peace.[2]

The secular power must protect the pure preaching of the gospel and in so doing protect the Church whose task this is. This means that the secular arm must prevent and punish all idolatry and blasphemy, and further, protect the cause of the Church, which means to provide for the ministers of the churches, the teachers of their schools, the guardians of their hospices, and not least, the universities. Calvin expected much of the civil power, though he deplored any encroachment on the spiritual sphere, such as he saw the German princes assume: the Church must work unhindered, unhampered and uncensured.

It is important for Calvin to emphasize the responsibility rulers have, never to allow the world to sink back to godlessness and sin. Christ is Lord of the secular world and secular rulers have to see that this dominion is maintained according to the Word of God. Calvin emphasized this heavy responsibility as well as the accountability one day before the solemn judgment seat of Christ, for all that they have done or left undone. Yet his words were not comfortless: God would always keep and uphold them, and the congregation pray for and support them.

Calvin urged the citizens to a full obedience to rulers as the servants of God, but at the same time assured them that the secular government was a demonstration of God's fatherly care and providence. With Luther (and Paul before them) he took the view that rebellion against authority was rebellion against God, a battle that any rebel will ultimately lose. Again, with Luther, this did not mean subservience. There was a reciprocal relationship: the people were subject to authority, but authority is subject to those whom it serves. And as this authority was an authority God had decreed, then this authority was circumscribed by God.

Calvin therefore set a prescribed limit to the authority of secular rulers.

[1] C.R. 13. 282.     [2] *Inst.* iv. 20. 2.

Rulers who pay no regard to the God who has actually called them to their service and who set themselves up in the place of God, cease to be legitimate rulers. Nevertheless, they are still rulers, and the worst tyranny is better than anarchy. Bad rulers spring from bad people, and the remedy is a change of heart and earnest prayer to God. God will ultimately prevail, and uses many means to break a wicked tyranny. Those means never envisage common rebellion, though he concedes official rebellion by responsible officers. Where rulers are godless and sacrilegious then they are not rulers in the authority of God but have forfeited their authority and are but ordinary men. It was better by far to be an exile in a land where God was honoured than to remain in one's fatherland whence Christ had been banished.

PART FOUR

*The Reformation in Britain*

CHAPTER XI

# THE REIGN OF HENRY VIII, 1509–47

## 1. The Background

THE BRITISH CHURCH HAD BEEN IN EXISTENCE SEVERAL CENTURIES before Augustine came to England in 597. There is a rhetorical reference of Tertullian (208) and a tradition from Bede around St. Alban (associated with the Diocletian persecution about 305), but the first historical references are to the British bishops who attended the Council of Arles (A.D. 314)[1] to discuss Donatism and that of Ariminum (359) to discuss Arianism. The Romans withdrew from Britain at the beginning of the fifth century, and when the Angles invaded later in the same century the British withdrew to their mountain steadfastnesses. So bitter was the hatred of the invader that the British never even offered them the gospel. Christianity was not completely unknown among the invaders: when Augustine, sent by Pope Gregory the Great to evangelize the English, began his Kentish mission in 597 he found a Christian queen, daughter of a Frankish prince, and the Romano–British Church of St. Martin in Canterbury, which she used for her devotions, was made available to him and his party. In 625 the Northumbrian king and his court accepted Christianity. Northumbrian Christianity was strongly influenced by Irish church practice,[2] and differed from the Roman pattern established at Canterbury in such matters as the reckoning of Easter; in 664 at the Synod of Whitby the northern province fell into line with the Roman practice.

In the eleventh century William of Normandy overcame the English king Harold and seized his crown; in spite of the improvements he brought, he yet found it necessary to displace Stigand, the Archbishop of Canterbury, in favour of Lanfranc, his own French nominee. All but one bishop was removed, and a long succession of French prelates sought to erode English independence and to bring the Church into the European orbit. Becket resisted the encroachments of the Norman kings but it was a

[1] H. Gee and W. J. Hardy (ed.), *Documents Illustrative of English Church History* (London, 1896). No. 1.
[2] Ireland was evangelized by Palladius (431) and especially by Patrick (d. 461). The territory north of the Roman frontier, later constituting the kingdom of Scotland, was evangelized by Ninian (397) and more effectively by Columba and his followers, from their base in Iona, to which Columba came from Ireland in 563. Aidan was sent from Iona as bishop to the Northumbrians in 635, and established his see at Lindisfarne. See F. F. Bruce, *The Spreading Flame* (London, 1958), pp. 353 ff.

resistance that brought the Church nearer Rome. The process continued until, with King John in 1213, England was in vassalage to Rome.[1]

This process disquieted many. It was the strong kings Edward I (1272–1307) and Edward III (1327–77) who made distinct efforts to limit papal encroachment.[2] A strong anti-papal movement developed in the upper classes and an equally strong anti-clerical movement in the middle and lower classes, two very different movements even though they were moving in the same direction. Wyclif (1324–84) with his teaching on the dominion of grace and his evangelical doctrine of the Church, allied with his heavy criticism of a demoralized, worldly church, worked untold damage on the papacy, and, but for the turn of political history, might well have inaugurated the breach with Rome that was to come a hundred and fifty years later.[3] All this shows that there was in the sixteenth century a long-standing tradition of aloofness in relation to Rome at both a spiritual and a national level. It was a relatively easy matter for Henry VIII to sever relations with Rome and carry the large part of England along with him.

The rupture with Rome in this country had little in common with the movements in Germany, Switzerland and France. When Henry severed the connection with Rome, he sought to maintain Catholicism without the Pope. In Europe the movement had been primarily theological and the fact that England turned away from the papacy on the issue of the divorce of Catherine can only be explained in the light of the long history of a thousand years: the divorce was merely the occasion, not the cause. The Reformation was much more than the divorce, but the theological movement could only develop when the hand of the papacy was stayed.

Lollardy had never died,[4] and there is much evidence that in the early sixteenth century the native revolt of Wyclif had been understood and appropriated by men like Cranmer, Hooper, Ridley and Bale before they read Luther. They disliked the papal supremacy as a great political hurt to the English people, declaimed against the secularized clergy, advocated a preaching ministry, and looked to the secular power to compel reformation on a reluctant church. Henry had all this behind him. In addition, the Christian Humanists, men much respected, poured scorn on superstitious abuses, pilgrimages, relic-worship and not least the monks. When Luther's works filtered into England the movement quickened and became theological. There is evidence of a long list of Luther's works in a bookseller's in Oxford in 1520; Erasmus refers to Luther's writings in England (1521); William Warham, the Archbishop of Canterbury, received letters from Oxford (1521) to the effect that the university was infected with Lutheran-

---

[1] Gee and Hardy, No. 25. See also 26, 27.
[2] Statute of Provisors, 1351, and Praemunire, 1353. Gee and Hardy, 35 and 34 n.
[3] Cf. G. H. W. Parker, The Morning Star (1965).
[4] See A. G. Dickens, The English Reformation (1964), pp. 22–37; A. G. Dickens, Lollards and Protestants in the Diocese of York (1959), for detailed study.

ism; and the Cambridge men were meeting at the White Horse Tavern to read and discuss Luther's writings.[1] And then in Europe following on the seventy-year scandal of the Avignonese Captivity the papacy took on the appearance of a corrupt foreign power, and when the Conciliar Movement showed that it was never going to succeed in bringing the papacy to heel, men began to realize as Wyclif and the Occamists foresaw that only the secular arm was going to be able to curb the spiritual. All these things add up to a great deal and go some way to explaining the preparedness of England for the Reformation and the strong support Henry received when he defied Rome.

## 2. The Breach with Rome

The divorce of course played an important rôle. There is no doubt that Henry was much troubled about the propriety of having married his brother's wife, Catherine of Aragon, when child after child of the marriage died, leaving Mary only to survive. There is no doubt either that Henry was much troubled at having no male heir. Henry worsened the situation by becoming involved with the highly unsuitable Anne Boleyn. It was known that Pope Clement VII had already considered dissolving the marriage but was afraid to move for fear of Charles V, Catherine's nephew, and further, that Clement had even considered bigamy as a way out of the difficulty.[2] When Englishmen realized that their pressing national problems were all subject to the shifting needs of one who in this respect was merely an Italian prince, the severance from Rome was imminent.

Henry now decided to resolve matters himself and called Parliament (November, 1529), to find the vast majority of his laity behind him. He carried out an anti-clerical policy and passed Probate, Mortuaries and Pluralities Acts. An order was published ordering the destruction of the works of Wyclif, Tyndale, Luther and Zwingli. At this time Cranmer had suggested that the king should take the matter of the divorce out of the hands of the Curia and consult the canonists of the European universities. It was found that the universities of Oxford and Cambridge, Paris, Orleans, Bruges and Toulouse, all declared the marriage invalid, an opinion which the universities of Ferrara, Padua, Pavia and Bologna all shared in spite of express commands to the contrary from the Pope.

At the Second Session of Parliament (January–March, 1531) Henry set himself the task of forcing the clergy into submission. Henry had struck a mortal wound at papalism when he arraigned the mighty Cardinal Wolsey before the common law and succeeded. It was but a small step

---

[1] See Dickens, *English Reformation*, 68 ff.; cf. also Letter to Luther, 30 May, 1519, Kidd, p. 54.

[2] Letters and Papers IV. iii. p. 2047, 2055.

when on a charge of praemunire[1] he fined the Canterbury clergy £100,000 and assumed the title "Supreme Head of the Church and of the clergy."

At the Third Session (January–May, 1532) Henry attacked the bishops and wrung out of them what is called "The Submission of the Clergy."[2] This meant that Convocation could meet only by the king's writ and that all canons were to be revised and authorized under royal licence. He further forced through the Annates Act[3] which stopped the practice of remitting the first year's benefice income to Rome: it also fixed fees. This made Sir Thomas More retire to private life from the Lord Chancellorship in which he had succeeded Wolsey in 1529. Warham died that year (1532) and Henry elevated the reluctant Thomas Cranmer, a known "Lutheran," to the archiepiscopal throne. Cranmer truly believed that the royal supremacy would cure the Church of ills the papacy was impotent to heal, and believed also that the marriage with Catherine was unlawful. Knowing this the papacy still ratified Cranmer's appointment. The marriage with Catherine was now annulled. Anne was crowned queen and gave birth not to a son, but a daughter, Elizabeth (1533), to Henry's disgust and chagrin.

At the Fourth Session (1533) Parliament passed the celebrated Restraint of Appeals Act,[4] by whose terms no appeals were to be allowed to go outside the realm. Following the decision of Cranmer's court which had declared the marriage between Henry and Catherine null and void, this Restraint Act was too much for the Pope. He reversed Cranmer's ruling, declared the marriage with Anne null and void and drew up the excommunication of Henry if Henry did not obey within ten days.

Henry answered by an appeal to a general council and a series of enactments of Parliament which made the definitive breach with Rome. At this Fifth Session (1534) the Annates Act was made absolute: there were to be no annates, no bulls, no pall. By the same Act the king was to nominate to bishoprics and the cathedral chapters were to accept his nomination. The submission of clergy and restraint of appeals was given statutable authority.[5] There were to be no dispensations to Rome or payments to Rome: all such matters had to be settled in England.[6] The Act for the Submission of the Clergy forbade Convocation to legislate except by licence of the Crown. The Act of Succession legitimized the marriage with Anne Boleyn and the right of the issue of Henry and Anne to succeed to the throne.[7] The Supremacy Act[8] declared the king Supreme Head of the Church of England (essentially a counter doctrine to the papal claim) and gave the king the right of ecclesiastical visitation

---

[1] The charge of taking claims to courts outside the realm, papal courts in this instance. See pp. 194, 248; cf. also G. S. M. Walker, *The Growing Storm* (1961), pp. 233 ff.
[2] Gee and Hardy, 48.     [3] ibid., 49.     [4] ibid., 50.     [5] Gee and Hardy, 51, 52.
[6] ibid., 53.     [7] ibid., 54, 56.     [8] ibid., 55.

and the power to redress ecclesiastical abuse, a dangerous power in the case of a monarch like Henry. It was made treasonable to deny the king any of these rights, or even to call the king a heretic or schismatic.[1] Finally, to complete the break, the convocations of Canterbury and York abjured the papal supremacy.[2] The effect of all these enactments was to finalize the breach with Rome. The kings of England had always exercised some control over the Church in England: the difference now was that Henry VIII assumed sole control and would share it with none. It was a *potestas jurisdictionis* not *potestas ordinis*. There was no change in doctrine. The essential difference lay in the fact that the Pope was no longer recognized. Those who objected were rejected. The heads of the Carthusians were executed: John Fisher (bishop of Rochester) and More, too, went to the block. Europe was horrified but helpless. At this stage Henry revived his intrigues with the Protestant states of Germany, but negotiations broke down for he would not accept the Augsburg Confession as a basis of agreement.

Thomas Cromwell was now the king's secretary and the most powerful man in the kingdom. For money he turned to the revenues of the monasteries. These were no longer pioneers in agriculture and learning. Men no longer believed in masses for deliverance of souls in purgatory, and yet it was for this reason that kings and nobles had bequeathed them their lands and wealth. Their ideal was out of date. Theological reformation was the last thing they wanted: they were in actuality hot-beds of papalism and reaction. Had the monasteries heeded the Reformers, instead of the sad ruins we see about the English countryside today we might have possessed a splendid and noble line of schools, universities and hospitals still within the living stream of Christianity. Dissolution was to go through as a political necessity, the price of having refused theological reform. Further, by the granting of the former lands of the monasteries to the gentry a party interest in the Reformation was established in these families. To them the Reformation was a good thing for the wrong reasons.

The Seventh Session met in February, 1536. It passed the Statute of Uses, an Act to prevent the ownership of land being severed from its enjoyment and to enable Henry to collect the dues more readily. At this time there was passed an Act for the dissolution of the smaller monasteries, a decision that was but the portent of events to come, for within four years all monasteries of any size were invested in the king.[3] It was one thing to dissolve the monasteries, another to destroy them. The Reformers had one view of the new rôle of the monasteries, the politicians and gentry another. The wanton destruction of buildings and treasures and the misappropriation of wealth that went with it were no part of the Reformation proper. The Reformers wanted these resources of the Church to be used

---

[1] ibid., 57.　　　[2] ibid., 58.　　　[3] Gee and Hardy, 61, 64.

to develop a proper parochial system to meet the now different spiritual, educational and social needs of the people; to establish a new system of university and school education; and in certain cases simply to restore the wealth to the families and people to whom it originally belonged. Instead, most of it went to the army and navy, or was sacrificed to the greed of Cromwell, Henry and his satellites, lost for ever to the purposes for which pious men originally bequeathed it.

In the midst of all these events (January, 1536) Catherine of Aragon died, an event Henry and Anne in characteristic coarseness and vulgarity celebrated with a carnival. But before the summer of that same year Anne found herself charged with adultery and incest, and went to the block in a tempestuous and black agony of despair. Ten days later Henry married Jane Seymour.

These corrupt and vile happenings had a grave effect on the people. In the north of England the Pilgrimage of Grace under Robert Aske received a sympathetic response in the hearts of ordinary people. The grievances were social, political and religious. Henry had appropriated to himself all the monastic property as well as the precious stones and metals from the shrines. These shrines and places of pilgrimage had meant much to the common folk: they had been holiday resorts as well as centres of spiritual expression and devotion, and the king's action caused popular unease. Further, enclosures of common lands in the interests of wool-growing, a more profitable activity than arable or stock farming, caused the rise of much poverty and unemployment. Taxation was rising. The people were growing tired of Cromwell and were beginning to prefer the safety and certainty of the old religious ways. Aske was invited to London for discussions, but in his absence there was a further outbreak of the movement which was cruelly and brutally repressed by an unknown number of executions, including many abbots of north country abbeys. The closing ten years of Henry's reign took on the nature of a reign of terror.

At this point reference may be made to the matter of Henry's concern for an heir. A third succession act (1536) settled the crown on the issue of the third wife, Jane Seymour, who in 1537 gave birth to Prince Edward only to die twelve days later. The humanist Cardinal Reginald Pole, closely connected with the royal family, who was an enlightened Catholic with much sympathy for Luther, and who was later to show a genuine concern to reform Catholicism, criticized Henry's policy in his treatise De Unitate Ecclesiae (1538). To save his life he fled the country. Henry's answer to this was to execute his brothers and his elderly mother who had remained in England (1541). In 1540, largely under the political manœuvrings of Cromwell to effect a better relationship with Protestant Europe, Henry married his fourth queen, Anne of Cleves, on January 6, 1540. At this time, however, Henry sensed that Cromwell was ahead of the people, and though they both desired a closer alliance with the German Protestants (Anne was sister-in-law of John Frederick, Luther's prince), when that alliance failed on theological grounds, Cromwell fell from grace. With him fell Anne, who had in any case fallen at first sight in Henry's eyes; but though Cromwell was executed, Anne was pensioned off and had the Teutonic good sense to keep out of the way of all these manœuvrings by quietly retiring to Leicestershire. Henry promptly married Catherine Howard (his fifth wife), who in 1542 followed her predecessor Anne Boleyn to the block. The next year he married Catherine Parr, and in 1544 had the fourth Succession Act passed whereby the crown was to be given to Edward, Mary and Elizabeth, in that order.

### 3. Formularies of Faith

More interesting than all these sordid and sad events is the consideration of the changes in religious faith and the drawing up of the formularies of faith during these years. The separation of England from Rome had not meant any change of doctrine at all. It only meant that the bishop of Rome was no longer *episcopus universalis* and that Henry was in sole control of the affairs of the Church of England. He delegated his jurisdiction to Cromwell and ordered all matters to be settled within the realm without appeal or reference to Rome. It was impossible, of course, for the English church to remain the same under these new circumstances. There began to be a stirring of the Reformation in the land. Cranmer was certainly evangelical and interested in Luther's theology. Cromwell was sympathetic to Reformation theology, and wanted a political alliance with the German Protestant princes. There was mooted the idea of a set of articles which would express the developing evangelical beliefs in England, but whilst men like Cranmer and Latimer, supported by Cromwell, sought to embody the reformed doctrine, it was found that the older bishops were conservative and resistant. This party was headed by Gardiner, Bishop of Winchester, who took the view that the rejection of papal supremacy was all that was needed and at the same time withstood all and every movement towards theological reform. Cranmer, on the other hand, saw increasingly beyond the mere rejection of the Pope to the reformation of doctrine and morals. In any case, he was a much abler theologian than Gardiner, and far more spiritual. The two movements were, and sometimes still are, designated the "old" and the "new" learning, but neither Cranmer nor his supporters accepted these terms, for the so-called "new" was biblical and catholic, while the "old" was essentially mediaeval and relatively recent. There was a further complication. The Anabaptists began to grow vociferous and acrimonious. Contemporary documents bear witness to the disquiet and disharmony that arose in the English Church owing to these three parties. Henry intervened and Convocation issued the Ten Articles of 1536[1] "to establish Christian quietness and unity in the land and to avoid contentious opinions."

It can hardly be claimed that the Articles establish any real advance towards Reformation theology, even if they do show signs of being influenced by the reform movement. They should be read alongside the Injunctions of 1536 and 1538,[2] when it becomes clearer that the Articles were intended, to say the least, to wean the people from the gross super-stitions of mediaeval religion. They have been described as "Romish articles with the Pope left out in the cold." They were rather a first attempt to construct a creed on which a pliant Lutheran and a pliant Romanist might agree. Their content was:

1. *Fundamentals.* The fundamentals of religion are comprehended in the Bible, the three creeds, and the first four general councils. This statement is directed not against the Romanists but against the Anabaptists, many of whom denied the Trinity and the Incarnation.

2. *Baptism.* Baptism is defended as of dominical authority, and therefore all, infants included, ought to be baptized. It is conceded that in the case of baptism of adults or of grown children, repentance and faith are necessary.

3. *Penance.* Penance is defended as a sacrament instituted by our Lord in the New Testament as necessary to salvation. It consists of contrition, confession, and amendment of life. Contrition is explained as a sorrowing for sin and a confidence in God's mercy whereby the penitent conceives hope and faith in God's forgiveness and justification, not on account of merit but through Christ. Confession means confession to a priest who gives absolution by authority of Christ. Penance consists in prayer, fasting, almsdeeds, restitution and other good works of charity. These must be diligently performed in order to obtain everlasting life and in order to deserve mitigation of pains and afflictions which God gives a man in this world on account of his sins.

4. *The Sacrament of the Altar.* The doctrine of the Real Presence is strongly taught, yet at the same time the Roman doctrine of Transubstantiation is not asserted.

5. *Justification.* Justification is defined as "remission of our sins, and our acceptation or reconciliation into the grace and favour of God, that is to say, our perfect renovation in Christ." After the theology has been explained two stipulations are given: "God

[1] C. Hardwick, *A History of the Articles of Religion* (1851), p. 237; C. Lloyd, *Formularies of Faith in the Reign of Henry VIII* (Oxford, 1825), XV. 1.
[2] Gee and Hardy, 62, 63.

requireth ... contrition, faith, charity ... to concur in remission
of our sins," and "after we be justified we must also have good
works of charity and obedience towards God. ..." The article
expresses a combination of the Lutheran view with the later
Tridentine view.

The second five articles relate to ceremonies.

6. *Images.* Images are permitted as "representers of virtue and good
example," but at the same time the clergy are commanded to
reform abuses. Bishops and preachers are enjoined to instruct
the people in the matter of censing, kneeling and offering to
images, to ensure that the honour is paid to God and not to the
image.

7. *Honouring the saints.* A modified reverence is sanctioned, though
not with the honour due to God. It is conceded that images may
be "advancers of our prayers and demands unto Christ."

8. *Praying to saints.* The article says, "It is very laudable to pray to
saints in heaven ... to be intercessors, and to pray for us and
with us ... We may pray to our blessed Lady, to St. John
Baptist, to all and every of the Apostles, or any other saint
provided that we do not think any saint more merciful, or will
hear us sooner than Christ, or that any saint serves for one thing
more than another." The article does assert that grace is of God
only through Christ, yet at the same time the concessions have
a modifying effect.

9. *Rites and Ceremonies.* Most of these are vindicated, for example,
holy water, candles, ashes, palms, creeping to the cross, exorcisms.
Nevertheless, a corrective is added when it is stated that none of
these ceremonies remit sin but lift up our minds to God who
alone forgives sins.

10. *Purgatory.* Prayers for the dead are commanded, and receive
justification with reference to the Second Book of Maccabees,
ancient doctors and church usage. Masses for the dead are justified
and it is claimed that they relieve the dead of their purgatorial
pains. The article bears witness to a general agnosticism on the
subject and an unwillingness to rebut as well as to assert, and
exhorts all to depend on the mercy of God. Flagrant abuses are
deplored, in particular, indulgences and special masses said at
shrines.

The *Injunctions* of Cromwell (1536)[1] commanded clergy to denounce
the usurped power of the Bishop of Rome as well as to explain the Ten

[1] H. Bettenson (ed.), *Documents of the Christian Church* 2nd ed., (Oxford, 1963), pp. 323 ff.;
Gee and Hardy, No. 62.

Articles. They announced the abolition of certain holy days. The clergy were forbidden to encourage pilgrimages, as well as to extol any images, relics or miracles. Charity was recommended as better than gifts to images, and man's normal daily occupation more pleasing to God than any pilgrimages. The clergy were commanded to teach all people the Creed, the Lord's Prayer and the Ten Commandments. They were to provide for the education of scholars and for a Bible (in Latin and English) to be set up in every parish church. One-fortieth of the income was to go to the poor, one-fifth for the repair of their own churches and vicarages. The clergy were also ordered to teach and to administer the sacraments more regularly, to set an example of moral living and to give themselves to the study of the Scriptures. The second set of *Injunctions* (1538)[1] went further. The clergy were again enjoined to provide a large Bible in church, and teach its contents diligently. They were to expound the Creed, the Lord's Prayer and the Ten Commandments a little at a time every week, to make the laity informed communicants. They were to preach at least once a quarter, when they were to declare the gospel and to exhort the people to those works of charity, mercy and faith especially prescribed in the Scriptures. They were to warn the people of the danger of non-scriptural practices such as pilgrimages, the offering of money or candles to images or relics, kissing images, reciting beads and suchlike superstitions. To avoid idolatrous practices, candles and tapers were not to burn before images. A register of births, marriages and deaths was to be kept.

At the same time it was thought good to have a manual of instruction to place in the hands of the lower clergy and the literate laity. This book, *The Institution of a Christian Man* (1537)[2] was a compromise piece of work, the evangelicals cautiously not going further than the conservatives were likely to accept. It is more conservative even than the Ten Articles, comprising some two hundred pages of text in four parts. It consisted of an exposition of the Creed, the Seven Sacraments (though retaining the pre-eminence of the Three),[3] the Ten Commandments, the Lord's Prayer, the Ave Maria, Justification and Purgatory. Henry remained aloof from the book, saying he had no time to read it, though he allowed it to be printed by the royal printer. The book was issued finally on the bishops' authority, and was popularly called the *Bishops' Book*.

The book gave a modicum of satisfaction to the conservatives in that it added four more sacraments to the three of the Ten Articles. Nevertheless, it refrained from imposing transubstantiation, and exposed abuses on the grounds of being non-scriptural. Other important points arise in the book. In its discussion of the Creed it argues splendidly the nature of

[1] Bettenson, 325 ff.; Gee and Hardy, 63.
[2] Text in C. Lloyd, *Formularies of Faith in the Reign of Henry VIII* (1825), pp. 21–212.
[3] Baptism, Penance and the Sacrament of the Altar (see pp. 60, 200).

the true Catholic Church. The Church is the elect people of God pre-destined by Him, and to speak of the Catholic Church is to speak of it in these terms, against which neither sin nor heresy can prevail. The Church is one throughout the world, constituted of free and national churches. Sinners there will always be, but they are yet called of God and belong to the Church. The section clearly argues that apostolic succession is a matter of succession of faith and doctrine, not sees. The whole is a magnificent treatment of the doctrine which Luther himself would have endorsed. The Ave Maria is permitted, but only within the framework of a careful historical account of Luke 1, followed by a theology of redemption in which Mary's rôle is outlined. Bishops and clergy are directed to instruct their people that the Ave Maria is not a prayer but a hymn of praise partly to Christ and partly to the Virgin. The doctrine of justification is explained as meaning remission of sins, reconciliation to God and renovation in Christ. Ideas of merit are disclaimed, but good works are demanded as necessary. On Purgatory it is argued that a man may pray for the souls of the departed and commit them to God, and reference is made to the relief of pain, though on this point considerable reserve is expressed. At the same time the associated abuses of indulgences and masses for the dead at special shrines are rejected.

Not the least important of the results of the Ten Articles and the *Injunctions* was the permission to read the Bible and to hear it read in the mother tongue. Wyclif's translation from the Vulgate had been heavily proscribed hitherto. Fired by the magnificent achievement of Luther, Tyndale set his heart on giving to his own people a like translation out of the Hebrew and Greek originals.[1] Finding he was unable to further the work in England he went in 1524 to Germany, his spiritual home, never to return. Under difficulties he produced two editions of the English New Testament (1525/6 and 1534), one with heavy marginal notes. Warham and More violently opposed this work, the latter describing it as "mischievous perversion ... intended to advance heretical opinions." The book was publicly burnt though the work was of the highest scholarship, accurate and in noble language. Vile emissaries were sent to hunt Tyndale down like a beast. By treachery and cunning he was seized, imprisoned, privately tried, strangled and burned at Vilvorde in October, 1536. By this time Cranmer had petitioned for a Bible in the vernacular and the *Injunctions* (1536) of Cromwell ordered one for every church. Cranmer had persuaded Coverdale to undertake the work a year earlier but it was based largely on Luther's and Zwingli's translations and current Latin versions. It lacked the accuracy and nobility of Tyndale's proscribed text, but had a large sale owing to the express command of the *Injunctions*. Cranmer was aware of all this and instituted a further translation which he

[1] See F. F. Bruce, *The English Bible* (London, 1961), pp. 28 ff.

sent to Cromwell with the request for a licence pending the bishops' producing a better, which would never happen this side of Judgment Day, as Cranmer expressed it. The history of this text was that Tyndale had entrusted to one of his friends, John Rogers (later the first of the Marian martyrs), his unfinished Old Testament translation (of which the Pentateuch and Jonah had been published in 1530 and Joshua to 2 Chronicles were ready in manuscript) and his completed New Testament translation. Rogers took this material, filled it out from Coverdale's version, and printed it under the signature of Thomas Matthew. This Matthew Bible was largely Tyndale's own fine scholarly translation. The text was found to be a little too pointed and evangelical (for certain conservative men in the government), but when duly revised by Coverdale it received the royal assent, to be set up in every parish church. This "Great Bible" (so called from its folio size) was published in April, 1539. From the preface which Cranmer wrote for the second edition (1540) it has sometimes been known as "Cranmer's Bible."[1]

## 4. Relations with the Continental Reformers

There was at this time a general sympathy between the German and English reformers. Both had suffered under the papal yoke; both had been concerned to eradicate mediaeval abuses; both had begun to despair of a general council; both realized that every prince would have to "redress his own realm."

A certain obstacle existed in that Henry VIII had quarreled with Luther, but both seemed very willing for Melanchthon to take up the rôle of mediator. The English realized by now that the Lutherans had steered clear of fanaticism as well as of political tumult, and had shown themselves as conservative of truth as they were destructive of perversion and error. The first accredited envoy (1535) was Robert Barnes[2] and the end in view was a religious-political treaty. Luther was always critical, often caustic, for he knew that Henry sought approval only of his divorce and had no genuine religion in him. The English concentrated on the gentle Melanchthon. Bishop Foxe and Archdeacon Heath accompanied Barnes to Schmalkald. There was much agreement and the representatives journeyed to Wittenberg. The theologians found Foxe "had the manner of prelates" and thought little of his learning, though they were charmed with the courtesy and learning of Heath. Luther liked Barnes, whom he affectionately referred to as "Saint Robert."

[1] See J. F. Mozley, *William Tyndale* (London, 1937) and *Coverdale and his Bibles* (London, 1953).

[2] Marcus Loane, *Pioneers of the Reformation in England* (1964), pp. 47–90; N. S. Tjernagel, *The Reformation Essays of Dr. Robert Barnes* (London, 1963).

There was more to the wrecking of the conference than the suspicion of the Germans. Catherine died, with honour unstained, on January 7, 1536, so the urgency of the proceedings was removed in Henry's eyes. Further, the English delegation was unable to accept the Augsburg Confession as the religious basis of the alliance. Still more, Bishop Gardiner, then ambassador in France, persuaded Henry that such an alliance would entangle him in the affairs of the German nation and that he would have to sacrifice his sovereignty to the Emperor as head of the churches in Germany. Henry heeded these warnings.

Nevertheless, Henry wrote again to the German Lutheran princes meeting in 1538, and the outcome was a delegation of Lutheran divines travelling to England to persuade Henry of the imminent perils of the Church and of the urgency for Henry to further unity among reforming princes and to discourage other princes from supporting the papal cause.

When the embassy arrived they conferred with a mixed team of divines, and after two months had managed to put down the agreed fundamentals in writing. The conference was wrecked on the matter of abuses. Henry still clung to communion in one kind, to private propitiatory masses, and to clerical celibacy. Cranmer grew rather disturbed, particularly when his fellow participants were pressing for seven sacraments. Cranmer realized that the anti-Reformation party, with Henry's support, were gaining ground at court. Henry pressed the Germans to return the following year to go further into these differences of opinion, but when they did return it was to find Henry further than ever estranged from the Reformation, having allowed Gardiner to push through convocation and Parliament the "reactionary Six Articles" of 1539. Henry was now excommunicate and seemed anxious to assure Europe of his catholic orthodoxy. Luther's judgment was proved right in the event.

The failure of these negotiations was an unmitigated disaster for the cause of Reformation. Nevertheless, the content of these Thirteen Articles,[1] as they were called, represents what theological and spiritual men were thinking at that time. The negotiations were a political failure, but the theology of the Articles lived through into the Thirty-Nine Articles later. The document was not official. It was lost for some three hundred years and was later found among Cranmer's papers. It bears a very close resemblance to the Augustana.

## 5. Reaction in Henry's Last Years

The reaction mentioned in the previous paragraph but one enacted the Six Articles Act of 1539,[2] called "the bloody whip with six strings." These

---

[1] Text in Hardwick, *History of the Articles of Religion* (Cambridge, 1861), pp. 251 ff.
[2] Gee and Hardy, pp. 303–19; Bettenson, pp. 328 f.

articles were forced through Parliament by the king himself who stayed to see that they were passed. Cranmer, Latimer and others resisted, but were compelled to yield. It was now certain that there was not the slightest prospect of any theological reform as long as Henry reigned. Article 1 maintained transubstantiation; Article 2 maintained communion in one kind; Article 3 enforced celibacy; Article 4 upheld monastic vows; Article 5 defended private masses; Article 6 defended auricular confession. All these dogmas, with the exception of transubstantiation, had been discussed with the Lutheran theologians, and it was particularly painful to Melanchthon to learn of this unilateral declaration opposed to the evangelical theology. Melanchthon actually wrote a strong letter of censure to Henry. There were all kinds of provisions for commissioners and heresy hunters built into the act, but fortunately it lay dormant.

Part of this same reactionary process was the drafting of the *King's Book* in 1543,[1] a catholic revision of the *Bishops' Book* of 1537 in splendid Elizabethan prose. The King appointed a committee of eight bishops and twelve theologians "to go into the things which pertain to the education of a Christian man." The eventual book was more than a revision: whole sections of the *Bishops' Book* were omitted, much new work was introduced. It represents essentially the theology of the Six Articles, yet at times the book is plainly evangelical.

The section on (1) faith is Cranmerian in style and content and may well have been Cranmer's work. Faith is explained as the gift of God, as that inner persuasion of belief in God, fulfilling itself in hope in God's promises, a love towards God and obedience to Him.

The passage on (2) the Creed emphasizes that when it comes to the point of expressing belief as belief *in*, then it is only of God, Christ and the Holy Spirit that we may use that term. It carefully explains Christ's work for man's redemption, and though it describes Christ as the only Mediator it yet concedes intercessions of the departed as effective. In the same context there is a splendidly expressed section on the doctrine of the Church. Here the Church is defined as the elect of God and distinguished by its ministry of word and sacrament. It is argued that the churches of other lands may have their own kind of ministry, order and government and yet still be part of the Catholic Church: nor are they compelled to acknowledge the Pope to retain that title. Catholic unity is described as a unity of scriptural and apostolic doctrine maintained by the Holy Spirit. All Christian people should obey their own Christian kings and princes as governors of their own particular church. The communion of saints is interpreted as the communion of the altar, though it is conceded that a saint is one called of God.

[1] Text in Lloyd, 221. See also modern edition by T. A. Lacey, *The King's Book* (S.P.C.K., 1932).

(3) The Seven Sacraments are taught. Baptism receives the generally accepted treatment. Penance is taught as meaning the offering of priestly absolution after the normal course of contrition, confession, satisfaction. The position is carefully safeguarded that man's satisfaction does not earn him forgiveness, though it indicates a willingness to show penitence. On the sacrament of the altar, transubstantiation is defended, as well as communion in one kind and fasting before reception. On matrimony, the priests are excepted. As for Orders, their necessity is maintained, and the ministrations of a wicked priest are not invalidated on the grounds of his wickedness. The claims of the Pope as head of Christendom are rejected on the grounds of being without patristic, conciliar or scriptural support. In this connection the temporal power of the Pope was denied as belonging to the secular prince. Confirmation is defended as apostolic, and Extreme Unction on the same grounds.

There then follows an exposition of (4) the Ten Commandments and (5) the Lord's Prayer. This is followed by an exposition of (6) the Ave Maria on the same lines as the *Bishops' Book*. (7) Free will is defended in the way that Erasmus defended it in his argument with Luther, though it is expressly stated that without the help of grace it cannot please God. Considerable changes are made in the section on (8) justification. Justification is interpreted as the making righteous on turning to God: it requires man's co-operation. It demands belief, repentance for sin, trust in the work of Christ, amendment of life and baptism as setting man in the first state. To fall into mortal sin subsequently requires penance to restore the former justification now lost. The section dismisses "the vain trust of predestination" and the assurance of election, and condemns fanaticism and speculation. It goes on to argue the necessity of good works alongside faith, and plainly denies justification by faith alone.

There then follows a section on (9) good works. These are described as of two kinds: the works and fruits of righteousness, and the works of penance which come of grace and attain justification. Good works are defended as not derogatory to grace, though the specifically religious good works of monks and nuns are criticized.

Finally (10) prayer for departed souls is defended, though warning is given against abuses, and all mention of purgatory disallowed. In this respect this article was more Lutheran than had been the corresponding article in the *Bishops' Book*.

One further development on the subject of formularies remains, Cranmer's Litany of 1544. He depended on the Sarum Litany, Luther's Litany of 1529 and the diaconal Litany of the Liturgy of St. John Chrysostom. This Litany is essentially the same as it appears in the Book of Common Prayer of 1549 and subsequent books, except for two important changes: the removal in 1549 of the three clauses invoking the saints;

the removal in 1559 of the clause relating to "the tyranny of the Bishop of Rome and all his detestable enormities."

The closing years of Henry's reign were marked by great social and political unrest as well as by a reaction against Cranmer and Reformation principles. Nevertheless, Henry supported Cranmer all along, and at the end it was Cranmer he sent for on his death-bed in 1547.

# CHAPTER XII

# THE REIGN OF EDWARD VI, 1547-53

THE HONOURABLE GENTLEMEN SITTING AT TRENT ARE SAID TO HAVE experienced a lively joy when they heard of the death of Henry VIII. Their joy was unseemly and injudicious. They did not realize that a vast part of Christendom was groaning for reformation, nor did they realize that Henry was no reformer. Henry had been against theological reformation and had merely sought catholicism without the Pope. His death, as far as England was concerned, gave an immense relief to the progressive forces, and released a movement the strength of which none had realized. Supported by an evangelical king and a reforming government, the natural impetus of the movement proved almost too fast in the event.

The man most responsible was Thomas Cranmer. In addition to his refurbishing the Church in England with a sound evangelical theology he resisted two movements: Roman corruptions and Puritanical fads. His pastoral kindness and gentle tolerance earned him much criticism for weakness and indecision, little of it just. His enemies called him Lutheran, and quite certainly his sympathies lay with Luther. Then so did those of all the pioneers of the Reformation in England, Frith, Barnes, Rogers, Bradford, and of all the masters, Bilney, Tyndale, Latimer, Ridley.

Yet when we are discussing the part these theologians played in the Reformation in England, we need to remind ourselves of the predominant part taken by the secular power, king, privy council and Parliament. This may seem regrettable to us in the twentieth century, but in its historical context it was unavoidable, even necessary. The Privy Council, as executors of the boy king, ordered all bishops to take out new licences to ensure their loyalty; authorized the Book of Homilies, a splendid evangelical work largely written by Cranmer; ordered the Paraphrases of Erasmus to be set up in churches; issued Injunctions whereby preaching and teaching the Bible was enjoined, church services were to be reorganized, the authority of the Pope replaced by the authority of the King. At this point Gardiner, Bishop of Winchester, and Bonner, Bishop of London, resisted and were imprisoned. Convocation (1547) revised canon law, ordered communion in both kinds, legalized the marriage of clergy, dissolved chantries, ruled the destruction of images, issued a new communion service, and regularized experimental services. In these matters the hand of Cranmer is clear. His new order of communion was a compromise designed to carry along with him the bishops of the old learning and not to lose them. This was strongly influenced by Lutheran experiments at liturgical reform. Parliament passed appropriate legislation: it enacted the repeal of Henry's Treason Acts, his Statute of Proclamation authorizing the Six Articles, heresy laws, the *congé d' élire*[1] system; it dissolved the chantries to found grammar schools and hospitals; it enacted the abolition of holy water, ashes, candles, palms and the like and the destruction of all images. It set up a commission to study and make ecclesiastical laws. The product of their labour, *Reformatio Legum*, remained in manuscript until 1571 and never received Parliamentary authorization.[2] It set up a commission to draw up a new Ordinal, wherein there were three orders, bishops, priests and deacons, and the stress was laid on the preaching and pastoral responsibilities. It further passed the Act of Uniformity (1549), legalizing the First Prayer Book of Edward VI, a book worked out on the principles of simplifying the services, holding them in English, basing them on Scripture and primitive use (the whole of the New Testament was read three times a year, the Old Testament once), one single usage throughout the country, the services to be congregational, the mass to be abolished. Instead of making for uniformity and peace, it made for unrest and rebellion. There was a rebellion of Devon and Cornish men (who knew no English) who wanted the restoration of the Six Articles and communion once a year in one kind and a general restoration of the old ways.

It was at this time, following the Interim of 1548 whereby Charles sought to bring religious matters in Germany under control (Luther now being dead, and the Lutheran princes defeated in war), that there was an influx of Protestant refugees. There was Martin Bucer, the Strasbourg reformer, a moderate Lutheran and a great ecumenical figure. He strongly criticized the 1549 Prayer Book and played a part in Cranmer's production of the 1552 Prayer Book. There were Peter Martyr, an Italian from Basel, strongly Protestant; Fagius, the German Hebraist; à Lasco, a Pole and strongly Zwinglian; and Pollanus, who with his weavers settled in Glastonbury. These foreign Protestants kept up a close correspondence with continental reformers.

To return to Cranmer, who was the most representative as well as the most influential mind in the English reformation: in the first year of the new reign he published a catechism which was in fact the translation of a translation of Luther's Catechism made by Justus Jonas.[3] On only one major point of theology did Cranmer differ from Luther, namely the Eucharist. Cranmer believed in a real presence, but the presence was in

[1] Permission to elect a bishop. Henry had claimed this as of royal prerogative. This act substituted the system of letters patent in the place of the royal prerogative.
[2] Modern edition by E. Cardwell( Oxford, 1850).
[3] See p. 94.

the heart of the believer, not in the elements. He rejected transubstantiation and consubstantiation as a variant of it. He sought a presence that was spiritual and sacramental, not corporal and substantial.

Cranmer's guiding principle was a quest for Catholicity.[1] It is ironic that Cranmer's last speech was an answer given to the summons of his judges to recant and to profess his Catholicism.[2] Catholicism he did profess, but it was a profession his executioners never expected. To him Protestantism was a quest for Catholicism, for historical, theological and spiritual continuity with the Church that Jesus founded. Notwithstanding the real desire for a reformation emanating from king, privy council and Parliament, the work of the genuinely religious reforming movement was that of church leaders. It was neither a lay reaction against ecclesiastical superstition and graft, nor an outbreak of nationalist sectarianism or schism, but a conscious attempt to restore to the Church of the West the Catholicity now long lost. To the Reformers, and to the Fathers, Catholicity was a theological and historical concept before it was a geographical or statistical one: they saw the essence of Catholicity as faithfulness to the gospel word and sacramental usage as from apostolic days. Cranmer judged that owing to papal absolution, priestcraft, the theology of the mass and neglect of the Bible, the Church has lost its biblical, apostolic, patristic Catholicism, and that his task was to restore the norm.

In this quest for Catholicism his thinking made three important developments. First, he arrived at the view of Luther that the papal claims of jurisdiction were null and void and that the Scriptures vest all powers in the civil head. Secondly, he accepted Luther's view of faith and justification. His *Notes on Justification*[3] consist of a collection of biblical, patristic and scholastic citations justifying this doctrine. Thirdly, it was from this position he worked out his doctrine of the eucharistic presence, which he saw in the believer, not in the elements. He argued that the gospel is not about sacraments, but sacraments are about the gospel, in that they visibly declare the gospel preached and appropriated by faith.

His theological life's work was the verification of Luther's theology (with the clear and important exception of his eucharistic theology) and to seek to restore English Christianity to a reformed Catholicism. He re-established the authority of scripture: formulated the doctrine of salvation in Christ alone; provided a doctrine of the Church; furnished a fresh doctrine of the eucharist. His clear doctrine of justification by faith alone gave him a Christology in which purgatory and the doctrine of the Mass fell aside as a broken cartwheel. This same doctrine inspired his liturgical work. It was a Catholic who said of him, "The rite of 1552 . . . is the only

[1] See introductory essay to J. I. Packer (ed.), *Thomas Cranmer* (1964), pp. x ff.
[2] ibid., 327-40.
[3] P. S. Miscellaneous Writings, pp. 203 ff.

effective attempt ever made to give liturgical expression to the doctrine of 'justification by faith alone'."[1] It was he who mooted in 1552 a pan-Protestant synod at which the reformed churches of Europe should compose their differences and testify to their unity in a common confession. Melanchthon was not so animated, and this statesmanlike move towards oecumenical unity did not come to fruition. Cranmer's basic concerns were to find a catholic consensus of biblical understanding running down the ages; to think through the doctrine of salvation christologically – it was vital to Cranmer to study salvation and the sacraments in relation to Christ and His work, and to find a sound doctrine of the Spirit in theology and devotion so that the Church might avoid ecclesiastical authoritarianism, barren formalism, and superstitious sacramentalism. This is how Cranmer formulated his work in 1556:

> ... it was never in my mind to write, speak or understand, anything contrary to the most holy Word of God, or else against the holy Catholic Church of Christ; but purely and simply to imitate and teach those things only which I had learned of the Sacred Scripture and of the holy Catholic Church of Christ from the beginning; and also according to the exposition of the most holy and learned Fathers and Martyrs of the Church.[2]

With all the foreign theologians then in England, the pulse of Protestantism began to beat still faster. Ridley, then Bishop of London, acting *ultra vires*, removed all stone altars to set tables in their place, and this action served as a kind of signal for others to do likewise. Hooper, who had been with Bullinger at Zürich, was the first of the English Puritans to refuse to wear a surplice or to kneel at communion. In this atmosphere many of the Romanist bishops were deprived, Heath of Worcester, Day of Chichester, Tunstall of Durham, and Gardiner of Winchester. In 1550 Cranmer had published *A Defence of the True and Catholic Doctrine*[3] which showed no belief in the corporal presence. Gardiner had attacked Cranmer on this, and justified his own view as being in accordance with the 1549 book. This made a revision imperative, and with pressure from Bucer, Martyr, Calvin and Bullinger, and others, the 1552 Prayer Book appeared.

It is interesting that the Forty-Two Articles did not appear until as late as 1553.[4] The reason behind this apparent delay was that Cranmer had been seeking all along to formulate a General Confessional Statement which would unite reformed Europe, only secondarily a confessional statement for the reformed church in England. As early as 1539 Melanchthon had shown his readiness, and with the help and support of Bucer and Calvin,

---

[1] Dom Gregory Dix, *The Shape of the Liturgy* (London, 1945), p. 672.
[2] *Answer to Gardiner. Works*, IV. 126.
[3] P. S. *Writings*, i ff., and Packer, *op. cit.*, pp. 45–231.
[4] Hardwick, 289 ff.

Cranmer had high hopes of success. The scheme was brought to nought by the defeat of the Lutheran princes by Charles V, by the difficulties in which Melanchthon was set, as well as by the difficulties inherent in such a grandiose scheme. The whole venture was abandoned in the reign of Elizabeth.

The Forty-Two Articles were based on the Augsburg Confession and directed to meet the needs of the day. Since Edward had come to the throne the Church in England had been tormented by Anabaptists, Arians, Socinians and those "fantastical spirits" that had so tried Luther's patience. In addition there were the domestic controversies of vestments and traditions. It was to this climate the articles addressed themselves to establish a more "godly concord in certain matters of religion."

This is shown by a synopsis of the articles.

1. *Of faith in the Holy Trinity* is taken almost verbatim from the Augsburg Confession and is directed against anti-Trinitarianism.
2. *The Incarnation* is taken from the Augsburg Confession and is directed against Anabaptism.
3. *On going down to Hell,* an answer to another controversy.
4. *The Resurrection of Christ,* which asserts the proper manhood as well as the resurrection.
5. *The Sufficiency of Scripture* asserts the necessity of scriptural proof for every doctrine of the Church in reply to scholastic and Tridentine errors on the subject of "the Word unwritten." It provided a safeguard against fanatical inspiration on the one hand, and on the other hand against the prevailing error which argued that each and every church usage must have clearly deducible Scriptural evidence before it could be validated.
6. *On Reverence for the Old Testament* – against the Anabaptists.
7. Accepts *The Three Creeds*.
8. On *Original or Birth Sin* against Pelagianism, but also directed against scholastic errors and Tridentine formulation.
9. *Of Free Will* – without grace a man cannot do good.
10. *Of Grace* – against a false doctrine of predestination.
11. *Justification* – as in the Augsburg Confession.
12. *Works before Justification* – to exclude merit (similarly Article 13).
14. *The Sinlessness of Christ* – impugns the Romish doctrine of the immaculate conception of the Virgin.
15. *Sin against the Holy Ghost* directed against Anabaptist theology and developed in Article 16.
17. *Of Predestination and Election.*
18. *Salvation in Christ Only* – directed against the schismatics.
19. *Defence of the Commandments* – directed against the Anabaptists.

20. *Of the Church*, taken from the Augsburg Confession and directed against the Romanist doctrine of Infallibility.
21. *The authority of the Church* explained as a witness to and a keeper of Scripture.
22. Argues the right of civil powers to convene councils, and states that councils may err.
23. *Purgatory, images and relics* are denounced as follies and figments.
24. Ministers must be lawfully called. Based on the Augsburg Confession and directed against Anabaptist lawlessness.
25. Services to be held in the mother tongue.
26. Sacraments: The sacraments are limited to two and their relationship to faith argued. Zwinglianism is rebutted.
27. The validity of a sacrament is not impaired by the unfitness of a minister.
28. Baptism: Defends a high view of baptism and retains infant baptism.
29. The Lord's Supper: Zwinglianism is avoided and transubstantiation condemned.
30. Christ's perfect sacrifice maintained in contradistinction to the repeated sacrifices of the mass.
31. The celibacy of the clergy is condemned.
32, 33. Disciplines and usages in the Church which had become contentions are discussed.
34. Commends the Homilies.
35. Commends the Prayer Book.
36. Of civil magistrates. Directed against papal supremacy and in support of civil authority.
37, 38. Directed against revolutionary spirits.
39-42. Directed against the Anabaptists.

The young king now lay dying. Northumberland saw the grave consequences of this event and made desperate schemes to persuade the young king to alter the succession his father had determined of Mary and Elizabeth. To effect this he arranged the marriage of his fourth son with Lady Jane Grey, an accomplished and godly young lady of Protestant persuasions, and with some claim to the throne in that her grandmother had been Henry VIII's sister. Northumberland persuaded Edward that Mary must never be allowed to succeed to the throne for she would change the religion and laws and set a Catholic foreigner on the throne as her consort. His fears were justified but his schemes were not. Lawyers and advisers argued strongly against the treasonable scheme. Neither council nor archbishop would consent. Only after the personal pressure of the king himself were the signatories persuaded to append their signatures. But the country was sick of intrigue and welcomed Mary, who had judiciously taken flight. When insurrection had broken out in the west under Sir Peter Carew, in Kent under Sir Thomas Wyatt, in Wales under Sir James Croftes and in the Midlands under the Duke of Suffolk, Mary was advised to adopt a policy of severity. Among the victims was the innocent Lady Jane, who had been forced into treason and usurpation. She had to witness her husband taken to the scaffold and his headless body brought back on a cart the same morning as she was taken to tread that bloody road. She was an innocent victim of desperate intrigue, high-principled and intelligent, made of the stuff of martyrs. Her death was an omen of still darker days to come.

# CHAPTER XIII

## THE MARIAN REACTION, 1553–8

THE COUNTRY WAS IN ECONOMIC DISTRESS, THE CHURCH HAD BEEN plundered, the universities were declining, politicians and courtiers were scheming rather than governing. Disquiet at this general background, the conservatism of the nation, economic distress and the dislike of foreign Protestants had all contributed to bring Mary to the throne amid popular applause. Would Mary bring peace again to a distracted church and a troubled land?

There were at this time three parties in the country: the Roman Catholics, the Protestants, and a middle party which was anxious to restore Catholicism provided the Pope was kept out. This party preferred Rome either to Wittenberg or Geneva, if there had to be a choice, and it was this party that enabled Mary to succeed to the throne. But she betrayed them, for though she might be described as the most attractive of the Tudors, she was an intolerant Catholic determined to restore Roman Catholicism to England. She released the imprisoned prelates, and allowed the foreign Protestants to leave the country unharmed. Many English Protestants accompanied them. Cranmer stood firm, as did Latimer, Ridley, Coverdale and Hooper.

The reaction was in two stages. First, the Edwardian legislation was repealed[1] and religion restored legally to the position left by Henry at his death in 1547. The Protestant bishops Cranmer, Latimer, Ridley and Coverdale were deprived and imprisoned, new bishops consecrated and the deprived Romanists Gardiner, Heath, Bonner and Day reinstated. Married clergy too were deprived. A disputation was held at Oxford on the subject of the mass when Cranmer, Latimer and Ridley were condemned. In 1554 the queen married Philip of Spain, and they were proclaimed king and queen of England.

The second stage began with the repeal by Parliament (November, 1554–January, 1555) of all laws enacted against the Roman See since 1529 and the revival of all the mediaeval laws against heresy. Cardinal Pole was brought back from Rome, and Parliament as a body received from him absolution when he received the kingdom "again into the unity of our Mother the Holy Church." The only limit to the tide of reaction was that the possessors of monastic lands were allowed to keep them.

In March, 1554, the Queen issued a series of *Injunctions*[1] to all bishops

---

[1] Gee and Hardy, 73.          [1] Gee and Hardy, 74.

giving detailed instructions to bring the Church again to the state it was in before the reforms of Edward VI. Bonner's Articles of Inquiry[1] of the same time, addressed to the clergy as well as laity, raised the minutest questions with the evident intention of restoring the mediaeval ceremonies and customs in detail. The laity received these moves with ominous discontent. Meanwhile the Visitations had been putting all this legislation into effect, and many of the reforming bishops and divines found themselves in prison, some under tolerable conditions, others under the most loathsome conditions of filth and famine. Ferrar, Hooper and Coverdale, Rogers, Bradford, Philpot, Crome, Saunders and others contrived to produce a signed confessional statement, drawn up almost certainly by Bradford. The document argued that they were being condemned for holding doctrine in accordance with Scripture, the Creeds, and the fathers; they affirmed justification by faith alone; they sought for a liturgy in the mother tongue; they disowned the invocation of saints, purgatory, and masses for the dead; they held the two sacraments and disavowed the doctrine of transubstantiation.

Cardinal Pole then ordered the prisoners to be tried for heresy. John Rogers, the translator of the Bible, was the first to go to the stake. The common English people did not like this; Rogers was cheered to his death. The envoy of Charles V warned Pole of the dangerous folly of this procedure. Persecutors always overreach themselves. Hooper, Saunders, Taylor, Ferrar and others lengthened the line of this noble army of martyrs. Ridley, the scholar, and Latimer, the preacher (now an old man), were proceeded against and burnt on October 16, 1555, in Broad Street, Oxford, a painful scene witnessed by Cranmer from the tower of his prison. Ridley, who in good conscience had spent the previous night in quiet rest and peace with God suffered unspeakable agonies owing to the dampness of the wood. It was at that moment that the elderly Latimer, a preacher even in his death, uttered words which belong to every schoolboy's repertoire: "Be of good comfort, Master Ridley, and play the man; we shall this day light such a candle, by God's grace, in England, as I trust shall never be put out."

Cranmer, being an archbishop, was amenable only to papal jurisdiction, and when he had been tried in St. Mary's Church, Oxford, a month prior to the martyrdom of Ridley and Latimer, it was before a papal commission on charges of adultery (he had been twice married), perjury (for breaking his oath to the Pope) and heresy (in denying the doctrine of transubstantiation).

Cranmer refused to acknowledge the jurisdiction of his judges but submitted to royal authority only. Back in prison he wrote to his queen on the scandal and degradation of appealing to an authority outside the realm to

[1] J. Strype (ed.), *Ecclesiastical Memorials* (Oxford, 1822), III. ii. 217.

try one of her own subjects. He followed this with a second, bolder letter declaring that Mary had broken her oath to maintain the laws, liberties and customs of this realm in maintaining the authority of the Pope. The charge of perjury he dismissed. His loyalty was to his country, not to the Pope, and Mary was in a contradictory position. The trial meanwhile was reported to Rome where the decree was promulgated that he was to be deposed, degraded, and punished as a heretic. Pole was set in his room a week later and Cranmer's effigy was burnt in Rome. When Cranmer heard the sentence he drew up an appeal to a General Council[1] on the lines of Luther's example.

In February, 1556, Bonner (Bishop of London) and Thirlby (Bishop of Ely) were commissioned with the task of degradation. Bonner carried out his commission with relish and bitter mockery, but Thirlby, to his credit, was much distressed at such distasteful and unnecessary brutality. Cranmer's mind must have been full of another occasion when soldiers mocked another, with sceptre reed and crown of thorns and robe of scarlet. Now a degraded layman (only in the eyes of his accusers and judges), the sensitive Cranmer went through the long humiliating indignity of degradation. Set up before them in mock robes and vestments and insignia, he was divested of each in turn. First his seven insignia were stripped from him; next, pall, mitre, crozier; everything was taken from him that man could take. The things that mattered were beyond their reach. Bonner taunted and mocked. But the last words are not with the Bonners of this world. The worst was yet to come, after he had been handed over to the secular authorities for execution.

In prison a long and carefully prepared softening up process of mental torture was inflicted on their condemned victim. Cranmer was given to understand that a measure of recantation could well free him from his imminent peril, and that he might be spared to heal the wounds of a divided Church. A series of recantations was imposed on him by authority of his queen, an authority he had argued as ultimate. The first four recantations were of a general kind, and Cranmer could sign them with a good conscience, confident that the world already knew how he interpreted such generalities. But the fifth and sixth recantations were grave confessions: Luther was anathematized, the Pope restored together with transubstantiation, the seven sacraments and purgatory. Mary, Pole and Bonner knew they could destroy the Reformers more easily than the Reformation, and their trump card in this gamble was to show the utter worthlessness of the movement in the ignominious collapse of its leaders. They never for a moment thought of sparing Cranmer. At the moment of their apparent victory God moved, and the frail body and broken spirit of Cranmer rose to the heights to which only God can raise a man, and in the few

[1] P.S., *Works*, ii. 445–56.

moments of his last act and last words Cranmer destroyed for ever in these shores the power of Romanism and made England a Protestant nation. It was a cruel irony that the man who had pleaded the cause of the little princess Mary to her father Henry VIII should be burnt by her when queen.

March 21, 1556, was fixed for the day of his burning. Cranmer was taken to St. Mary's Church, Oxford, and made to stand on a platform opposite the pulpit to hear from Dr. Cole what is generally described as "the sermon". It makes odious reading today as Cole sought to justify before God the deeds of which history can never acquit him and his associates. The climax, all carefully rehearsed, was to call Cranmer himself to testify to the people his conversion to Catholicism.[1]

Cranmer prayed at some length that God would have mercy on him, closing with the Lord's Prayer. He then addressed the people and exhorted them: first, that they let not the love of this present world blind them to the reality of the eternal world; secondly, that they obey the King and Queen as ministers of God; thirdly, that they give themselves to brotherly love in the country; fourthly, that the rich should help the poor.

Then Cranmer turned to his own condition, standing on the brink of eternity as he was. This was not the hour for dissembling. He confessed his faith in God, and in every article of the catholic faith, and every word of the Old and New Testaments. He continued

> And now I come to the great thing that so much troubleth my conscience, more than anything that ever I did or said in my whole life; and that is the setting abroad of writings contrary to the truth . . .[2]

So far all proceedings were running according to plan. He was now expected to conclude with a declaration of the Queen's just title to the crown and a retraction of his books and writings on the sacrament of the altar. But he continued:

> which [writings] now here I renounce and refuse, as things written with my own hand, contrary to the truth which I thought in my heart, and written for fear of death, and to save my life, if it might be; and that is, all such bills and papers which I have written or signed with my hand since my degradation; wherein I have written many things untrue. And forasmuch as my hand offered, writing contrary to my heart, my hand shall first be punished therefore; for, may I come to the fire, it shall be first burned.
>
> And as for the Pope, I refuse him, as Christ's enemy and Antichrist, with all his false doctrine.
>
> And as for the sacrament, I believe as I have taught in my book against the Bishop of Winchester; the which my book teacheth so true a doctrine of the sacrament, that it shall stand at the last day before the judgment of God, where the papistical doctrine, contrary thereto, shall be ashamed to show her face.

[1] Hillerbrand, pp. 352 ff.
[2] P. S. *Works and Writings*, 224.

"Here the standers by were all astonished. . . . It was a world to see the doctors beguiled of so great a hope . . . never was cruelty more notably or better in time deluded and deceived."[1] An uproar broke out. Cranmer was pulled down from the stage. He virtually ran to the fire with the Spanish friars shrieking at him to make one last recantation. These he ignored. At the scaffold he stood in his shirt barefooted and bareheaded on that cold, wet March day, as steadfast as the stake to which he was chained. He shook hands with a few bystanders. When the wood was kindled and began to burn he put his right hand into the flames and unflinching, watched it burn first, and in that heroic deed gave voice to his undying faith. With the words of Stephen, "Lord Jesus, receive my spirit," he went forth from this life with the dignity of the ancient martyrs.

Had Cranmer the robustness of Luther his death might have been less eloquent. Here was no Hercules triumphing over supernatural difficulties, but a man of human frailty, gentle, forgiving, peace-loving, considerate and merciful, elderly, non-dramatic, hardly the human stuff of heroes. Yet his frail humanity paradoxically revealed the strength of his cause. When men saw the fine features of that noble head, the sad eyes with tears standing in them and the long venerable white beard of their aged and scholarly primate, his Christ-like demeanour, his final heroism shone the brighter for it was seen to be not his own. He who had been the only man in the realm to oppose Henry with courage enough to plead for Princess Mary, for Thomas Cromwell, for those who even now stood as his accusers, had none to plead his cause. The candle that Latimer and Ridley lit was now a beacon, and that beacon no man can put out. It is the bush that burns but is never consumed (Ex. 3:2). When a man stops and turns aside to study this beacon he will hear God call him – by name (Ex. 3:4). Here is the Great Light – the subject and content of this book.

A long succession of burnings followed Cranmer's, three hundred in all, not counting those miserable, captive, nameless victims whom famine and disease claimed ingloriously. Mary restored all property confiscated by the Crown to the Church and restored the "first fruits" of benefices to the papacy. She attempted to restore the monastic institutions but failed dismally. She reintroduced the pilgrimages to shrines, but too many of the populace had been disabused of their purpose for them to be re-established. The new Pope, Paul IV (1555–9) made things difficult for Mary, for, apart from his own narrow anti-Protestant complex and his maniacal bad temper, he had a personal hatred for Philip her husband, and a dislike of Pole, her archbishop.

Mary died on November 17, 1558, wretched and unhappy, execrated by her people. Her life had been bitter and tragic. Daughter of a great king and born of one of Europe's noblest princesses, at one time the bride-

[1] From John Foxe's account in *History of the Acts and Monuments of the Church* (1563).

elect of the Emperor, she was a young lady of great beauty and colour. At the gentle age of seventeen her life was prematurely blighted – her father, her government, her country, set her aside as illegitimate. Twenty years of brooding on this in virtual exile could not be set aside when she was called to the throne at thirty-seven. She was already embittered, sallow, prematurely old with a harsh voice: only her dark and lovely eyes told the world of the beauty she once possessed. She loved her husband, but he grew tired of living with her. She yearned for children but none were given: so great was her longing that she interpreted the first symptoms of her final and fatal disease as conception, and actually prepared written announcements of the birth of a prince never even conceived. The Church to which she was utterly devoted seemed not to care, the Pope for whom she had given so much was indifferent. To the English people who but five short years ago had welcomed her back, and whom she genuinely loved, she was "Bloody Mary." All the troubles of herself and her nation she mistakenly imagined as the wrath of God inflicted on England for its faithlessness, a wrath she had sought to appease with martyrs' blood. The truth was other. Her sterile and disastrous reign, fortunately of short duration, was dogged by a myopic and obstinate wrongheaded passion to restore England to papal suzerainty. She was also foolishly obsessed with the fond fancy of her Spanish blood, disastrously determined to marry a Spaniard or nobody. It would be hard to conceive any policy more inappropriate at that hour in nationalist Tudor England. Mary crumbled among the ruins she had herself created. At the same hour Pole lay dying: he followed her to her death within twelve hours. It was a fitting close to a great tragedy. Catholic reaction was a total and ignominious failure.

England now needed a new monarch and a new archbishop: a fresh start for both Church and nation. All eyes turned to Elizabeth.

# CHAPTER XIV

# SCOTLAND: SAVIOUR OF THE REFORMATION

SO FAR WE HAVE SAID NOTHING OF EVENTS IN SCOTLAND. NOT THAT these were unimportant. On the contrary, Scotland was to prove the saviour of the Reformation in England, her one-time enemy. But before that story can be told we should go back a little in Scottish history and seek to relate these events to the story we have just been telling so that we can understand the mighty Scottish story in relation to England and her struggle.

Historians describe the Scotland of the early sixteenth century as a country four centuries behind the rest of Europe.[1] The authority of her kings had been too long weakened by a record of assassinations, infant regencies, intrigue, and baronial lawlessness. Her so-called Parliament was a feudal assembly with parties jockeying for power and was ineffectual in the one thing expected of it, just and stable constitutional legislation.[2] Her Church was wealthy and secularized, and more corrupt than anywhere else in Europe. Her numerous and idle clergy, "dumb dogs" and "idle bellies" as reforming men named them, had prepared a fertile seed-bed for the new pastors, men called of God, men sent with a biblical and evangelical theology in the power of the Holy Spirit. Nowhere did men feel more betrayed by those who should have been their ministers and pastors.[3]

But Scotland seems always to have been marked by a native ability as well as by a long history of belief in education. She was bound to break her captivity one day. This belief in education may well have come from the remarkable influence of the old Celtic Church, distinguished by its missionary zeal and educational fervour. There were in existence old Celtic ecclesiastical rules which expressly stated that it was as important to teach boys and girls to write and read as to dispense the sacraments. The Scottish student wandering in Europe was a well-known figure of the Middle Ages. Scottish students listened to Occam and Dubois, and when Lollardy was at its height great numbers were to be found in Oxford. No fewer than eighty-one attended lectures in Oxford in 1365.

Lollardy was brought from Oxford in this way and made progress in

---

[1] T. M. Lindsay, *History of the Reformation* (Edinburgh, 1907), II, p. 274.
[2] J. H. Burns, *The Political Background of the Reformation. Innes Review*, 1962, pp. 1 ff.
[3] Matthew Mahoney, *The Scottish Hierarchy 1513–65. Innes Review*, 1962, pp. 39 ff. See a fine, spirited account of this background in the Introduction to William Croft Dickinson, *John Knox's History of the Reformation* in Scotland (Edinburgh, 1949).

Scotland, according to the documents of the time.[1] (An English Lollard, James Reseby, was burnt at Perth in 1407.) This development attracted the attention of the Hussites in Bohemia, and one of their agents, Paul Craw, was seized and burnt at St. Andrews in 1433 on the grounds of denying transubstantiation, auricular confession, and prayers to departed saints. At his execution his mouth was stopped with a brass ball in case he preached to the bystanders. But the movement was not stamped out. There were Lollards in Kyle in 1491, and not long afterwards a Scots edition of the later Wycliffite Bible (John Purvey's version) was prepared by Murdoch Nisbet. The same spirit survived into the sixteenth century as the presses of Sir David Lindsay testify, and "the good and godly ballads" of the Wedderburns bear witness.

It was not until preachers began to come from Wittenberg and men had begun to study the writings of Luther and other reformers, together with the Scriptures, that the great evangelical themes of sin and salvation began to stir men's hearts. The east coast ports of Aberdeen, Leith, Dundee, and Montrose had traded with the Continent and in this way books and tracts began to seep into the life of the country. In 1525 the authorities had begun to express alarm at the infiltration of Luther's books and views into Aberdeen. It was apparent to all that the new movement was stirring Scotland, particularly when it was learned that Tyndale's Bibles were being smuggled in by merchants. By 1535 an Act was passed prohibiting all but clergy to possess heretical books: those who had them were to hand them over to the authorities. Several Lutherans were burnt.

The first Scottish martyr was Patrick Hamilton, the young and well born Abbot of Ferne, who had studied at Paris and Louvain. He was studying in Paris in 1520 when Luther's writings were causing such a stir, but when he returned to Scotland with this theology he found he was compelled to flee the country from his accusers. He seems to have gone to Wittenberg and thence to Marburg certainly, where he was present at the opening of Philip of Hesse's new Evangelical University (1527) actually drafting the theses of the first academic disputation. He returned to Scotland to testify against the Church of his native land. His fresh and true theology met with instant success, to the jealousy and anger of the ecclesiastics. The latter enticed him to St. Andrews and left him unmolested for a month to preach in church and dispute in the University. Suddenly one morning he was arrested and tried in the Cathedral, and by midday found himself tied to a stake to die a lingering and cruel death (February 27, 1528).

"The reek of Patrick Hamilton infected many."[2] He converted one of his accusers, Alexander Alane (or Aless, latinized Alesius), who eluded his captors and escaped to the Continent to become the friend of Melanchthon.

---

[1] Lindsay II. 276 f.          [2] Knox, I, 18.

There was a succession of martyrs: Henry Forrest (1533), David Stratten and Norman Gourlay (1534), Simpson, Forrester, Keillor, Beverage, Forret, Russell, and Kennedy (1539). George Buchanan managed to escape from prison. John MacAlpine escaped to Copenhagen to become a professor of theology there.[1] In 1540 the Scots Parliament and Privy Council came to the rescue of the Church by a series of enactments, proof of the widespread nature of the growing theological revolt. Enactments were made ordering the reverence of the Virgin, prayers for the prosperity of the King, the triumph of the catholic faith and the loyalty of the people to the Church. Prayers were to be made to the saints, and to impugn papal authority by word or deed meant confiscation of goods and death. Images were to be left in churches. No heretic, even repentant, was to have any office of any kind. Anybody who assisted a heretic would merit the utmost severity of the law. Even so, the new movement was not blocked.[2]

These reforming forces were checked more by the long-standing hatred of England than any other factor. The more anti-Catholic Henry VIII became, the more Catholic grew his nephew James V. His catholic leanings made him dependent on the clergy who failed him in his hour of need and brought about his premature death on December 14, 1542. He left his infant daughter Mary (whose mother was Mary of Lorraine),[3] to succeed him when she was six days old. Scotland again had the tragedy of an infant sovereign, a sovereign Henry was planning to marry to Edward, his own infant son. Many Scotsmen thought this a sensible way forward to bring unity to the two peoples, but David Beaton, the dissolute but clever Cardinal Archbishop of St. Andrews, led the party for Scotland with the Papacy against this policy of England with the Reformation.

At first the English party prevailed. The nobles elected the Earl of Arran (a remote cousin of the Queen) as regent (January 3, 1543), and Beaton was imprisoned. The Governor selected two reformers as his chaplains, modified the measures against heretics and permitted the reading of the Bible. At this juncture Henry VIII blustered in, but all his schemes of bringing about the marriage, getting rid of Cardinal Beaton, and annexing Scotland, carried out with pillage and bloodshed, came to nought. Arran could not hold out against Rome and Beaton, who in 1543 became Chancellor of Scotland. Beaton revoked the reforming policy and set up again all the old mediaeval legislation. Persecution revived, the ground

[1] His surname was latinized (by Melanchthon) as Maccabaeus. His wife, Agnes Macheson, was the sister of Coverdale's wife; at MacAlpine's request, the Danish King persuaded Mary Tudor in 1555 to release Coverdale from prison (see p. 216) and allow him to leave England for Denmark.

[2] Lindsay, II, 281.

[3] Also called Mary of Guise. The house of Guise was a cadet branch of the house of Lorraine. Mary was daughter to Claude, first Duke of Guise, whose father and eldest brother were Dukes of Lorraine.

gained was lost, and the little queen was sent to France to ensure a catholic education that would remain with her for life.

Yet it should be seen that, though the Reformation was losing ground in courts of queens and prelates and among the nobility, it was gaining steadily and certainly in the spiritual quickening of the common people, a not unexpected pattern for evangelical theology. George Wishart, who had fled from persecution in 1538, now returned from the Continent in 1543, to preach the gospel, but eventually he was imprisoned and tried by Beaton and condemned to the stake on March 1, 1546.[1] He had been often defended by the then unknown John Knox who used to stand by Wishart's side with a two-edged sword in his hand ready to cut anybody in two who interfered with the preaching. He would have stood by his side to the end but Wishart had other plans. The reforming party counter attacked within three months, raided the castle of St. Andrews and slew Archbishop Beaton. The castle was held by the rebels whom the government failed to dislodge. John Rough the reformer was recalled, and John Knox called to preach, an invitation he accepted reluctantly. Knox was a taciturn, dour Scot with no ambition to play a leading rôle, yet his first sermon showed that he was to be the reformer of Scotland. He at once outshone all that Wishart had been, and men feared for the future of the reformer, now a marked man.

What the government could not effect, the French fleet did. The walls of the city were pounded to rubble until the castle had no choice but to surrender. The conditions were that the rebels would be spared, though they would be exiled from their native land. The promises were broken and Knox with others found himself condemned to the galleys. For nineteen months he endured this revolting cruelty. Chained to a seat with the vilest malefactors he spent night and day unreleased, exposed to all weathers and the overseer's whip. Eventually the good offices of the English government obtained their release and Knox returned to Edward's England on April 7, 1549, to become eventually the great preacher of the Reformation and indeed its organizer in Scotland. He flourished under the new régime of Edward VI and actually declined episcopal office in it. He doubtless influenced Cranmer towards a reformed position in the Prayer Book of 1552. When Mary Tudor came to the throne, and most other reformers had fled the country, he firmly stayed in London and had the lion-hearted audacity to rebuke the crowds rejoicing at her entry into the capital.

Save for a ten-month visit to Scotland from September, 1555, to July, 1556, during which he spread reformation doctrine and practice, Knox spent the duration of Mary's reign on the Continent, with Calvin in

---

[1] See *The Condemnation and Martyrdom of George Wishart* in John Knox's *History*, Appendix III (Vol. II, pp. 233 ff.).

Geneva and with Bullinger in Zürich, and possibly a period in Germany. He learnt a great deal from his friends, and away from Britain began to see, more clearly than those embroiled in the events, that the future of the Reformation lay in a Protestant England united with a Protestant Scotland. By December, 1557, the Protestants of Scotland had organized themselves into what might be called a confederation to maintain the Word of God and His Church and to seek ministers of Christ's gospel and sacraments to serve His people, the first of the famous covenants.[1] This was in the great Scottish tradition but the covenant was now charged with a fresh theology, and with fresh power. The confederates wrote to Knox at Geneva, as well as to Calvin, urging the return of Knox to his home country. They resolved that in the parishes the Book of Common Prayer should be used and the Bible read, but further made the decision to allow house churches, where the Word of God would be preached and sound doctrine taught, until the government granted the Church the freedom of a true, pastoral and preaching ministry. These steps caused considerable alarm to the Queen Mother, who urged the Archbishop of St. Andrews to take steps to defeat these plans.

No man ever defeated God. The men who accepted the Reformation in Scotland adopted for themselves the word Congregation, an exact parallel of the Continental usage. The "Congregation of Jesus Christ" (the reformed Church) now stood over against the "Congregation of Satan" (the Catholic Church). This evangelical community or assemblage ordered themselves into a Church, elected leaders, and promised loyalty and obedience to them.[2] They then sought recognition of this emergency "organization" to allow themselves to worship publicly as well as to reform their wicked clergy. Not finding satisfaction, they requested the suspension of the heresy laws until a General Council be called and petitioned Parliament for the right to go ahead with the Reformation as they thought fit, adding that since the reformation of abuses in religion was right and proper, any outbreaks of violence would be blamed on those who refused reformation.

Meanwhile Knox had responded to the appeal of the confederates but was much distressed on his return journey to Scotland to find awaiting him in Dieppe letters counselling him that he must delay his return as Mary Tudor was doing all she could to destroy the Reformation in England, and Queen Mary of Guise was compelling the Archbishop of St. Andrews to do the same in Scotland. He sat down and wrote his notorious *First Blast of the Trumpet against the Monstrous Regiment of Women* (1558),[3] a book that permanently damaged his career and effectiveness as a reformer.

---

[1] J. H. S. Burleigh, *A Church History of Scotland* (London, 1960), pp. 134, 161; Lindsay, II, 289.

      [2] Lindsay II. 290.        [3] *Works*, Vol. IV, 349 ff.

Mary Tudor died, but when Elizabeth Tudor read it she felt that it applied to her, too, and never forgave the forthright Scot for his vehement *Blast*.

When Mary Tudor was dead Knox returned home to his native land early in 1559 to find the Queen opposing the Lords of the Congregation. He hurried from Edinburgh to Dundee, now a stronghold of reformed theology. The Queen ordered the preachers to cease and to appear before her. They retaliated with a letter from "The Professors of Christ's Gospel in the Realm of Scotland" (May 6, 1559).[1] The letter stated the reformers' principles and is worth looking at in some detail. They begin by saying that they expected of the Queen that she would maintain the preaching of the Word and true worship, would defend Christian men, and destroy all idolatry, abomination and superstition in the realm. They regretted she had done the reverse, and had thereby put herself in the position of usurping a false power, in confusing civil and spiritual jurisdiction. They questioned her authority to inhibit men clearly sent by God to preach God's Word. Believing men must disobey such mistaken authority, but they were not thereby guilty of sedition and rebellion, nor were they disobedient subjects. They would go forward in their reformed theology and would never return to the abomination of the old religion under any circumstances. Finally they professed due obedience to her, praying that God would lead her by His Spirit in the way acceptable to Him.

The people were now rising up against the Queen Regent and her prelates, and in the skirmishes the people suffered most, for she was supported by crack French troops. A regrettable feature of these skirmishings was the destruction of images and the like in the churches, an activity which did much harm to the Protestant cause (as Luther had seen forty years earlier). Neither preacher nor magistrate could restrain the "rascal multitude,"[2] and in this situation, the truth which Knox had sensed in his exile, namely that the Reformation could be secured only by Scotland and England together, received convincing proof. Others, too, were seeing that both countries should free themselves from the intrigues and toils of foreign potentates, find a common friendship, and unite on the basis of a reformed religion. The next few years were critical, critical even for Europe.

The issue was this. If Knox could prevail in Scotland and Cecil keep England Protestant, then the Reformation was won for all Britain, and a new Protestant united nation born. If Knox were defeated and Scotland kept for France and Romanism, and if Mary Queen of Scots could establish her claim to the throne of England, then the Reformation was lost to all Britain and Romanism would prevail. Men of vision saw too that the struggle for Protestantism in Scotland epitomized the struggle of Europe. If reaction triumphed in Scotland, it would then triumph in

[1] Hay Fleming, *The Scottish Reformation*, p. 44.　　　[2] A favourite phrase of Knox's.

England. If Britain relapsed to Romanism then the Reformation would be crushed in the Netherlands and in Germany. Cecil needed Knox and Knox needed Cecil: both knew they needed each other, for both saw that a Scotland controlled by the Guises spelt the death of the Reformation.

Yet in 1559 the situation was by no means favourable to the Protestants nor the outcome certain. The Kings of France and Spain had concluded at Cateau-Cambrésis (April, 1559) a treaty binding them to crush the Protestantism of Europe, a treaty which gave great disquiet to the Prince of Orange, who in his turn, determined to free his fatherland of the Spaniard. A fresh impetus was given to the movement by Henry II, prodded by the Duke of Guise, the Cardinal of Lorraine, and Diana of Poitiers. Observers in Europe read the signs of the times. Mundt, ambassador in Strasbourg, warned Cecil of grave developments: the proposed conquest of Denmark, the Emperor's commands against his household attending Protestant services, the general build-up of anti-Protestant movements. He further advised Cecil that the fate of Scotland was the most important issue in Europe. Throckmorton, ambassador in Paris, was of the same mind, urging Cecil to support Knox and the Lords of the Congregation. Yet Cecil needed no persuading for he saw that "Elizabeth's crown and Parker's mitre depended on the victory of Knox in Scotland,"[1] as the Scottish historian T. M. Lindsay so aptly expressed it. Cecil's problem was how and when to do so. Even then, Elizabeth did not like Knox and his Calvinism.

Throckmorton continued writing from Paris. "Beat the iron when it is hot," he pleaded. Cecil did. An English fleet entered the Firth of Forth, an English army beleaguered the French in the fort of Leith. The French were finished and the Treaty of Edinburgh signed on May 10, 1560. The conquering English army left Scottish soil with praises in their ears and prayers that Scotland would never again enter into hostilities against the realm and nation of England. The French had been compelled to relinquish all hold on Scotland. Scotland was wisely left to settle her own affairs.

This was the moment for Knox, who of course had not been idle. A year earlier at Perth the congregations of Fife, Perth, Dundee, Angus, Mearns and Montrose had dedicated their life and property against any powers that threatened the cause of Reformation, a covenant renewed at Stirling and at Edinburgh. These reforming Scots knew that they were no match for the French in the field; the strength of their position was in the hearts of the people. The commonalty were drawing their own conclusions about the rapine and insolence of the foreign troops, and had begun to realize that only English arms would deliver them from the foreigner, a deliverance which would mean freedom to follow the Reformation. In fact, the Congregations were so much alive to the situation that they met in

[1] Lindsay, II. 297.

Edinburgh before the English or French troops had left, and consequently had to adjourn till the soldiers had actually gone.

At this hour Knox rose to his greatest heights in the pulpit of St. Giles where he preached the Word of God daily. A mighty service of thanksgiving was arranged in St. Giles there and then and the Scots began to set their own house in order. Eight fully constituted churches were arranged and five superintendents appointed. They petitioned Parliament for a Reformation settlement. Parliament invited Knox to prepare a confession of faith, which was ratified and approved. Within a week Parliament decreed that the Bishop of Rome had no power or jurisdiction in the land; they repealed all previous acts contrary to the reformed faith; they abolished the mass.[1]

The men who had compiled with Knox the confession of faith were now asked to draft a constitution. After discussion copies were sent in translation to Calvin, Viret and Beza for their opinion. The draft was read by the politicians who hankered after uniformity, an ideal that was to cause much division in later generations, and which was as unnecessary as it was mistaken. The *Confession of Faith and Doctrine* was translated into Latin under the title of *Confessio Scoticana* and was displaced only by the *Westminster Confession* of 1647 in the interests of uniformity. It has a human warmth and personal quality about it not normally characteristic of confessional statements. It confesses the faith of the four oecumenical councils and adds the special Reformation emphases of grace and pardon, as well as the doctrines of the Word and the Holy Spirit. Interesting Lutheran emphases reveal themselves: for instance, Luther's handling of scripture and revelation as promise; the treatment of election as of grace, and as proof of God's power in salvation. The characteristics of the Church are the preaching of the Word of God, the administration of the sacraments, and a proper discipline, a particularly Calvinist note. It stresses the authority of Scripture in that Scripture is of God not man. The document received moving and unanimous approval before it was sent to Cecil for his.

The authors were invited to draw up a system of Church government and produced the *First Book of Discipline*.[2] It provided for the government of the Church by kirk sessions, synods and general assemblies. It recognized as officers the four Calvinist categories of ministers, teachers, elders and deacons, to which it added superintendents and readers. Superintendents were necessary as organizing authorities in a very unsettled country; readers owing to the grave shortage of minsters as well as to the very high standard they conceived a minister should fulfil. The *Book* contains a chapter on the spending of the Church's patrimony on church

---

[1] Cochrane, *Reformed Confessions*, 159–184; Knox, *History*, I, 338 ff.
[2] Dunlop, *Collection of Confessions*, II, 515 ff.; Lindsay, II, 304 ff.

needs, education and the care of the poor. The barons found difficulty with this section for they had misappropriated too much of the patrimony already. The General Assembly of the Reformed Church of Scotland met for the first time in 1560, a date which marks the completion of the Reformation in Scotland.

Yet the victory was won only in principle, hardly in reality. Mary and Francis refused to ratify these Acts, Acts which were only ratified when Mary was deposed in 1567. Francis II died in December 1560, and the young widowed Queen returned to Scotland in August 1561.

The reformers were alarmed but alerted. They knew that Mary was the Stuart Queen, and had been involved from childhood in the worst kind of scheming Romanism. One of the sinister features of the Roman Catholics of this period was less their wrong theology than their political machinations. Mary was also utterly unscrupulous and seemed to believe that feminine charm, with which she was richly endowed, was a gift for winning men to her own political ends. The shrewd Scots saw through Mary, none more penetratingly than John Knox. Intrigue, passion and power politics proved her eventual undoing, but there is no doubt that it was John Knox and John Knox alone who stood in her way.

Cecil in England was anxious about the course of events. He was simply reminded that Knox was there. When Mary attended Mass in her chapel read by a French priest it was with great difficulty that the threatening mob was restrained from breaking in and disrupting the service. Vast, serious-minded crowds were listening to Knox's sermons. The Queen temporized and retained the Mass in her own chapel whilst allowing the law of its abolition to stand. Some of her leading men began to be persuaded that Mary would adopt the Reformation if only Knox would walk delicately. Only Knox knew how wrong they were, and Knox had the support of the commons in Scotland.

The famous duel between the young and fascinating Queen and the stern preacher now began. One is sometimes tempted to feel sympathetic to the beautiful Queen on natural grounds of humanity, sometimes simply sentimentality, but we need to remember that they were protagonists in a revolution that was convulsing Europe. It is a shallow judgment which speaks of Knox's rudeness. He was utterly deferential, never once sought the royal presence but was commanded there, and it was only when the themes touched the religious concerns of his life, that Knox spoke with staggering sternness and certainty. The importance of these interviews is that autocratic and despotic royalty was faced with a representative and spokesman of the divine right of the common people. Here is epitomized the conflict between autocratic power and the civil and religious rights and dignities of the common man. Modern man owes a lot to the Luthers and Knoxes of the sixteenth century who knew where, when, and how to stand.

It is not easy to make proper, even non-controversial judgments on Mary and her reign, for the source material is a mass of conflicting evidence where the reported facts are too often coloured by emotion and desire,[1] but it is not impossible to discuss the main events as they happened and in so far as they have a bearing on our subject.

There was some concern that the young widowed Queen should find the "right" husband, and after a scrutiny of the short list, her cousin, Henry Stuart, Lord Darnley, was despatched from the Elizabethan court. Some saw in this match the future possibility of the union of England and Scotland, a hope eventually realized in their son, the future James VI of Scotland and James I of England. But Darnley was a lewd, licentious lout of a youth, of the baser sort; vulgar, stupid, almost imbecilic, childish, moody, arrogant, utterly untrustworthy and irresponsible, without physical, moral or spiritual strength. A man of this kind could never create a relationship as responsible as marriage, and was never fitted to wear a crown. Mary seemed to have loved him at first, but the marriage resolved itself into its natural doom. Apart from the damage it wreaked on her own personal life it shattered responsible government under Lethington. At first, Mary had adopted the commendable policy of peace with the Congregation and toleration of the Protestants, but now began to adopt an irresponsible and intolerable confusion of personal politics and private intrigue. The Earl of Murray,[2] her other chief minister with Lethington and leader of the Protestant lords, realized there was no place for responsible government as he saw it, and fled the country. Rejecting now both Scottish politics as well as her husband, Mary confided more and more in her Italian secretary, David Rizzio. Darnley, in one of his uncontrollable rages, broke into the Queen's chamber one night with a reckless gang, dragged Rizzio out, and murdered him, or had him murdered (1565). This was perpetrated on Mary when she was with child with the future James VI; it may have been intended to precipitate a miscarriage. Mary's mind was consumed with a passion for revenge, and feigning affection for Darnley, she wheedled out of the childish nincompoop the names of the accomplices, whereupon they found themselves dismissed and the Earl of Murray restored. Within a year, perceiving that Darnley's one virtue in her eyes, namely a claim to her consuming passion to succeed to the English throne, was now not likely to have much weight in England, Mary determined to be rid of him. Darnley fell sick again towards the end of the year (1566) and feigning a great show of wifely love Mary took him to the remote house of Kirk o' Field, just outside

---

[1] Mary's reign has now almost become a special branch of historical science. A considerable amount of detailed documentary evidence is given in the valuable work D. Hay Fleming, *Mary Queen of Scots* (2nd edn., 1898), pp. 177–543.

[2] James Stuart, an illegitimate son of James V and therefore Mary's half-brother.

Edinburgh, to convalesce. Sitting up late by his bedside one night she suddenly remembered that there were wedding festivities of one of her maids she had promised to attend, and assuring her husband that the next night she would surely sleep with him, soothed him and left the house. Meanwhile, a conspiracy of Scottish lords, led by the wildest and most uncouth of them all, James Hepburn, Earl of Bothwell, now Mary's favourite, was at that moment piling up gunpowder in the room underneath the King's, and when Mary was safely away, the whole house was blown up sky-high. Mary's complicity in the plot, in the nature of the case, cannot be proved, but there is damaging evidence of her cognizance. Even this plot cannot certainly be disentangled,[1] for there is weighty evidence that the King was not blown up at all, but was strangled in the garden, where his body was found at some distance from the house, uncharred and undamaged. He was buried at night, and nobody allowed to view the corpse.

Within the year Bothwell was divorced from his wife and married to Mary, with dire consequences to Mary's reputation: she allowed herself to be seized, if not raped, by the dissolute and boorish brute, who carried her off to Dunbar where they lived together until the divorce was granted. Thereupon, they were married legally, and with a Protestant service. Such conduct staggered Europe, whose crowned heads felt they could hardly now support such a catholic queen. If it staggered royal Europe, it sealed her fate with the Scots – murder, adultery, and the wrong religion to boot, was more than they would stand. If Mary has had many defenders since her death, she had too few at that hour. The national and religious life of the country was at stake, and men could not afford the luxury of romanticism and sentimentalism, as could a later age non-involved with the tragedy played before their eyes. The Protestant lords and her people rose up against her. Her wretched supporters put up a lamentable fight, though Mary herself displayed considerable courage and fortitude. Defeated at Carberry Hill, she was imprisoned in Lochleven Castle where she was compelled to abdicate in favour of her son James and to nominate Murray as regent (1567). Meanwhile Bothwell saved his skin by fleeing the country, and still showing considerable spirit, Mary refused to re-

---

[1] *Editor's note:* Three plots seem to have got their lines crossed. The gunpowder plot that Darnley and Co. had laid to blow up Mary so as to win the kingdom for himself and papal reaction was discovered by Bothwell, who fired the train in order to hoist Darnley with his own petard; but Darnley, escaping into the garden in the nick of time, was (with his page) murdered there by some of the Douglases (cousins on his mother's side: hence his last cry, "Pity me, kinsmen, for the love of Him who pitied all the world!"). For alleged complicity in this murder one of the Douglases who was not actually present, the Earl of Morton, later Regent, was executed in 1581 (see p. 246). The "official" version of Darnley's murder and attendant events, which gained general credence once the primary witnesses were safely out of the way, lies open to serious doubt; see, e.g. R. H. Mahon, *The Tragedy of Kirk o' Field* (Cambridge, 1930); R. Gore-Browne, *Lord Bothwell* (London, 1937); M. H. A. Davison, *The Casket Letters* (London, 1965).

nounce her marriage with him. In 1568 she escaped from Lochleven, mustered an army, but was defeated at Langside.

Of all places it was to Protestant England she fled, appealing to Elizabeth for help against what she termed "rebels". The reason she appealed to Elizabeth must lie in the fact that she sought sanctuary, for neither France nor Spain were very happy about her recent conspiracies and marital misadventures, and were not disposed and hardly able to offer any real practical help. Mary's flight to England put Elizabeth into an impossible position. She could not return her to Scotland without jeopardizing the cause of Protestantism there, and losing the valuable and growing friendship of the Scots. She could not let her go to France, for that would restore the dangerous position of 1560. She could not simply leave her in England for that would have left a growing point for Roman Catholic rebellion and disaffection.

Elizabeth's tactics were marked by delay and duplicity, perhaps simply uncertainty, and eventually she consented to hear both sides not in a trial but in a kind of general examination. The lords were required to produce evidence of the charges they made against the queen of murder and adultery, the queen of the lords' rebellion. The hearing was first at York, later London (1568-9). It was at this examination that the lords produced the famous "Casket Letters", allegedly found after Mary's flight, and which contained proof of the most humiliating charges of being Bothwell's mistress and a collaborator with the murderers of Darnley. Mary refused to answer to such charges, and her supporters refuse to admit these letters, but when all is coolly considered, even if the letters were genuine they hardly affect the case materially, for the evidence of her fond and foolish passions for bad men, bad values and bad religion do not depend on these letters. The verdict of the commission was that no case of rebellion could be established against the Scottish lords, but that the case against Mary lacked completeness. An ugly verdict, on any account. Mary came out better than was expected. She was sentenced to close but honourable confinement. Murray returned to save Scotland for Protestantism and Elizabeth preserved the now real and growing unity between the two nations. Two wholesome consequences out of a sordid scandal.

Yet Mary, even in prison, continued to be a grave concern to Elizabeth. Mary, who had been a menace in Scotland, now became a permanent danger in England. She could, at any moment, be the head of a Catholic conspiracy, a rôle she played once too often. Elizabeth could not stoop to murder nor even open execution, for she was too humane and womanly and had too deep a respect for royal blood. There were plots, conspiracies and intrigue all the time. In 1571-2 there was a particularly sinister plot to have Mary's marriage with Bothwell annulled to enable her to marry the Duke of Norfolk. This exfoliated in a Catholic rising in the North, and its failure was followed by the execution of Norfolk. Elizabeth once more saved Mary from the nation's fury. Until 1585 she was imprisoned in Sheffield where she had to handle the redoubtable Bess of Hardwick, the spouse of her guard, the Earl of Shrewsbury. In Sheffield she was treated with honour and respect as a queen, captive though she was, but when again the ugly Throckmorton plot came to light, the parliamentary association formed to liberate her, and the assassination of William of Orange, matters came to a head, and she was transferred to the Puritanical care of Tutbury Castle in 1585, where she was treated by her Puritan keeper, Sir Amias Paulet, as an evil and traitorous woman. Almost at once another plot came to light followed by the Babington conspiracy. This conspiracy was aimed at the assassination of Elizabeth and the release of Mary, and when the sordid affair came to light in 1586 the conspirators were tried, found guilty and executed. All save Mary.

Mary, being a queen, faced a special commission in October, 1586, and though she was found guilty, Elizabeth was still of the same mind not to exact the penalty of death. But the nation and the council were now determined on their course: they had had all they could stand, queen or no. Elizabeth was finally compelled to sign the death warrant in February, 1587, yet refused to let it from her hand. The council finally acted without the Queen's knowledge and despatched the warrant a week later. When she learned of their unilateral action she went wild with rage, almost to distraction. She threatened the council with a prosecution for murder, threw the Secretary of State into the Tower after fining him mercilessly, and it was some considerable time before Elizabeth was mollified sufficiently to forgive these men for assuming the responsibility for the execution of Mary.

Hurt though the Scots were at this tragic and ill-timed death of their former queen, whose courage on the scaffold was so memorable as to create a kind of sentimental catharsis which washed away all her sins, the English felt that a traitor in their midst had been removed, and their own queen safe at long last. Whatever the romanticists now say, Mary was the cause and figure-head of a national and religious threat to Elizabethan Britain, a threat continually breaking out into ugly pustules and tolerated by Elizabeth for close on twenty years. When all is said, Mary could have retired in royal dignity and washed her hands of the cloak-and-dagger techniques of Catholic reaction. In that she pursued her former foolish ways she created for herself and for Britain an impossible situation. In the words of G. R. Elton, the council cut the knot that there had been no way of untying.[1]

It was a pitiful even disgraceful story. From this none of the actors emerges with any credit. Mary draws from all much personal sympathy,

[1] G. R. Elton, *England under the Tudors* (London, 1955).

but this should not blind us to the cause which she sought to further by any and every means. It is yet some compensation that her infant son, this "native prince of this our realm," was destined at the death of Elizabeth in 1603 to realize the dream of a peaceful union of the Scottish and English Crowns on terms honourable to both peoples.

But it is to Elizabeth we must turn before we can complete our story. We must therefore go back to the beginning of her reign and attempt to explain the situation she faced in England, and how, with the help of the Scottish victory just described, she was enabled to bring about the Elizabethan Settlement in spite of foreign threats and dissensions within.

# CHAPTER XV

# ELIZABETH, 1558–1603

LIZABETH WAS VERY DIFFERENT FROM HER SISTER MARY, IN MANY WAYS inferior. She had inherited a good deal of Tudor craft and guile, and circumstances had developed a remarkable capacity of self-preservation. She was illegitimate to both Protestant and Romanist alike. Her early life had been passed in the shadow of the block. She was soon to realize the virtue of self-mastery, caution and dissembling; the avoidance of any extremes; the art of keeping open a ready retreat of withdrawal. Her own perils were a reflection of those of the nation, and the country soon found in her an almost providential queen.

It is true that the life of England was becoming slowly Protestant of its own. Young English intellectual life was growing remarkably alive, remarkably Protestant. Young ladies of the upper classes were reading Latin, Greek and Italian, sometimes Hebrew, an activity which led not only to Protestantism but even the more rigid forms of Calvinism or Puritanism. The common people were openly developing an anti-Romanist outlook, and were disrespectful of papist customs and papist personages. The fanatical burnings of the Protestant martyrs, not least that of Archbishop Cranmer, had stirred the indignation of the populace in Southern England, and this animadversion was spreading to the north and to remote country areas. Further, every Englishman had hated the subjugation of his country's life to the interests of Spain during Mary's reign. In these matters Elizabeth was utterly at one with her people.

Yet, though it is true that there was this slow landslide in England, it is important to understand the perils which threatened Elizabeth. So grave were these perils that the conclusion is forced upon the reader that the religious convictions of Elizabeth and Cecil were a more compelling factor in the Settlement than many historians appreciate. Lesser conviction would certainly have sought readier compromise. First, there was danger of civil war. Germany had been ravaged with civil war and many realized that the worst was yet to come. Catholics and Huguenots had begun their internecine warfare in France, and everybody feared that the strife was only in its early stages. England might well repeat this desolating conflict. The economic position of England was not strong at the beginning of the reign. There were serious and longstanding agrarian troubles, the coinage was debased, trade was stagnant. The plague had broken out again. The war in France had drained England of men and money, resulting in a loss of prestige as well as territory.

Another great peril to the Settlement was the change in the mood of Romanism. The Popes had now been "reconverted to Christianity." Instead of the vicious and licentious dilettantes that had brought Rome into disrepute, there now walked through the curia men of strong religious faith and purpose. This was a direct result of Luther's protest (though they would not admit it). The Counter-Reformation was beginning to transform Catholicism and had developed an aggressive, militant mood. The Council of Trent, now in its closing sessions, had certainly reformed the general level of morality and integrity in the Church and cleansed the Augean stables. It effected no real theological reformation in the sense the Reformers sought, though it certainly changed the theological climate. The Index served most effectively to stop the spread of evangelical theology and free scholarship simply by not allowing the books to be seen or read, or even printed. Still worse were the wicked techniques of the Inquisition where the accused were allowed no defence, no opportunity to recant, and charges and punishments multiplied even after the victim's death. Two examples will suffice to remind us of its horror. In Spain, during the eighteen years rule of Torquemada as Inquisitor-General (c. 1480–98) it was conjectured by Llorente that 114,000 persons were accused, 10,220 were burnt and 97,000 condemned to perpetual imprisonment or public penance.[1] It was less revolting in Italy, in that it was on a smaller scale, but there were continuous burnings in all the cities. Venice ran a variation on the burning by laying the victim on a plank between two gondolas and ordering the boats to row slowly apart, to watch the victim drown. An unyielding congregation of Waldensians in Calabria was attacked; some perished by the sword, some were hurled over cliffs, some sent to the galleys, some to prisons and some to mines. The elderly women, a hundred of them, were tortured and then slain. The few who survived were sold into slavery. But there was more to the Counter-Reformation than the negative Index and destructive Inquisition, neither of which was approved by the best Catholics. The most effective force was the rise of the Jesuits under Ignatius Loyola. They brought into decaying Catholicism faith, enthusiasm, devotion, and appeared as preachers, pastors, missionaries and educationists. They rolled back the days of darkness from the Mediterranean lands right up to Germany. They sought to educate the young and founded schools, and thus won the young back to catholic practice, even to the confessional. They sought to revive higher places of learning, now utterly deserted, always attempting to establish catholic discipline and practice. Above all they sought the

[1] These figures are now generally believed to be greatly exaggerated. Several historians estimate the burnings as nearer 2,000.

young nobility. Soon there was a new generation devoted to the one great mission, the extirpation of Protestantism.

Another factor that imperilled Elizabeth's position was the hostility of foreign states. The Counter-Reformation could count upon the secular forces of the King of France, and Philip, lord of Spain, the Netherlands and the Indies. Philip was a fanatical Romanist and Europe realized that neither of these Catholic monarchs would stand idly by while Protestantism established itself in England. It was Scotland that saved the situation (see p. 227 f.). England was genuinely afraid of foreign invasion. And when Pius V issued his bull of excommunication in 1570 and released Roman Catholic Englishmen from allegiance to Elizabeth this fear intensified. It was only with the ignominious rout of the Armada in 1588 that England felt the threat was removed.

Fourthly, Elizabeth's title to the throne was sullied. In the eyes of Catholics (and Protestants) she was the illegitimate child of Anne Boleyn, and Mary, Queen of Scots (also Queen of France from July, 1559, to December, 1560), had an attractive alternative claim. Many men toyed with the idea of a united England and Scotland under Mary. The union, of course, would have been Catholic, and would have destroyed Protestantism. Too many Englishmen had their eyes open to this danger, and so had Elizabeth.

Yet, not all of the difficulties worked against Elizabeth. French strength was seriously dissipated by the distressing Huguenot wars. Philip's strength was severely occupied with the depredations of the Turks, the revolt of the Moors, and the rebellion of the Dutch. Still more important was the intense antagonism of the Valois and the Hapsburg dynasties. Philip had every reason to fear Mary's being put on the throne of England instead of Elizabeth, for this would have aligned both France and England against him. All this indicates how delicately affairs are often balanced, and how the real issues, in this case religious, are often settled in relation to, even as secondary to, nationalist, political or social forces. The decisive factor at this moment was the revival of Calvinism in Scotland under Knox, the driving out of the French from Scotland, and the establishment of the Reformation there. When Elizabeth's army and navy had helped to drive out the French from Scotland, the future of the Reformation settlement was secured in these shores once and for all.

Important as the national problems were, nevertheless the most important for Elizabeth was the religious settlement. Her position was difficult for the issues were not clear. Many Catholics had disliked the events of Mary's reign but there was a great number of English people unwilling on that account to turn from Roman ways. Then the Protestant refugees were returning from the Continent, and many of these were Calvinist rather than Lutheran, desiring the Reformation to proceed on

Calvinistic lines. By these men, the Second Prayer Book of Edward VI was regarded merely as a first step, and now that they had drunk deeply of Calvin's intoxicating theology, they were in no mood for half measures. They wanted to strip English Christianity of the "rags of popery" she still clutched round her and clothe her in the pure robes of Reformed Christianity. These men, had they prevailed, would have stripped the ancient English Church of her continuity and her Catholicism, and reformed the English Church on the lines of Geneva. The Romanists wanted to preserve the Marian settlement. At this time, the Pope showed himself willing to accept all that had happened in England, if England would recognize his supremacy and herself as part of the Church Catholic.

Elizabeth could not be described as a spiritually minded person, in the way her sister undoubtedly was. She was Protestant and anti-papal, almost of national necessity, rather than of deep religious conviction. Her first proclamation[1] of December 27, 1558, forbade preaching and teaching on the grounds that it created contentions and public disorder. She allowed the exposition of the gospel or the epistle of the day and the Ten Commandments, and ordered the continuance of all the old services until everything was regularized by lawful authority. The Roman Mass remained legal. She promised to advance religion and virtue, and to promote unity among her people. The document is by no means a Reformation blast, and must have caused misgivings, though no one seems to have doubted her Protestantism. She had her position regularized and legalized by the following April in her Supremacy and Uniformity Acts.[2]

The Queen was crowned on January 15, 1559. The ceremony was performed by the Bishop of Carlisle, there being no Archbishop of Canterbury, and Heath, the Archbishop of York, declining. Parliament was called almost immediately and effected the Act of Supremacy and the Act of Uniformity. This was the beginning of the religious settlement forced through by lay government in defiance of bishops and Convocation, and forced upon a reluctant and unwilling clergy, for the clerical establishment was now Marian. By the Supremacy Act (April, 1559) Elizabeth claimed the title of Supreme Governor in this realm of all causes spiritual and temporal, a *jus potestatis* not a *jus ordinis*. By this same Act she revived ten Acts of Henry VIII and one of Edward VI, confirmed the repeal of six Acts of Henry VIII, and repealed the Heresy Act of Philip and Mary. Penalties for first and second offence were fines and imprisonment but a third offence was to be considered treason against the Queen, the penalty being death. By this Act the Crown had rights of visiting and correcting heresies, abuses and offences. Immediately after this the Act of Uniformity was passed, repealing Mary's Act and reauthorizing the Second Prayer Book of Edward VI and his Act of Uniformity. Three

[1] Gee and Hardy, No. 77.          [2] Gee and Hardy, Nos. 79, 80.

changes were made in the Prayer Book: the offensive clause about the Bishop of Rome was removed from the Litany; the words of administration of the Holy Communion combined the words used in the books of 1549 and 1552, and the Ornaments Rubric added whereby clergy were instructed to wear the vestments in use in the second year of Edward VI. This last clause was not made operative: in fact it was very difficult to persuade the clergy to wear even a surplice. For disobedience the clergy faced a penalty of a fine of one year's salary plus six months imprisonment; a second conviction resulted in dispossession and one year's imprisonment; a third conviction meant dispossession with life imprisonment. Every person was to attend service on Sunday under pain of censure and a fine of one shilling, the money to be given to the poor. Machinery was established to administer the Act. While these Acts were in process of going through the Houses of Parliament a conference was arranged between Roman Catholic and Protestant divines. The disputation was to deal with three questions: (1) Whether a particular church can change rites and ceremonies; (2) Whether public worship must be conducted in Latin; (3) Whether the Mass is a propitiatory sacrifice. The conference began at Westminster before the Privy Council, Lords, Commons and the commonalty, but when the Romanist divines withdrew, as they had often done in Europe, their cause suffered most in the public estimation.

To ensure that these Acts of Supremacy and Uniformity were given effect a royal visitation was begun and guidance given by the Royal Injunction of 1559.[1] A clean sweep was made of almost all the ornaments, a policy approved of by men like Grindal and Sandys, then bishops of London and Worcester respectively, later to become Archbishops of Canterbury and York. All the crosses, images and altars were removed from St. Paul's and the other London churches, and a great number of rood figures, crosses, books and banners burnt at Smithfield. The same sort of thing happened in the provinces. The Injunctions gave instructions in the matter of preaching, reading of homilies, teaching and Bible reading as well as pastoral visitations and the care of the poor. Clergy were to be licensed, recusants to be reported. Parish registers were to be kept. Sundays were to be suitably observed and sinners excluded from communion. Superstitious practices were condemned:

> They shall take away, utterly extinct, and destroy all shrines, coverings of shrines, all tables, candlesticks, trindals, and rolls of wax, pictures, paintings, and all other monuments of feigned miracles, pilgrimages, idolatry and superstition, so that there remain no memory of the same in walls, glass windows, or elsewhere within their churches and houses.[2]

[1] Gee and Hardy, No. 78.          [2] Injunction 23.

Instructions follow on all kinds of church matters: concerning an alms chest; the proper apparel of clergymen; regulations for clerical marriage; teaching of children; oversight of church attendance; careful regulation of printed matter; stone altars (closely identified with the doctrines of the sacrifice of the mass and with transubstantiation) were to be destroyed under proper authority and control, and wooden tables to be set in their place; plain bread without figures thereon to be used in communion. There can be no doubt in the mind of an unprejudiced reader that Elizabeth and her advisers were set on a Protestant régime.

The clergy were recalcitrant, for all the bishops (and most of the higher clergy) were Marian and mediaevalist. They refused to take the oath in which papal rule was abjured and the Queen declared supreme in the realm, and England was virtually without bishops. Some of the old deprived Edwardian bishops returned and new men were appointed. The lower clergy were easier to handle: all except 200 accepted "the alteration of religion." The change was effected quietly and without riotings. The 200 were in the end deprived, whereas in Mary's reign one-third of the beneficed clergy were removed. Three reasons may account for this. First, the visitors were given careful instructions to deal compassionately with the clergy, and secondly, England was now fast becoming Protestant. But thirdly, it must be the theological balance and the literary beauty of the Book of Common Prayer which more than any other single factor kept English churchmen together, as it still does today.

By now Elizabeth had settled on Matthew Parker as successor to Cardinal Pole as Archbishop of Canterbury. Parker had been a chaplain to Henry VIII but had lived in obscurity during Mary's reign. Most reluctantly he was constrained to take this arduous responsibility and on December 17, 1559, he was consecrated at Lambeth by the rites of the Ordinal of 1552, carefully safeguarding continuity and succession by having two bishops consecrated by the old Roman rite (Barlow and Hodgkins), as well as Coverdale and Scory (consecrated by the reformed rites of 1550). Within a few months eleven new diocesans were consecrated.

Many clergy were feeling the need for some clear doctrinal statement as a guide and standard of belief. Parker was a learned and practical man, not dissimilar to Cranmer. He promulgated Eleven Articles (1559),[1] which were meant as a temporary expedient of a simple and practical nature to meet this situation. The subject matter of these articles is as under:

1. The doctrine of the Trinity.
2. The sufficiency of Scripture and the recognition of the Three Creeds.

[1] Text in Hardwick, Appendix IV, 357 ff.; see also 118 ff.

I

3. The Church: where the Word of God is preached, the Sacraments duly administered and "the keys" duly used. The right of existence of national churches maintained.
4. Due calling to the ministry.
5. The Royal Supremacy.
6. The papal monarchy contrary alike to scripture and tradition.
7. The Prayer Book defended as catholic, apostolic, and agreeable to Scripture.
8. Exorcism and oil to be abolished.
9. Private masses condemned as not primitive, and the doctrine of a propitiatory sacrifice to deliver souls from purgatory is founded neither on Christ's nor on apostolic foundation.
10. Communion to be in two kinds.
11. Disallowance of images, relics and other superstitions.

The whole country was now beginning to return to Reformation doctrine, with the exception of the clergy. Parker continued working on the Articles. He took the Forty-two Articles of Edward (1553)[1] and revised them with the help of Grindal (London), Horn (Winchester) and Cox (Ely). They used the Confession of Württemberg (1552) in their revision, which again demonstrates the determining influence of Lutheran theology on Anglicanism, though the sacramental teaching was more Reformed than Lutheran. These revised articles were submitted to Convocation, where they were reduced to thirty-nine. The Queen removed one and they were published as the Thirty-Eight Articles of 1563.[2]

It is interesting to note the changes these articles underwent. Strong Lutheran influences can still be traced; certain controversial elements were omitted which were originally directed against sectaries; four were added by Parker, on the Holy Ghost, Good Works, Communion in both kinds and the non-participation of the wicked in the Body of Christ; certain safeguards on church and sacraments were made. The articles indicate a fuller and more general acceptance of Reformation doctrine. A striking feature of these Articles is the increased anti-Roman character. It is commonly asserted that Elizabeth sought to conciliate Rome during the first ten years of her reign but the evidence is to the contrary. Elizabeth sought not to conciliate Rome but to unite the Protestants in England, and this on a Lutheran basis, the doctrine of Holy Communion excepted. When she retained crosses and candles in her own chapel it was not to conciliate Romanists but to maintain herself under the aegis of the Peace of Augsburg against the threat of papal excommunication. Be that as it may, Parliament desired to make these articles authoritative in England. Elizabeth temporized in her efforts to read the signs of the times but eventually they were given their definitive form as the Thirty-Nine

[1] Hardwick, 66 ff.          [2] Hardwick, Appendix II, 289.

Articles of 1571. Article XXIX was inserted: this excluded the Real Presence in the Lutheran sense as well as the Roman. In support of these Articles there was published a reformed canon law of 1571.

Nevertheless, the country was in a grave state of spiritual destitution, she had undergone too much. The parishes were under-staffed, often badly staffed; learning was at a low ebb and the universities depleted; many bishops were lax, unspiritual and worldly; laymen retained much of the Church's property. Men realized that reform was a slow, painful and costly process. They hoped to withstand the reactionary forces of Rome and the narrowing influence of Puritanism, and to let learning and spiritual life revive. It was the open Bible, the Prayer Book and the English divines themselves that contributed most to this healing stream.

Amidst all this uncertainty John Jewel, Bishop of Salisbury, composed in 1560 a splendid statement to clarify the position of the Church of England in relation to Rome.[1]

He argued that truth had always been persecuted down the ages and that Rome was now persecuting and preventing the spread of Reformation doctrine on the grounds that evangelical doctrine was heretical. The cause was not his own but that of Christ, the Apostles and the Church fathers, and Jewel was compelled to reply.

He stated that the Church of England believed in a Triune God, in one single Catholic Church, and in a threefold ministry of bishops, priests and deacons. It believed that the Scriptures were the basis, criterion and norm of all doctrine. It accepted the sacrament of Baptism and the Lord's Supper, and these he expounded evangelically to the expulsion of all the foolish fables associated with the mass, not least the teaching about purgatory. Public worship was now based on apostolic tradition and legitimate historical development, and always held in the mother tongue. This worship was centred on Christ, not on his mother or his saints. The Church of England taught that all men were sinners saved only by the forgiveness offered by God in Christ; that all men were justified by faith alone; that all such men would rise again at the Last Day.

The Romanists argued that the Church of England had separated itself from the Church and forsaken the Catholic faith. Yet the Church of England had never swerved from the Word of God, from the Apostles, the primitive Church and the holy fathers. For its part it did not despise the Roman Church nor had it parted willingly, but if Rome is compared with the primitive Church and refuses to reform, a Christian man could but soberly and decently withdraw to Christ, the Apostles and a true Church.

[1] Jewel's *Apologie of the Church of England* (Parker Society, 1840), III. 1. See abridged text in Parker, L.C.C., Vol. XXVI, pp. 14 ff.

To say that such matters could not be settled by England unilaterally but only in general council is to advise what all the Reformers requested and were refused. The Church of England did not despise councils. It was because Rome would not accede to this proper demand that England was compelled to act in the only way possible, by lawful provincial synod. Jewel concluded: "We departed from him [the Pope] to whom we were not bound and who had nothing to say for himself."

# CHAPTER XVI

# THE CHURCH UNDER ELIZABETH

## 1. *The Elizabethan Settlement and the Papacy*

THE ACTS OF SUPREMACY OF 1559 AND 1563 VIRTUALLY PLACED THE property and lives of the Romanists in the hands of the government, though it is fair to add that the Romanists enjoyed in actual fact a large measure of immunity. By now schoolmasters, lawyers and Members of Parliament were brought within the terms of the Acts. A refusal to take the oath meant the forfeiture of goods and liberty for the first conviction, but if persisted in, could mean a charge of treason. Nevertheless, England moved forward with characteristic clemency, sense and toleration. If contemporary man is critical he should compare England at this time with France or Spain or any other country in Europe. It was essential to maintain order in the country and unity among Englishmen: religious toleration would have meant national chaos or anarchy. Romanists were fined for non-attendance at Church. Frequently they were imprisoned and released. It varied from place to place. In the north of England and the remoter parts the older ways prevailed and many of the justices of the peace and the country gentry, themselves Romanist, found no reason to enforce the Acts.

The real change came in 1570 when Pius V made the foolish and fanatical decision to excommunicate and depose the Queen and to release Englishmen from their allegiance to her and to England.

> And the nobles, subjects and peoples of the said realm, and all others who have taken an oath of any kind to her we declare to be absolved for ever from such oath and from all dues of dominions, fidelity and obedience. . . .[1]

He went further: he commanded that Romanists were in no circumstances to attend the services of the English Church, otherwise they would involve themselves in the sin of schism. Pius was acting *ultra vires*, and such autocratic handling of men and nations was already long out-dated, especially when he ordered Spain and France to put the bull into effect. Romanists thus put themselves in the wrong. Every Elizabethan at this time was either one of Elizabeth's men or a traitor. It was neither crime nor sin to be a papist, but the papists largely took the wrong road and associated themselves from now on with plots, conspiracies and treasonable activities

Up till 1570 the English Romanists were of two main kinds. The

[1] Bettenson, 338f.

moderates accepted the settlement, went to their parish church, tolerated what they got there, and whenever the opportunity occurred went secretly to mass. The other kind realized that this would spell the death of Catholicism in these shores, for the next generation would be absorbed into the national Church. The vital activity was to keep up a flow of Roman priests into this country, particularly when the Marian clergy were ageing. William Allen, a Fellow of Oriel, saw this situation and took steps to meet it. He founded at Douay in 1568 his famous seminary for the training of Englishmen for the Catholic ministry. The training was on the lines of the strictest Tridentine theology balanced with contemporary learning. These men were to be smuggled into England, to minister to the adherents of the old faith, when their rigorous training was complete. One of Allen's earliest, if not most famous, pupils was Edmund Campion. By 1574 these enthusiastic priests, fired with missionary zeal and excited by the danger of the mission began to land in England. No fewer than a hundred had returned by 1579. These seminarists were strengthened by the now vigorous Jesuitic movement of the Counter-Reformation a movement that was having a remarkable influence in Europe as the arresting, ornate church buildings of the time still testify to our eyes. Campion was now a trained Jesuit, and joined by Robert Parsons, came to England in 1580. England might have accepted this spiritual and intellectual zeal, but the zealots seemed difficult to distinguish from Vatican-inspired political intriguers. It was one thing to tolerate a Christian man who was a Catholic; it was another if he was intriguing with a foreign power to overthrow the Queen and the established order of Church and State.

These plots, intrigues and risings began to take on a very ugly shape. The year 1569 saw the risings of the old families of the Percys and the Nevilles in Northumberland and Durham, and plots in which Norfolk was involved at the cost of his life. Ireland, Scotland and Spain were all used in unsuccessful attempts to overthrow Elizabeth and bring England under Roman influence. In 1579, Sanders attempted to raise Ireland with the assistance of Spanish and Italian troops. In 1579–81 a plot was hatched to restore Scotland to Catholicism; the Protestant Earl of Morton, Regent from 1572 to 1580, was executed in 1581 for alleged complicity in the murder of Darnley, the King's father, fourteen years before.[1] Endless intrigues centred round Mary Queen of Scots who was imprisoned by Elizabeth in 1568. Until her execution in 1587 she was constantly involved in sordid conspiracies inspired by the Guise family and by Philip. The two last-named conspiracies had the assassination of Elizabeth as their prime purpose.

---

[1] The Regent Murray (see p. 231) had been assassinated in 1570, as was also his successor, the Earl of Lennox (Darnley's father). The next Regent was the Earl of Mar, who on his death in 1572 was succeeded by Morton.

Englishmen began to be grimly aware that Roman Catholicism was not simply another way of understanding Christianity but was too closely involved with intrigue and high treason. And then the Continental Catholics gave conclusive proof of what Protestants might expect at the hands of a triumphant Catholicism. The Massacre of St. Bartholomew (1572), when 70,000 Huguenots met their death in France, was received in England with a shock – and as a warning. The atrocities of Philip in Spain and the Netherlands served as a grim reminder of a fate from which only Elizabeth and a Protestant England could save them.

Prior to these events there was little severity in the Elizabethan Settlement. The government had not pried into men's consciences and had demanded a decent conformity. The Pope's bull of 1570, the misguided activities of the Jesuits, the intrigues of Mary Queen of Scots and her foolish conspirators had all served to make Romanism a treasonable political activity. The spiritually minded Romanist was slowly forced into an impossible and unnecessary position between loyalty to his faith and loyalty to his queen. When the Pope authorized English Roman Catholics to take their oath of loyalty to the crown with a secret reservation to be loyal only to the moment when resistance became practicable, he not only did them a gross disservice, but he gave immoral advice. He virtually compelled them to be traitors, if not in fact, then in intent. It was from this moment that the severe laws found themselves on the Statute Book.

Following the papal bull of 1570 it was declared high treason to deprive the Queen of her title to the throne, and also to introduce papal bulls into the country. In 1581 it was declared high treason to be reconciled to the Roman Church and to help anybody else to seek reconciliation. Fines for non-attendance at Church were raised. In 1585 the Act against Jesuits and seminaries[1] was passed, the first Act directed against Jesuits as such, though they had come under the penalties of earlier Acts. The Act describes the purpose of such seminary priests as

> . . . not only to withdraw her highness's subjects from their due obedience to her majesty, but also to stir up and move sedition, rebellion, and open hostility within the same her highness's realms and dominions, to the great endangering of the safety of her most royal person, and to the utter ruin, desolation, and overthrow of the whole realm. . . .

By its terms all Jesuits and seminary priests were banished from the realm on pain of death. Any who knowingly harboured them was guilty of a felony, and were to suffer "death, loss and forfeit." All Englishmen abroad in training in Jesuit establishments or seminaries were to return to England and take the oath of allegiance: failing that, they would be

[1] Gee and Hardy, No. 85.

adjudged traitors, guilty of high treason, and receive the same condemnation. By the same Act any person helping seminarists abroad, or sending young people abroad to such places for education, would commit *praemunire*[1] under the penalty of £100. Provision was made for Jesuits and seminarists to return home and take the oath of allegiance before a bishop or a responsible crown officer, though such men were never to be within ten miles of the Queen for ten years after their submission. It is clear that the concern of the country in the matter of Catholics was not that they were Catholics but lest they became traitors. In fact, religious faith and practice does not even receive mention in the Acts. In 1593 a further Act was passed against the recusants[2] forbidding them to travel more than five miles from home under pain of forfeiture of all possessions.

The inevitable effect of this legislation was to declare seminarists traitors by English Law. And, of course, when they were caught and had the stock question put to them, "If the Pope and the King of Spain landed in England for whom would you fight?", they faced a painful dilemma. As individuals these missionaries of the English mission were heroes, martyrs, often saints, but there is no escaping the ugly fact that they were sent by their superiors and rulers with the clear and illegitimate intention of using their mission to impose forcibly upon England a Catholic monarch. Equally, the difficulty of the government was to discriminate between that minority of Catholics hatching plots against the Queen, and the majority who wanted to combine their loyalty to both Church and Crown, and who actually proved this loyalty to their fellow Englishmen when the Armada sailed against England in 1588.

These unfortunate men were cruelly ground to death between the lower millstone of patriotic necessity and the upper millstone of papist diplomacy. Some two hundred men paid the extreme penalty and died as traitors. An ugly feature of the defeat of this inglorious mission was that the saints too often suffered while the intriguers went scot free. One example of this painful tragedy will suffice. In 1580, as has been said, two of the Jesuits who came to these shores on the English Mission were Edmund Campion and Robert Parsons. Campion was a saintly man, gifted, and of noble Christian character. He was caught and executed in 1582. Parsons, a schemer and an intriguer, lived to a ripe old age into the Stuart dynasty. It is foolish fancy to pretend that these men suffered for their religion. The mildness of Elizabeth's rule until the fatal folly of the Pope in 1570 is proof of that. After 1570 Romanism had gathered her forces against the Queen, forces of a very mixed kind, including the assassin's knife alongside the missionary zeal of spiritual priests, foreign

---

[1] Technically the taking of English cases to papal courts, but often extended to include any kind of papal encroachment.
[2] Gee and Hardy, No. 87

governments alongside internal conspiracies. Every Romanist came to be regarded as part of this multifarious power marshalled to destroy the Queen and to overthrow the hard-fought-for established order of Church and State. Yet many Romanists were never part of this, and many were identified with it unwillingly. Sometimes the government showed mercy on the moderates and sought to drive a wedge into the Catholic body. And, of course, many moderate men were wholly opposed to calling in the Spanish enemy to restore the old faith. To Elizabethan Englishmen the problem was not so much recusancy as its association with the assassination plots against the Queen and the threat of foreign Catholic invasion. These associations strained to breaking point the loyalty of Catholic Englishmen. To attempt to convert Protestant Elizabethan England from foreign bases, and to associate that with armed invasion as well as conspiracy was to attempt the impossible, and neither the splendid devotion of the Catholic laity nor the saintly heroism of its priesthood could bring such a cause to fruition. The whole movement was contained by the end of the reign. It had never been strong and had stemmed largely from conservative country families who had retained their Catholicism and maintained it in their servants and tenants. The seminarists and Jesuits haunted these country houses and would have had short shrift in open villages, or in towns and cities.

## 2. The Rise of Puritanism

Romanism was not the only problem in the making of Church co-extensive with nation. Though the Puritans were not the political danger the Romanists were, though they were stiffly embattled against the fanatical Romanism of Spain and supported the throne when the Armada threatened, nevertheless, many Englishmen were suspicious of Puritanism and thought it divisive of national unity. It has often been described as a backwater in the national life by the older historians, but recent writers are bringing a fresh and more kindly judgment to bear on Puritanism.[1] Puritanism had the theological intensity of Calvin and brought to bear in the national life the theocentricity of Calvin's theology, his high doctrine of election and grace, his uncompromising sense of the authority of the Bible, the dignity and nobility of the secular life, and a doctrine of the State that made it subserve the Church or at least compelled the State to Christian obedience. Puritanism was in the nature of the case a body of thinking disaffected with the Elizabethan compromise. It represented a constant criticism and dissatisfaction with the settlement and found itself

[1] "Puritanism belonged to the mainstream of the Reformation" (A. G. Dickens, *The English Reformation* (London, 1964), pp. 314–15. Cf. S. B. Babbage, *Puritanism and Richard Bancroft* (S.P.C.K., 1962).

too often opposed to both Church and society, and too strongly sectarian, even fanatical. Most Englishmen recoiled from the intensity and the uncompromising nature of the Puritans' theological thinking, for their theology set it in opposition to the compromise position of the general level of Anglicanism as well as to the prevailing morals of society. Puritanism has been too often caricatured, and too often led itself into indefensible positions, but it should be seen as a very powerful and clear theological position resulting in a pure and noble morality. At one time, Puritanism was the only course for converted and high-minded men to take, attracting many of the best minds and noblest characters, but it should not be seen as in opposition to Anglicanism. Parker, Jewel, Grindal and others were in a real sense forerunners of that balanced position at which Hooker arrived. It would be truer to say that those Elizabethans who truly cared about religion would be either Romanists or Anglican Puritans. Englishmen were not happy about the world-renouncing, almost Manichaean view of material things, and the seeking of God apart from any external means. Puritanism had a quality of oriental mysticism about it, and this mystic strain and dismissal of externalities made Puritans ruggedly individualistic. Nevertheless, the biblical and theological nature of Puritanism made it a constituent part of the English Reformation, to which it still belongs.

The death of Mary Tudor and the accession of Elizabeth had brought back streams of theological refugees from Europe,[1] but already within Protestantism there were deep theological differences. There was the approach which may be called "Lutheran" in that it represented Luther's views, namely, the reformation of the old theology and the old tradition in the light of Scripture, patristic tradition and sound learning. This is really a "catholic" way forward. There was the approach which may be labelled "Calvinist" for the same reasons, but is now known as "reformed" in distinction to Luther's which is called "evangelical." The reformed position was more radical than Luther's, and sought to build a new church on the pattern of the early Church, with the precise structure of biblical theology. The approach of Bucer at Strasbourg was a balance of these two positions not unlike the Anglican. Most of the refugees had been in reformed towns not evangelical, and consequently their theology was Calvinist, often uncompromising. When they returned to England many of them found themselves unable to accept the Elizabethan Settlement, and a reformed, separatist movement began to crystallize out. There were the moderate men, the men who accepted the leadership of a Jewel, a Sandys, and a Grindal (who later as Archbishop of Canterbury allowed

---

[1] Some 800 leading men of Protestant opinion including Richard Cox, Laurence Humphrey, Thomas Leaver, James Pilkington, Edwin Sandys, Sir John Cheke, Sir Anthony Choke and John Jewel.

the Puritans a great deal of freedom to the open displeasure of the Queen).
Nevertheless, there were the more extreme men who sought to change the
Settlement. In the early stages of Puritanism there was no desire to leave
the Church of England. The more extreme Puritans (a name we are really
anticipating and which did not yet exist) sought to capture control of the
Church of England in the hope of forwarding the reformation of its
liturgy and practice by the ultimate introduction of simpler and purer
forms (as they conceived them). Consequently, in its first phase (1559–70)
we find the concerns centred round the externals of worship. These men
resented robes or vestments at Holy Communion and thought of them
as the rags and relics of popery. Yet all the evidence indicates that all that
was used was a surplice, occasionally a cope. Many of them would not
even wear a surplice. They also took a strong line against many customs
and ceremonies that had grown up in church life, for example the signing
of the cross at baptism or the use of a ring in marriage. Many of them saw
great danger in kneeling at communion as being a form of adoration of
the elements. Their argument was that nothing should be allowed which
was not taught or sanctioned by Holy Scripture. But many Englishmen
believed that not everything needed the support of biblical texts, but that
honourable customs could grow up from historical or geographical origins,
and if not repugnant to reason, should be retained. This view eventually
prevailed in England. It was Luther's view precisely, and in the midst of
these unnecessary disputes, both Bullinger and Beza from the Continent
advised the disputants that it were better to conform than allow Romanists
to step into the places they themselves were refusing to occupy.

To this situation Archbishop Parker directed his thought and energy.
He composed Articles in 1564, but after two unsuccessful efforts to procure
the Queen's signature eventually published them on his own authority.[1]
The people were "to be knit together in one perfect unity of doctrine,
and to be enjoined in one unity of rites and manners," as the preface
defines the aims of the document. The first six articles were on the subject
of doctrine and preaching: preaching was to be regularly performed by
competent persons with the avoidance of controversial issues. In this
context the sacraments of baptism and holy communion were to be regularly and reverently performed. Then follow fourteen articles on the
administration of prayer and sacraments. Common prayer was to "be
said or sung decently and distinctly." Clergy not admitted by the bishop
were not allowed to preach but were to read the Homilies. Then follow
instructions about the wearing of a cope in cathedrals at communion and
of surplice and hood at choir office, as well as the proper conduct of
church services. Sunday is ordered as a day without work and without
business. Then follow eight articles of instruction on the selection and

[1] Gee and Hardy, No. 81.

training of ordinands, and nine more on clerical outdoor dress. Finally, there are eight articles on the conduct of the ministry, to which clergy were to subscribe, the final one prohibiting secular employment. Many Puritans refused to comply even with these moderate requirements and were deprived or in some cases imprisoned. This actually marked a transition into a new policy, for certain of the deprived ministers sought to set up their own meeting houses. They were not successful by and large for most Puritans sought to remain within the Anglican Church and to remodel it on reformed lines working from within.

The deeper question in Puritanism was not in these externals but in the matter of Church government. Thomas Cartwright (1535–1603), the most gifted, learned and able of the Puritans, argued that the ultimate authority of episcopacy was the papacy, and that to retain prelacy, which in any case was unscriptural, was to hold on to the vestiges of popery. Arguing on a New Testament basis he pleaded for the "parity of ministers." At this time the Puritan party gained a measure of strength in Parliament, and we now begin to see attempts to presbyterianize the Church of England by legislation. It was never the Queen's wish to allow Parliament any voice in the life of the Church; she preferred to rule with Convocation; yet in 1571 Parliament enacted the Thirty-Nine Articles, to which all clergy must subscribe on pain of deprivation.[1] Clauses were added about the age, competency and education of clergy. A certain stiffening of policy is now clearly discernible by the bishops and Ecclesiastical Commission, who were now insisting on clergy declaiming their allegiance to the Book of Common Prayer as being agreeable to the Word of God, on their wearing the surplice, and on their declaring the Articles as containing true Christian doctrine. This pressure from Church leaders set up an opposite pressure from the Puritans. Thomas Cartwright and Walter Travers[2] now begin to show their aims and ideals, though as men they were utterly different. Cartwright was the prophet of Puritanism, a learned man, and undoubtedly deeply religious, but was at the same time intolerant. He had taken a strong line, when Professor of Divinity at Cambridge, against the surplice, a course which cost him his Chair and his fellowship. He could descend to depths of scurrility and bitterness, along with many other sixteenth-century men, but his arguments contrasted unfavourably with the balanced good sense of Hooker. Travers, on the other hand, hardly less able, hardly less religious, maintained a consistent debate at high level and achieved fame in his controversy with the great Hooker whom he had assisted at the Temple. The debate carried through by these two men typifies the nature of the Puritans' growing

---

[1] See Gee and Hardy, No 83; Hardwick, Chap. xi.
[2] See *Elizabethan Nonconformist Texts*, ed. A. Peel and L. H. Carlson, Vols. i–v (London, 1951–66).

unease with the Elizabethan Settlement, as well as the Puritans' programme for continuing the Reformation.

The Puritans persisted in their view that the Elizabethan Settlement was retaining popery, and instanced the use of the surplice because it was white, and the clerical cap because it was square. They found the Prayer Book too close to the old Roman rites, and still objected to the use of the ring, the sign of the cross and kneeling at communion. They saw papistical relics in the retention of saints' days, in the continuance of confirmation and private baptism, in the retention of psalms, canticles and organs and in the maintenance of bishops, priests and deacons. They contended that a compromise position was unsatisfactory and that the only safe policy was a thoroughgoing reformed course. Hooker eventually gave his views defending the Establishment, maintaining that practices were not necessarily bad because they were practised by Rome and that it was both a misuse and misunderstanding of Scripture to insist that all usages must have the authority of Scripture.[1]

There was more to the Puritan criticism than this. They were undoubtedly right to emphasize the urgency of a competent preaching ministry. Perhaps their prophesyings were not the way to go about this at the time, but it is incontrovertible that without a preaching ministry under the Word of God the Reformation has lost its tap-root. Further, the quality of the lives of many of the clergy was no better than in the old pre-Reformation days. There was the old pluralism and non-residence, and far too much scandalous living. The ecclesiastical courts were no better than before, excommunication was used as a procedural course, penance commuted for money and archiepiscopal dispensations dispensed. On all of these matters the Puritans were incontrovertibly right. Such abuses do not belong to the Elizabethan Settlement as such, but that settlement had fallen victim to them as the old unreformed Church had done, and the call was for a clearer insight into the meaning of reformation.

The Puritans' own programme of reform was positive. They sought primarily to re-establish the nature of the ministry in relation to the congregation on strict New Testament lines. "Parity of ministers" was their cry, and, therefore, the abolition of the episcopacy the necessary corollary. Each congregation was to call and elect its own minister, who was to serve with the elders in the form of a consistory, and who was to be admitted to his office on the authority of the wider conference. The minister and his elders were to serve their own congregation and exercise a Christian discipline. Congregations were to have the service of deacons, unordained men, whose special care was the poor. The ultimate authority was to be a national synod. All this was modelled on New Testament lines. Not only was the theory carefully worked out, but the procedure too.

[1] Hooker's Works, V. 5–10.

It was slowly and deliberately planned to conform outwardly to the Church of England but inwardly to prepare the way for its presbyteriani-zation. Puritanism was a real force. The clergy were now accustomed to regular meetings for the exposition of Scripture, but through these meet-ings, "prophesyings" as they were called, these men saw an opportunity of inculcating their biblical theology and realizing their wish to presby-terianize the Church. Elizabeth saw this as a grave threat to the establish-ment (1574), and she was undoubtedly right. But Grindal refused to condemn the "prophesyings" and sought primarily to regularize them, a resistance which cost him his throne (1577). Grindal sought to preserve the good and at the same time eliminate what was offending the Queen. He sought to bring them under episcopal control, to exclude laymen and deprived ministers, and to mollify the Puritan opposition to authority. Elizabeth would listen to no such half measures. Grindal stood firm. He emphasized the value of the prophesyings, bluntly refused to eradicate them and then concluded by advising the Queen to consult her theologians on matters such as these in the way she consulted her judges on legal matters. The Queen overrode Grindal and sent her orders directly to the bishops after sequestrating the Archbishop and bringing him into disgrace. Grindal did not yield till his death, and the deprived Church of England battled through the storms captainless.

Matters worsened. Oppression begat resistance: resistance polemics and extremism: resistance more oppression. The satirical and violent polemics of the Martin Marprelate tracts of 1588 gave rise to much bitterness. By 1593 we find the Act against Puritans[1] directed against the "wicked and dangerous practices of seditious sectaries and disloyal persons." By terms of this Act to refuse to attend church, to challenge the Queen's title, or attend any conventicle was to face imprisonment until the recalcitrant conformed. Obstinate offenders were to be banished the realm, and the determinedly disobedient treated as felons. Full opportunity was given for open submission by offenders. To harbour an offender (unless related by kindred) was to face a penalty of a fine of £10, a third part of which was to be given to charity.

In the meantime a separatist tendency had been growing within Puri-tanism, and these events served to quicken that movement and bring to birth Independency. Independency was the third and final stage of the development of Puritanism, and its story belongs to the next volume. Yet the rise of Independency belongs to the Elizabethan story even if its story belongs to the seventeenth century. Discontent with the Establishment had now developed into hostility, and the Puritan leaders were now convinced that episcopacy needed to be swept away in favour of Presbyterianism. The zealots were seeking to impose a sabbatarianism on society, objecting

[1] Gee and Hardy, No. 86.

to the fairs and relaxations which had been normal practice after Church on Sunday, even to organs and choirs in the churches. But many people still liked the organ in the church and the maypole on the green, and had little sympathy with the world-renouncing nature of Puritanism. Puritan inspired moves in Parliament were unsuccessful though a petition of the Queen by the Commons, through the Privy Council at first but later direct to the Queen, caused her to acknowledge the protest. The Commons showed concern about the incompetence of the clergy and the abuse of discipline by ecclesiastical lawyers. Convocation joined the chorus and petitioned the bishops for reform. The Queen sent for Edwin Sandys, Archbishop of York, who startled her by saying the matter was so momentous as to require Parliamentary legislation. The Queen refused and allowed a few proposals through on the education of the clergy and their preaching responsibilities, neither of which met the gravity of the situation. Nevertheless, the Commons continued to "exhibit" their complaints, and a reading of these shows how strong a hold Puritanism had over the minds of the clergy. They were virtually demanding what was a Genevan discipline on Cartwright's or Travers's lines, a discipline the bishops were now resisting, even if they were tightening up their pastoral control in their dioceses. There was, too, the problem of presbyterian orders, and the evidence of non-episcopally ordained men exercising high office in the Church (Wittingham, Dean of Durham, for example) shows how far Puritan views had permeated the Elizabethan Church.

It was but a step for Robert Browne to slight his episcopal licence and raise the whole question of the validity of non-episcopal orders. Here began independency. He sought a new and true reformation which would yield a truly spiritual Church free of all these sickening abuses. Browne was more than a mere nonconformist. He knew the reformation he desired demanded separation and the reorganization of the Church "from the worthiest, were they never so few." The step was inevitable, a step the nonconformists were to be compelled to take. Joined by Robert Harrison they caused great unrest in East Anglia. Their cry was "Reformation without tarrying for any." This wing of the Puritan party rejected the divine right of the Presbyterian system. They rejected outright the whole idea of the royal supremacy. They would not recognize the historic church in England as a church at all: they believed it was corrupt and contaminated with non-believers and evil livers, conceiving a church as consisting only of the elect saints in the New Testament sense. The Brownists fell foul both of Presbyterianism and Anglicanism. Following on the disorders of East Anglia, Browne fled to Holland to join the Puritan English colony of Middelburg, where he found the theological climate less congenial than the Anglican he had so roundly abused. At Middelburg the Puritan nonconformists, assembled under the banners of Cartwright and

Fenner, cared not for Browne's fantatical exclusivism: the Nonconformist wished to cling to the outward organization of the Church while seeking to reform it from within; the Separatist had the sectary's view of the spiritual church as a body of believers, and condemned the Nonconformist's allegiance (or subservience) to civil authority. Browne returned to England in 1591 and actually died as an English rector. It was the refusal to accept the Royal supremacy which brought in the death of the first Protestant martyrs in East Anglia (Coppin and Thacker, June, 1583) as well as a bonfire of Browne's books, and when Henry Barrow (1550-93) and John Greenwood (d. 1593) took up the leadership of the movement they faced execution in 1593 on the same charge of sedition for refusing to acknowledge the royal supremacy.

It was this final stage of Puritanism which compelled the leaders of the Church of England to define their position. It brought the battle out of the Law Courts and out of the Commons into the pulpit, the Puritans' own ground. It was Bancroft's sermon at Paul's Cross in 1589 that began the campaign. He had earlier denounced the Puritans for their attack on the Church as well as the Marprelate tracts. In 1593 he published his two books, *A Survey of the Pretended Discipline* and *Dangerous Positions*,[1] which were exposures of the principles and practices of Puritanism. Bancroft, though hardly a great theologian, elevated the controversy from matters of vestments, ceremonies and ecclesiastical courts, to the issue of episcopacy versus presbyterianism. Many found the bishop's case too strongly stated, for in certain quarters the view had gained ground that though England had maintained the episcopacy it was a mere matter of convenience or historic accident. Not so Bancroft. Bancroft was supported by others, among whom was the distinguished Dutch scholar, Hadrian Saravia, drawn with other learned foreigners to England on account of the very English Reformation the Puritans were seeking to change. The Puritans made several abortive attempts in Parliament (1589, 1593, 1597, 1601) to advance their cause, but in fact the most part of the business was done in convocation. Here Whitgift (Grindal's successor at Canterbury) was supported in his efforts to remedy pluralism, absenteeism and other abuses, and succeeded in laying the foundations of the canon law of 1604.

It then emerged in the Law Courts that the conspiracy to substitute presbyterianism for the Elizabethan system was far more powerful and more widely organized than had been realized. The negotiations with John Johnson of Northampton and Edmund Snape revealed that these unlawful assemblies had declared themselves against the dumb ministry, episcopal ordination and government, and that Snape had mutilated the Prayer Book and even renounced his orders in favour of a call from a

---

[1] A. Peel (ed.), *Tracts ascribed to Richard Bancroft* (1953). Bancroft was to become Bishop of London (1597-1604) and Archbishop of Canterbury (1604-10).

classis.[1] A deep disagreement emerged in the matter of the oath *ex officio*. This empowered a bishop to take action on the basis of a spiritual relation rather than a judicial, but when this power was denied the matter was referred to the Law Officers of the Crown. They viewed the matter as a judicial not a spiritual issue, and determined that in cases of disobedience of such a kind, a prosecution in the court of Star Chamber and a sentence of banishment was the only procedure. Cartwright, Snape and others faced actions, but the lawyers allowed the wider theological issues to be ignored in favour of the precise, legally enforceable, matter of the oath. The prisoners would not respond to this illegitimate narrowing of the issue and found themselves imprisoned, deprived and degraded. It was only the following year that Whitgift himself, who held Cartwright in high regard, eventually secured their release.

Certain issues come to light in this matter. It became clear that the Puritans, though under oath to the bishop, and under licence of the established church, were using their position as a cloak to cover their Puritanism. In actual fact they were managing their parishes according to the *Book of Discipline*[2] not the *Book of Common Prayer*. Their commission they were taking from presbyterian committees, not their bishops, and their directions from presbyterian synods not convocation. They used the parts of the Prayer Book they liked, wore what clothes they liked, did what they wanted, destroyed what they wanted. They accepted ministerial posts of the Church, enjoyed her revenues and properties, and used the place and its resources to pervert that to which they had taken oaths. This is a remarkable phenomenon for men of such conscientious scruples, and the only explanation is that they enjoyed the support of a public opinion which preferred the high earnestness of the Puritans to the grave laxity and open scandal of the establishment.

When Whitgift secured the release of Cartwright the battle ended. Cartwright intended to resume the fight when Elizabeth died, and we find him drawing up the Millenary Petition in London in March, 1603. He was to have been the great protagonist at the Hampton Court Conference, but died in December, 1603, in the midst of his final preparations. The loss to the party was enormous, his place could not be filled. In Cartwright died the noblest Puritan of his generation, perhaps the most learned and cultured of all Puritans.

Another important development should be noted. In the closing years of the century, men began to turn away from all the disputes about externalities and discipline, and more to the matters of doctrine. Hitherto Calvin's theology had dominated the Puritans, but the distinguished Lady Margaret Professor of Divinity at Cambridge, the French Calvinist Baro,

[1] From κλῆσις, a meeting called together. It sometimes meant a presbytery.
[2] Text in Calderwood. II. 51-120, III 529-55.

a disciple of Calvin, ordained by the master himself, had begun to modify his Calvinism, particularly in the matter of the doctrine of predestination. One of his pupils on praying for his B.D. degree precipitated the process of modification in a sermon preached in 1595. The archbishop, in an effort to allay harmful doctrinal controversy, produced a set of articles proposed by Whitaker the Regius Professor, to rebut Baro's "Arminianism." These Lambeth Articles caused Baro to demur, and on examination Baro justified his formal assent but the archbishop accepted Baro's explanations and allowed him to continue in office. In the meantime Whitaker died, to be succeeded by Overall, one of the younger rising Anglican men, who saw the issues differently from their rather Calvinistic older contemporaries. In fact Overall was responsible for having these Lambeth Articles pigeon-holed; he even foiled the Puritan attempts to bring them out again in 1604.

## 3. The Anglican Compromise

This illustrates a change, broader and wider, that was coming over the Church in England. With Hooker in Oxford, and Andrewes and Overall at Cambridge, a fresh and abiding development took place in Anglicanism. These men, and others, formulated and led the appeal against dominant Calvinism, and introduced – and this is said without any odious comparison with Calvin – a typically English kind of settlement, mature and sane. This conception was based on the appeal to scripture, on the appeal to the catholic undivided Church of East and West, and on sound, informed reason. These principles Luther himself had enunciated, and none had held with clearer logic and more effective power than Calvin. Yet they needed digesting, making our own, and developing into our national life. This is only what Cranmer and all the others had seen, but circumstances had hitherto prevented.

Hooker's work needs special mention in this context. It will be remembered how at the Temple he had engaged in noble polemics with his younger colleague Travers, and how men marked the voice of Canterbury in the morning and Geneva in the afternoon. Hooker retired to the country to seek the chance of formulating his views and left, regrettably unfinished before his death, his superlative Elizabethan apologia for the English Church, his *Ecclesiastical Polity*,[1] of which Pope Clement VIII declared,

> it had in it such seeds of eternity that it would abide till the last fire shall consume all learning.[2]

Hooker met an anarchic Protestantism with a high theory of order and law, whose "seat is the bosom of God and her voice the harmony of the

[1] Hooker's Works, Vol. I, 71.        [2] Hooker's Works III. i. 10.

world." He saw this law as behind the papal decrees, behind Scripture itself, and expressing itself in both. God he saw as revealing Himself in many ways, and he expected man not only to learn to know God from the Scriptures but by a number of concurrent means and faculties. Puritans restricted themselves to the Bible only. Hooker encouraged men to see that it was no disparagement of Scripture to admit the guidance of the Holy Spirit in the history of the Catholic Church and in the drawing up of her great conciliar creeds. He believed that a church had every right to order its own rites and ceremonies, and that the Church in England was a true part of the Church Catholic. He claimed the right to reform the Church in England by the Christian men who lived within its shores, and granted that right to others in other lands. "We unchurch nobody," he said.

> To reform ourselves is not to sever ourselves from the church we were of before; in the church we were and we are so still.[1]

Unlike many Protestants or rather contemporary Puritans he did not seek to disparage the old church in order to make the new appear better. Nor would he have former practices dismissed as "popish dregs," for he would never think other than that God had been in His church all the centuries, even when the Church was at its lowest ebb. Similarly, he refused to exalt the primitive apostolic order of the Church alone as the divine, unalterable unchangeable norm and roundly denied that the original form had been presbyterian. He saw the ministry as a matter of administration and order, a matter of historical necessity, even accident. Many Anglicans have not accepted his view of the Church as a kind of social evolution. Nor have they admitted his acceptance of Continental non-episcopal orders, and with it his view of apostolic succession as a matter of succession of apostolic doctrine, nor a mere tactual transmission of orders. In other places Hooker has a more exalted view of the priesthood and the episcopacy as having authority from God rather than from the Christian society, nevertheless, these other views are clearly expressed. He also discusses in the Fifth Book a very fine doctrine of the Incarnation,[2] together with a doctrine of the Holy Communion, where he says that

> these holy mysteries do instrumentally impart into us, in true and real though mystical manner, the very person of our Lord Himself, whole, perfect and entire.[3]

Nevertheless, he does express a virtualist and receptionist view of the sacrament, as Cranmer did:

> the real presence of Christ's most blessed Body and Blood is not to be sought for in the Sacrament, but in the worthy receiver of the Sacrament.

[1] Hooker, V. l. 1 ff.  [2] Ibid. V. lxvii. 8.  [3] Ibid. V. lxvii. 6.

It will be seen that Hooker represents a conservative reaction from the rigours and excesses of the earlier days, a reaction that was continued under Andrewes, Herbert and Laud. But these men belong to another age, and another writer must relate their story. Certainly Hooker rescued theological controversy from the gutter and invested it with a peculiar and abiding Englishness, a richness and a grandeur that was to last a long time, and which still belongs to the ethos of the Church of England.

Hooker was working during those years when the spiritual struggles of his countrymen were slowly beginning to abate. The country had been through terrible days of war, poverty, weakness, upheaval, disunity. Religion had sunk to a low ebb: decency in worship and dignity in ministration had been the first casualties. At one time hatred of Rome and Spain had done duty for national religion. These days were over. Churches were now being cared for as centres of worship and prayer, and services beginning to revive. There are signs that confession reappeared, books of devotion were printed, and a general rise in English spirituality developed, but how this real spirituality developed and maintained itself will be the work of another writer. When Queen Elizabeth died on March 24, 1603, she brought a great church era to an end.

Anglicanism may be understood as an attempt to settle in England the religious disputes raised by the Reformation. It was a genuine attempt to meet on the one hand the demands of the Protestants by a precise appeal to Scripture, and on the other the demands of the Catholics by a critical appeal to tradition. It was an attempt to reform Catholicism by an appeal to its own original foundations, an attempt to keep the Reformation within Catholicism. Above all it was an attempt to keep this settlement one and the same for all Englishmen, a single united Church embracing all: one Church, one people. The nation at large accepted the Anglican compromise, though often for different reasons. The Catholic Anglican saw in it a reasonable continuation of the old faith: the Protestant Anglican a clear enough challenge to Rome and her practices. But there was (and still is in Anglicanism) a strong third party less theologically committed. They liked (and like) Anglicanism as a form of Christianity granting them more liberty of thought than any other known form, and support it on this pragmatic ground. Extremists from both sides opposed it for exactly the same reason. They saw the settlement as a weakening of the fibre of religion, a snare alike to the weak Catholic and the unenthusiastic Protestant. Nevertheless, the unification of Protestant and Catholic under Scripture, Catholic tradition and sound reason, with a single prayer book and balanced articles and formularies is a significant historical achievement. It eventually proved itself incapable of realizing its purpose fully, for the extreme Catholics withdrew to Roman Catholicism, the extreme Protestants to found Independency and the Free Churches. Nevertheless, in

Laud's memorable phrase, religion before and after the Reformation was like Naaman before and after his cure. But "it was the same Naaman, leprous with them (the Romanists), cleansed with us (the Anglicans)."

It was the intention of Cranmer and of all the English reformers that the Anglican Settlement should be a provisional stage in the creation of a new, truly oecumenical Catholicism, purged of its accretions and impurities, and purified by the perpetual, critical activity of evangelical theology. Catholicism and Protestantism fell asunder because Christendom could not receive as a single living communion the divine disturbance we call the Reformation, and could not meet as a single living communion the challenge of holding them together in one Church.

# CHRONOLOGICAL TABLES

## POPES (1492–1605)

| | | | |
|---|---|---|---|
| Alexander VI | 1492–1503 | Paul IV | 1555–1559 |
| Pius III | 1503 | Pius IV | 1559–1566 |
| Julius II | 1503–1513 | Pius V | 1566–1572 |
| Leo X | 1513–1521 | Gregory XIII | 1572–1585 |
| Adrian VI | 1522–1523 | Sixtus V | 1585–1590 |
| Clement VII | 1523–1534 | Urban VII | 1590 |
| Paul III | 1534–1549 | Gregory XIV | 1590–1591 |
| Julius III | 1550–1555 | Innocent IX | 1591–1592 |
| Marcellus II | 1555 | Clement VIII | 1592–1605 |

## EMPERORS OF THE HOLY ROMAN EMPIRE OF THE GERMAN NATION

| | | | |
|---|---|---|---|
| Maximilian I | 1493–1519 | Ferdinand I | 1556–1564 |
| Charles V | 1519–1556 | Maximilian II | 1564–1576 |
| | (died 1558) | Rudolf II | 1576–1612 |

## KINGS OF FRANCE

| | |
|---|---|
| Louis XII | 1498–1515 |
| Francis I | 1515–1547 |
| Henry II | 1547–1559 |
| Francis II[1] | 1559–1560 |
| Charles IX | 1560–1574 |
| Henry III | 1574–1589 |
| Henry IV | 1589–1610 |

## RULERS OF ENGLAND

| | |
|---|---|
| Henry VII | 1485–1509 |
| Henry VIII | 1509–1547 |
| Edward VI | 1547–1553 |
| Mary I | 1553–1558 |
| Elizabeth I | 1558–1603 |
| James I | 1603–1625 |

## RULERS OF SCOTLAND

| | | | |
|---|---|---|---|
| James IV | 1488–1513 | Mary | 1542–1567 |
| James V | 1513–1542 | | (died 1587) |
| | | James VI | 1567–1625 |

[1]First husband of Mary, Queen of Scots.

263

## LIST OF ABBREVIATIONS

| | |
|---|---|
| C.R. | *Corpus Reformatorum.* |
| L.C.C. | Library of Christian Classics. |
| P.C.H. | Paternoster Church History. |
| P.S. | Parker Society. |
| W.A. | *Weimarer Ausgabe* (Weimar edition of Luther's works.) |
| W.A.Br. | Weimar edition of Luther's Letters *(Briefe).* |
| W.M.L. | *Works of Martin Luther* (Philadelphia). |

See also pp. 267–8.

# BIBLIOGRAPHY

## I. WORKS OF REFERENCE

Aland, Kurt, *Hilfsbuch zum Lutherstudium* (Guetersloh, 1956).

*Calvin Bibliographie*, Wilhelm Niesel. 1901–59 (Munich, 1961).

*Catholic Encyclopedia*, 15 vols. + Index (New York, 1907–14).

Cross, F. L. (ed), *The Oxford Dictionary of the Christian Church* (London, 1957). Valuable for bibliographies. Not good on the Reformation articles.

*Dictionary of English Church History*, ed. S. L. Ollard and G. Grosse (London, 1902) and M. F. Bond (London, 1948).

*Dictionary of National Biography*, eds. G. Smith, L. Stephen and S. Lee, repr. 21 vols. with Supplements (London, 1908–9).

*Histoire de l'Église*, ed. A. Fliche and V. Martin. Vol. 16. *La crise religieuse du 16e siècle*, E. de Moreau (Paris, 1950).

*Lexikon für Theologie und Kirche*, ed. M. Buchberger. 10 vols. (Freiburg im Breisgau, 1930–38).

*New Cambridge Modern History*, Vol. 1. Potter, G. R., *The Renaissance 1493–1520* (Cambridge, 1957).

Vol. 2. Elton, G. R., *The Reformation* (Cambridge, 1958).

Parker, T. H. L., Calvin Bibliography 1900–40. *The Evangelical Quarterly*, April 1946, pp. 123–31.

Pastor, L., *The History of the Popes from the Close of the Middle Ages*, English translation. 40 vols. (London, 1891–1957).

Read, Conyers, *Bibliography of British History: Tudor Period 1485–1603* (Oxford, 1933).

*Realencyklopaedie fuer Protestantische Theologie und Kirche*, J. J. Herzog und A. Hauck. 21 vols. (Leipzig, 1896–1913). (Supplements 2 vols., Leipzig, 1913).

*Religion in Geschichte und Gegenwart*, ed. 2, H. Gunkel and L. Zscharnack. 5 vols., 1927–31; ed. 3, K. Galling, 6 vols. + Index vol. (Tübingen, 1957–65).

## II. TEXTS

Bancroft, Richard, *Tracts*, ed. Albert Peel (Cambridge, 1953). *Die Bekenntnisschriften der evangelisch-lutherischen Kirche* (Göttingen, 1959).

Bettenson, Henry, *Documents of the Christian Church* (London, 1943).

Brandt, Otto H., *Der Grosse Bauernkrieg. Zeitgenosse Berichte* (Jena, 1926).

Brandi, Karl, *Briefe und Akten zur Geschichte des XVI Jahrhunderts* in *Beiträge zur Reichsgeschichte 1546–55*. Vol. 4 (Munich, 1873).

Bucer, *Martini Buceri Omnia Opera. Martin Bucers Deutsche Schriften* ed. François Wendel *et al.* (Paris and Guetersloh 1960–   ).

Melanchthon and Bucer, L.C.C., Vol. 19, ed. F. J. Taylor (appearing).

Calvin, *Corpus Reformatorum*, Vols. 29–87 (Braunschweig, 1863–1900), *J. Calvini Opera Selecta*, 5 vols. (Munich, 1926–52)

*Institutes of the Christian Religion*, ed. J. T. McNeill, L.C.C. Vols. 20–21 (London, 1961).

*Theological Treatises*, ed. J. K. S. Reid, L.C.C. Vol. 22 (London 1954).

Calvin's Commentaries (Edinburgh, 1846 ff.). (Being reprinted by Eerdmans, Grand Rapids, 1948–   .)

Commentaries, ed. Joseph Haroutunian, L.C.C. Vol. 23.

*Letters of John Calvin* (Philadelphia, n.d.).

*Calvin Treasury.* Preface by T. F. Torrance (London, 1963).

*Tracts and Treatises,* 3 vols. Repr. of 1844 edn. (Edinburgh, 1958).

Cardwell, Edward, ed., *Reformatio Legum Ecclesiasticorum,* 1552–3.

Cardwell, Edward, ed., *Documentary Annals of the Reformed Church of England 1546–1716* (Oxford, 1839).

Cochrane, Arthur (ed.), *Reformed Confessions of the 16th century* (London, 1966).

*Concilium Tridentinum* (ed.), Societas Goerresiana (Freiburg, 1901– ).

*The Book of Concord,* Trans. and ed. Theodore G. Tappert (Philadelphia, 1959).

*Corpus Schwenckfeldianorum,* 14 vols. (Leipzig, 1907–36).

Cowan, Ian B., *Blast and Counterblast. Contempory Writings in the Scottish Reformation* (Edinburgh, 1960).

W. Croft Dickinson and Gordon Donaldson, *Source Book of Scottish History,* 3 vols. (London, 1950–54).

Dunlop, William, *Collection of Confessions of Faith, 1719, 1775, 1857* (Edinburgh).

Ellis, Henry, *Original Letters illustrative of English Church History,* 3 series (London, 1825–46).

Erasmus, *Desiderii Erasmi Opera Omnia,* 10 vols. (Leiden, 1703–6).

P. S. Allen, *Opus Epistolarum Desid. Erasmi Roterodami,* 11 vols. (Oxford, 1893–1947).

*Discourse on Free Will,* Trans. and ed. Ernest F. Winter (Ungar, 1961).

Foxe, John *Acts and Monuments,* 1563. 8 vols. (London (1870?)).

Gee. H., and Hardy, W. J., *Documents Illustrative of English Church History,* 3rd ed. (London, 1914).

Goldsmid, Edward, *Collection of Documents Illustrative of the Reigns of the Tudor and Stuart Sovereigns* (Edinburgh, 1886).

Hardwick, C., *History of the Articles of Religion 1536–1615.* (Cambridge, 1861. rev. 3rd ed., London, 1904.)

Herminjard, A. L., *Correspondance des Réformateurs,* 9 vols. (Geneva, 1866–97).

Hillerbrand, H. J., *The Reformation in its own Words* (London, 1964).

Hooker, Richard, *The Works of Richard Hooker,* 3 vols., ed. John Keble (Oxford, 1836).

Kidd, Benjamin J., Documents illustrative of the Continental Reformation (Oxford, 1911).

The King's Book, ed. T. A. Lacey (London, 1932).

John Knox: Works, Collected and edited by David Laing, 6 vols. (Edinburgh, 1846–64).

Leishmann, Thomas, *Liturgy of John Knox (Book of Common Order)* (Edinburgh and London, 1868).

Letters and Papers, *Calendar of Letters and Papers, Foreign and Domestic of the Reign of Henry VIII,* eds. J. Brewer, J. Gairdner, R. Brodie. 20 vols. (London, 1862–1910).

*Calendar of State Papers: Edward VI, 1547–53,* ed. William B. Turnbull (London, 1861).

*C.S.P. Mary 1553–58,* ed. William B. Turnbull (London, 1861).

*C.S.P. (Domestic Series) Edward VI, Mary and Elizabeth*, ed. Robert Lemon (London, 1856–72).

*C.S.P. (Foreign) Queen Elizabeth*, eds. J. Stevenson, A. J. Crosby, A. J. Butler, S. C. Lomes and Allen B. Hinds (London, 1863–1950).

Luther, D. *Martin Luthers Werke*, Weimar 1883–
    Quoted. WA.      volume, page, line.
          WABi    (Bible) volume, page, line.
          WABr.   (Letters) volume, number.
          WATi.   (Table Talk) volume, number.

*Works of Martin Luther*, Philadelphia, 1915–32. Quoted WML. Volume, page. (Called Philadelphia Edition.)

*Luther's Works*, St. Louis and Philadelphia 1957 ff. Quoted AE. Vol., page. (Called American Edition.)

*The Whole Workes of W. Tyndall, John Frith, and Doctor Barnes*, ed. John Day (London, 1573).


Other useful translations generally available:

Martin Luther, *Reformation Writings*, 2 vols., translated B. Lee Wolf (London, 1952).

Martin Luther, *Selections from his Writings*, John Dillenberger. (Chicago, 1961).

Smith, Preserved, and Jacobs G. M., eds., *Luther's Correspondence*, 2 vols. (Philadelphia, 1913–18).

*Commentary on Galatians*, re-ed. P. S. Watson (Edinburgh, 1953).

Martin Luther, *Letters of Spiritual Counsel*, ed. Tappert, Theodore (Philadelphia, 1955).

Packer, J. I., and Johnston, O.R., eds., *The Bondage of the Will* (London, 1953).

Scheel, Otto, *Dokumente zur Luthers Entwicklung bis 1519* (Tübingen, 1929).

Lloyd, C., ed., *Formularies of the Faith* (Oxford, 1825).

Loescher, Valentin Ernst, *Vollständige Reformationsacta und Dokumente*. 3 vols. (Leipzig, 1720–29).

*Library of Christian Classics*. London and Philadelphia (quoted: L.C.C.).

Vol. 14. *Advocates of Reform: from Wyclif to Erasmus*, ed. Matthew Spinka (1953).

Vol. 15. Luther, *Lectures on Romans*, ed. Wilhelm Pauck (1961).

Vol. 16. Luther, *Early Theological Writings*, ed. James Atkinson (1962).

Vol. 18. Luther, *Letters of Spiritual Counsel*, ed. Theodore Tappert (1955).

[Appearing Vol. 19. Melanchthon and Bucer, ed. F. J. Taylor?].

Vols. 20, 21. Calvin, *Institutes*, ed. John T. McNeill (1961).

Vol. 22. Calvin, *Theological Treatises*, ed. J. K. S. Reid (1954).

Vol. 23. Calvin, *Commentaries*, ed. Joseph Haroutunian (1958).

Vol. 24. *Zwingli and Bullinger*, ed. G. W. Bromiley (1953).

Vol. 25. *Spiritual and Anabaptist Writers*, eds. G. H. Williams and Angel M. Mergal (1957).

Vol. 26. *English Reformers*, ed. T. H. L. Parker (1966).

Macgregor, M. B., *The Sources and Literature of Scottish Church History* (Glasgow, 1934).

*Marprelate Tracts*, 1588, 1589, ed. William Pierce (London, 1911).

*Melanchthons Werke*, ed. Robert Stupperich et al. (Guetersloh, 1951–    ).

Melanchthon: *Selected Writings*, trans. Charles L. Hill (Augsburg, 1962).

*Monumenta Historica: Societas Jesu*, 89 vols. (Madrid, 1894 ff.). (Indispensable source-book.)

Murray, Iain, *The Reformation of the Church* (Collection of Reformed and Puritan documents) (London, 1965).

Niemeyer, Hermann Agathon, *Collectio Confessionum* (Leipzig, 1840).

Peel, A., and Carlson, L. H., *Elizabethan Nonconformist Texts* (London, 1951–   ).

Parker Society Publications. 53 vols. (Cambridge, 1841–53).

Reich, Emil, *Select Documents illustrating Medieval and Modern History* (London, 1905).

*Deutsche Reichstagsakten, jüngere Reihe* I (1893), Kluckhorn ed.; II–IV (1896–1908), Wrede ed.; VII (1935) Kühn ed. (Gotha).

Routh, C. R. N., *They saw it happen. An Anthology of Eye-Witness Accounts of Events in British History, 1485–1688* (Oxford, 1957).

Schaff, Philip, *The Creeds of Christendom*. 3 vols. (New York, 1877).

Sehling, Emil, ed., *Die evangelischen Kirchenordnungen des XVI Jahrhunderts* (Tübingen, 1965–   ).

Strype, J., *Annals*. 4 vols. (Oxford, 1824).

Calendar of State Papers. Public Record Office (London)
    Papers preserved in Rome, 2 vols., ed. J. M. Rigg, 1916–26.
    Papers preserved in Spain, 15 vols., ed. G. A. Bergenroth, 1862–54.
    Papers preserved in Venice, vols. 1–9, ed. Rawdon Brown, 1864–1947.

Torrance, T. F., *The School of Faith: Catechism of the Reformed Church* (London, 1959).

Zwingli, *Huldreich Zwinglis Sämtliche Schriften*. Corpus Reformatorum, Vols. 88 ff. (Leipzig, 1905).

Huldreich Zwingli, *Hauptschriften*, ed. Künzli (Zürich, 1940 ff.).

Köhler, Walther, *Das Buch der Reformation Huldreich Zwingli* (Munich, 1926).

Ulrich Zwingli, *Eine Auswahl aus seinen Schriften*, eds. G. Finsler, W. Köhler, A. Ruegg (Zürich, 1918).

The following English translations are useful:

Bromiley, G. W., *Zwingli and Bullinger*, L.C.C. 24 (Philadelphia and London, 1953).

Jackson, Samuel M. (ed.), *Selected Works of Huldreich Zwingli* (Philadelphia, 1901).

Jackson, Samuel M. (ed.), *The Latin Works and Correspondence of Huldreich Zwingli*. 3 vols. (New York, 1912; Philadelphia, 1922, 1929).

## III. General Works

* = Specially commended

Allen, P. S., *Erasmus, Lectures and Wayfaring Sketches* (Oxford, 1934).

*Althaus, Paul, *The Theology of Martin Luther* (Gütersloh, 1962, trans. 1966). Weighty, scholarly.

Andreas, Willy, *Deutschland vor der Reformation* (Stuttgart, 1948).

Atkinson, James, *Rome and Reformation* (London, 1966).

Babbage, Stuart Barton, *Puritanism and Richard Bancroft* (London, 1962).

Bagley, J. J., *Henry VIII* (London, 1962).

Bainton, Roland, *Bibliography of the Continental Reformation* (Chicago, 1935).

Bainton, Roland, *Here I Stand* (New York, 1950) (Theologically thin).

Bainton, Roland, *The Medieval Church* (Princeton, 1962).

Bainton, Roland, *Studies on the Reformation* (Boston, 1963; London, 1964).

Beza, Theodore, *Life of John Calvin* (1564). Trans. Henry Beveridge (Edinburgh, 1844).

*Bindoff, S. T., *Tudor England* (Pelican) (London, 1950).

Birt, Norbert, *The Elizabethan Religious Settlement* (London, 1907).

Blaarer, Ambrose (or Blarer, or Blaurer). A. Blarer, *Die Schwäbische Reformation* (Stuttgart, 1860).

Black, J. B., *The Reign of Elizabeth, 1558–1603* (Bibliographies) (Oxford, 1936).

Boehmer, Heinrich, *Road to Reformation* (London, 1946, 1957).

Boehmer, Heinrich, *The Jesuits* (Philadelphia, 1928).

Boettner, Loraine, *Roman Catholicism* (London, 1966).

Booty, John E., *John Jewel as Apologist of the Church of England* (London, 1963).

Bornkamm, Heinrich, *Luther's World of Thought* (St. Louis, 1958).

Bouyer, Louis, *The Spirit and Forms of Protestantism*. Trans. A. V. Littledale (London, 1956).

Brandi, Karl, *Charles V* (1937). Eng. trans., C. V. Wedgwood (London, 1939).

Broderick, James, *The Origins of the Jesuits* (London/New York, 1940).

Broderick, James, *The Progress of the Jesuits* (London/New York, 1947).

Broderick, James, *St. Francis Xavier (1506–52)* (New York, 1952).

Brown, P. Hume, *John Knox*. 2 vols. (London, 1895).

Bruce, F. F., *The English Bible* (London, 1961).

Bruce, F. F., *The Spreading Flame*, P.C.H. Vol. 1 (London, 1958, 1961).

Burleigh, J. H. S., *A Church History of Scotland* (London, 1960).

Burns, J. H., *The Political Background of the Reformation*. Innes Review, 1962, pp. 1 ff.

Butterworth, Chas C., *The English Primers 1529–45* (Philadelphia, 1953).

Calderwood, D., *The History of the Kirk of Scotland*. 8 vols. (Edinburgh, 1842–9).

Cardwell, E., *Documentary Annals of Church of England 1546–1716* (Oxford, 1854).

Carlson, Edgar M., *The Reinterpretation of Luther* (Philadelphia, 1948).

Caspari, F., *Humanism and the Social Order in Tudor England* (Chicago, 1954).

Chadwick, Owen, *Pelican History of the Church*, Vol. 3. *The Reformation* (London, 1964).

Chambers, R. W., *Thomas More* (London, 1935).

Courvoisier, Jacques: *Zwingli, a Reformed Theologian* (London, 1963).

Creighton, Mandell, *Queen Elizabeth* (London, 1896).

Dakin, A., *Calvinism* (London, 1941).

Daniel-Rops, H., *The Protestant Reformation* (London/New York, 1961).

Daniel-Rops, H., *The Catholic Reformation* (London/New York, 1962). (Both well written, but with Catholic bias.)

Darby, H. S., *Hugh Latimer* (London, 1953).

Dawley, P. M., *John Whitgift and the English Reformation* (New York, 1954).

Denifle, Heinrich, *Luther und Luthertum* I, II, III (Mainz, 1904–9). Trans. *Luther and Lutherdom* (Somerset, Ohio. Torch Press, 1917). (Violently anti-Protestant.)

Dickens, A. G., *The English Reformation* (New York, 1964).

Dickens, A. G., *Lollards and Protestants in the Diocese of York 1509–1558* (London, 1959).

Dickens, A. G., *Reformation and Society in 16th Century Europe* (London, 1966).

Dickinson, William Croft, *John Knox's History of the Reformation in Scotland* (Edinburgh, 1949).

Dillenberger, John, and Welch, Claud, *Protestant Christianity* (New York, 1954).

Dix, Dom Gregory, *The Shape of the Liturgy* (London, 1945).

Dixon, R. W., *History of the Church of England*. 6 vols. Vol. 5. 1558–63 (1902); Vol. 6. 1564–70 (1902) (London and Oxford, 1878–1902).

Donaldson, Gordon, *The Scottish Reformation* (Cambridge, 1960).

Dowey, E. A., *The Knowledge of God in Calvin's Theology* (New York, 1952).

Dowey, E. A., *Studies in Calvin and Calvinism. Church History* 24 (1959); 29 (1960).

Duffield, G. E., ed., *John Calvin* (Abingdon, 1966).

Duffield, G. E., ed., *William Tyndale* (Abingdon, 1964).

Dugmore, C. W., *The Mass and the English Reformers* (London, 1958).

Dumont, Jean, *Corps Diplomatique*. 8 vols. (Amsterdam, 1726–31).

Eells, H., *Martin Bucer* (New Haven, 1931).

*Elton, G. R., *England under the Tudors* (London, 1955). (Excellent Bibliographies.)

*Elton, G. R., *King or Minister? The Man behind the Henrician Reformation* (History, 1954).

Enders, E. L., and Kawerau G. (ed.), *Luther's Correspondence,* 19 vols. (Frankfurt-am-Main, 1884–1932).

Ehrenberg, Hans (ed,), *Luther Speaks* (London, 1947).

*Farner, Oskar, *Huldrych Zwingli*. 4 vols. (Zürich, 1943–59). (The best work on Zwingli available. German difficult.)

*Fife, Robert H., *Young Luther* (New York, 1928).

Fife, Robert H., *The Revolt of Martin Luther* (New York, 1957). (Massive, detailed, scholarly, documented.)

Fleming, D. Hay, *The Reformation in Scotland* (London, 1910).

*Fleming, D. Hay, *Mary Queen of Scots*. (London, 1898).

Foxe, John, *Acts and Monuments*. 8 vols. (London, 1841).

Franz, Günther, *Der Deutsche Bauernkrieg* (Darmstadt, 1956).

Froude, James A, *Life and Letters of Erasmus* (Lectures, delivered 1893–4, publ. London, 1927).

Gairdner, James, *Lollardy and the Reformation in England*. 4 vols. (London, 1908–13). (Not sound on Tudor Lollardy.)

Garrett, C. H., *The Marian Exiles* (Cambridge, 1938). (Useful facts but most questionable conclusion.)

Gee, Henry, *The Elizabethan Clergy and the Settlement of Religion 1558–1564* (Oxford, 1898).

George, C. H., and George, K., *The Protestant Mind of the English Reformation* (Princeton, 1961).

Green, V. H. H., *Luther and the Reformation* (London and New York, 1964). (Useful bibliographies.)

*Grim, Harold J., *The Reformation Era* (New York, 1954).

Grisar, Hartmann, *Luther* (English). 6 vols. (London, 1913–17). (First publ. 1911–12 in Freiburg.) (Violently anti-Protestant.)

Haile, M., *Life of Reginald Pole* (Edinburgh, 1910).

Harnack, Theodosius, *Luthers Theologie*. 2 vols. (Erlangen, 1862–86). (Very old but masterly in its treatment.)

Harrison, D., *Tudor England* (New York, 1954).

Hassinger, Erich, *Das Werden des neuzeitlichen Europa 1300–1600* (Braunschweig, 1959).

Hermelinck, Heinrich, *Reformation und Gegenreformation* (Tübingen, 1931).

Henry VIII, *Assertio septem sacramentorum*. Translated Louis O'Donovan (New York, 1908).

Henry VIII, *Luther's Reply to King Henry VIII*, trans. E. S. Buchanan (New York, 1928).

Higham, Florence, *Catholic and Reformed. A Study of the Anglican Church 1559–1662* (London, 1962).

Hildebrandt, Franz, *Melanchthon, Alien or Ally?* (Cambridge, 1946).

Holl, Karl, *Gesammelte Aufsätze zur Kirchengeschichte* (Tübingen, 1932).

*Homilies* (Oxford, 1832).

Hopf, Konstantin, *Martin Bucer and the English Reformation* (Oxford, 1946).

*Hughes, Philip, *The Reformation in England*. 3 vols. (London, 1950). (Bibliographies. R.C. bias, nevertheless important.)

Hughes, Philip E., *Theology of the English Reformers* (London, 1965). (Not same author as above.)

Hunt, R. N. Carew, *Calvin* (London, 1933).

Hunter, A. M., *The Teaching of Calvin*. 2nd ed. rev. (London, 1950).

Janelle, P., *The Catholic Reformation* (Milwaukee, 1949).

Jansen, J. F., *Calvin's Doctrine of the Work of Christ* (London, 1956).

*Jedin, Hubert, *History of the Council of Trent*. 2 vols. Trans. Ernst Graf (London, 1951–61).

Jewel, John, *Apologie of the Church of England 1560*. Parker Society. Jewel. Vol. 3. Abridged text. L.C.C. Vol. 26 (1966).

Jones, Rufus M., *Spiritual Reformers in the 16th and 17th centuries* (London, 1914).

Keith, R., *The History of the Affairs of Church and State of Scotland*. 3 vols. (Edinburgh, 1884). (Contains many documents.)

*Knappen, M. M.: *Tudor Puritanism* (Chicago, 1939).

Knowles, David, *The Religious Orders in England*. Part III: *The Tudor Age* (Cambridge, 1959).

Knox, D. B., *The Doctrine of Faith in the reign of Henry VIII* (London, 1961). (Bibliography.)

*Knox, John, *History of the Reformation* (Glasgow, 1586–7). Ed. W. Croft Dickinson. 2 vols. (Edinburgh, 1949). (Valuable introduction and appendices, including *The Scots Confession*, and *The First Book of Discipline*.)

Köhler, Walther, *Zwingli und Luther: Quellen und Forschungen zur Reformationsgeschichte*, VI (Leipzig, 1924).

Köhler, Walther, *Dokumente zum Ablassstreit von 1517* (Tübingen, 1901, 1934).

Köstlin, Julius: *Luthers Theologie*. 2 vols. (Stuttgart, 1901).

Köstlin, Julius: *Life of Luther* (Trans.) (London, 1883).

*Köstlin, Julius, and Kawerau, Georg, *Martin Luther*. 2 vols. (Berlin, 1903).

Kramm, H. H., *The Theology of Martin Luther* (London, 1947).

Küng, Hans; Barth, Karl, *et al.*, *Christianity Divided* (London, 1961).

Lacey, T. A., *The King's Book* (London, 1932).

Lau, Franz, *Luther*. Trans. Robert H. Fischer (London, 1963).

Lea, H. C., *History of the Inquisition in Spain*. 4 vols. (New York, 1922).

*Lechler, Gotthard Victor, *John Wiclif and His English Precursors*. 2 vols. Trans. P. Lorimer (London, 1878).

Leff, Gordon, *Medieval Thought from Augustine to Aquinas*. Pelican (London, 1958). (Philosophical rather than theological.)

Leff, Gordon, *Heresy in the Later Middle Ages*. *1250–1450* (Manchester, 1967).

*Lindsay, T. M., *History of the Reformation*. 2 vols. (Edinburgh, 1907). (Old, but valuable.)

Linklater, Eric, *Mary Queen of Scots* (Edinburgh, 1934). (Special pleading.)

Loane, Marcus L., *Pioneers of the Reformation in England* (London, 1964).

Loane, Marcus L., *Masters of the English Reformation* (Bilney, Tyndale, Latimer, Ridley, and Cranmer) (London, 1954).

Locher, Gottfried W., *Die Wandlung des Zwingli-Bildes Zwingliana II* (1963).

Lorimer, Peter, *Patrick Hamilton* (Edinburgh, 1857).

*Lortz, Joseph, *Die Reformation in Deutschland*, 2 vols. (Freiburg, 1962). (Balanced R.C.).

Mackie, J. D., *The Earlier Tudors*. *1485–1558* (Oxford, 1952). (Oxford History of England, Vol. 8.)

McCrie, Thomas, *Life of John Knox* (Edinburgh, 1812). (Sometimes written Maccrie in catalogues.)

McCrie, Thomas, *Life of Andrew Melville*. 2 vols. (Edinburgh, 1819).

McFarlane, K. B., *John Wycliffe and the Beginnings of English Nonconformity* (Teach Yourself History) (London, 1952).

McGregor, Geddes, *The Thundering Scot* (Philadelphia, 1952).

McKinnon, James, *Luther and the Reformation*. 4 vols. (London, 1925–30). (Old but still valuable.)

McNeill, J. T., *Thirty Years of Calvin Study* (*Church History* 17, 1948).

McNeill, J. T., *The History and Character of Calvinism* (New York, 1954).

McRoberts, David (ed.), *Essays on the Scottish Reformation 1513–1625*. *Innes Review* (Glasgow, 1962).

Mahoney, Matthew, *The Scottish Hierarchy 1513–65* in the *Innes Review* (Glasgow, 1962), pp. 39 ff.

Maitland, F. W., *The Anglican Settlement and the Scottish Reformation* (Camb. Modern Hist. Vol. 11).

*Manschrek, Clyde L., *Melanchthon: The Quiet Reformer*, 2 vols. (Chicago, 1958). (Good.)

Mattingly, G., *Catharine of Aragon* (London, 1942).

*Mennonite Encyclopedia*. 4 vols. (Scottdale, 1955–9). (Invaluable.)

Meyer, A. O., *England and the Catholic Church under Elizabeth*. Trans. J. R. McKee (London, 1916). (Lutheran author.)

Meyer, Carl S., *Elizabeth I and the Religious Settlement of 1559*. (St. Louis, 1960).

Moeller, Bernd (ed.), *Ambrosius Blarer* (Konstanz, 1964).

Moorman, J. R. H., *A History of the Church in England* (London, 1953).

Mourret, F., *A History of the Catholic Church.* Vol. 5. (St. Louis, 1930).

Mozley, J. F., *William Tyndale* (London, 1937).

Murray, Iain, H., *The Reformation of the Church* (Collection of Reformation and Puritan documents. Bibliographies) (London, 1965).

Murray, Robert Henry, *Erasmus and Luther* (London, 1920).

*Neale, J. E., *Queen Elizabeth* (London, 1934).

Neale, J. E., *The Elizabethan House of Commons* (London, 1949).

*Neale, J. E. *Elizabeth I and her Parliaments.* Vol. 1. 1559-81; Vol. 2 1584-1601 (London, 1953-7).

Neale, J. E., *Essays in Elizabethan History* (New York, 1958).

Nichols, John G. (ed.), *Narrative of the Days of the Reformation* (Westminster, 1859).

Niemeyer, H. A., *Collectio Confessionum* (Leipzig, 1840).

*Niesel, Wilhelm, *The Theology of John Calvin* (Philadelphia, 1956).

Niesel, Wilhelm, *Calvin Bibliographie 1901-59* (Philadelphia, London, 1960).

Olin, J. C., *A Reformation Debate* (Harper, New York, 1966). (Calvin's debate with Sadoleto.)

*Packer, James I. (ed.), *Cranmer* (Abingdon, 1964).

Parker, G. H. W., *The Morning Star.* P.C.H. Vol. 3 (London, 1965).

Parker, T. M., *The English Reformation to 1558* (London, 1950).

Parker, T. H. L., *The Oracles of God* (London, 1947).

Parker, T. H. L., *Portrait of Calvin* (London, 1954).

Parker, T. H. L., *The Doctrine of the Knowledge of God* (Edinburgh, 1952).

Pauck, Wilhelm, *The Heritage of the Reformation* (Boston, 1950).

Pearson, A. F. Scott, *Thos. Cartwright and Elizabethan Puritanism 1535-1603* (Cambridge, 1925).

Percy, Lord Eustace, *John Knox* (London, 1937).

Pfürtner, Stephanus, *Luther and Aquinas* (London, 1964).

Plass, Ewald M., *What Luther Says.* 3 vols. (St. Louis, 1959).

*Pollard, A. F., *Thomas Cranmer and the English Reformation* (London and New York, 1904).

Pollard A. F., *Henry VIII* (London, 1902).

Pollard A. F., *Wolsey* (London, 1929).

Porter, H. C., *Reformation and Reaction in Tudor Cambridge* (Cambridge, 1958).

Prescott, H. F. M., *Mary Tudor* (London, 1952).

Quinlan, David, *Roman Catholicism* (London, 1966).

Quistorp, H., *Calvin's Doctrine of the Last Things.* Trans. (London, 1955).

Read, Conyers, *The Tudors* (New York, 1949).

Read, Conyers, *Mr. Secretary Walsingham and the Policy of Queen Elizabeth.* 3 vols. (London, 1925).

Read, Conyers, *Mr. Secretary Cecil and Queen Elizabeth* (London, 1955).

Reich, Emil, *Select Documents illustrative of Medieval and Modern History* (London, 1905).

Reid, J. K. S. ed., and trans., *Concerning the eternal predestination of God* (London, 1961).

Ridley, Jasper, *Thomas Cranmer* (Oxford, 1962).

Ridley, Jasper, *Nicholas Ridley* (London, 1957).

Rilliet, J. H., *Zwingli: Third Man of the Reformation* (London, 1964).

Ritter, Gerhard, *Luther*. Trans. J. Riches (London, 1963).

Ritter, Gerhard, *Die Neugestaltung Europas im 16. Jahrhundert* (Berlin, 1950).

Ritter, Gerhard, *Why the Reformation occurred in Germany. Church History*, 27 (1958), pp. 99–106.

*Rowse, A. L., *The England of Elizabeth* (London, 1950).

Rowse, A. L., *The Expansion of Elizabethan England* (London, 1955).

*Rupp, E. Gordon, *The English Protestant Tradition* (Cambridge, 1949).

*Rupp, E. Gordon, *Luther's Progress to the Diet of Worms* (London, 1951).

*Rupp, E. Gordon, *The Righteousness of God: Luther Studies* (London, 1953).

*Rupp, E. Gordon, *The Old Reformation and the New* (London, 1967). (The Cato Lectures.)

Savine, A., *English Monasteries on the Eve of the Dissolution* (Oxford, 1909).

Scheel, Otto, *Dokumente zur Luthers Entwicklung bis 1519*. 2nd ed. (Tübingen, 1929).

Scheel, Otto, *Martin Luther. Vom Katholizismus zur Reformation*. 2 vols. (Tübingen). Vol. I. *Auf der Schule und Universität* (1921). Vol. II. *Im Kloster* (1930).

Schenk, W., *Reginald Pole* (London and New York, 1950). (Useful notes on source material.)

Schroeder, H. J., *The Canons and Decrees of the Council of Trent* (St. Louis and London, 1951).

Schwiebert, Ernest G., *Luther and His Times* (St. Louis, 1950).

Sehling, Emil, *Die Evangelischen Kirchenordnungen*. 2 vols. (Berlin and Leipzig, 1922–7).

de Senarclens, Jacques, *Heirs of the Reformation* (London, 1963).

Servetus, Michael, *Two Treaties on the Trinity* (1531). Trans. E. M. Wilbur. *Harvard Theological Studies XVI* (Cambridge, Mass., 1932).

Smith, Maynard H., *Henry VIII and the Reformation* (London, 1948).

*Smith, Maynard H., *Pre-Reformation England* (London, 1938).

Smith, Preserved, *The Life and Letters of Martin Luther* (Boston and New York, 1911).

Smith, Preserved, *Erasmus* (New York and London, 1923).

Smith, Preserved, *Luther's Correspondence* (Philadelphia, 1952).

Smyth, C. H., *Cranmer and the Reformation under Edward VI* (Cambridge, 1926).

Stählin, Ernst, *Quellen zur schweizerischen Reformationsgeschichte*. Re-edited by Oskar Farner (Zürich, 1901).

Stephens, W. R. W., and Hunt, William: *A History of the English Church*. 9 vols. (London, 1912). (To be used with greatest caution on the matter of the Reformation.)

Stone, Darwell, *A History of the Doctrine of the Holy Eucharist*. 2 vols. (London, 1909).

Strype, John, *Ecclesiastical Memorials*. 3 vols. (Oxford, 1822).

Strype, John, *Annals of the Reformation*. 4 vols. (Oxford, 1824).

Stupperich, Robert, *Melanchthon* (Berlin, 1960) Trans. Robert H. Fischer (London, 1966).

Tappert, Theodore, *Book of Concord* (Philadelphia, 1959).

Thiel, Rudolph, *Luther*. 2 vols. (Berlin, 1933, 35).

Tjernagel, N. S., *The Reformation Essays of Dr. Robert Barnes* (London, 1963).

Tjernagel, N. S., *Henry VIII and the Lutherans* (St. Louis, 1965).

Todd, J. M., *Martin Luther* (London, 1964). (R.C. work: fair in its judgments though unoriginal.)

Torrance, T. F., *Calvin's Doctrine of Man* (Lutterworth, 1949).

Torrance, T. F., *Kingdom and Church* (Edinburgh, 1956). (On Luther, Calvin and Bucer.)

Usher, R. G., *The Reconstruction of the English Church.* 2 vols. (New York, 1910).

Van Buren, P., *Christ in our Place: The Substitutionary Character of Calvin's Doctrine of Reconciliation* (Edinburgh, 1957).

Verduin, Leonard, *The Reformers and their Stepchildren* (Exeter, 1966).

Walker, G. S. M., *The Growing Storm.* Vol. 2. P.C.H. (London, 1961).

Wallace, R. S., *Calvin's Doctrine of the Word and Sacrament* (Edinburgh, 1953).

Wallace, R. S., *Calvin's Doctrine of the Christian Life* (Edinburgh, 1959).

*Watson, P. S., *Let God be God* (London, 1947).

Wernle, Paul, *Paulus Gerhardt. Religionsgeschichtliche Volksbücher.* IV. 2 (Tübingen, 1907).

*Wendel, François, *Calvin: Origin and development of his religious thought* (Paris, 1950). Trans. (London and New York, 1963). (Excellent. Bibliography.)

Whale, J. S., *The Protestant Tradition* (Cambridge, 1955).

Wilbur, Earl Morse, *A History of Unitarianism, Socinianism and its Antecendents* (Cambridge, 1945).

Williams, G. H., *Spiritual and Anabaptist Writers* (London and Philadelphia, 1957).

Williams, G. H., *The Radical Reformation* (London, 1962).

Williamson, J. A., *The Tudor Age* (London, 1953).

Workman, H. B., *John Wyclif.* 2 vols. (Oxford, 1926).

# INDEX